# STAMPINGS

# ON

# SHOTSHELLS

by
Ken J. Rutterford

Published 2011 by arima publishing

www.arimapublishing.com

ISBN 978-1-84549-475-9

© Ken J. Rutterford 2011

All rights reserved

This book is copyright. Subject to statutory exception and to provisions of relevant collective licensing agreements, no part of this publication may be reproduced, stored in a retrieval system, or transmitted in any form or by any means, without the prior written permission of the author.

Printed and bound in the United Kingdom

This book is sold subject to the conditions that it shall not, by way of trade or otherwise, be lent, re-sold, hired out, or otherwise circulated without the publisher's prior consent in any form of binding or cover other than that which it is published and without a similar condition including this condition being imposed on the subsequent purchaser.

arima publishing
ASK House, Northgate Avenue
Bury St Edmunds, Suffolk IP32 6BB
t: (+44) 01284 700321

www.arimapublishing.com

# COPYRIGHT

All of the head-stamp drawings in this book are of my own copyright. I do expect that cartridge collectors may wish to copy them so as to use in listing their own collections. Or the cutting them out and sticking them on to the fronts of draws in cartridge cabinets, etc. What the publishers and I will not tolerate is having them copied and used for gain, or given away as a complete set. If one should wish to use them for any other genuine reason, then please be so kind as to seek my permission in writing via the publishers.

Ken J. Rutterford.

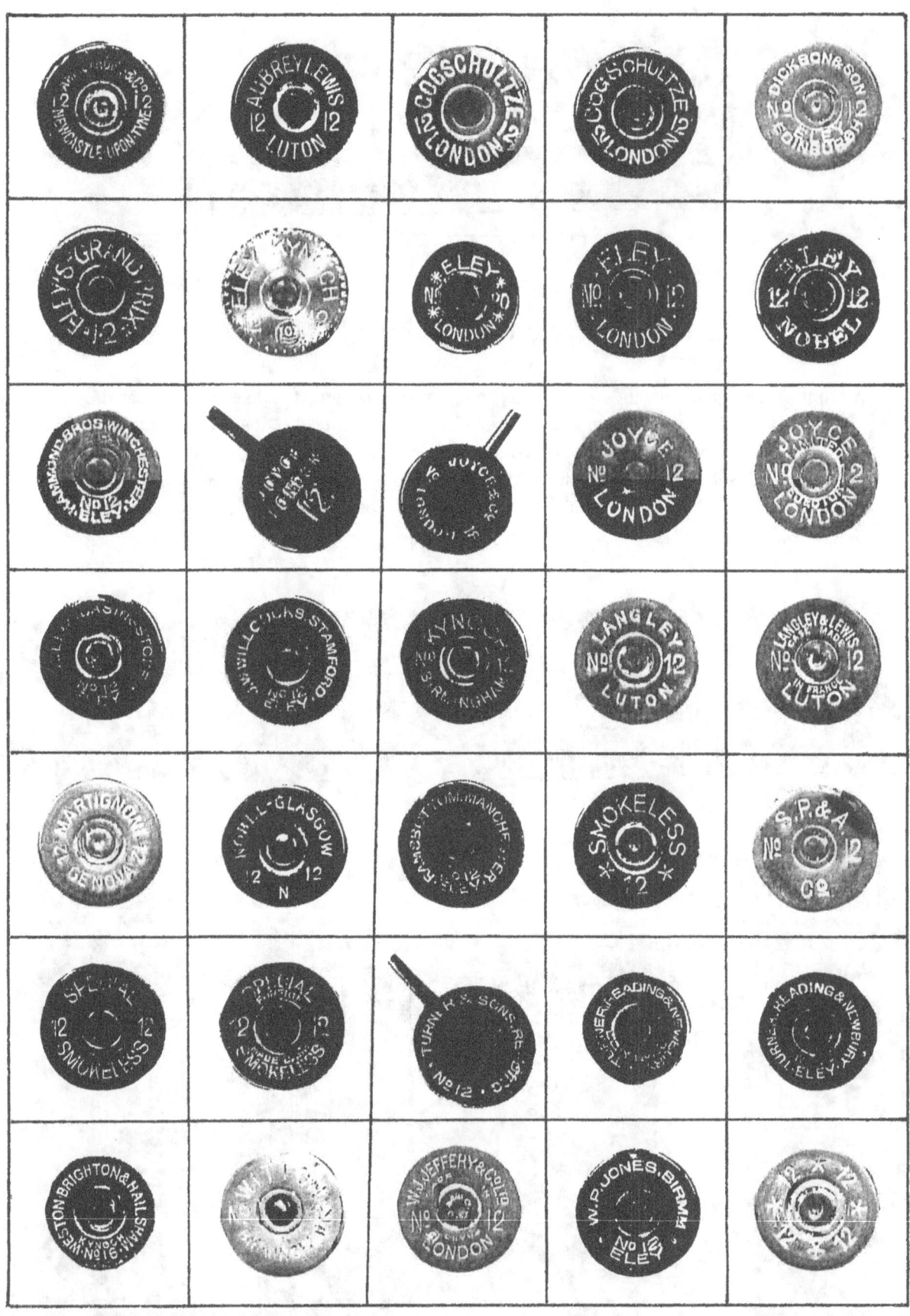

These headstampings were obtained by using photo copy machines. This was just another way that I have been able to secure accuracy for making some of my drawings.

# ACKNOWLEDGEMENTS

The material that I have made use of in making the headstamp drawings I have obtained from many sources throughout the last half century. There has been so many helpful people that have contributed by letting me photograph their cartridges or to make foil rubbings from them. Also I have been sent photographs and sketches of cartridge stampings by many people. I first started drawing these headstamps when I once owned a large cartridge collection. When much younger, I would go metal detecting and I then drew many from my finds. Many other people have, and still do, save me old cartridge remains which they have unearthed while metal detecting. Because there has been so many people that have kindly helped me over a long period of time I have decided against writing out a long list of names.

Within the pages of this book you will see that I have made use of a lot of American material. Because of this it is only right that I mention just a few names. To start with, the late Dale Hedlund who helped me and kindly welcomed me to stay in his home each time I made a visit to the U.S.A. Two other Americans were the late Don Steagall and Windy Klinect. I do not know if Windy is still with us as I lost contact with him many years ago. Both of these gents sent me so much material over the past years and they both kindly gave me permission to use any of it if I so wished. I will include a copy of a letter that was once sent to me by Windy.

I feel that it is only right to mention two people who love metal detecting. These are Angie and Dave Stone. I have never met these people but together they filled a sack with old cartridge remains and passed them on to Neville Cullingford. Neville kindly took on the task of sorting through the contents of the sack and then sending me parcels of stampings that he thought may be new to me. These finds were from in Hampshire and Sussex. From these parcels I have now drawn very many more. If only I could have got finds like this from all over the country then there would have been hundreds more.

To those people that I have just mentioned and to everyone who has contributed in helping me, I here thank all of you. By doing so you have helped in recording a little of our past and you have given many other people the chance to view them. By looking through this book you may then get to know of other stampings that will be new to you. Please, do enjoy.

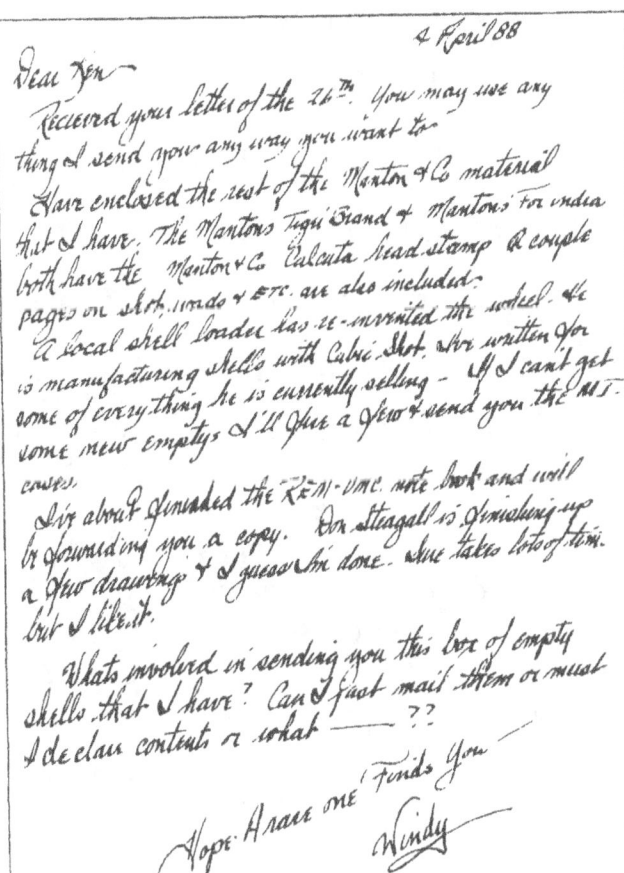

# CONTENTS

## FIRST SECTION

Copyright III; Acknowledgements V; Foreword VII; Introduction VIII; The Abbreviations X; International Registrations as used in this book XI; Reading The Drawings, also, A Guide To Reading The Head-stamps XII; Initials on Head-stampings XIII; Treasures From Beneath Our Feet XVII;

## SECOND SECTION

### PINFIRES IN ORDER BY LETTERS

Nil 2; A 4; B 5; C 6; D 8; E 9; F 13; G 15; H17; I 18; J 19; K 21; L 22; M 23; N 25; O 25; P 26; R 27; S 28; T 30; U 31; V 31; W 32;

### CENTRE-FIRES IN ORDER BY LETTERS

(From 360 up to 4 Gauge)

Nil 33-44; A 45-61; B 62-69; C 70-90; D 91-98; E 99-126; F 127-136; G 137-149; H 150-163; I 164-167; J 168-179; K 181-194; L 195-204; M 205-218; N 219-228; O 229; P 230-245; Q 246; R 247-265; S 266-287; T 288-295; U 296-309; V 310-312; W 313-342; X 343; Y 344; Z 345;

### OTHER HEAD-STAMPINGS

THE BIG BOYS (Larger than 4 Gauge), 346-348; POWDER TRANSPORTATION 349; WILHELM COLLATH & SOHNE'S CARTRIDGES 350; GREENER POLICE GUN CARTRIDGES 351; GARDEN GUN RIMFIRES 352; SOME ODDITYS 352;

### THE SIDE ELEVATIONS Pages 353-358.

### BELATED ADDITIONS

(Listed in alphabetical order with all the letters grouped)

From Nil and then from A up to Z 360-371;

### OTHER ITEMS

BUCK & CO. Adv 4; CARTRIDGE EXPLODES 22; W. COX & SON, Adv 7; CURTIS'S & HARVEYS CARTRIDGES 345; DARLOWS CARTRIDGES 352; ELEY SHOTGUN CARTRIDGES 99; ELEY-KYNOCH I.C.I. PINFIRE CARTRIDGES Adv 14; ELEY NONEKA CARTRIDGES 194; ELEY ROCKET (TRACER) CARTRIDGES 18; ELEY CARTRIDGES Circa 1970's 27,29,30; GERMAN PINFIRES 287; F. JOYCE & CO, LTD Adv 21; KYNOCH SHOTGUN CARTRIDGES 180; LEFT HANDED CARTRIDGES 25; MANTON'S CARTRIDGES 25; TYPICAL IRONMONGERS SHOPS 309; UNITED STATES CARTRIDGE CO 17; WIN THE WAR DAY IN 1918, 216;

# Foreword

The wordings found on the base of shotshells or shotgun cartridges, call them which you will, is what this book is all about. In this book you will find well over 6,000 drawings of headstampings. The information on these stampings is just as important to the cartridge collector as what the markings on coins are to the coin collector. In the early days of breech loading, any information to be found on a cartridge was stamped in to the bases of the brass heads. Here one must not get confused. The headstamp is to be found on the base of the cartridge this being the head of the cartridge. Years ago most of these were made from brass, but today they are usually made from thin steel and often brass lacquered over. Being made from steel they then rust right away within around five years when discarded in the countryside. The top of a shotgun cartridge is the end where the shot is retained.

Now just a few words on how all of these different gauge sizes came about. In those early days of breech loading some very odd sizes got used. What few of these that remain today are now very much sought after by cartridge collectors. Eventually standardisation took place with many more gauge sizes in use than what there are today. Gradually these gauge sizes got whittled down to just 10, 12, 16, 20 and 28. The measurement of the calibre, gauge or bore, call it which you wish was introduced from one pound of pure lead. A Spherical ball of lead weighing just one pound that would just fit a barrel would be a one gauge. One twelveth of this pound of lead made into a spherical ball that would just fit the barrel would be a twelve gauge. As there are sixteen ounces in a pound a similar ball of lead that would fit the barrel of a sixteen gauge gun would weigh just one ounce. It was established that a four bore would be 1·052 inch and a fourteen would be ·410 inch. The 9 mm garden gun being 9 mm.

Many of to days shooting folk do not realize the vast amount of history that has gone in to the making of the modern cartridge. One reason for producing this book is to record some of this past history so that it will not be lost to future generations. Back in the 1980's and up until the first world war, most towns in the UK had at least one firm that bought in his ready printed and often stamped cartridge cases. Quite often some of these would be imported. These old firms, gunsmiths, gunmakers and also ironmongers would then load up and sell their own celebrated brands of shotgun cartridges. The paper tubes were often printed, but for just a little extra cost they could have their name and that of the town stamped in to the brass heads. It was not all of the firms that sold their own cartridges would go to these expenses. If they required to place their name on the cartridge without a high cost they would just buy the over-shot cards ready printed.

In those bygone days the more expensive cartridges would have their brasses up to one inch high. Those considered best for the then new ejecting guns would have brasses nearly to the tops of them. On the other hand, some very cheap imported cases would have their brass heads only just above the rims. Like today, you generally got what you paid for.

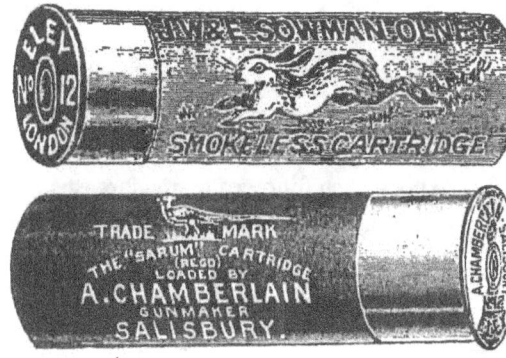

# INTRODUCTION

Throughout my lifetime I have been a keen collector of shotgun cartridges, or shotshells, call them which ever you will. Although I no longer have a large collection, I still take a great interest in them and of the very many firms of long ago that once sold them. I am now in my eighties and hopefully as I write this, that this will be my fourth book to have published on collectors cartridges. In my last book, 'Cartridge Drawings Now and Then from The Pen of Ken' and kindly published for me by arima publishing, I included in it a section of head-stampings. This proved popular and since then people have contacted me and have told me of stampings that I did not show. This is not that surprising as there has been thousands of them. It is certain that there are thousands more of them that I and most other people will now never get to know of. By producing this book it will record just another small portion in our history that could well have been lost forever. By using a semi-alphabetical order it has compiled these stampings in one place where they can more easily be found. These are alphabetically placed by using the first main letter of the stamping and not by a firms name which might also be included in that stamping.

When I first started to draw head-stampings I often had a cartridge to work from in front of me. In the past I have taken a multitude of photographs of stampings with the kind thanks of many other collectors. By placing a small portion of metallic cooking foil over a cartridge head and by using a finger or a pencil eraser has enabled me to make imprints which I have then been able to bring home and accurately work from. Drawings that I have made from methods like these I have called, First Hand. Now in order to show so many other stampings that I will never ever get a chance to draw first hand I have had to use many other peoples sketches. Very many of these are anything other than, well rough. Drawings that I have made from this kind of material I have called Second Hand. On the bottom line of each head-stamp drawing I have given it a reference number. For those drawings in the book mentioned above I have retained the same numbers but to the front of each I have placed three capital letters. H standing for head-stamp. This followed by F or S standing for first hand or second hand whichever it happened to be. The third letter being either C centre-fire, E electrical-fire, P in-fire or R rim-fire. All S type drawings can only be as accurate as what that person made them when he drew the sketch. They should be of the correct lay-out but the sizes to their lettering, gauge size and percussion cap could be way out. At the end of a number where /R is shown refers to that stamping is known to be a raised pressing.

Many of the F class drawings have been made from cartridge remains that have been dug out of the ground by kind persons using metal detectors. When I was a much younger chap I indulged in this hobby myself. Other people doing likewise could not understand why I was getting thrilled about what they were throwing away. I did manage to educate one or two of them but it was very difficult.

As this is a book about head-stampings I feel that I should try to explain just what is a head-stamp. Try as I may, I cannot think of any other thing than a cartridge that has a head at its bottom. The base of a cartridge is known as its head. This being so, when you stand a cartridge up you are standing it on its head. With the old rolled turn-over paper case walled cartridge the over-shot card is often referred to as the top wad. This then establishes the shot load end of the cartridge as its top. Therefore the head of the cartridge has to be at its bottom. This then makes the stamping on its bottom the head-stamping.

Within this book I have placed various stampings in sections. The first section deals with the pin-fires. This is then followed by the largest section, the centre-fires. In these two sections they are shown semi-alphabetically and also by their gauge sizes starting with ·360 up until 4 gauge.

Alphabetically not by firm but by the leading letter of the stamping. All stampings without letters as NIL precede the letter A. I do not like to see blank spaces as to me it is a waste of good paper. In such places I have purposely filled them with old cartridge advertisements or pictures of cartridges taken from out of them. This then helps in separating each letter and can give an added interest. Due to the need of space, gauges larger than 4 are shown under the title, 'The Big Boys'. Following on from this are some other small sections and one of these are the rim-fires.

Towards the end of this book you will find 'Belated Additions'. I have thought hard about this one but decide in the end that it should be included. All of the stamping drawings illustrated in this book were first drawn at size x2 (double size) and then reduced back by half. Each one has then been carefully cut out and alphabetically stored in small tins. This method worked well for most of them but due to static, the odd interesting one got stuck below another and found its self in the wrong letters tin. This then caused it to lose its alphabetical slot. Many other interesting oldies that came my way through kind people with metal detectors also missed their alphabetical slots. Then through the post thanks to the kindness of our club's Peter McGowan came a wad of several hundred sketches. You will see for yourself, 'Belated Additions' just had to go in. Please remember that if you are looking for some stamping in the main sections and cannot find it, then it is worth taking a look in the back of this book. As this book is alphabetically illustrated I have decide not to include an index.

Although I have referred mostly to older cartridges, modern stampings are also shown in the listings. There is so much that I do not know and never will know. Likewise, some things that you don't know and may never know, I just might know. For reasons like this I am unable to date all of the illustrations. All the same, I do have a good idea as to many of them. Please also remember that many of the stampings were used over many years such as SPECIAL SMOKELESS and SMOKELESS GASTIGHT. Prior to the large explosives firms merger in 1918, G. Kynoch & Co and Messrs Eley Brothers were hard at it in competition with each other. This will then date many of these cartridges to pre World War One. That great war which was supposedly to have ended all wars. In between the boxes under each drawing I hope I have given you a few clues. To start with Pla is the abbreviation for plastic. Where you will see this you will know that it would be dated well after World War Two.

DRAWINGS x 2.
Twice full size.

IX

## The Abbreviations

C......Centre fire cartridge . Used in the headstamp number.

F......First hand drawing. Drawn from the actual item or from a photograph.

H......Indicating that it is a headstamp number.

P......Pin fire cartridge. Used in the headstamp number

R......Rim fire cartridge Used in the headstamp number.

R/....Raised stamping. To the end of the headstamp number.

?......Do not know if the percussion cap has an insert cup.

Abc..Seen on an all brass case. May also have been on others.

Adv..Drawing made from an advert or a cartridge box.

Alu..Seen on an all aluminium case. May also have been on others.

Apc..Seen on an all plastic case. May also have been on others.

Asc..Seen on an all steel case. May also have been used on others.

Dps..Department stores.

Ejt..Seen on an ejector brass cartridge. May also have been used on others.

Eng.. Seen on an engine starter cartridge.

Fwk.. Firework or a pyrotechnic manufacturer.

Gnm..Gunmaker or gunmakers.

Hws.. Hardware stores.

Irm.. Ironmonger or ironmongers business.

Pap..Seen on a paper tubed cartridge. May have been used on others.

Pla..Seen on a plastic tubed cartridge. May have been used on others.

Ww1.. World War One.

Ww2.. World War Two..

# INTERNATIONAL REGISTRATIONS AS USED IN THIS BOOK

I have used these marks to abbreviate the countries shown within the stamping drawings. They are taken from those carried on the rear of motor vehicles whilst driven in other countries. The letters GB stand for Great Britain. To these letters I have added an extra one of four letters. E, England. I, Northern Ireland. S, Scotland and W, Wales. The first letter group is the country of the firm. In some cases this is followed by a second group. This second group is the country in which the cartridge case was probably made. I have used the word probably as in some cases I am making a guess.

| | | | | | |
|---|---|---|---|---|---|
| A | Austria | GBI | Northern Ireland | PAK | Pakistan |
| AUS | Australia | GBS | Scotland | PL | Poland |
| B | Belgium | GBW | Wales | R | Rumania |
| BR | Brazil | GR | Greece | RA | Argentina |
| BUR | Burma | H | Hungary | RC | China |
| C | Cuba | I | Italy | RL | Lebanon |
| CDN | Canada | IND | India | S | Sweden |
| CH | Switzerland | IRL | Republic of Ireland | SU | Russia |
| CS | Czechoslovakia | J | Japan | SUD | Sudan |
| CY | Cyprus | MEX | Mexico | TR | Turkey |
| D | Germany | MOZ | Mozambique | USA | United States of America |
| DK | Denmark | N | Norway | VN | Vietnam |
| DZ | Algeria | NL | Netherlands | YU | Yugoslavia |
| E | Spain | NZ | New Zealand | YV | Venezuela |
| F | France | P | Portugal | ZA | South Africa |
| GBE | England | | | | |

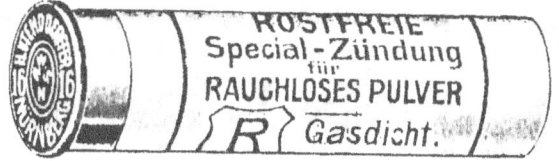
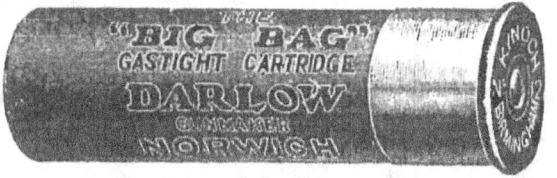

XI

# Reading The Drawings

Having drawn many old cartridges I did not always have the need to draw the same headstamp again and so I made myself a bank of these stampings that I could utilize. These I gave a number starting with the letters HN. These standing for Headstamp Numbers. In my book, 'Cartridge Drawings Now and Then from the Pen of Ken' I included ninety-six pages of headstamp drawings. These I numbered from 1 to 2,237. I made the decision to include all of these drawings in this book as I considered that they should all be included in just one book. This being so, I have kept their same numbering and have added on to it. To the front of each number I have placed three capital letters. These start with H to indicate that it is a headstamp number. The next letters are either F or S. F standing for First Hand. This a drawing made when I had its full details in front of me. The S standing for Second Hand. These drawings have been made from other persons sketches and are not so accurate. The following letter being either a C, P or R. These letters standing for Centre-fire, Pin-fire or Rim-fire respectively.

Below each drawing are four boxes. The bottom box is the reference number that I have given to it. Working upwards, the next is the country of the firm where known. Please remember that some stampings were used in several countries. If there is a follow on, then this is the country of the case manufacturer. Many firms would import their cartridge cases. Due to a lack of space, I have shown the countries by their vehicle international registration letters. A list of these can be found at the rear of this book. Being British, I have added an extra letter to our GB. These extra letters are E, I, S and W. These indicate that the firms were from either England, Northern Ireland, Scotland or Wales respectively. Below is a guide which I hope you may find helpful.

## A Guide To Reading The Headstamps

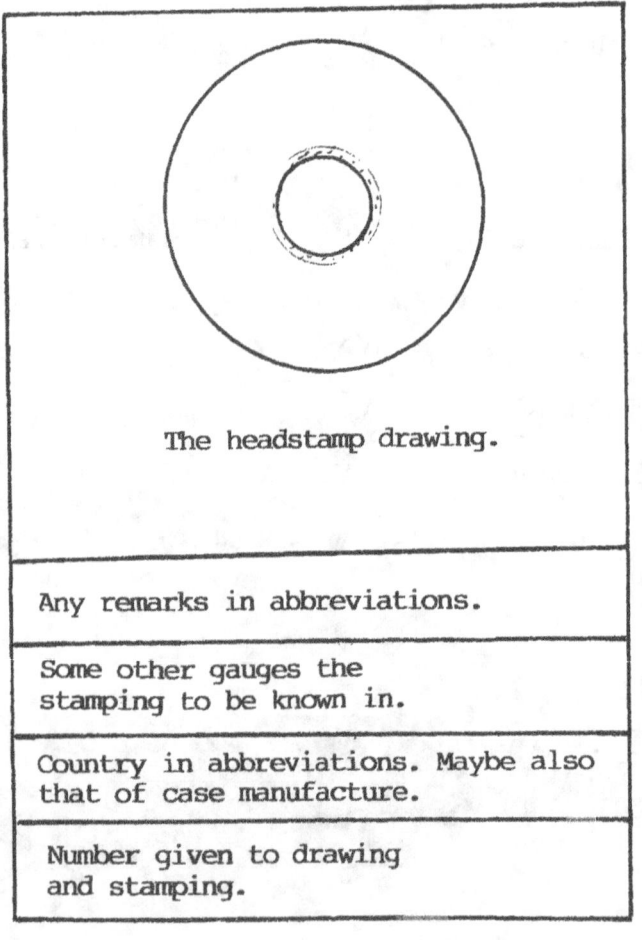

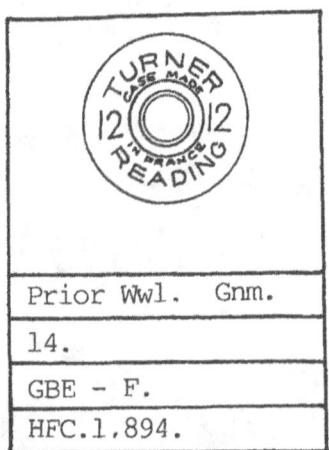

THE ABOVE EXAMPLE

1. Prior to World War One. Gunmaker.
2. Other gauge size seen in, may have been in others.
3. The firm as in Great Britain (England). Case made in France.
4. The stamping number. If it had been followed by /R, it would have had a raised up stamping.

# INITIALS ON HEAD-STAMPINGS

A.A.CO. AMERICAN AMMUNITION CO. Oak Park & Chicago, Ill, U.S.A. Also at, Muscatine, Iowa. Circa, 1910.

A.B.C. AMERICAN BUCKLE & CARTRIDGE CO. West Haven, Conn, U.S.A. (Purchased in 1889).

A.C.CO. AUSTIN CARTRIDGE CO. Cleveland, Ohio, U.S.A. (1890-1908).

ACE. GAMBLES STORES INC. U.S.A.

ALCAN. ALLIED MUNITIONS CO. Kansas City, Missouri, U.S.A.

A.L.H. A.L.HOWARD & CO. (Box 399) New Haven, Conn. U.S.A. Circa, 1885.

A.M.C.& CO. AMERICAN CARTRIDGE & AMMUNITION CO. Hartford, Conn, U.S.A. (1901-1906).

A & N.C.S.L. ARMY & NAVY CO-OPERATIVE SOCIETY, LTD. Westminster, London, England. Also, Bombay, India. Circa, 1909.

A.W.G. A.W.GAMAGE, Holborn, London, England.

AZOT. BAIKAL, U.S.S.R.

B.E.L.L. BRASS EPTRUSION LABORATORIES, LTD. U.S.A.

B.P.D. BOMBRINI PARODI DELFINO. Italy.

B.R.I. BALLISTIC RESEARCH INDUSTRIES. Soquel, California, U.S.A.

B.S.A. BIRMINGHAM SMALL ARMS B.S.A., LTD. Birmingham, Midlands, England.

C.A.C. COLONIAL AMMUNITION CO. Auckland, New Zealand.

C.A. CO. Also as, C.A & CO. CHICAGO ARMS CO. Chicago, Ill, U.S.A.

C.A.I. CONVERSION ARMS, INC. Yuba City, California, U.S.A.

C & B. CRAMER & BUCHHOLZ. Germany.

C.C.C. CREEDMORE CARTRIDGE CO. Barberton, Ohio, U.S.A. Circa 1890.

C.C, CO. CENTRAL CARTRIDGE CO. U.S.A.

C.C, CO. CLINTON CARTRIDGE, CO. U.S.A.

C.C & T, CO. CHAMBERLIN CARTRIDGE & TARGET, CO. Cleveland, Ohio, U.S.A. (Purchased by Remington Arms, Co in 1930).

CF CARTOUCHERIE FRANCAISE. France. (Seen on pin-fires. Merged in 1978 with Gevelot and became, Societe de Munitions.

C.F.C & CO. C.F.COOK & CO. U.S.A.

C.H.M.C. COGSWELL & HARRISON MANUFACTURING, CO. London, England.

C.I.L. CANADIAN INDUSTRIES, LTD. Brownsburg, Quebec, Canada. (1902 onwards).

D (Within a diamond). DELAWARE CARTRIDGE, CO. U.S.A. (See line below).

D.C, CO.   THE DELAWARE CARTRIDGE, CO. Wilmington, Delaware. U.S.A.

D.C,CO.   DOMINION CARTRIDGE, CO. Brownsburg, Quebec, Canada.

D E.   Was used by the DELAWARE CARTRIDGE, CO. U.S.A.

D.P.I.   DANSK PATRON INDUSTRI, Roskilde, Denmark.

ECLAIR. (French word for Lightning).

E-K   ELEY-KYNOCH. Witton, Birmingham, Midlands, England. Also in, Australia and New Zealand. (1926 onwards).

E.T.L.   EXPLOSIVES TRADES, LTD. Witton, Birmingham, Midlands, England. (1918-19190).

F.   FRANKFORT ARSENAL, Philadelphia, Pa, U.S.A.

F.C.   FEDERAL CARTRIDGE, CO. Minneapolis, Minnesota, U.S.A.

F.D & CO.   F.DRAPER & CO. U.S.A.

F.N.   FABRIQUE NATIONALE de 'ARMES de GURRE, Belgium.

G.C.C.   GORDON CARTRIDGE CO. Sydney, N.S.W, Austra

GECCO.   GUSTAV GENSHOW & CO. Durlach, Germany.

G-F.   GIVLIO FIOCCHI. Lecco, Italy.

G & H.   GATHMAN & HERMAN. U.S.A.

G.K & CO.   GEORGE KYNOCH & CO. Witton, Birmingham, Midlands, England. (Prior to 1919).

H.A, CO.   HUNTER ARMS CO. U.S.A.

H.K.   HAERENS KRUDTVAERK. Denmark.

H.S.A.   HAMMERSTOM'S SMALL ARMS. Regina, Saskatchewan, Canada.

H.S.B & CO.   HIBBARD SPENCER 7 BARTLETT, CO. Chicago, Ill, U.S.A. (Hardware distributors).

I.C, CO.   SPORTSMAN'S INTERNATIONAL CARTRIDGE, CO. Kansas City, U.S.A.

I.C.I.   IMPERIAL CHEMICAL INDUSTRIES, LTD. (METAL DIVISION). UK, Also in Australia & New Zealand. Parent firm at Witton, Birmingham, UK. Circa, 1926-1970.

I.C.I.A.N.Z.   IMPERIAL CHEMICAL INDUSTRIES of AUSTRALIA & NEW ZEALAND. (1936-1956)

I.F.S.   INTERNATIONAL FLARE SIGNAL, CO. Tippecanoe City, Ohio, U.S.A.

I.M.I.   IMPERIAL METAL INDUSTRIES (AUSTRALIA), LTD. Melbourne, Vic, Australia (1970 +).

IXL   AMERICAN BUCKLE & CARTRIDGE, CO. U.S.A.

J   F.JOYCE & CO. London, England.

J.A,R.E & BROS.   JACK A.R. ELLIOTT & BROTHERS. U.S.A.

| | |
|---|---|
| J.G.R. | J.G.R. GUNSPORT, LTD. Toronto, Ontario, Canada. |
| J.P & S. | J.PAIN & SON. Salisbury, England. (Firework and signal cartridges). |
| K | G.KYNOCH or KYNOCH & CO. Witton, Birmingham, Midlands, England. |
| K.C.CO. | KELSEY CARTRIDGE, CO. U.S.A. |
| KGH | KONGELIG GRONLANSKE HANDEL. Greenland. (Gyttorp, Sweden). |
| L.B. | LEON BEAUX. Milan, Italy. |
| L.B.C. | LEON BEAUX & CO. Milan, Italy. |
| L.B & CO. | LEWIS BROTHERS, Montreal, Canada. |
| L.C.M & CO. | LATIMER CLARK MURIHEAD & CO. Millwall, London, England (Founded 1887). |
| L.D.F. | LIBERTY DISPLAY FIREWORKS, CO. Danville, Ill, U.S.A. |
| L.M. | ELM CITY MANUFACTURING, CO. U.S.A. |
| LRB. | PENGUIN INDUSTRIES, INC. U.S.A. |
| M.F.A, CO. | MERIDAN FIREARMS MANUFACTURING, CO. Meridan, Conn, U.S.A. Circa, 1900. |
| M.G.M. | MANUFACTURE GENERALE de MUNITIONS. Bouge Le Valence, France. |
| N.A & A. CO. | THE NATIONAL ARMS & AMMUNITION CO. Birmingham, England. (1919-1921). |
| N.A.C. CO. | NORTH AMERICA CARTRIDGE, CO. Canada. |
| N.C.S. | NOUVELLE CARTOUCHERIE de SURVILLIERS. Survilliers, France. |
| N.F.I. | NURNBERG FURTHER INDUSTRIEWK. Nurnberg, Germany. |
| N.I. | NOBEL INDUSTRIES, LTD. Witton, Birmingham, Midlands, England. (1919-1921). |
| NIKA | NEDERLANDSE INDUSTRIE VOOR KUNSTSTOFFEN. (Netherlands Industry for plastic ammunition. |
| NYC | A.L.HOWARD & Co. U.S.A. |
| N.Y.C. | NEW YORK CARTRIDGE, CO. New York, U.S.A. |
| N.Z. | COLONIAL AMMUNITION, CO. Auckland, New Zealand. (1938-1945). |
| P.C. also, P.C.C. | PETERS CARTRIDGE, CO. Cincinnati, Ohio, U.S.A. (1890 onwads). |
| R.A. | REMINGTON ARMS, CO. Bridgeport, Conn, U.S.A. (1943 on tracer shells). |
| REM-UMC | REMINGTON PETERS, CO. Bridgeport, Conn, U.S.A. Also in Canada. |
| R.F. | ROCKLAND FIREWORKS, CO. Boston, Mass, U.S.A. |
| R.G & MFC, CO. | RAWBONE GUN & MANUFACTURING, CO, LTD. Toronto, Ontario, Canada. |
| R.H.A.CO. | ROBIN HOOD AMMUNITION, CO. Swanton, VT, U.S.A. (Purchased by Remington UMC in 1916. |

| | | |
|---|---|---|
| R.H.L. | H.A. LOCKWOOD ET AL. U.S.A. | |

R.H.L.	H.A. LOCKWOOD ET AL. U.S.A.

R.H.P.CO.	ROBIN HOOD POWDER, CO. Swanton, VT, U.S.A.

R.M.C.	RODEN MANUFACTURING. Capetown, South Africa.

R.W.S.	RHEINISCHE WESTFALISCHE SPRINGSTOFF. Germany.

S,B. Also S & B and also SBP. SELLIER & BELLOT. Prague, Czechoslovakia.

S.C.CO.	SOUTHERN CARTRIDGE, CO. Georgia, U.S.A.

S.C.CO.	STRONG CARTRIDGE, CO. New Haven, Conn, U.S.A.

S.D & G.	SCHOVERLING, DALY & GALES. U.S.A.

S.F. also S.F.M.	SOCIETE FRANCAISE des MUNITIOS de CHASSE et de GUERRE. France.

SG	Second grade.	U.S.A.

S.G.	WORCESTER CARTRIDGE, CO. U.S.A.

S.G.CO.	SCHULTZE GUNPOWDER, CO. Eyeworth, Hants & Bucklersbury, London, England. (Prior 1914.

S.G.D.G.	Found on some GEVELOT. Stood for, SANS GUARANTEE du GOVERNMENT. Patent is protected by the government. France.

S.I.C.CO.	SPORTSMANS INTERNATIONAL CARTRIDGE, CO. Kansas City, U.S.A.

S.K.D.	Seen on CARL SCHOLTZ of Brisbane, Queensland, Australia.

S.M.I.	SOCIETA METALLURGICA ITALIANA. Italy.

S.O.C.CO.	SOUTHERN CARTRIDGE, CO. Houston, Texas, U.S.A.

SP	SWARTKLIP PRODUCTS, LTD. Cape Town, South Africa.

S.P & A. CO.	SMOKELESS POWDER & AMMUNITION, CO. England.

S.Q.	WINCHESTER REPEATING ARMS, CO. New Haven, Conn, U.S.A. (Used on specials).

S.R & A.CO.	SEARS ROEBUCK & CO. U.S.A.

ST	ARTHUR L. HOWARD. U.S.A.

ST.	DELAWARE CARTRIDGE, CO. Delaware, U.S.A.

SUPER	SUPER CARTRIDGE, CO. Raleigh Rd, Maribyrnong, Victoria, Australia.

S & W.	SMITH & WESSON CHEMICAL, CO. Rock Creek, Ohio, U.S.A. Circa 1974.

S.W.F.	SMITH WESSON & FIOCCHI. U.S.A.

T.E.I.	TRIUMPH EXPLOSIVES, CO. INC. U.S.A.

U.F.	UNITED FIREWORKS MANUFACTURING, CO. U.S.A.

U.M.C.CO.	UNION METALIC CARTRIDGE, CO. Boston & Bridgeport. U.S.A.

U.S.C.CO.    UNITED STATES CARTRIDGE, CO. Lowell, Mass, U.S.A. (Terminated in 1929).

V.F.M.    VITALE FIREWORKS MANUFACTURING, CO. U.S.A.

V.L & A.    VON LENGERKE & ANTONIE. Chicago, Ill, U.S.A.

V.L & D. Also V.L & D.N.Y.    VON LENGERKE & DETMOLD. New York City, U.S.A.

W.A.    WESTERN AUTO STORES. U.S.A.

W.C.C. also W.C.CO.    WESTERN CARTRIDGE, CO. East Alton, Ill, U.S.A.

W.H.E.    ECKHARDT. U.S.A.

W.M.C.    W.M.COOPER. Sydney, New South Wales, Australia.

W.R.A.CO.    WINCHESTER REPEATING ARMS, CO. New Haven, Conn, U.S.A. (1884 onwards).

W-W.    WINCHESTER-WESTON DIV, OLIN CORP. New Haven, Conn, U.S.A. Also in Australia and Italy.

X    Was used by, DELAWARE CARTRIDGE, CO. Delaware, U.S.A.

TREASURES FROM BENEATH OUR FEET

Thanks to the metal detector. Also thanks to those kind people who had passed on to me these cartridge remains, I now own this pile of rubbish. Ah yes, but what rubbish. Hidden within this mound are many rare head-stampings. Some of them are of firms long gone that no collector has ever seen a cartridge by them. Without these remains we would never have known that these old firms marketed their own brands of shotgun cartridges. Thanks to these remains, I have now been able to make some accurate drawings so preserving this past history. Sadly, all of them are beyond preservation. If only they could have been dug up some fifty years earlier.

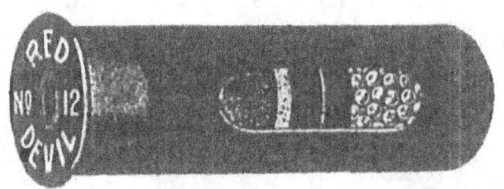

SARSON WOOD, AMPORT, HAMPSHIRE

It was in 1930 that my interest in cartridges started here.

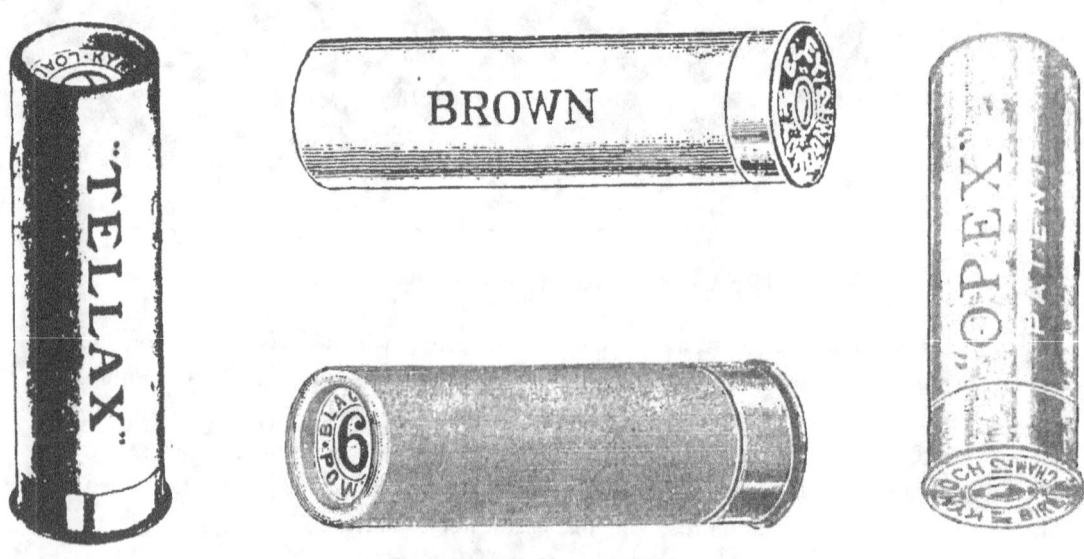

XVIII

# THE HEAD-STAMPINGS

These are placed in a semi-alphabetical order and each leading letter of the alphabet starts with a fresh page. Cartridge drawings taken from old advertisements help in separating them. They are also listed in order of gauge size. Smallest is shown first and the largest is last.

**THE PIN-FIRE SECTION IS FOLLOWED BY THE CENTRE-FIRE SECTION**

| | | | |
|---|---|---|---|
| .410. | 24 gauge. | 24 gauge. | 20 gauge. |
| 12. | 12. | | |
| HFP.3. | HFP.12. | HFP.13. | HFP.21. |
| 16 gauge. | 16 gauge. | | 16 gauge |
| | D/D | | D/D |
| HFP.5,079. | HSP.5,080. | HFP.5,081. | HSP.5,082. |
| 16 gauge. | | | 16 gauge. |
| 12. | | | |
| HSP.5,083. | HFP.28. | HFP.29/R. | HFP.30/R. |
| 16 gauge. | | 16 gauge. | 12 gauge. |
| 16 gauge. | | 12. | .410. |
| | D/D | D/D | |
| HFP.34. | HFP.5,084. | HFP.31. | HFP.95. |

| | | | |
|---|---|---|---|
| ![12] | ![12] | ![12] | ![12] |
| 12 gauge. | | | 12 gauge. |
| | | | |
| HFP.96/R. | HFP.5,085/R. | HFP.5,086. | HFP.97. |
| ![12 12] | ![12 12 12 12] | ![12 12] | ![Nº 12] |
| 12 gauge. | | | 12 gauge. |
| | 16. | | 16. |
| HFP.5.087. | HFP.100. | HFP.98. | HFP.99. |
| ![12] | ![star 12] | ![Nº 12] | ![Nº 12] |
| 12 gauge. | | | 12 gauge. |
| | 24. | | GBE/ |
| HFP.102. | HFP.101. | HFP.103. | HFP.104. |
| ![12 stag] | ![10] | ![8] | |
| 12 gauge. | 10 gauge. | 8 gauge. | |
| D/D | | | |
| HFP.105. | HFP.189. | HSP.5,088. | |

| | | | |
|---|---|---|---|
| 18 gauge. | 16 gauge. | 16 gauge. | Gnm, 12 gauge. |
| | | | |
| HSP.5,089/R. | HFP.5,090. | HSP.5,091. | HSP.5,092. |
| 12 gauge. | 12 gauge. | | |
| GBE | GBE | | |
| HSP.5,093. | HSP.32. | | |

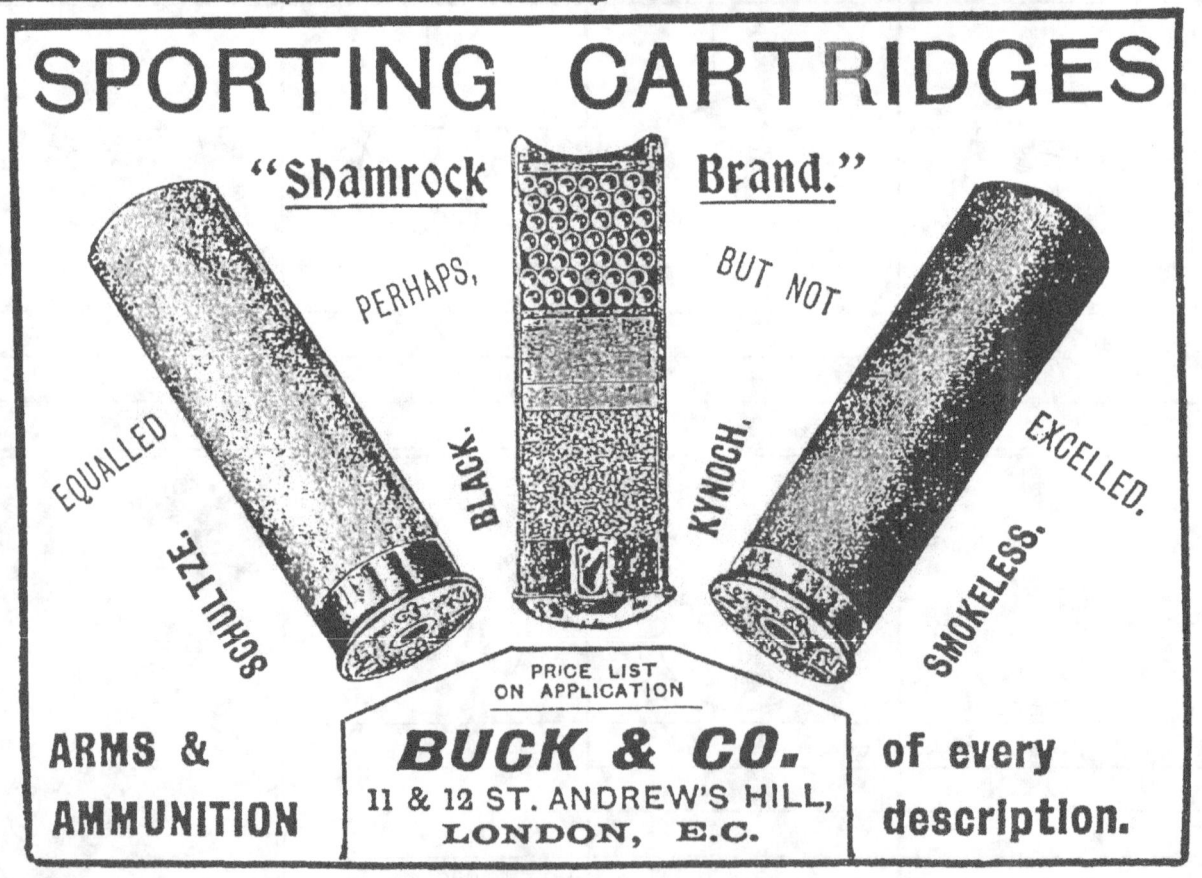

# SPORTING CARTRIDGES
## "Shamrock Brand."

PERHAPS, BUT NOT
EQUALLED, EXCELLED.
SCHULTZE. BLACK. KYNOCH. SMOKELESS.

PRICE LIST ON APPLICATION

ARMS & AMMUNITION

**BUCK & CO.**
11 & 12 ST. ANDREW'S HILL,
LONDON, E.C.

of every description.

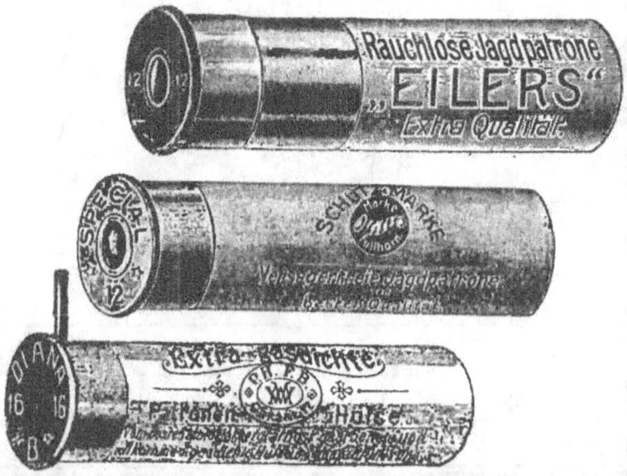

| | | | |
|---|---|---|---|
| 20 gauge. | 18 gauge. | 16 gauge. | 16 gauge. |
| | | D/D | I/I |
| HSP.5,094. | HSP.5,095. | HFP.5,096. | HFP.5,097. |
| 16 gauge. | 16 gauge. | 14 gauge. | 12 gauge. |
| | | 12. | 14. |
| D/D | D/D | F | F |
| HFP.36. | HFP.35. | HFP.77. | HFP.106. |
| 12 gauge. | 12 gauge. | 12 gauge. | Aluminium head. |
| B/B | | | |
| HFP.107. | HSP.5,098/R. | HFP.108/R. | HSP.5,099. |
| 8 gauge. | | | |
| HFP.200. | | | |

| | | | |
|---|---|---|---|
| 12mm /.410. | 14mm. | 14mm. | 28 gauge. |
| B/B | B/B | B/B | B/B |
| HFP.1/R. | HSP.5,100. | HSP.5,101. | HSP.5,102. |
| 24 gauge. | 20 gauge. | 20 gauge. | 16 gauge. |
| F/F | B/B | | |
| HFP.14. | HSP.5,103. | HFP.22. | HFP.38. |
| 16 gauge. | 16 gauge. | 16 gauge. | 16 gauge. |
| F/F | B/B | B/B | B/B |
| HFP.39. | HFP.41. | HFP.5,104/R. | HFP.40. |
| 12 gauge. | 12 gauge. | 12 gauge. | 12 gauge. |
| | 10. | 10. | |
| | USA | USA | B/B |
| HFP.109. | HSP.5,105/R. | HSP.5,106/R. | HFP.110. |

| | | | |
|---|---|---|---|
| CHAMBERS No 12 CARDIFF | CHAS. W. STEPHENS No 12 LEDBURY | CHAS. W. STEPHENS No 12 LEDBURY | C L 12 L |
| Gnm, 12 gauge. | 12 gauge. | 12 gauge. | 12 gauge. |
| GBW | GBE | GBE | B/B |
| HSP.5,107. | HSP.5,108. | HSP.5,109. | HFP.111. |

| | | | |
|---|---|---|---|
| C. PINDER & Co. No 12 BASINGSTOKE | C. D. LEET SPRINGFIELD MASS 10 | CHAUDUN Fs MONTMtre 7 PARIS 8 | 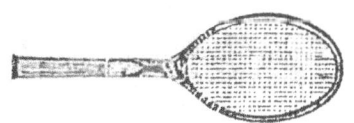 |
| Irm, 12 gauge. | 10 gauge. | 8 gauge. | |
| | 12. | | |
| GBE | USA | F | |
| HFP.112. | HSP.5,110/R. | HFP.201/R. | |

## W. COX & SON LTD.   28 High Street SOUTHAMPTON

Telephone 140Y    Branch—7 Bernard Street    Estd. 1830

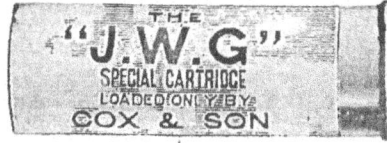

**GUNMAKERS** Sole Manufacturers of the "J.W.G." Cartridges. Repairs and overhauls by our own workmen a speciality.

**SPORTS OUTFITTERS** Leading Outfitters for Football Clubs, Cricket and Tennis Clubs. Country Clubs receive personal attention. Sole Agents in the United Kingdom for special Imperial Football. Ace Cricket Balls. Ace Tennis Ball. Repairs by post sent back per return.

**CUTLERS & SILVERSMITHS** We hold a large stock of cutlery and plate for hotels and clubs. Special quotations on application.

FISHING TACKLE MERCHANTS

SPECIAL LISTS
CARTRIDGES · · TENNIS · · · ·
FOOTBALL · · CROQUET · · ·
CRICKET · · · INDOOR GAMES

WHOLESALE · · PYROTECHNISTS

1920 Advert.

FIREWORK DISPLAYS DESIGNED FOR FETES & SPECIAL OCCASIONS

| | | | |
|---|---|---|---|
|  |  |  |  |
| 20 gauge. | 16 gauge. | 16 gauge. | 16 gauge. |
| | | | 12. |
| | | | |
| HFP.25. | HFP.42/R. | HFP.5,111. | HFP.5,112. |
|  |  |  |  |
| Wells-next-Sea. | 12 gauge. | 12 gauge. | 12 gauge, Gnm. |
| | | 16. | |
| GBE | | | GBS/GBE |
| HSP.5,113. | HFP.113/R. | HFP.114. | HSP.5,114. |

8

| .410 | 32 gauge. | 28 gauge. | 20 gauge. |
|---|---|---|---|
| GBE/GBE | GBE/GBE | | GBE/GBE |
| HFP.4/R. | HFP.9. | HFP.10. | HFP.5,115. |
| 20 gauge. | Manufacturer. | Eley Bros. | 16 gauge. |
| GBE/GBE | GBE/GBE | GBE/GBE | GBE/GBE |
| HFP.5,116/R. | HSP.5,117/R. | HFP.43/R. | HFP.44/R. |
| 16 gauge. | Manufacturer. | Eley Bros. | 16 gauge. |
| GBE/GBE | GBE/GBE | GBE/GBE | |
| HFP.45/R. | HSP.5,118. | HFP.5,119/R. | HSP.5,120. |
| 16 gauge. | | Manufacturer. | 16 gauge. |
| | On other gauges. | | |
| | GBE/GBE | GBE/GBE | GBE/GBE |
| HFP.46. | HFP.5,121/R. | HSP.5,122/R. | HFP.5,123/R. |

| | | | |
|---|---|---|---|
| 16 gauge. | Last of pins. 12. | Eley Bros. | 16 gauge. |
| GBE/GBE | GBE/GBE | GBE/GBE | GBE/GBE |
| HFP.47. | HFP.48. | HFP.5,124. | HFP.49. |
| Manufacturer. | Nobel Industries. | 16 gauge. | 16 gauge. |
| GBE/GBE | GBE/GBE | | |
| HSP.5,125. | HSP.5,126. | HFP.51. | HFP.50/R. |
| Rare 15 gauge. | 14 gauge. | Eley Bros. On other gauges. | Manufacturer. |
| GBE | GBE/GBE | GBE/GBE | GBE/GBE |
| HFP.75/R. | HSP.5,127/R. | HFP.78. | HFP.79/R. |
| 14 gauge. | Manufacturer. | Eley Bros. | 14 gauge. On other gauges. |
| GBE/GBE | GBE/GBE | GBE/GBE | GBE/GBE |
| HFP.5,128/R. | HFP.5,129/R. | HFP.80. | HFP.81. |

| | | | |
|---|---|---|---|
| 14 gauge. | 12 gauge. | Eley Bros. | 12 gauge. |
| GBE/GBE | GBE/GBE | GBE/GBE | GBE/GBE |
| HFP.5,130. | HFP.1.151/R. | HFP.116/R. | HFP.117. |
| Gnm. | 12 gauge. | Manufacturer. | 12 gauge. |
| GBE | D | GBE/GBE | GBE/GBE |
| HFP.118. | HFP.119. | HFP.5,131/R. | HFP.120/R. |
| 12 gauge. | Manufacturer. | | Last pinfires. 16. |
| GBE/GBE | GBE/GBE | GBE/GBE | GBE/GBE |
| HFP.122/R. | HFP.121/R. | HFP.5,132. | HFP.123. |
| 12 gauge. | Eley Bros. | Eley Bros. | 12 gauge. |
| GBE/GBE | GBE/GBE | GBE/GBE | GBE/GBE |
| HFP.124/R. | HFP.125/R. | HSP.5,133. | HFP.126. |

| | | | |
|---|---|---|---|
| 12 gauge. | Eley Bros. | Manufacturer. | 12 gauge. On other gauges. |
| GBE/GBE | GBE/GBE | GBE/GBE | GBE/GBE |
| HFP.128. | HFP.127. | HFP.129. | HFP.5,134. |
| Nobel Industries. | 12 gauge. | 12 gauge. | 10 gauge. |
| GBE/GBE | | | GBE/GBE |
| HFP.130. | HFP.131/R. | HFP.132/R. | HSP.5,135. |
| 10 gauge. | Manufacturer. | | Eley Bros. |
| GBE/GBE | GBE/GBE | GBE/GBE | GBE/GBE |
| HFP.5,136/R. | HFP.190/R. | HFP.191/R. | HFP.192. |
| 8 gauge. On other gauges. | Eley Bros. On other gauges. | 4 gauge. On other gauges. | |
| GBE/GBE | GBE/GBE | GBE/GBE | |
| HFP.202/R. | HFP.203. | HFP.205/R. | |

| | | | |
|---|---|---|---|
| (Fabrique Gevelot Paris 14 Millim) | (Fabrique Gevelot Paris 16) | (Favorito * 16 *) | (Favorito ☆ 16 ☆) |
| 14 mm. | 16 gauge. | 16 gauge. | 16 gauge. |
| F/F | F/F | | |
| HFP.5. | HFP.53. | HSP.5,137. | HFP.5,138. |
| (F F 16 ♦ 16 ◇◇◻) | (Fortuna 16 16 ✻ K ✻) | (Fortuna 16 16 ✻ K ✻) | (Fortuna 16 16 × K ×) |
| 16 gauge. | | | 16 gauge. |
| | D/D | D/D | D/D |
| HFP.52. | HFP.54. | HFP.55. | HSP.5,426. |
| (Fabric Italiana 14 14 Piloni Bernardo) | (Fabrique C&D A Paris 14) | (Fabrique G&D A Paris 14) | (F.A. Bales, Ipswich No 12 Eley) |
| 14 gauge. | 14 gauge. | 14 gauge. | Frank Bales, Gnm. |
| I/I | F/F | F/F | GBE/GBE |
| HFP.82. | HSP.5,139. | HFP.83. | HFP.133. |
| (Fabrication Garantie P12F) | (Fabrique Gevelot 12 Paris) | (F. Joyce & Co 12 London) | (F. Joyce & Co No 12 London) |
| 12 gauge. | Manufacturer. | Manufacturer. | 12 gauge. |
| | F/F | GBE/GBE | GBE/GBE |
| HSP.5,140. | HSP.5,141. | HSP.5,142/R. | HSP.5,143. |

|  |  |  |  |
|---|---|---|---|
| ![headstamp F.WOOD.SALISBURY No 12 ELEY] | ![headstamp FABRIQUE GEVELOT 10 PARIS] | ![headstamp FABRIQUE GEVELOT 10G10 PARIS] | |
| Fwk. Pre Wwl. | 10 gauge. | 10 gauge. | |
| GBE/GBE | F/F | F/F | |
| HFP.134. | HFP.193. | HFP.194. | |
| ![headstamp FABRIQUE GEVELOT 8 PARIS] | ![headstamp FABRIQUE GEVELOT 8 PARIS] | ![headstamp Francse des MUNITIONS PARIS 4] | ![headstamp FABRIQUE GEVELOT 32 MILLIM PARIS] |
| 8 gauge. | Manufacturer. | 4 gauge. | 32 mm. |
| F/F | F/F | F/F | F/F |
| HSP.5,144. | HSP.5,145. | HFP.206. | HFP.207/R. |

SHOTGUN CARTRIDGE CASES

### ELEY "BROWN PIN-FIRE"

A paper cartridge case, metal lined, with ⅜″ brass.

| Gauge | Length | Colour |
|---|---|---|
| 12 | 2½″ | Light brown |
| 16 | 2½″ | Light brown |

NOTE. The loading of smokeless powder into pin-fire cases is not recommended.

| | | | |
|---|---|---|---|
| (GARANTIE 28) | (GARANTIE 24) | (GIULIO FIOCCHI 24 24 LECCO) | (GAUPILLAT & Co PARIS 20) |
| 28 gauge. | 24 gauge. | 24 gauge. | 20 gauge. |
| D | D | I/I | F/F |
| HFP.11. | HFP.16/R. | HSP.5,146. | HSP.5,147. |
| (GARANTIE 16 16 B) | (GARANTIE CROCODILE 16) | (GAUPILLAT 16 16 PARIS) | (GERMANIA C.16) |
| 16 gauge. | 16 gauge. | 16 gauge. | 16 gauge. |
| D | D | F/F | D |
| HFP.5,148. | HSP.5,149. | HSP.5,150. | HSP.5,151. |
| (GEVELOT 16 16 PARIS) | (16 GJ PARIS) | (GALE ELEY BARNSTAPLE) | (GIULIO FIOCCHI 14 14 LECCO) |
| Manufacturer. | | 14 gauge. | 14 gauge. |
| F/F | F/F | GBE/GBE | I/I |
| HFP.56. | HFP.57. | HSP.5,152. | HFP.85. |
| (14 GJ) | (GALE No 12 ELEY BARNSTAPLE) | (GASTIGHT JOYCE LONDON No 12) | (G & C BISSET & Co 12 LONDON) |
| 14 gauge. | 12 gauge, Gnm. | Manufacturer. | 12 gauge, Gnm. |
| | GBE/GBE | GBE/GBE | GBE |
| HFP.86/R. | HSP.5,153. | HSP.5,154. | HFP.135/R. |

| | | | |
|---|---|---|---|
| 12 gauge, Gnm. | 12 gauge. | Manufacturer. | 12 gauge. |
| GBE | GBE | I/I | I/I |
| HFP.5,155/R. | HSP.5,156/R. | HFP.136. | HSP.5,157. |
| 12 gauge, Irm. | George William, Gnm. | 10 gauge. | 10 gauge. |
| GBE | GBE | F/F | F/F |
| HSP.5,158. | HFP.137/R. | HFP.195. | HFP.196. |

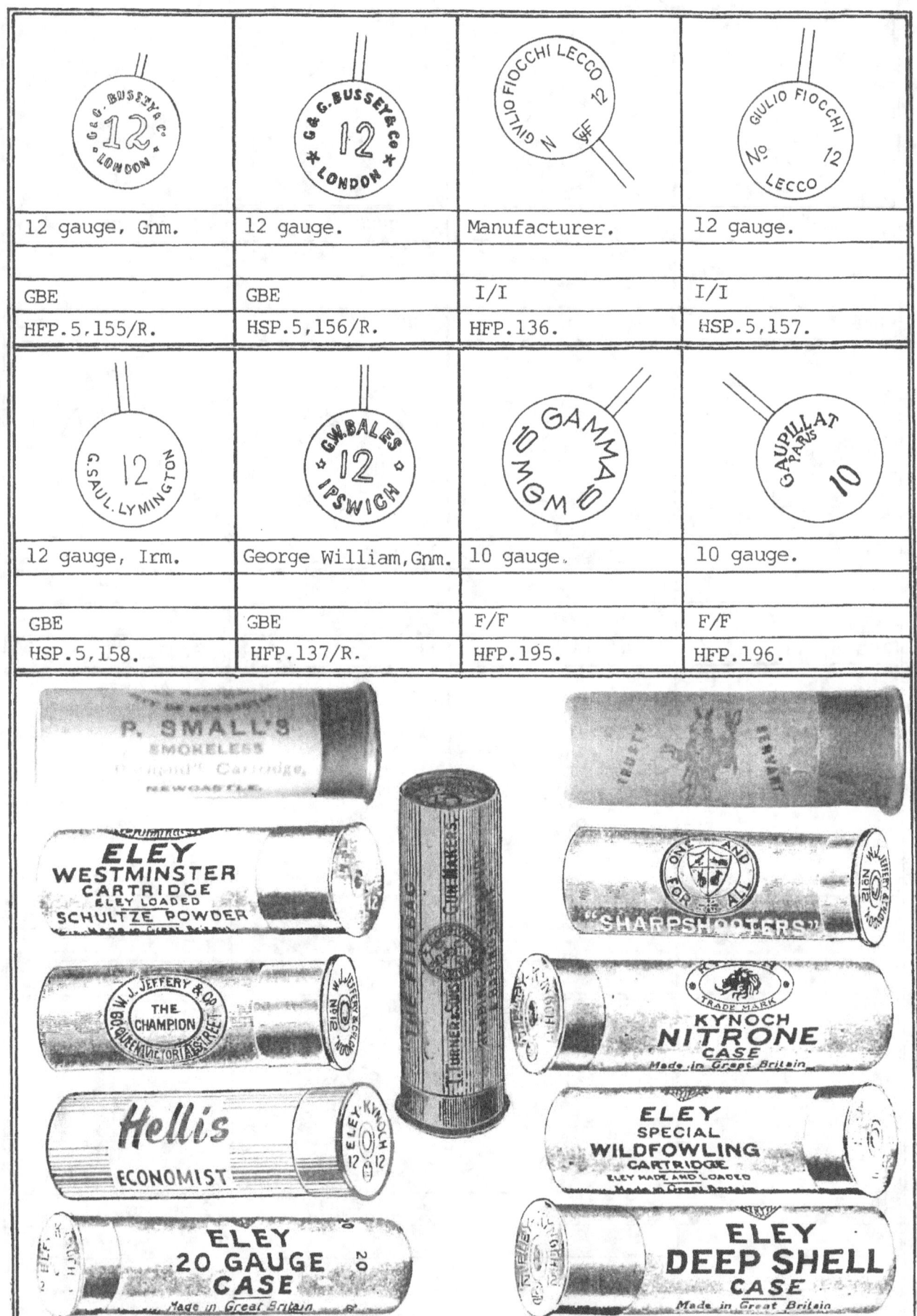

| | | | |
|---|---|---|---|
| HIRTENBERG 18 * * | HIRTENBERG 16 * * | HIRTENBERG 16 K&C | Z.H.UTENDOERFFER No NURNBERG |
| 18 gauge. | 16 gauge. | 16 gauge. | 16 gauge. |
| | | | D/D |
| HSP.5,159/R. | HFP.58. | HFP.59. | HSP.5,160. |
| HAMMOND 12 WINCHESTER | No HAMMOND BROS 12 WINCHESTER | HAZEL.DORCHESTER No 12 ELEY | HUBERTUS .12 |
| 12 gauge, Gnm. | Irm. | Irm. | 12 gauge. |
| GBE | GBE | GBE/GBE | D |
| HFP.5,161/R. | HSP.5,162. | HFP.138. | HFP.139. |

## U. S. CARTRIDGE COMPANY,
### LOWELL, MASS.

**U.S. "CLIMAX"** WATERPROOF PAPER SHOT SHELLS

**EVERLASTING** BRASS SHOT SHELL CLIMAX NO. 12.

PATENTED OCT. 4, 1884. PAPER SHOT SHELL CLIMAX BRAND.

PATENTED OCT. 14, 1884. **WATERPROOF** PAPER SHOT SHELL FIRST QUALITY.

**BRASS SHOT SHELL** NO. 10.

PATENTED OCT. 14, 1884. PAPER SHOT SHELL STAR BRAND.

U.S. **FIRST QUALITY** BRASS SHOT SHELL.

17

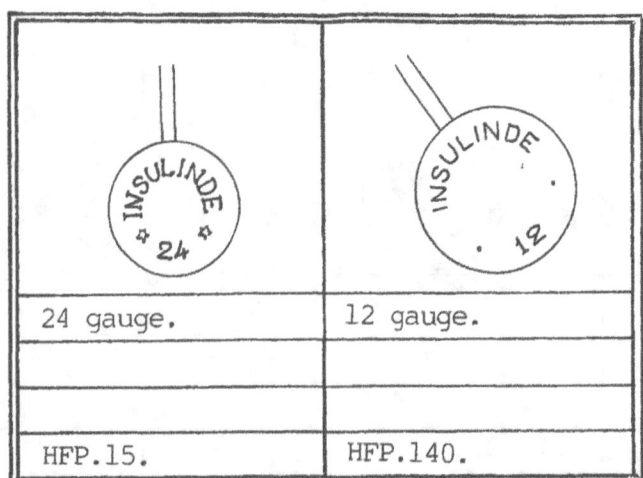

| 24 gauge. | 12 gauge. |
|---|---|
| HFP.15. | HFP.140. |

# "ROCKET"
## (TRACER) CARTRIDGES

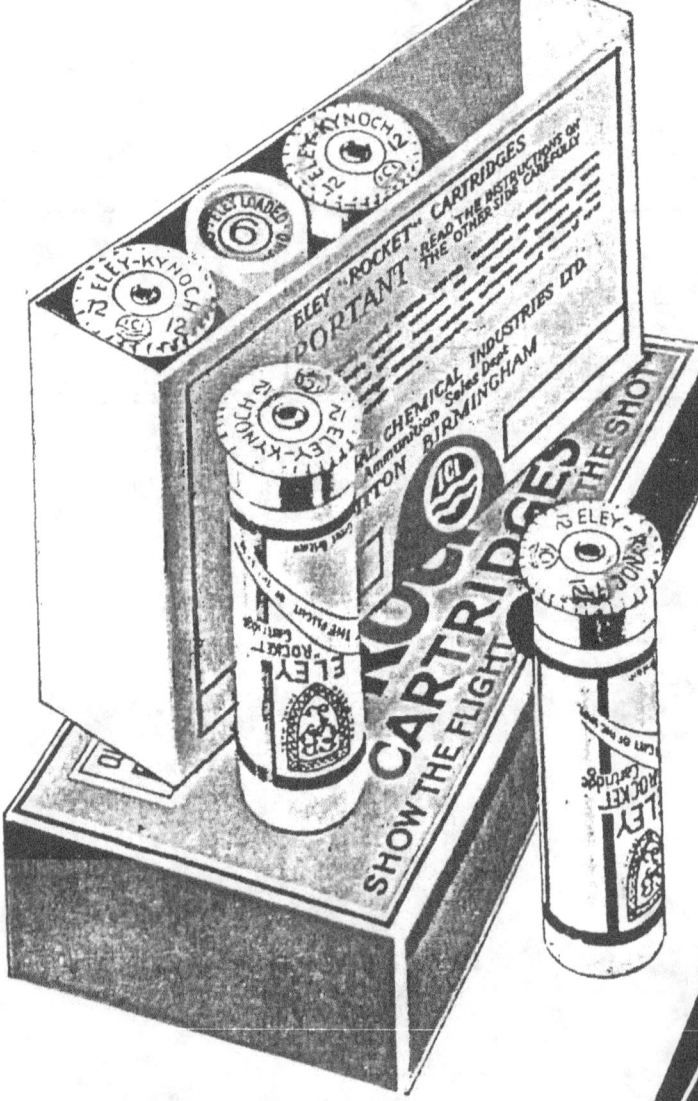

Packed in cartons of five; 12, 16 and 20 bore, 2½ in. length, and 12 bore, 2¾ in. length, with ⅝ in. brass head. The special milled heads, grey tubes and blue printing are designed to distinguish "Rocket" cartridges from standard cartridges.

⬤ ⅝ in. brass, milled head, loaded with "Smokeless ◇ Diamond" (12 gauge) or "Schultze" (16 and 20 gauge). Colour: Grey. The Improved "Rocket" cartridge contains a tracer pellet that marks out the path of the shot charge by the emission of a bright spot of light, so that errors of aim can be detected and corrected. For clay pigeon shooting and for game shooting. The composition used in the tracer element has no harmful effect on the flesh of game shot with it.

*"Rocket" advert circa 1936.*

| | | | |
|---|---|---|---|
| JUPITER C 18 * L * | JAGD 16 16 B | J.HALL.STATION.RD.WIGTON KYNOCH No 16 | JOYCE LONDON 16 |
| 18 gauge. | 16 gauge, | 16 gauge. | 16 gauge. |
|  | D | GBE/GBE | GBE/GBE |
| HSP.5,163. | HFP.5,164. | HFP.60. | HFP.5,165/R. |
| JOYCE No 16 LONDON | JOYCE & Co No 16 LONDON | JOYCE & Co No 16 LONDON | F. JOYCE & Co 14 LONDON |
| Manufacturer. | 16 gauge, Pre Ww1. | Manufacturer. | 14 gauge. |
| GBE/GBE | GBE/GBE | GBE/GBE | GBE/GBE |
| HSP.5,166. | HFP.61. | HFP.5,167. | HFP.84/R. |
| JOYCE & Co LONDON No 14 | J.AMES LLOYD.LEWES No 12 | No JEFFERY 12 GUILDFORD | JEFFERY.GUILDFORD No 12 ELEY |
| 14 gauge. | 12 gauge, Gnm. | Samuel R. Gnm. | 12 gauge, Gnm. |
| GBE/GBE | GBE | GBE | GBE/GBE |
| HFP.87. | HSP.5,168. | HFP.141. | HSP.5,169. |
| J.HALL.STATION.RD.WIGTON KYNOCH No 12 | J.HANSON.LINCOLN No12 ELEY | J.LANG LONDON 12 E.G.P. | JOYCE 12 LONDON |
| 12 gauge, Pre Ww1. | John. Cycle. Gnm. | Joseph H. Gnm. | Manufacturer. |
| GBE/GBE | GBE/GBE | GBE | GBE |
| HFP.142. | HSP.5,170. | HSP.5,171/R. | HSP.5,172/R. |

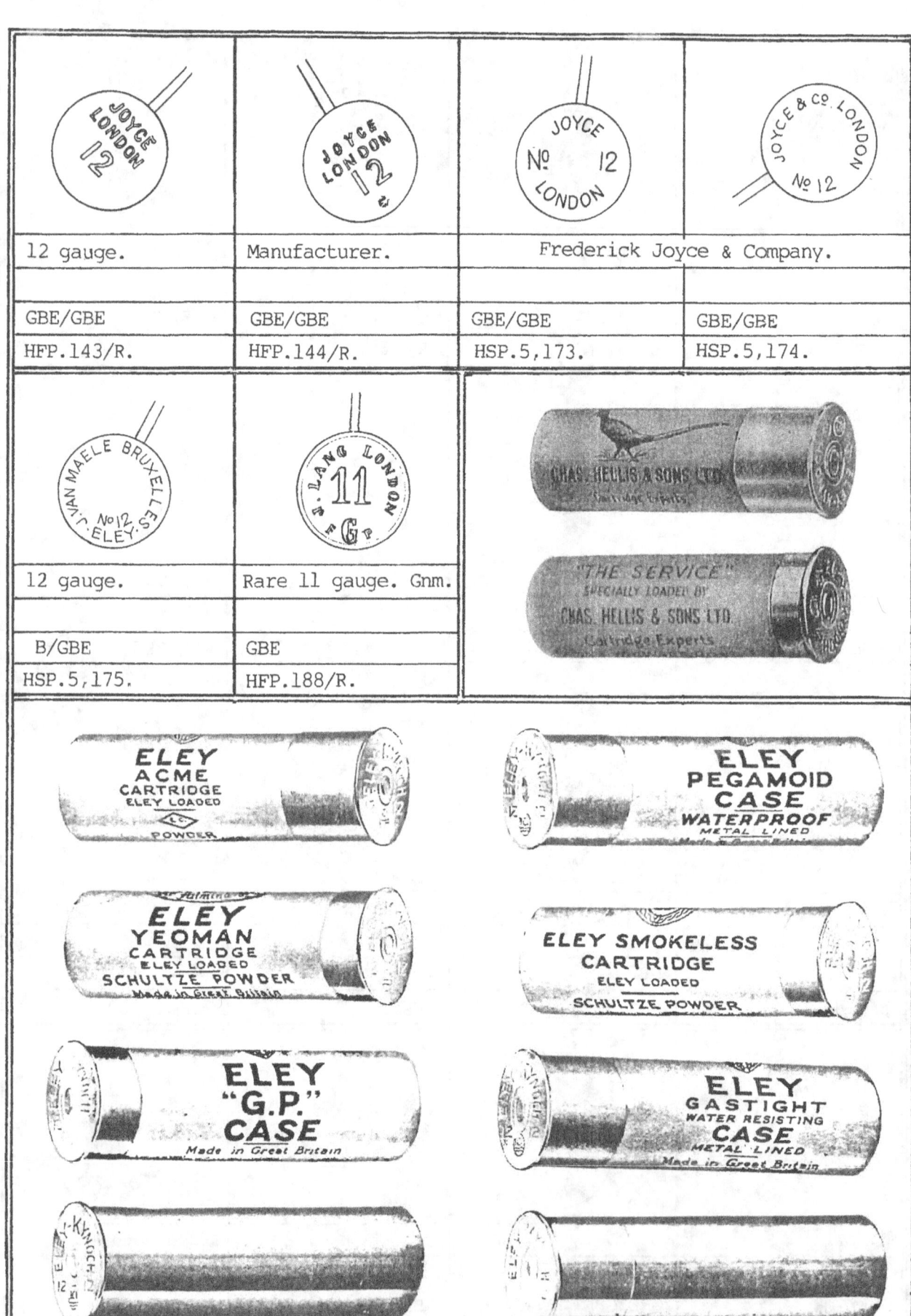

| | | | |
|---|---|---|---|
| 20 gauge. | 16 gauge. | 16 gauge. | 14 gauge. |
| | | | On other gauges. |
| GBE/GBE | D | GBE/GBE | GBE/GBE |
| HFP.23/R. | HSP.5,176. | HSP.5,177. | HFP.88. |
| 14 gauge. | Irm, Pre Wwl. | Manufacturer. | Pre Wwl. |
| | | On other gauges. | |
| GBE/GBE | GBE | GBE/GBE | GBE/GBE |
| HFP.5,178. | HFP.145. | HFP.146. | HFP.5,179. |
| 12 gauge. | 10 gauge. | 10 gauge. | |
| | | On other gauges. | |
| GBE/GBE | GBE/GBE | GBE/GBE | |
| HFP.147. | HFP.197. | HFP.198. | |

# F. JOYCE & CO. Ltd., London

SPORTING and MILITARY...

## AMMUNITION

...of all kinds.

"ROYALTY" Cartridges a Speciality. The Highest Class Manufactured.

Australasian Representative—EDWARD PARRY, Paling's Buildings, Sydney

| | | | |
|---|---|---|---|
| ⊙ LENIL 12% | ⊙ L.M.&Co 18 WIEN | ⊙ LUX 16 16 D | ⊙ LANG LONDON 15 G |
| 12 mm / .410. | 18 gauge. | 16 gauge. | Rare 15 gauge. |
| | A | | GBE |
| HFP.2. | HSP.5,180. | HFP.5,181. | HFP.76/R. |
| ⊙ L.M.&Co 14 WIEN | ⊙ LB 12 ★★★ | ⊙ L.BACHMANN 12 BREVETE 12 | ⊙ 12 LERCAE |
| 14 gauge. | 12 gauge. | 12 gauge. | 12 gauge. |
| A | I/I | | |
| HSP.5,182. | HFP.148/R. | HFP.149/R. | HFP.150/R. |
| ⊙ L.M.&Co 12 WIEN | | | |
| 12 gauge. | | | |
| A | | | |
| HFP.151/R. | | | |

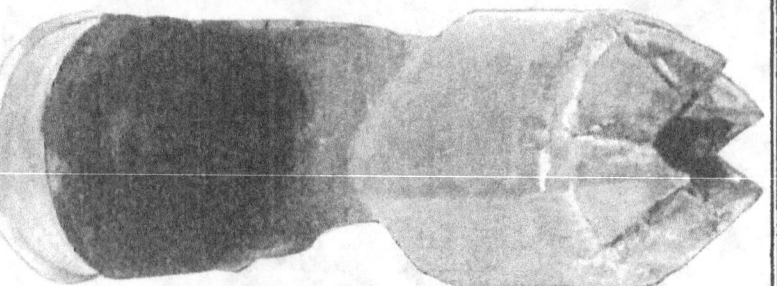

**A CARTRIDGE EXPLODES**

SIR. A party of four guns was standing on the roadway beside a car preparatory to moving off to the shoot. A No. 6 cartridge was accidentally dropped. It landed on a piece of gravel and exploded.

The attached photograph shows the result. No-one was injured, nor was there any paint chipped from the car beside which we were standing. The four guns total about 120 years' experience of shooting between them, but none had ever seen or heard of this happening before. They all agreed that it was a most unpleasant experience, but only suffered the inconvenience of having to shake No. 6 hail out of their clothing and hair!

J. A. McKINNEY
Vernon Grove, Rathgar, Dublin.

**FROM OUT OF MY SCRAP BOOK**
Why be afraid of pinfire cartridges.
One accidentally dropped on its pin
might explode very similar.

| | | | |
|---|---|---|---|
| 14 mm. | 24 gauge. | HFP.24. | 24 gauge. |
| | F/F | F/F | F/F |
| HFP.6. | HFP.17. | HFP.18. | HFP.19. |
| 24 gauge. | | 20 gauge. | 18 gauge. |
| | 12. | | |
| HFP.5,183/R. | HFP.24. | HFP.5,184. | HSP.5,185. |
| 18 gauge. | 16 gauge. | 16 gauge | 16 gauge. |
| | | | 20,12. |
| | | F | F/F |
| HSP.5,186. | HFP.62. | HSP.5,187/R. | HSP.5,188. |
| 16 gauge. | Gnm. | | 12 gauge. |
| F/F | GBS | F/F | B |
| HFP.63. | HSP.5,189/R. | HFP.5,190. | HFP.152. |

| | | | |
|---|---|---|---|
| 12 MARKE BLITZ 12 / 12 | MARQUE DEPOSEE B / U PARIS / 12 | MC 12 12 C A | M<sup>re F</sup> D'ARMES St ETIENNE 12 12 |
| 12 gauge. | 12 gauge. | 12 gauge. | 12 gauge. |
|  |  |  | 20, 16. |
|  | F | D | F/F |
| HFP.153. | HPF.154/R. | HSP.5,191. | HSP.5,192. |
| M.F 12 12 ST. ETIENNE | 12 M.G & C<sup>IE</sup> 12 PARIS | MOORE & GREY 12 LONDON | MOORE & GREY 12 LONDON |
| 12 gauge. | 12 gauge. | 12 gauge. Gnm. | 12 gauge. Gnm. |
|  |  |  |  |
| F/F | F/F | GBE | GBE |
| HFP.155. | HFP.156. | HSP.5,193/R. | HSP.5,194. |
| M<sup>re F<sup>se</sup></sup> D'ARMES DE ST ETIENNE 12 12 | MUNITIONS 12 12 M.G.M | MARQUI AU LION 10 | 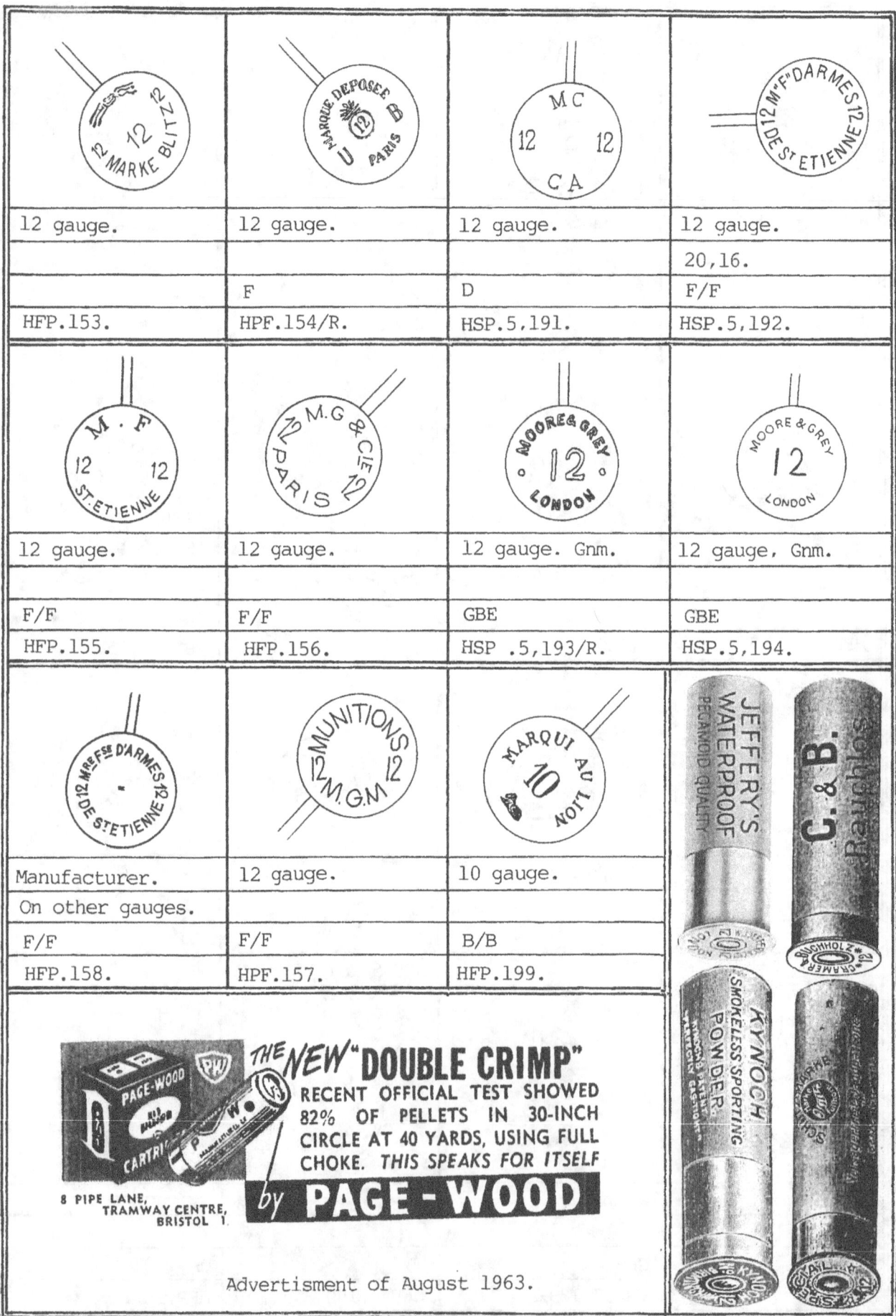 |
| Manufacturer. | 12 gauge. | 10 gauge. |  |
| On other gauges. |  |  |  |
| F/F | F/F | B/B |  |
| HFP.158. | HPF.157. | HFP.199. |  |

THE NEW "DOUBLE CRIMP"
RECENT OFFICIAL TEST SHOWED 82% OF PELLETS IN 30-INCH CIRCLE AT 40 YARDS, USING FULL CHOKE. THIS SPEAKS FOR ITSELF
by PAGE-WOOD
8 PIPE LANE, TRAMWAY CENTRE, BRISTOL 1

Advertisment of August 1963.

| | | | |
|---|---|---|---|
| NEWNHAM No 14 LANDPORT | NIMROD 16 | N ARQUE 12 AU LION | ND 12 |
| 14 gauge, Gnm. | 16 gauge. | 12 gauge. | 12 gauge. |
| GBE | D | B/B | |
| HFP.5,195. | HFP.64. | HFP.159. | HFP.5,196. |

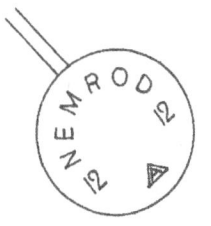

12 gauge.

HFP.160.

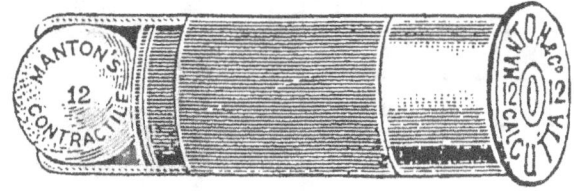

| | |
|---|---|
| 14 ØRN 14 | OAKES & Co MADRAS No 12 ELEY |
| 14 gauge. | 12 gauge. |
| | IND/GBE |
| HFP.89. | HFP.161. |

### LEFT HANDED CARTRIDGES

**After years of research and development we have produced the LEFT HANDED CARTRIDGE.**

Available only from the London Gun Co, in trap 7s or Skeet 9's at

**£75.00 per 1,000**

**WARNING:** These cartridges should only be used by LEFT HANDED PEOPLE

Phone 01-575 2934 ask for Doug Florent

Our club is at West End Road, Northolt just a few minutes from the shop

November, 1982

An advertisment from my scrap book.

| | | | |
|---|---|---|---|
| 20 gauge. | 16 gauge, Gnm. | 16 gauge. 12. | 16 gauge. |
| F/F | GBE | F/F | F/F |
| HFP.26. | HSP.5,197/R. | HFP.65. | HSP.5,198/R. |
| 16 gauge. | 16 gauge. | 12 gauge. 16. | 12 gauge. |
| I/I | | F/F | D |
| HFP.66. | HFP.67. | HFP.162. | HFP.163/R. |
| 12 gauge, Irm. | Gunsmith. | 12 gauge. | 12 gauge. |
| GBE | GBE | I/I | |
| HFP.164. | HFP.165. | HFP.166. | HFP.167. |
| 12 gauge, Gnm. | 12 gauge, Gnm. | | |
| GBE | GBE | | |
| HFP.168/R. | HFP.169/R. | | |

| | | | |
|---|---|---|---|
| R.W.S 16 16 GASDICHT | REILLY LONDON 14 G. | R.W.S ♥ ♥ 14 | RODON 12 |
| 16 gauge. | 14 gauge. | 14 gauge. | 12 gauge. |
| D/D | GBE | D/D | |
| HFP.68. | HSP.5,199. | HSP.5,200. | HFP.170. |
| ROWE No BARNSTAPLE 12 | R.W.S ♥ ♥ 12 | R.W.S. 12 GASDICHT 12 | R.W.S 8 |
| W.W. Rowe, Gnm. | Rheinische Westfalische Springstoff. | | 8 gauge. |
| GBE | D/D | D/D | D/D |
| HFP.5,201. | HFP.171. | HFP.172. | HFP.204. |

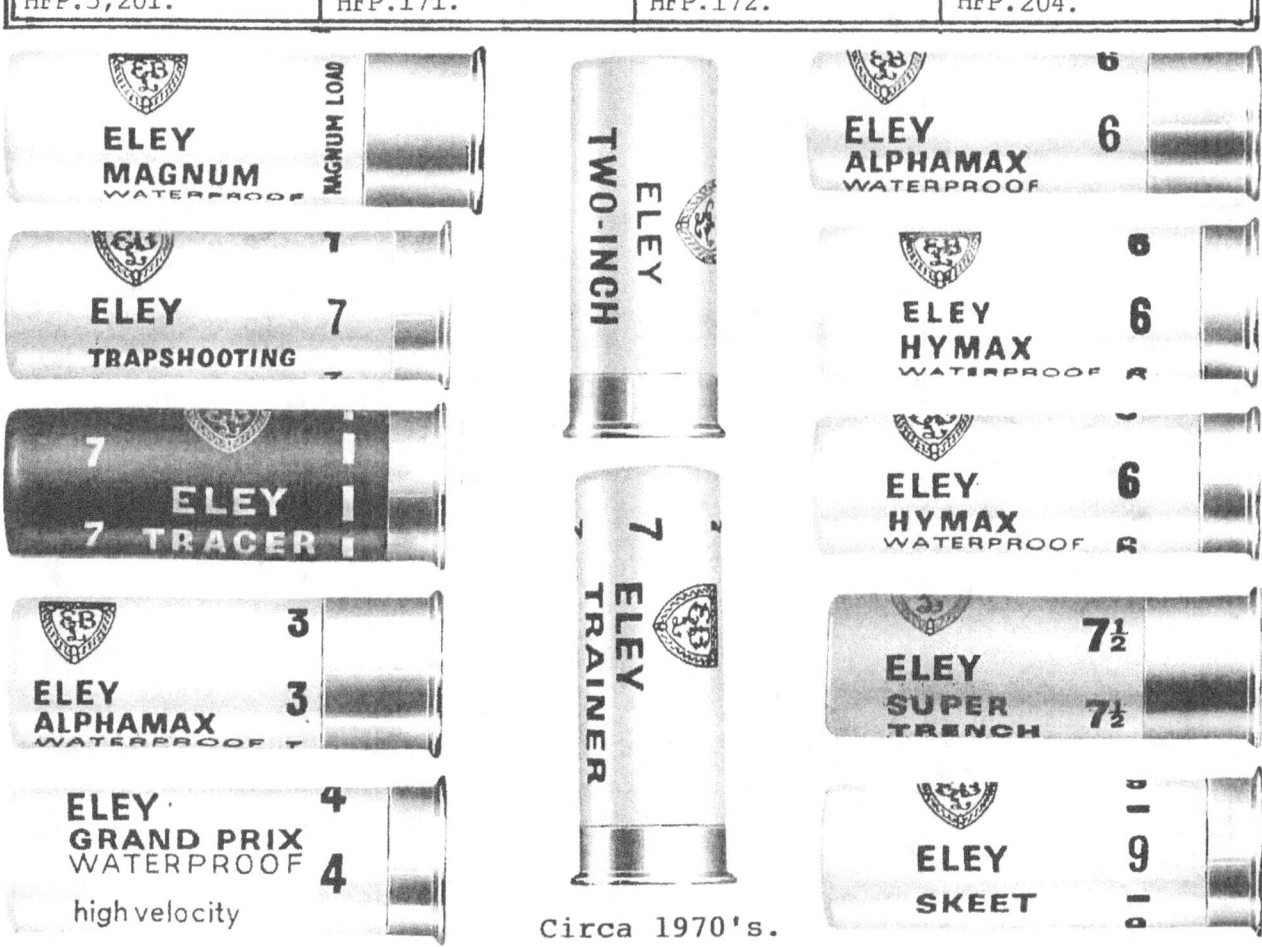

Circa 1970's.

27

| | | | |
|---|---|---|---|
| 14 mm. | Manufacturer. | 20 gauge. | 20 gauge. |
| | F/F | F | F |
| HFP.7/R. | HFP.5,427. | HSP.5,202. | HSP.5,203. |
| 20 gauge. | 18 gauge. | Manufacturer. | 18 gauge. |
| F/F | CS/CS | CS/CS | CS/CS |
| HSP.5,204. | HSP.5,205/R. | HSP.5,206. | HSP.5,209/R. |
| 16 gauge. | Manufacturer. | 16 gauge. | 14 gauge. |
| | | | 12. |
| | F/F | D | |
| HFP.70. | HFP.69. | HSP.5,208. | HSP.5,207. |
| 14 gauge. | 14 gauge. | 14 gauge. | 12 gauge. |
| | | | 14. |
| CS/CS | CS/CS | | |
| HFP.90. | HFP.91. | HFP.92. | HSP.5,210/R. |

| | | | |
|---|---|---|---|
| SELLIER & BELLOT 12 | SELLIER & BELLOT 12 | SHARLAND BROS. WELLINGTON No.12 ELEY | SPALE ARM 12 |
| 12 gauge. | Manufacturer. On other gauges. | 12 gauge. | 12 gauge. |
| CS/CS | CS/CS | NZ/GBE | |
| HSP.5,211. | HSP.5,212. | HSP.5,213. | HFP.173. |
| Ste Francse des MUNITIONS PARIS 12 12 | Ste Fse des MUNITIONS PARIS 12 12 | STENNER & Co. TIVERTON No.12 ELEY | STEPHEN GRANT 12 LONDON |
| 12 gauge. | Manufacturer. | | 12 gauge, Gnm. |
| F/F | F/F | GBE/GBE | GBE |
| HSP.5,214. | HFP.174. | HFP.175. | HSP.5,215/R. |
| 12 ST.ETIENNE 12 | SVEA 12 | SELLIER & BELLOT 8 | Ste Francse des MUNITIONS 32mm 32mm |
| 12 gauge. | 12 gauge. | 8 gauge. | 32 mm. |
| F/F | | CS/CS | F/F |
| HFP.176. | HFP.177. | HSP.5,216. | HFP.5,217. |

Circa 1970's.

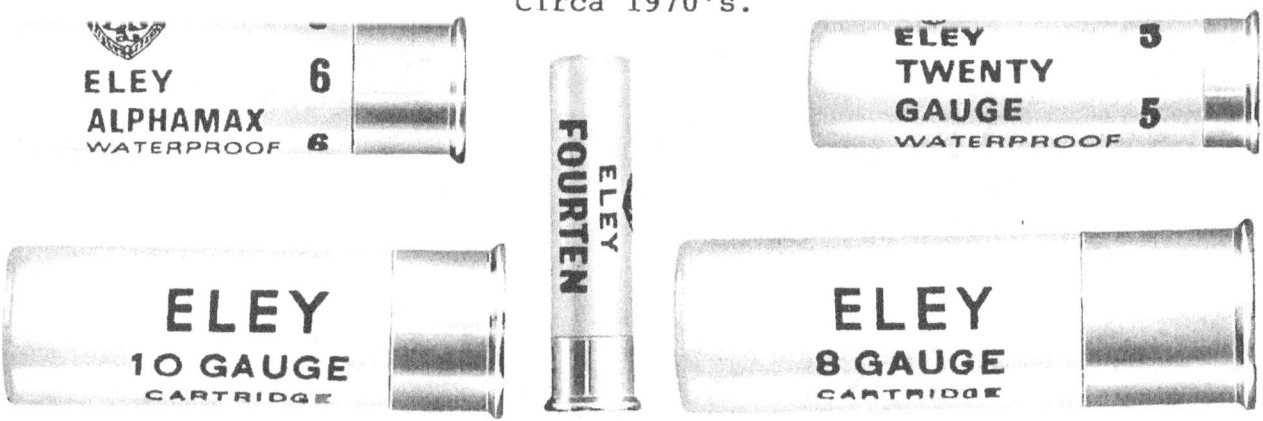

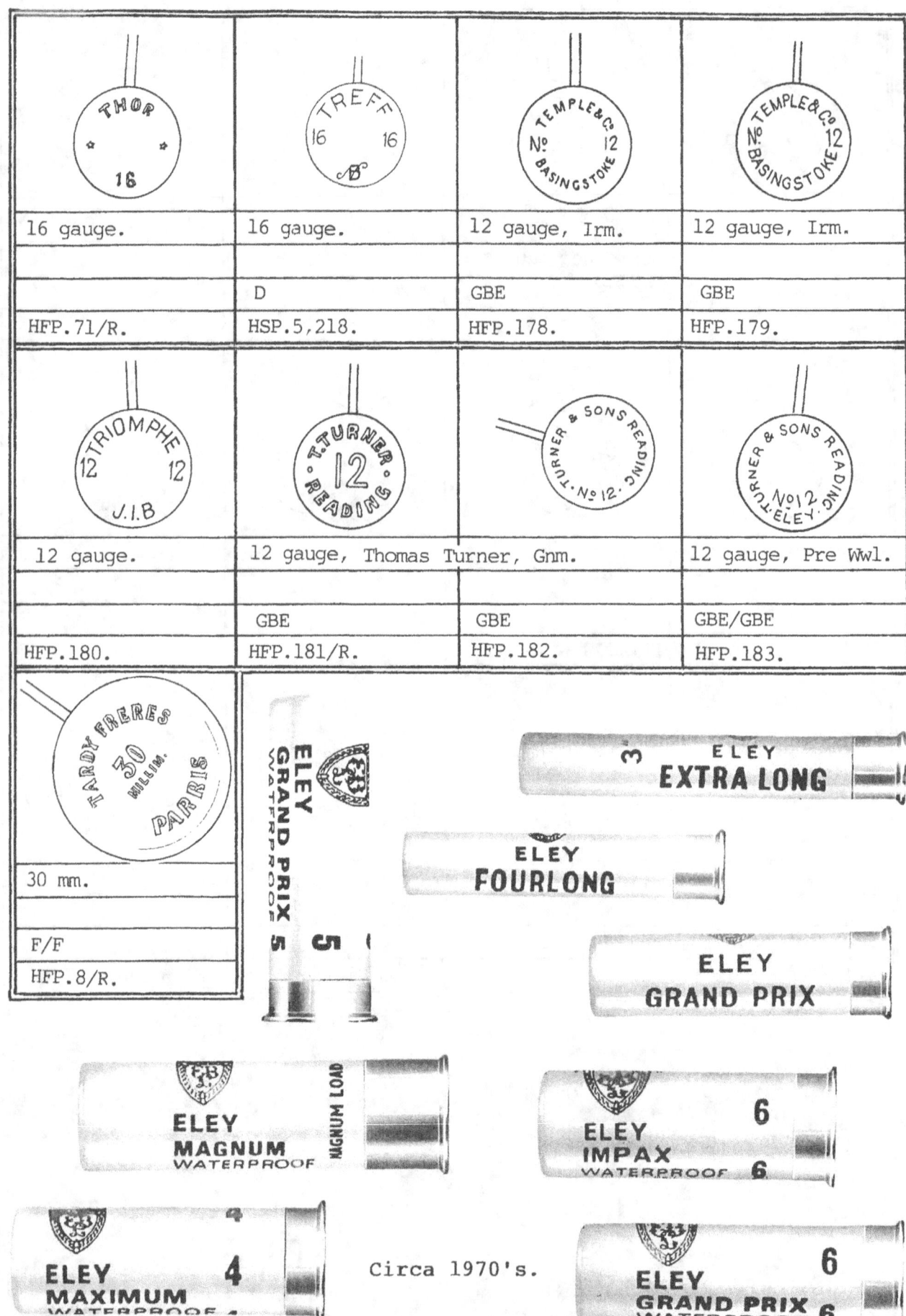

| | | | |
|---|---|---|---|
| 16 gauge. | 16 gauge. | 12 gauge, Irm. | 12 gauge, Irm. |
| | D | GBE | GBE |
| HFP.71/R. | HSP.5,218. | HFP.178. | HFP.179. |
| 12 gauge. | 12 gauge, Thomas Turner, Gnm. | | 12 gauge, Pre Wwl. |
| | GBE | GBE | GBE/GBE |
| HFP.180. | HFP.181/R. | HFP.182. | HFP.183. |
| 30 mm. | | | |
| F/F | | | |
| HFP.8/R. | | | |

Circa 1970's.

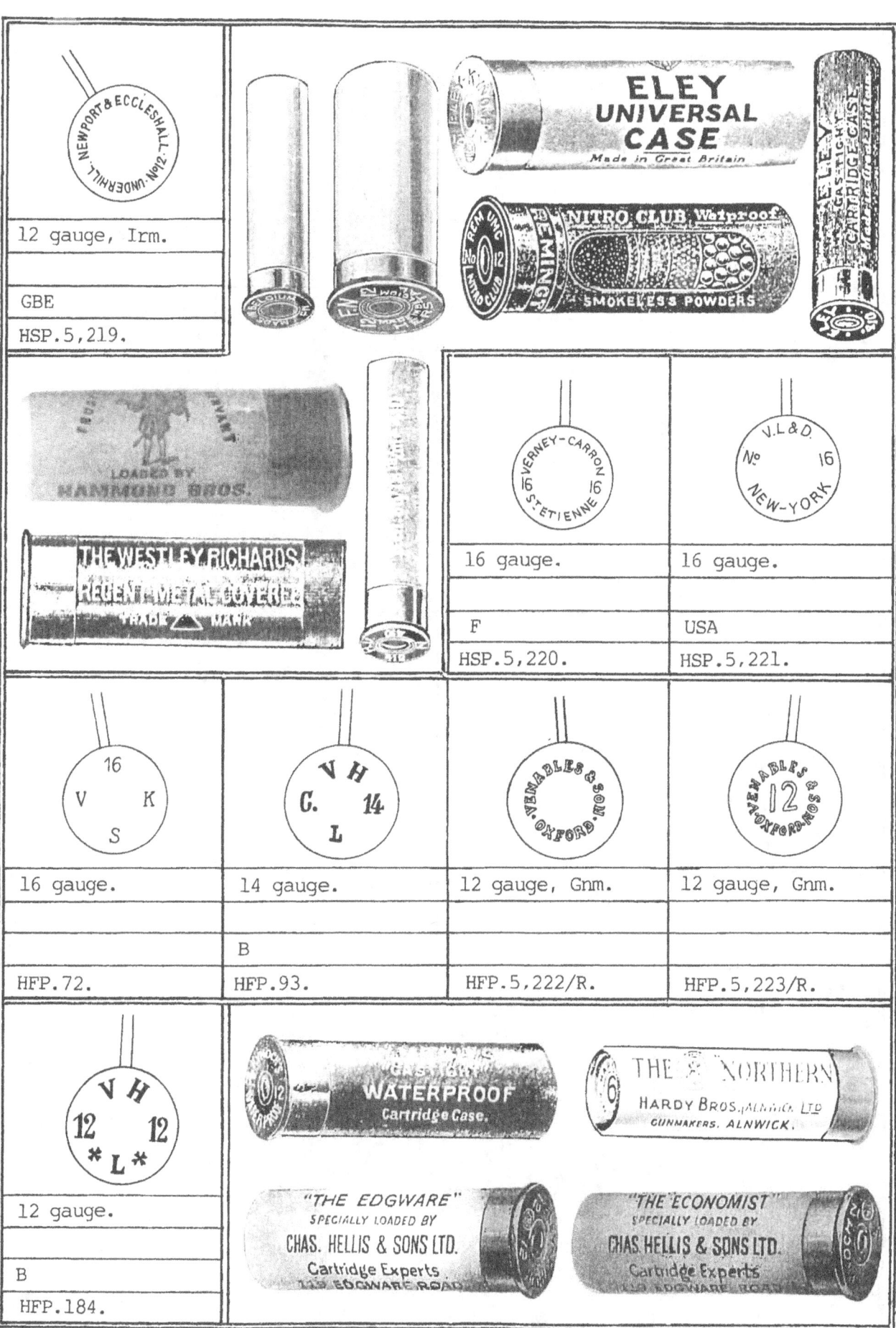

| | | | |
|---|---|---|---|
| WM 24 B | W.BURGESS.MALVERN WELLS | W.BURGESS.MALVERN WELLS.W.16.S | WM 16 16 |
| 24 gauge. | 16 gauge alarm gun. | 16 gauge, Irm. | 16 gauge. |
| | GBE | GBE | D |
| HFP.20. | HSP.5,224. | HSP.5,225. | HSP.5,226. |
| WM FABRIK BISCHWEILER | WM 16 FABRIK BISCHWEILER | WM | W.LEECH CHELMSFORD 12 |
| | | Believed 14 gauge. | |
| D | D | D | GBE |
| HSP.5,227. | HFP.73. | HFP.74. | HFP.185/R. |
| WM 12 B | W.M. FABRIK BISCHWEILER | WM 12 FABRIK BISCHWILLER | W.R.PAPE No 12 NEWCASTLE |
| 12 gauge. | Believed 12 gauge. | 12 gauge. | 12 gauge, Gnm. |
| D | D | D | GBE |
| HFP.186. | HFP.94. | HFP.187. | HSP.5,228. |
| W.R.PAPE No 12 ELEY NEWCASTLE | | | |
| Gnm, Eley case. | | | |
| GBE/GBE | | | |
| HSP.5,229. | | | |

| | | | |
|---|---|---|---|
| ·360 | ·410 | 12mm / ·410. 32, 28. | Pla.   ·410 |
| HFC.218. | HFC,2,243. | HFC.2,136. | HFC.2,244. |
| 12mm / ·410. | 12mm / ·410.  Pla. | 12mm / ·410.  Pla. | 12mm / ·410. |
| HSC.2,247. | HFC.2,246. | HFC.2,245. | HFC.219. |
| Remington Arms Co. USA | | | |
| HSC.2,242. | HFC.221. | HFC.222. | HFC.2,248. |
| | Pap. | | |
| HFC.2,249. | HFC.2,250. | HFC.2,238. | HSC.2,239. |

| | | | |
|---|---|---|---|
| P.C.C. | W.R.A.Co. | 14mm / 32 gauge. | 14mm / 32 gauge. |
| | | .410, 28 gauge. | |
| USA | USA | | |
| HSC.2,240. | HSC.2,241. | HFC.2,137. | HFC.240. |
| Pla. | Remington Arms Co. | W.R.A.Co. | 28 gauge. |
| | USA/USA | USA/USA | .410, 32 gauge. |
| HFC.2,251. | HSC.2,252. | HSC.2,253. | HCF.2,140 |
| | | | Remington Arms Co. |
| | | | USA/USA |
| D | | | |
| HSC.2,254. | HFC.247. | HSC.2,255. | HSC.2,256. |
| Pla. | | | |
| On other gauges. | On other gauges. | | |
| | | | D |
| HFC.2,257. | HFC.248. | HFC.246. | HSC.2,258. |

| | | | |
|---|---|---|---|
| ☆/24 mark | N° 24 mark | small circle | 20 mark |
| | | 20 gauge. | |
| | F | | D |
| HFC.269. | HSC.2,259. | HFC.274. | HSC.2,260. |
| 20 with stars | N° 20 with stars | 20 • 20 | 20 ☆ 20 ☆ |
| | | 16. | On other gauges. |
| | | D | |
| HFC.275. | HFC.276. | HSC.2,261. | HFC.277. |
| 20 ☆ 20 | 20/20/20 | 20/20/20 | 20☆20☆20 |
| | On other gauges. | On other gauges. | On other gauges. |
| HFC.2,262. | HFC.278. | HFC.279. | HFC.280. |
| N° 20 | N° 20 | N° 20 | N° 20 |
| | Remington Arms Co. | Remington Arms Co. | Remington Arms Co. |
| | On other gauges. | On other gauges. | |
| | USA | USA | USA |
| HFC.2,266. | HSC.2,263. | HSC.2,264. | HSC.2,265. |

| | | | |
|---|---|---|---|
| 18 gauge. | 18 gauge. | 16 gauge. | |
| | D | | D |
| HSC.2,267. | HSC.2,268. | HFC.2,269. | HSC.2270. |
| | | | |
| 20. | | | |
| D | | | |
| HSC.2271. | HFC.429. | HFC.430. | HFC.2,272. |
| | | | |
| Remington Arms Co. | Remington Arms Co. | | |
| On other gauges. | On other gauges. | | |
| USA | USA | | |
| HSC.2,273. | HSC.2274 | HFC.342. | HFC.431. |
| | | | |
| | On other gauges. | | On other gauges. |
| | | NZ | |
| HSC.2275. | HFC.434. | HSC.2276. | HFC.433. |

| | | | |
|---|---|---|---|
| (image) | (image) | (image) | (image) |
| On other gauges. | On other gauges. | | 12. |
| HSC.2,277. | HFC.2,278. | HSC.2,279. | HSC.2,280. |
| (image) | (image) | (image) | (image) |
| | | | 14 gauge. |
| | D | D | |
| HFC.2,281. | HSC.2,282. | HFC.435. | HFC.2,283. |
| (image) | (image) | (image) | (image) |
| | 12 gauge. | 12 gauge. | 12 ga. Circa 1875. |
| 24, 20, 18. | | | |
| D | | | |
| HSC.2,284. | HFC.637. | HFC.629. | HSC.2,285. |
| (image) | (image) | (image) | (image) |
| 12 ga. W.R.A.Co. | Confetti filled. Pla. | 12ga. Pla. Scare. | 12 gauge. Pla. |
| USA | USA | | |
| HSC.2,286. | HSC.2,287. | HFC.2,289. | HSC.2,288. |

37

| | | | |
|---|---|---|---|
| HFC.2,290. | HFC.639. | HFC.638. | HSC.2,291. |
| | | 20, 16.<br>D | |
| HSC.2,292. | HFC.2,293. | HSC.2,294. | HFC.646. |
| | | | |
| HFC.653. | HFC.644/R. | HFC.645/R. | HFC.630. |
| | | | |
| HFC.631. | HFC.2,154. | HFC.649. | HFC.647. |

| | | | |
|---|---|---|---|
| 12 ⊙ 12 | 12 ⊙ 12 | 12 ⊙ 12 | 12 ⊙ 12 |
| | | | |
| HFC.648. | HFC.650. | HFC.2,155. | HFC.652. |
| 12 ⊙ 12 | 12 ⊙ 12 | 12 ⊙ 12 | Nº ⊙ 12 |
| | Pla. | | |
| | | | USA |
| HFC.651. | HFC.654. | HSC.5,428. | HSC.2,295. |
| Nº ⊙ 12 | Nº ⊙ 12 | Nº ⊙ 12 | Nº ⊙ 12 |
| | | | |
| HFC.640. | HFC.641. | HFC.2,296. | HSC.2,297. |
| Nº ⊙ 12 | 12 ⊙ 12 | 12 ⊙ 12 | 12 ⊙ GA |
| Remington Arms Co. | | | |
| On other gauges. | | | |
| USA | | | |
| HFC.642. | HSC.2,298. | HFC.5,429. | HFC.633. |

| | | | |
|---|---|---|---|
| HFC.632. | HSC.2,299. | HFC.2,300. | HFC.655. |
| HFC.656. | HFC.657. | HFC.635. | HSC.2,301. |
| | | Pla. | Pla. |
| HFC.634. | HFC.659. | HFC.660. | HFC.658. |
| HFC.661. | HFC.662. | HFC.663. | HFC.664. |

| | | | |
|---|---|---|---|
| HFC.665. | HSC.2,302. | HFC.691. | HSC.2,303. |
| HFC.666. | HFC.667. | HFC.668. | HFC.669. |
| HFC.2,304. | HFC.671. | HFC.673. | HFC.672. |
| NZ<br>HSC.2,305. | HFC.670. | HFC.692. | Remington Arms Co.<br>On other gauges.<br>USA<br>HFC.2,306. |

41

| | | | |
|---|---|---|---|
| | | On other gauges. | On other gauges. | |
| HFC.2,307. | HFC.679. | HFC.680. | HFC.678. |
| | | | |
| HFC.675. | HFC.674. | HFC.676. | HFC.2,308. |
| | | | |
| HFC.687. | HFC.688. | HFC.2,309. | HFC.2,310. |
| | | | |
| HFC.693. | HFC.690. | HFC.689. | HFC.686. |

| | | | |
|---|---|---|---|
| | | | |
| | Pla. | | 12 gauge. |
| | | | |
| HFC.643. | HSC.2,311. | HFC.685. | HSC.2,312. |
| | | | |
| 12 gauge. | | Pla. | 12 gauge. |
| SU | | | |
| HSC.2,313. | HSC.2,314 | HFC.684. | HFC.682. |
| | | | |
| 12 gauge. | 12 gauge. | 12 gauge. | |
| | | | |
| HSC.2,315. | HFC.681. | HFC.683. | HSC.2,316. |
| | | | |
| | A.L.Howard. 10ga. | Coiled steel tube. | 10 gauge. |
| B | USA | | D |
| HSC.2,317. | HSC.2,318. | HSC.2,319. | HSC.2,320. |

| | | | |
|---|---|---|---|
| № ○ 10 | № ○ 10 | № ○ 10 | № ○ 10 |
| | 10 gauge. | 10 gauge. | Remington Arms Co. |
| | | | On other gauges. |
| USA | | | USA |
| HSC.2,326. | HSC.2,321. | HSC.2,322. | HSC.2,323. |
| № ○ 10 | № ○ 8 | № ○ 8 | |
| Remington Arms Co. | Abc. | | |
| | | On other gauges. | |
| USA | | USA | |
| HSC.2,324. | HSC.2,325. | HFC.2,097. | |
| ○ | | | |
| 4 gauge. Eng. | | | |
| Electric detonation | | | |
| HFE.2,114. | | | |

44

| | | | |
|---|---|---|---|
| (AB-LEIBNITZ 20) | (ACTIV 20) | (No 20 EAGLE) | (No 20 EAGLE) |
| | Apc. | Manufacturers. | Manufacturers. |
| | | 16, 12. | 16, 12. |
| | | USA/USA | USA/USA |
| HFC.281. | HFC.2,327. | HSC.2,328. | HSC.2,329. |
| (AGUILA 20 20 CDM) | (A.HAJI DOSSUL & SONS-KARACHI ELEY No 20) | (ALCAN 20 20) | (ALCAN 20 20 MADE IN ITALY INCORPORATED) |
| | | | |
| | | | |
| MEX | PAK/GBE | USA | USA/I |
| HSC.2,330. | HFC.282. | HFC.283. | HFC.284. |
| (ALFA 20 20) | (AMERICAN No 20 EAGLE) | (AMRON 20 GA G&W) | (ARROW 20 GA EXPRESS) |
| | Manufacturers. | | Remington Arms Co. |
| | 16, 12. | 12. | 16, 12. |
| D | USA/USA | USA | USA/USA |
| HSC.2,331. | HSC.2,332. | HSC.2,333. | HSC.2,334. |
| (ASHI-SEIKI 20 20 AOA) | (ALFA 18 18) | (A.B.C. No 16) | (A.C.CO. 16 GA ALERT) |
| | 18 gauge. | 16 gauge. | 16 gauge. |
| 16, 12. | | 12, 10. | 12, 10. |
| J | D | USA | USA |
| HFC.2,335. | HSC.2,336. | HSC.2,337. | HSC.2,338. |

45

| | | | |
|---|---|---|---|
| A.C.Co. 16 GA BANG | A.C.Co. 16 GA CRACK SHOT | A.C.Co. 16 GA CRACK SHOT | A.C.Co. 16 GA FLASH |
| Manufacturers. | Manufacturers. | Manufacturers. | Manufacturers. |
| 12, 10. | 12, 10. | 12, 10. | 12, 10. |
| USA | USA | USA | USA |
| HSC.2,339. | HSC.2,340. | HSC.2,341. | HSC.2,342. |
| A.C.Co. 16 GA FLASH | A. DE ARMEROS V 16 | A. DE ARMEROS 16 A 16 | ADLER-MARKE 16 |
| Manufcturers. | | | |
| 12, 10. | | | |
| USA | | | D |
| HSC.2,343. | HSC.2,344. | HSC.2,345. | HSC.2,346. |
| No 16 EAGLE | HAJI DOSSUL & SONS, KARACHI No 16 ELEY | A.H.RUTT.NORTHAMPTON 16 ELEY | ALCAN 16 16 MADE IN USA INCORPORATED |
| Manufacturers. | | Alfred Rutt. Gnm. | |
| 20, 12. | 15 ? | | |
| USA | PAK/GBE | GBE/GBE | USA/I |
| HSC.2,347. | HFC.436. | HSC.2,348. | HFC.437. |
| ALCAN 16 16 USA | ALFA 16 16 | ALTA 16 16 HIGH | AMERICAN No 16 EAGLE |
| Manufacturers. | | | Manufacturers. |
| | | | |
| USA/USA | D | MEX | USA/USA |
| HFC.2,349. | HSC.2,350. | HSC.2,351. | HFC.2,352. |

| | | | |
|---|---|---|---|
| (Army & Navy C.S.Ld Bombay No 16) | (Arthur Dennis Dunmow No 16) | (A.Sanders, Maidstone. Eley. No 16) | (Ashi-Seiki 16 16 AOA) |
| Dps. | | Gnm. | |
| | | | 20, 12. |
| IND | GBE | GBE/GBE | J |
| HSC.2,353. | HFC.438. | HFC.439. | HSC.2,354. |
| (Atkin No 16 Eley's Ejector) | (Austin 16 G Ct.ge Co.) | (Alfa 14 14) | (A.A.Hodgson No 12 Kynoch Louth) |
| Henry Atkin. Gnm. | Manufacturers. | 14 gauge. | |
| GBE/GBE | USA | D | GBE/GBE |
| HFC.440. | HSC.2,355. | HSC.2,356. | HFC.695. |
| (A.Allan No 12 Glasgow) | (A.Allan No 12 Glasgow) | (A.A.M.Co.Ld No 12 London) | (A.Barnes No 12 Ulverston) |
| Arthur Allan. Gnm. | Arthur Allan. Gnm. | | |
| GBS | GBS | GBE | GBE |
| HFC.696. | HFC.2,357. | HSC.2,358. | HFC.697. |
| (Abarto 12 12 Espana) | (A.B.C. No 12) | (A.B.C. No 12) | (A.B.C. No 12) |
| | Manufacturers. | Manufacturers. | Manufacturers. |
| | | | 16, 10. |
| E | USA | USA | USA |
| HFC.698. | HSC.2,359. | HSC.2,360. | HSC.2,361. |

47

| | | | |
|---|---|---|---|
| A.B.&C.CO. No 12 PAT.MAR.3-85 | A.B.&C.CO. No 12 | AB-LEIBNITZ 12 | ЗАВОД 12 56 АЗОТ |
| Manufacturers. | Manufacturers. | | Baikal. 1956. |
| USA | USA | | SU/SU |
| HSC.2,362. | HFC.2,363. | HFC.699. | HSC.2,364. |
| ЗАВОД 12 60 АЗОТ | ЗАВОД 12 61 АЗОТ | ЗАВОД 12 61 АЗОТ | A.B.WYLIE No 12 WARWICK |
| Baikal. 1960. | Baikal. 1961. | Baikal. 1961. | |
| SU/SU | SU/SU | SU/SU | GBE |
| HFC.694. | HSC.2,365. | HFC.2,366. | HFC.700. |
| ACCLES,LIMITED No 12 BIRMINGHAM | A.C.CO. 12 GA ADVANCE | A.C.CO. 12 GA ALERT | A.C.CO. 12 GA BANG |
| Manufacturers. | Austin Cartridge Co 16, 10. | Austin Cartridge Co 16, 10. | Austin Cartridge Co 16, 10 |
| GBE | USA | USA | USA |
| HFC.701. | HSC.2,367. | HSC.2,368. | HSC.2,369. |
| A.C.CO. 12 GA BANG | A.C.Co. No 12 CRACK SHOT | A.C.CO. 12 GA CRACK SHOT | A.C.CO. 12 GA FLASH |
| Austin Cartridge Co 16, 10. | Austin Cartridge Co 16, 10. | Austin Cartridge Co 16, 10. | Austin Cartridge Co 16, 10. |
| USA | USA | USA | USA |
| HSC.2,370. | HFC.2,371. | HSC.2,372. | HSC.2,373. |

| | | | |
|---|---|---|---|
| (A.C.CO. 12 GA INVINCIBLE) | (A.C.CO. 12 GA INVINCIBLE) | (A.C.CO. 12 GA RELIANCE) | (A.C.CO. 12 GA WINNER) |
| Austin Cartridge Co | Austin Cartridge Co | Austin Cartridge Co | Austin Cartridge Co |
| 16, 10. | | 16, 10. | |
| USA | USA | USA | USA |
| HSC.2,374. | HSC.2,375. | HSC.2,376. | HSC.2,377. |
| (A.CHAMBERLAIN.SALISBURY No12 ELEY) | (A.CHAMBERLAIN KYNOCH'S PATENT GROUSE EJECTOR No12 SALISBURY) | (ACME G.I.Co 12A) | (STANDARD 12A A.C.HOBBS PAT.OCT.31.76) |
| Arthur Chamberlain. | Gnm. Ejt. | | |
| GBE/GBE | GBE/GBE | | USA |
| HFC.702. | HFC.703. | HSC.2,378. | HSC.2,379. |
| (A.CONYERS BLANDFORD No12 ELEY) | (ACTIV 12) | (ACTIV·12·ACTIV·12·) | (ADAMS & Co. FINSBURY LONDON No12) |
| Gnm. | | | |
| GBE/GBE | | | GBE |
| HFC.704. | HFC.705. | HFC.706. | HFC.707. |
| (A DE ARMEROS 12 R 12) | (ADGEY & MURPHY FRENCH No 12 MADE CASE BELFAST) | (ADKIN & SONS BEDFORD No12 ELEY) | (ADLER-MARKE 12) |
| Apc. | | Gnm. | |
| | GBI/F | GBE/GBE | |
| HSC.2,380. | HFC.708. | HSC.2,381. | HFC.709. |

| | | | |
|---|---|---|---|
| (No 12 EAGLE) | (No 12 EAGLE) | (A.E.1301 INT.PAT.) | (A.E.RINGWOOD 12 12 BANBURY) |
| Manufacturers. | Manufacturers. | 12 gauge. | Gnm. |
| 20, 16. | 20, 16. | | |
| USA | USA | | GBE |
| HSC.2,382. | HSC.2,383. | HFC.710. | HFC.711. |
| (A.E.RINGWOOD 12 12 BANBURY) | (A.E.WARREN No 12 KYNOCH WINDSOR) | (A.F.PUNTER No 12 BASINGSTOKE) | (A.F.PUNTER No 12 BASINGSTOKE) |
| Gnm. | Gnm. | Arthur Punter. Irm. | Arthur Punter. Irm. |
| GBE/B | GBE/GBE | GBE | GBE |
| HFC.712. | HFC.713. | HFC.715. | HFC.714. |
| (A.F.SMITH No 12 HAILSHAM) | (AGNEW & SON EXETER No.12) | (AGNEW & SON No 12 ELEY EXETER) | (12 12 AGUILA) |
| A. Fisher Smith. | Gnm. | Gnm. | |
| GBE | GBE | GBE/GBE | MEX |
| HFC.716. | HFC.717. | HFC.718. | HFC.719. |
| (AGUILA 12 12 CDM) | (A.HILL No 12 HORNCASTLE) | (A HILL No 12 KYNOCH HORNCASTLE) | (A.H.KING.BALLARAT No12 ELEY) |
| | Arthur Hill. Gnm. | Arthur Hill. Gnm. | |
| 20. | | | |
| MEX | GBE | GB/GBE | AUS/GBE |
| HSC.2,384. | HFC.720. | HFC.2,156. | HFS.2,385. |

| | | | |
|---|---|---|---|
| (A.H.RUTT.NORTHAMPTON No12 ELEY) | (A.J.DUKES.RUGBY No12 ELEY) | (A.J.JEWSON No12 KYNOCH HALIFAX) | (A.J.RUDD.NORWICH No12 ELEY) |
| Alfred H. Rutt. Gnm | | Gnm, outfitters. | Gnm. |
| GBE/GBE | GBE/GBE | GBE/GBE | GBE/GBE |
| HSC.2,386. | HFC.721. | HFC.722. | HSC.2,387. |
| (A.J.RUSSELL&SONS No12 KYNOCH MAIDSTONE) | (AKRILL No12 BEVERLEY) | (ALASKAN 12 GA CARTRIDGE) | (ALASKAN 12 GA CARTRIDGE B) |
| Gnm. | H.Esau Akrill. Gnm. | | Pla. |
| GBE/GBE | GBE | USA | USA |
| HFC.723. | HSC.2,388. | HSC.2,389. | HSC.2,390. |
| (ALCAN 12 12) | (ALCAN 12 12 ALCAN) | (ALCAN MADE IN USA 12 12 ALCAN) | (ALCAN 12 USA) |
| Manufacturers. | Manufacturers. 20. | Manufacturers. | Manufacturers. |
| USA | USA | USA | USA |
| HFC.2,391. | HFC.2,392. | HFC.725. | HSC.2,393. |
| (ALCAN 12 USA) | (ALCAN 12 12 INCORPORATED) | (ALCAN MADE IN USA 12 12 INCORPORATED) | (ALCAN MADE IN USA 12 12 INCORPORATED) |
| Manufacturers. | Post Ww2. | Manufacturers. | Manufacturers. |
| USA | USA | USA | USA |
| HFC.2,394. | HFC.724. | HFC.726. | HSC.2,395. |

| | | | |
|---|---|---|---|
| ALCAN MADE IN USA 12 12 TARGETMAX | ALCAN 12 12 USA | ALCAN 12 12 USA | ALCAN 12 12 MADE IN ITALY INCORPORATED |
| Manufacturers. | Manufacturers. | Manufacturers. | Manufacturers. |
|  | 16. |  | 20, 16. |
| USA | USA | USA | I |
| HSC.2,396. | HSC.2,397. | HSC.2,398. | HSC.2,399. |
| ALCOCK & PIERCE No 12 MELBOURNE | ALCOCK & PIERCE No 12 ELEY MELBOURNE | ALCOCK & PIERCE No 12 KYNOCH MELBOURNE | ALCOCK & PIERCE ELEY No 12 LONDON MELBOURNE |
|  |  |  |  |
| AUS | AUS/GBE | AUS/GBE | AUS/GBE |
| HSC.2,400. | HSC.2,401. | HFC.727. | HFC.728. |
| ALCOCK & PIERCE PTY LTD MELBOURNE 12 | ALCOCK & PIERCE PTY LTD MADE IN GERMANY MELBOURNE 12 | ALDER-MARKE 12 | A.LECLERCQ 12 12 COUVIN |
|  |  |  |  |
| AUS | AUS/D | D | B |
| HSC.2,402. | HSC.2,403. | HSC.2,404. | HCS.2,405. |
| ALFA 12 12 | A.L.H No 12 | A.L.H No 12 | A.L.HOWARD No 12 NEWHAVEN CT |
|  | A. L. Howard. | A. L. Howard. | Manufacturers. |
| D | USA | USA | USA |
| HSC.2,406. | HSC.2,407. | HSC.2,408. | HSC.2,409. |

| | | | |
|---|---|---|---|
| (ALMA 12 12) | (ALTHAM & SON. PENRITH. No.12. ELEY.) | (Am.C&A.Co 12 GA * No 40 *) | (AM.C.&A.CO 12 GA * No 45 *) |
| | Pre-Ww1. | Manufacturers. | Manufacturers. |
| | | | |
| | GBE/GBE | USA | USA |
| HSC.2,410. | HFC.5,430. | HSC.2,411. | HFC.2,412. |
| (AMERIA MASINA 12 12 CARACUS) | (AMERICAN 12 GA EAGLE) | (AMERICAN No 12 EAGLE) | (AMERICAN No 12 EAGLE) |
| | Manufacturers. | Manufacturers. | Larger cap. |
| | | 20, 16. | |
| YV | USA/USA | USA/USA | USA/USA |
| HSC.2,413. | HFC.2,157. | HSC.2,414. | HSC.2,415. |
| (AMERICAN 12 GA EAGLE) | (AMERICAN No 12 EAGLE) | (AMERICAN JACK No 12 RABBIT) | (AMERICAN No 12 STANDARD) |
| Manufacturers. | Manufacturers. | | |
| | | | |
| USA/USA | USA/USA | USA/USA | USA/USA |
| HSC.2,416. | HSC.2,417. | HSC.2,418. | HSC.2,419. |
| (AMER ROCK 12 12 EXPRESS) | (AMER.ROCK 12 12 EXPRESS) | (AMER ROCK 12 12 EXPRESS) | (AMER ROCK 12 12 EXPRESS) |
| | | | |
| | | | |
| USA | USA | USA | USA |
| HFC.2,420. | HSC.2,421. | HFC.2,422. | HSC.2,423. |

| | | | |
|---|---|---|---|
| AMER ROCK EXPRESS 12 | AMMO-HOUSE No 12 | AMRON 12 GA GW | AMRON 12 GA G&W |
| | | | 20. |
| USA | NZ | USA | USA |
| HFC.730. | HSC.2,424. | HSC.2,425. | HSC.2,426. |
| A.&N.C.S.L? No 12 BOMBAY | A.&N.C.S.L? No 12 BOMBAY | A.&N.C.S.L. No 12 LONDON | A.&N.C.S.L. No 12 LONDON |
| Dps, Gnm. | Dps, Gnm. | Dps, Gnm. | Dps, Gnm. |
| IND | IND | GBE | GBE |
| HFC.732. | HFC.731. | HFC.733. | HSC.2,427. |
| A.&N.C.S.L? No 12 KARACHI | A.&N.C.S.L? ELEY No12 LONDON | A.&N.C.S.LTD No12 ELEY | A.&N.C.S.LTD No 12 KYNOCH |
| Dps, Gnm. | Dps, Gnm. | Dps, Gnm. | Dps, Gnm. |
| PAK | GBE/GBE | GBE/GBE | GBE/GBE |
| HFC.2,158. | HFC.734. | HSC.2,428. | HFC.735. |
| ANGLIA CARTRIDGE Co. 12 | ANGLIA CARTRIDGE Co. 12 | FRANCE·ARMES 12 | ARMSTRONG & Co. NEWCASTLE No12 |
| Manufacturers. | Manufacturers 16. | | |
| GBE | GBE | F | GBE |
| HFC.737. | HFC.736. | HFC.738. | HFC.739. |

| | | | |
|---|---|---|---|
| (Armstrong & Co Newcastle-upon-Tyne 12) | (Armstrong & Co Newcastle-upon-Tyne 12) | (Armstrong Eley No 12 Newcastle-on-Tyne) | (Armstrong Newcastle Eley No 12) |
| Dps. | Dps. | Dps. | Dps. |
| | | | 16. |
| GBE | GBE | GBE/GBE | GBE/GBE |
| HFC.740. | HFC.2,429. | HFC.741 | HFC.2,430. |
| (Armstrong Newcastle-on-Tyne Eley No 12) | (Armstrong's Pressure Reducing Case Kynoch No 12) | (Armstrong & Co Recoil Reducing Newcastle-upon-Tyne 12) | (Armunit-S 12) |
| Dps. | Dps. | Dps. | |
| | | | |
| GBE/GBE | GBE/GBE | GBE | |
| HSC.2,431. | HFC.742. | HFC.743. | HFC.744. |
| (Armuriers Professionnels 12) | (Armuriers Professionels 12) | (12 Armuriers 12 Professionnels) | (Armusa 12 12 Armusa) |
| | Pla. | | |
| | | | E |
| HFC.745. | HSC.2,432. | HFC.746. | HFC.747. |
| (Armusa 12 12 Armusa) | (Armusa 12 12 Spain) | (Army & Navy C.S.Ld Eley No 12) | (Army & Navy C.S.Ld No 12 Eley London) |
| | | Dps. Gnm. | Dps, Gnm. |
| | | | |
| E | E | GBE/GBE | GBE/GBE |
| HFC.748. | HFC.749. | HSC.2433. | HSC.2,434. |

| | | | |
|---|---|---|---|
| ARMY & NAVY C.S. Ld No 12 ELEY BOMBAY | ARMY & NAVY C.S. Ld No 12 ELEY BOMBAY | ARMY & NAVY C.S. Ld No 12 ELEY BOMBAY | ARMY & NAVY C.S. Ltd No 12 ELEY |
| Dps, Gnm. | Dps, Gnm. | Dps, Gnm. | Dps, Gnm. |
| | 16. | | |
| IND/GBE | IND/GBE | IND/GBE | GBE/GBE |
| HSC.2,435. | HSC.2,436. | HSC.2,444. | HFC.750. |
| ARMY & NAVY C.S. Ld No 12 LONDON | ARMY & NAVY C.S. Ld No 12 LONDON | ARMY & NAVY C.S. Ld No 12 LONDON | ARMY & NAVY STORES LONDON No 12 ELEY |
| Dps, Gnm. | Dps, Gnm. | Dps, Gnm. | Dps, Gnm. |
| | | | |
| GBE | GBE | GBE | GBE/GBE |
| HFC.751. | HSC.2,437. | HSC.2,438. | HFC.2,439. |
| ARROW 12 GA EXPRESS | ARTHUR ALLAN No 12 GLASGOW | ARTHUR ALLAN No 12 GLASGOW | ARTHUR DENNIS No 12 DUNMOW |
| Remington Arms Co. | Gnm. | Gnm. | |
| | | | |
| USA | GBS | GBS | GBE |
| HFC.752. | HSC.2,440 | HFC.753. | HFC.2,441. |
| ARTHUR TURNER SHEFFIELD No 12 | ARTHUR TURNER No 12 SHEFFIELD | ASAHI 12 12 SKB | ASAHI 12 12 SKB |
| Gnm. | Gnm. | | |
| | | | |
| GBE | GBE | | |
| HFC.2,442. | HSC.2,443. | HFC.754. | HFC.755. |

| | | | |
|---|---|---|---|
| A.SANDERS.MAIDSTONE No 12 ELEY | ASHI-SEIKI 12 12 AOA | A.T.FITCHEW No 12 RAMSGATE | ATKIN.2.JERMYN ST.S.W. No 12 ELEY |
| Gnm. | Also Fwk. 20, 16. | | Gnm. |
| GBE/GBE | J | GBE | GBE/GBE |
| HSC.2,445. | HSC.2,446. | HFC.756. | HFC.757. |
| ATKIN.2.JERMYN ST.S.W. No 12 ELEY | ATKIN.41.JERMYN ST.S.W. No 12 ELEY | ATKIN.41.JERMYN ST.S.W. No 12 ELEY | ATKINSON & GRIFFIN.KENDAL No 12 ELEY |
| Gnm. 16. | Gnm | Gnm. | |
| GBE/GBE | GBE/GBE | GBE/GBE | GBE/GBE |
| HFC.2.159. | HFC.758. | HFC.759. | HSC.2,447. |
| ATKINSON No 12 LANCASTER | ATKINSON No 12 ELEY LANCASTER | No. ATKINSON 12 LANCASTER&KENDAL | No ATKINSON 12 LANCASTER&KENDAL |
| Gnm. | Gnm. | Gnm. | Gnm. |
| GBE | GBE/GBE | GBE | GBE |
| HFC.2,448. | HFC.761. | HFC.760. | HFC.762. |
| ATKINSON 12 ELEY LANCASTER&KENDAL | AUBREY LEWIS 12 12 LUTON | AUBREY LEWIS 12 12 LUTON | AUBREY LEWIS CASE MADE IN 12 BELGIUM 12 LUTON |
| Gnm. | Gnm. | Gnm. | Gnm. |
| GBE/GBE | GBE | GBE | GBE/B |
| HFC.763. | HFC.764. | HFC.2,449. | HFC.765. |

| | | | |
|---|---|---|---|
| (A.U.DUKES.RUGBY No.12 ELEY) | (AURE LE PAGE F.DUMOND Sen 12 PARIS 12) | (AUSTIN 12 G CT'GE CO.) | (AUSTIN No 12 CT'GE CO.) |
| | Gnm. | Manufacturers. | Manufacturers. |
| | | | 10. |
| GBE/GBE | F | USA | USA |
| HFC.766. | HFC.2,160. | HSC.2,450. | HSC.2,451. |
| (AUSTIN'S No 12 EXTRA SPECIAL) | (AUSTIN'S No 12 EXTRA SPECIAL) | (12 GA AUSTRALIA) | (AUTOCRAT 12 12 R.H.A.CO) |
| Manufacturers. | Manufacturers. | Winchester AUS Pty | Robin Hood. |
| USA | USA | AUS/AUS | USA |
| HSC.2,452. | HFC.2,161. | HFC.767. | HFC.768. |
| (AUTOMATIC 12 12 R.H.A.CO) | (AUTOMATIC 12 12 R.H.A.CO) | (AUTOMATIC No 12 EJECTOR) | (AUTOMATIC No 12 EJECTOR) |
| Robin Hood. | Robin Hood. | | |
| USA | USA | | |
| HSC.2,453. | HSC.2,454. | HSC.2,455. | HSC.2,456. |
| (AVERILL & SON No 12 EVESHAM) | (AVORENKAMP 12 12 GRONINGEN) | (LOADED IN LONDON FOR A.W.GAMAGE CO CASE MADE IN GERMANY No 12 HOLBORN.E.C.) | (AZOT 12 12 MADE IN USSR) |
| | | Dps. | Baikal. |
| GBE | | GBE | SU/SU |
| HFC.769. | HFC.770. | HFC.771. | HFC.773. |

| | | | |
|---|---|---|---|
| Baikal. | Baikal. | Baikal. 1961. | Baikal. 1961. |
| SU/SU | SU/SU | SU/SU | SU/SU |
| HFC.774. | HSC.2,457. | HFC.2,458. | HSC.2,459. |
| Baikal. 1963. | Baikal. 1964. | Baikal. 1966. | Baikal. 1968. |
| SU/SU | SU/SU | SU/SU | SU/SU |
| HFC.772. | HSC.2,460. | HFC.775. | HSC.2,461. |
| Baikal. 1968. | Baikal. 1970. | Baikal. 1970. | 10 gauge. |
| SU/SU | SU/SU | SU/SU | USA |
| HFC.2,462. | HSC.2,463. | HSC.2,464. | HFC.2,465. |
| Manufacturer. | Manufacturer. | 10 gauge. | Manufacturer. |
| USA | USA | USA | USA |
| HSC.2,466. | HSC.2,467. | HFC.2,468. | HSC.2,469. |

| | | | |
|---|---|---|---|
| A.B.C. No 10 | A.B.C. No 10 | A B C No 10 | A.B.C. No 10 |
| Manufacturer. | Manufacturer. | Manufacturer. | Manufacturer. |
| | | | |
| USA | USA | USA | USA |
| HSC.2,470. | HSC.2,471. | HSC.2,472. | HSC.2,473. |
| A.B.C. No 10 | A.B.C. No 10 | A.C.CO. 10 GA BANG | A.C.CO. 10 GA BANG |
| Manufacturer. | Manufacturer. | Manufacturer. | Manufacturer. |
| | | 16, 12. | 16, 12. |
| USA | USA | USA | USA |
| HSC.2,474. | HSC.2,475. | HSC.2,476. | HSC.2,477. |
| A.C.CO. 10 GA FLASH | A.C.CO. 10 GA INVINCIBLE | A.C.CO. 10 GA KRACKSHOT | ACME G.I.CO. 10 A |
| Manufacturer. | Manufacturer. | Manufacturer. | |
| 16. 12. | | | |
| USA | USA | USA | USA |
| HSC.2,478. | HSC.2,479. | HSC.2,480. | HSC.2,481. |
| ACME S.I.CO. 10 A | ALCAN MADE IN USA 10 10 ALCAN | ALFA 10 10 | A.L.H No 10 |
| | Manufacturer. | | A. L. Howard. |
| | | | |
| USA | USA | D | USA |
| HSC.2,482. | HFC.2,483. | HSC.2,484. | HFC.2,485. |

| | | | |
|---|---|---|---|
| Manufacturer. | Manufacturer. | | Remington Arms Co. |
| | | | 20, 16, 12. |
| USA | USA | USA | USA |
| HSC.2,486. | HSC.2,487. | HSC.2,488. | HSC.2,489. |
| Manufacturer. | Manufacturer. | 4 gauge. | |
| | | | |
| USA | USA | USA | |
| HSC.2,490. | HSC.2,491. | HSC.2,492. | |

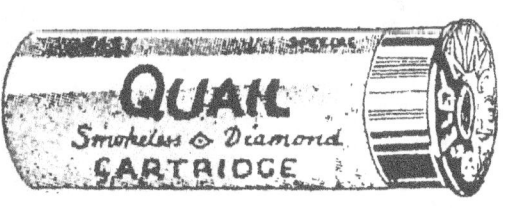

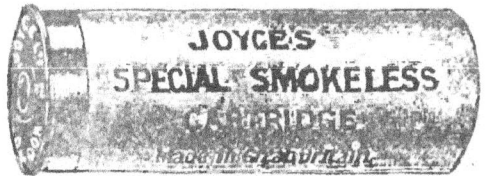

| | | | |
|---|---|---|---|
| .410 | .410 | 20 gauge. | 20 gauge. |
| | | | |
| CDN or B | CDN or B | B | CDN or B |
| HSC.2,493. | HSC.2,494. | HSC.2,495. | HFC.285. |
| 20 gauge. | 18 gauge. | 18 gauge. | 16 gauge. |
| D | D | D | I |
| HSC.2,564. | HFC.423. | HSC.2,496. | HSC.2,497. |
| Gnm. | 16 gauge. | 16 gauge. | Gordon Cartridge Co |
| GBE/GBE | D | D | AUS |
| HSC.2,498. | HFC.2,499. | HSC.2,500. | HSC.2,501. |
| | | 12 gauge. | 12 gauge. |
| | 12. | | |
| | D | B | B |
| HSC.2,502. | HSC.2,503. | HFC.776. | HSC.2,504. |

| | | | |
|---|---|---|---|
| BACHMANN BRUXELLES No. 12 | BACHMANN BRUXELLES 12 12 | BAIKAL 12 12 MADE IN USSR | BAIKAL 12 12 MADE IN USSR |
| 12 gauge. | 12 gauge. | Manufacturer. | Manufacturer. |
| B | B | SU/SU | SU/SU |
| HFC.2,505. | HFC.2,506. | HSC.2,507. | HFC.779. |
| BAIKAL 12 12 MADE IN USSR | BAIKAL 12 12 65 | BAILEY No12 GAS-LEAK-PROOF | BAKER No 12 DARLINGTON |
| Manufacturer. | Manufacturer. | | |
| SU/SU | SU/SU | | GBE |
| HFC.778. | HFC.777. | HFC.780. | HFC.781. |
| BAKER KYNOCH'S PATENT GROUSE No 2090 No 12 LONDON | BAKER STEEL CONE 12 G | BAKER & Co. 12 | BALLS BROS No 12 NEWTON ABBOT |
| Ejt. | | | Irm. |
| | 10. | 10. | |
| GBE/GBE | USA | USA | GBE |
| HFC.782. | HSC.2,508. | HSC.2,509. | HFC.783. |
| BALMFORTH, ORMSKIRK. No 12 ELEY | BARNARD & LEVET No C.H.M.C. 12 LICHFIELD | BARNES No 12 CALNE | BARRATT No 12 BURTON ON TRENT |
| Engineers, Irm. | | Irm. Kynoch case. | |
| GBE | GBE/GBE | GBE/GBE | GBE |
| HFC.784. | HFC.785. | HFC.786. | HSC.2,510. |

63

| | | | |
|---|---|---|---|
| (BARRATT BURTON ON TRENT No.12 ELEY) | (BARTRAM BRAINTREE No ELEY 12) | (Pellagri 12 baschieri &) | (Apc. 12 gauge) |
| | George T. Gnm. | | Apc. 12 gauge, |
| | | | |
| GBE/GBE | GBE | | |
| HFC.2,511. | HSC.2,512. | HFC.787. | HFC.788. |
| (12 BB) | (BEAUX MILANO 12 12) | (BEAUX MILANO 12 12) | (BEESLEY LONDON No12 ELEY) |
| | | | Gnm. |
| | | I | GBE/GBE |
| HFC.789. | HFC.790. | HSC.2,565. | HSC.2,162. |
| (BEESLEY No 12 ELEY LONDON) | (BEESLEY KYNOCH'S PATENT GROUSE No 2080 LONDON 12) | (B.E.L.L. No 12) | (BEST No 12) |
| Gnm. | Gnm. Ejt. | | |
| | | | 10. |
| GBE/GBE | GBE/GBE | USA | USA |
| HSC.2,566. | HFC.792. | HFC.2,567. | HFC.2,568. |
| (BIRDFRITE) | (BISLEY 12 12 BISLEY) | (BISLEY 12 12 BISLEY) | (B&J.V.COULTAS No 12 GRANTHAM) |
| 12 gauge. | | | |
| | | | |
| AUS | GBE | GBE | GBE |
| HSC.2,569. | HFC.793. | HFC.794 | HFC.796. |

| | | | |
|---|---|---|---|
| B.&J.V.COULTAS Nº12 GRANTHAM | BLANCH & SON. LONDON Nº 12 | Nº BLANCH&SON 12 LONDON | BLANCH&SON.LONDON Nº12 ELEY |
| | Gnm. | Gnm. | |
| GBE | GBE | GBE | GBE/GBE |
| HFC.795. | HSC.2,570. | HFC.797. | HSC.2,571. |
| Nº BLAND & SONS 12 LONDON | BLAND & SONS 12 12 LONDON | BLITZ 12 12 BLITZ | BLUE CHEST Nº 12 |
| Gnm. | Gnm. | | |
| GBE | GBE | | USA |
| HSC.2,572. | HSC.2,573. | HFC.798. | HSC.2,574. |
| BLUE RIVAL 12 12 | BLUE RIVAL 12 12 | BLUE SEAL 12 12 SMOKELESS | BLUE SEAL 12 12 SMOKELESS |
| | | | |
| GBE | GBE | AUS | AUS |
| HSC.2,575. | HFC.2,576. | HSC.2,577. | HSC.2,578. |
| BMD 12 | B.MEGGINSON Nº 12 ATHERSTONE | BOMBRINI-PARODI-DELFINO ROMA 12 | BOND THETFORD Nº12 ELEY |
| | | Pla. | Gnm. |
| D | GBE | I | GBE/GBE |
| HSC.2,579. | HFC.2,580. | HSC.2,581. | HFC.2,163. |

| | | | |
|---|---|---|---|
| BOND & SON No 12 THETFORD | BOND & SON, THETFORD No 12 ELEY | BOND & SON No 12 ELEY THETFORD | BOND & SON No 12 ELEY THETFORD |
| Gnm. | Gnm. | Gnm. | Gnm. |
| GBE | GBE/GBE | GBE/GBE | GBE/GBE |
| HFC.799. | HSC.2,582. | HFC.800. | HFC.801. |
| BOREHAM No 12 COLCHESTER | BORNACHI 12 12 ITALY | BORNAGHI 12 12 ITALY | BOSS LONDON No 12 |
| Field sports. | | | Gnm. |
| GBE | I | I | GBE |
| HFC.802. | HFC.803. | HFC.804. | HSC.2,583. |
| BOSS LONDON No 12 | BOSS No 12 LONDON | BOSS LONDON No 12 | BOSS & Co No 12 LONDON |
| Gnm. | Gnm. | Gnm. | Gnm. |
| GBE | GBE | GBE | GBE |
| HFC.2,584. | HFC.805. | HFC.2,585. | HFC.806. |
| BOSS & Co No 12 LONDON | BOSS & Co LONDON No 12 ELEY | BOSS & Co LONDON No 12 ELEY | BOSS & Co No 12 LONDON |
| Gnm. | Gnm. | Gnm. | Gnm. |
| GBE | GBE/GBE | GBE/GBE | GBE/GBE |
| HFC.807. | HFC.2,164. | HFC.808. | HFC.809. |

| | | | |
|---|---|---|---|
| (headstamp) | (headstamp) | (headstamp) | (headstamp) |
| Gnm. Cancelation. | Gnm. Ejt. | Gnm. Ejt. | |
| GBE/GBE | GBE/GBE | GBE/GBE | I |
| HFC.810. | HFC.811. | HFC.2,586. | HFC.812. |
| (headstamp) | (headstamp) | (headstamp) | (headstamp) |
| | | Gnm. | Gnm. |
| I | I | GBI | GBI |
| HFC.813. | HFC.814. | HFC.815. | HSC.2,587. |
| (headstamp) | (headstamp) | (headstamp) | (headstamp) |
| Gnm. | Gnm. | Gnm. | |
| GBI/GBE | GBE/GBE | GBI/F | GBS |
| HFC.2,588. | HSC.2,589. | HSC.2,590. | HSC.2,591. |
| (headstamp) | (headstamp) | (headstamp) | (headstamp) |
| Pla. | Pla. | | |
| | USA | | GBE |
| HSC.2,592. | HSC.2,593. | HFC.816. | HFC.2,594. |

| | | | |
|---|---|---|---|
| (BRITISH MADE LONDON 12 12) | (BRITISH MADE LONDON 12 12) | (BRITISH MAKE 12 12) | (BROWN No 12 MORPETH) |
| Cogswell & Harrison | Cogswell & Harrison | | |
| GBE/GBE | GBE/GBE | GBE | GBE |
| HFC.818. | HFC.817. | HFC.819. | HFC.820. |
| (BROWN No 12 MORPETH) | (BROWNING 12 12 BROWNING) | (BRUNDLE HOBART No12 ELEY) | (BSA 12) |
| | Manufacturer. On other gauges. | | Post Ww2. Gnm. |
| GBE | CDN | ?/GBE | GBE |
| HFC.821. | HFC.823. | HSC.2,595. | HFC.825. |
| (BUFFALO MADE IN USA 12 12 BUFFALO) | (BUFFALO MADE IN USA 12 12 BUFFALO) | (BULLS EYE 12 12 G.C.C.) | (BULLS-EYE No12 ELEY) |
| | | Gordon Cartridge Co | Gordon Cartridge Co |
| USA | USA | AUS | AUS/GBE |
| HSC.2,596. | HFC.826. | HSC.2,597. | HFC.827. |
| (BURROW.PRESTON No12 ELEY) | (BURROW.PRESTON & CARLISLE No12 ELEY) | (BURY 12 12 SUPER-SPEED) | (BUSSARD 12 12 *JB*) |
| | 12 gauge, Ejt. | | 16. |
| GBE/GBE | GBE/GBE | F | D |
| HFC.828. | HSC.2,598. | HSC.2,599. | HSC.2,600. |

68

| | | | |
|---|---|---|---|
| ELEY BUYERS ASSOCIATION LONDON No12 | B.WARREN No 12 KYNOCH WINDSOR | BYCROFT No ? 12 PALMERSTON | BYCROFT No 12 PALMERSTON |
| | Gnm. | | |
| | | | |
| GBE/GBE | GBE/GBE | NZ | NZ |
| HSC.2,601. | HFC.829. | HSC.2,602. | HSC.2,603. |
| BAKER 10 | BAKER & CO. 10 | BAKER STEEL CONE 10 G | BEST No 10 |
| 10 gauge. | 10 gauge. | Manufacturer. | |
| 12. | 12. | | 12. |
| USA | USA | USA | USA |
| HSC.2,514. | HSC.2,513. | HSC.2,515. | HFC.2,517. |
| No BLATCHFORD 10 CARTRIDGE | BOSS No 10 | BOSS No 10 | |
| | Gnm. | Gnm. | |
| | | | |
| USA | GBE | GBE | |
| HFC.2,518. | HSC.2,516. | HSC.5,431. | |

| | | | |
|---|---|---|---|
| (CASE MADE IN GERMANY 410) | (C.C.CO .410 MALLARD) | (C.C.CO .410 XTRA-RANGE) | (Imperial 410) |
| ·410 | Manufacturer. | Manufacturer. | ·410 |
| D | USA | USA | CDN |
| HFC.2,519. | HSC.2,520. | HSC.2,521. | HFC.223. |
| (COOPPAL POWDER 410) | (COOPPAL WETTEREN 410) | (C R C 35) | (COOPPAL WETTEREN 28 28) |
| | Pla. | Pap. ·410. | Pla. 28 gauge. |
| B | B | | B |
| HSC.2,525. | HFC.2.523. | HFC.2,524. | HSC.2,522. |
| (C L C. 24 L) | (CAMPO 20 20 FIELD) | (CARTOUCHERIE FRANÇAISE ·20·) | (CARTOUCHERIE FRANÇAISE C F PARIS ·20·) |
| 24 gaug. | | | |
| B | MEX | F | F |
| HSC.2,2526. | HSC.2,527. | HFC.287. | HFC.286. |
| (CARTOUCHERIE FRANÇAISE C F PARIS 20 20) | (CARTOUCHERIE NATIONALE 20 20) | (C B C 20 20 C B C) | (CHARLES DALY 20) |
| | | | |
| F | F | | |
| HSC.2,2528. | HFC.288. | HFC.289. | HFC.290. |

| | | | |
|---|---|---|---|
| (CHEDDITE 20) | (CHURCHILL FOREIGN MADE CASE LONDON 20 20) | (C.&H. WESTON No 20 BRIGHTON) | (C·I·L CANUCK 20 20) |
| 20 gauge. | Gnm. | Gnm. | |
| On other gauges. | On other gauges. | | |
| | GBE | GBE | CDN |
| HFC.291. | HFC.292. | HFC.2,141. | HFC.293. |
| (C·I·L IMPERIAL 20 20) | (CLEVER VERONA 20) | (CLEVER VERONA ·20·) | (CLIPPER R.H.A.CO. 20 20) |
| | | | Robin Hood. |
| CDN | I/I | I/I | USA |
| HFC.294. | HFC.295. | HFC.296. | HSC.2,529. |
| (C L C 20 L) | (COGSWELL & HARRISON 20 20 LONDON) | (COMET 20 20 R.H.A.CO.) | (COOPPAL ☆ ☆ 20) |
| | Gnm. | Robin Hood. | |
| | On other gauges. | | |
| B | GBE/GBE | USA | B |
| HSC.2,530. | HSC.2,531. | HSC.2,532. | HSC.2,533. |
| (C.T. C. 20) | (C.T. C. 20) | (C.T. C. 20 L) | (CURTIS'S & HARVEY LD ELEY No 20 LONDON) |
| | | | Powder Co. |
| B | B | B | GBE/GBE |
| HSC.2,534/R. | HFC.2,535. | HFC.2,536. | HSC.2,537. |

71

| | | | |
|---|---|---|---|
| 18 Gauge. | 16 gauge. | Robin Hood. | 16 gauge. |
| | | | |
| B | NZ | USA | F |
| HSC.2,538. | HSC.2,539. | HSC.2,540. | HSC.2,541. |
| | | | |
| Pla. | | | |
| F | F | F | LV |
| HSC.2,542. | HSC.2,543. | HSC.2,545. | HSC.2,546. |
| | | | |
| | Gnm. | | |
| LV | GBE | CH | I. |
| HSC.2,547. | HFC.442. | HSC.2,548. | HSC.2,549. |
| | | | |
| Gnm. | Gnm. | | |
| GBE/F | GBE/ | CDN | CDN |
| HFC.445. | HFC.444. | HSC.2,550. | HSC.2,551. |

| | | | |
|---|---|---|---|
| (H.CLARKE & SONS. LEICESTER EXPRESS CARTRIDGE No 16) | (CL 16 16 LIEGE MADE IN BELGIUM) | (CLIPPER 16 16 R.H.A.CO.) | (C.O & C. ? 16) |
| Gnm. | | Robin Hood. | |
| GBE | B | USA | |
| HSC.2,552. | HSC.2,553. | HSC.2,554. | HSC.2,555. |
| (LANG COCKSPUR ST. No 16) | (COL.AMM No 16 COY.LTD.) | (COLONIAL AMMUNITION No 16 COMPANY LIMITED) | (COOPAL & CIE. STE.AN. WETTEREN No 16 EB) |
| Gnm. | Manufacturer. | Manufacturer. | |
| GBE | NZ | NZ | B/GBE |
| HSC.2,556. | HSC.2,557. | HSC.2,558. | HSC.2,559. |
| (COOPPAL 16 16 WETTEREN) | (COX & SON No 16 SOUTHAMPTON) | (COX & SON. SOUTHAMPTON No 16 C.ELEY.) | (CRESCENT 16 16 R.H.A.CO.) |
| | Gnm. | | Robin Hood. |
| B | GBE | GBE/GBE | USA |
| HFC.466. | HFC.447. | HFC.2,560. | HSC.2,561. |
| (CRESCENT 16 16 R.H.A.CO.) | (CURT'IS'S & HARLEY.LD. ELEY. No 16. LONDON) | (C.LANCASTER. LONDON No 14.) | (CAB 12 12) |
| Reverse arrows. | Powder Co. | 14 gauge. | 12 gauge.  Pla. |
| USA | GBE/GBE | GBE | |
| HSC.2,562. | HSC.2,563. | HFC.611. | HSC.2,604. |

73

| | | | |
|---|---|---|---|
| C.A.BOGARDUS No 12 CHAMPION | C.A.BOGARDUS No 12 CHAMPION | C.A.C. No 12 | CAC 12 12 CAC |
| 12 gauge. | 12 gauge. | 12 gauge. | Manufacturer. |
| USA | USA | NZ | NZ |
| HSC.2,605. | HFC.2,166. | HFC.2,606. | HFC.830. |
| CAC 12 12 CAC | CAC 12 12 CAC | C.A.C. No 12 CHAMPIONSHIP | C.A.C. No 12 ELEVEN FIFTY |
| Manufacturer. | Manufacturer, Pla. | Manufacturer, | Manufacturer. |
| NZ | NZ | NZ | NZ |
| HSC.2,607. | HSC.2,608. | HSC.2,609. | HFC.2,167. |
| CAC 12 12 GAUGE | C.A.C. No 12 GUN CLUB | C.A.C. No 12 LONG RANGE | C.A.C. No 12 NEW ZEALAND |
| Manufacturer. | Manufacturer. | Manufacturer. | Manufacturer. |
| NZ | NZ | NZ | NZ |
| HFC.2,168. | HFC.2,169. | HFC.2,170. | HFC.2,610. |
| CAC 12 12 N.Z | CAC 12 12 N.Z | CAC 12 12 N.Z | C.A.C. 12 12 N.Z |
| Manufacturer. | Manufacturer. | Manufacturer. | Manufacturer. |
| NZ | NZ | NZ | NZ |
| HFC.831. | HFC.833. | HFC.2,171. | HFC.832. |

| | | | |
|---|---|---|---|
| 12 gauge. | Manufacturer. | Manufacturer. | Manufacturer. |
| NZ | NZ | NZ | NZ |
| HSC.2,611. | HFC.2,172. | HFC.834. | HFC.835. |
| Manufacturer. | Manufacturer. | | |
| NZ | NZ | USA | |
| HFC.2,173. | HFC.2,174. | HSC.2,612. | HFC.2,175. |
| Pla. | | Pla. | |
| HSC.5,432. | HFC.836. | HSC.2,613. | HSC.2,614. |
| Pla. | | Pla. | Kynoch case. |
| LV | GBI | P | RA |
| HSC.2,615. | HSC.2,616. | HSC.2,617. | HSC.2,618. |

| | | | |
|---|---|---|---|
| CANUCK 12 12 CANADA | CAPITAL 12 12 R.H.A.CO. | CAPITAL 12 12 R.H.A.CO. | CAPSULERIE LIEGEOISE 12 LIEGE 12 |
| | Robin Hood. | Robin Hood. | |
| CDN | USA | USA | B |
| HSC.2,619. | HSC.2,620. | HSC.2,621. | HSC.2,622. |
| CARLSBAD No 12 AMMO.CO. | CARLSBAD No 12 AMMO CO | CARR BROS No 12 ELEY HUDDERSFIELD | CARR&Co No 12 KYNOCH NOTTINGHAM |
| | | Gnm. | Gnm. |
| USA | USA | GBE/GBE | GBE/GBE |
| HFC.837. | HSC.2,176. | HFC.2,177. | HFC.2,178. |
| CART!eBELGE 12 12 LEIGE | CARTLANG 12 12 FRANCE | CARTOUCHERIE FRANCAISE C.F. PARIS -12- | CARTOUCHERIE FRANCAISE -12- |
| | Pla. | | |
| B | F | F | F |
| HSC.2,623. | HSC.2,624. | HFC,2,625. | HFC.838. |
| CARTOUCHERIE FRANCAISE 12 PARIS 12 | CARTOUCHERIE 12 12 NATIONALE | CARTOUCHERIES 12 12 PYRKAL | CARTRIDGE No 12 GASTIGHT |
| | Monaco. | Pla. | |
| F | P | | |
| HSC.2,626. | HSC.2,627. | HSC.2,628. | HFC.2,179. |

| | | | |
|---|---|---|---|
| (CASA CANEDO 12 12 BUENOS AIRES) | (CASE MADE IN GERMANY No 12) | (CASIMIR WEBER 12 12 ZURICH) | (CASSADY No 12) |
| | | | 10. |
| RA | GBE/D | CH | USA |
| HSC.2,629. | HFC.2,184. | HSC.2,630. | HSC.2,631. |
| (CASSADY No 12) | (CASTLE Bros No 12 KYNETON) | (CATRON 12 12 CARMEL CAL) | (CATRON 12 12 CARMEL CAL) |
| | | | |
| USA | AUS | USA | USA |
| HSC.2,632. | HSC.2,633. | HSC.2,634. | HSC.2,635. |
| (CAVIM CAL. 12) | (CBC 12 12 CBC) | (CBC 12 12 S.PAULO) | (C.B.C. 12 12 S.PAULO) |
| | | | |
| | BR | BR | BR |
| HFC.839. | HFC.840. | HSC.2,636. | HSC.2,637. |
| (C.B No 12 KYNOCH) | (C.BOSWELL No 12 126 STRAND) | (C.BOSWELL No 12 KYNOCH 126.STRAND) | (C.BOSWELL KYNOCHS PATENT CA No 02090 126 STRAND 12) |
| Manufacturer. | Gnm. | Gnm. | Gnm. Ejt. |
| GBE/GBE | GBE | GBE/GBE | GBE/GBE |
| HFC.2,180. | HSC.2,638. | HFC.841. | HFC.842. |

| | | | |
|---|---|---|---|
| | | 16, 10. | 10. |
| | | USA | USA |
| HFC.843. | HFC.848. | HSC.2,639. | HSC.2,640. |
| | | | |
| USA | USA | USA | USA |
| HSC.2,641. | HSC.2,642. | HSC.2,643. | HSC.2,644. |
| | | | Latvian alphabet. |
| | 10. | | |
| USA | USA | GBI/GBE | |
| HSC.2,645/R. | HSC.2,646/R. | HFC.845. | HSC.2,647. |
| | Pla. | | |
| | | USA | GBE |
| HSC.2,648/R. | HSC.2,649. | HSC.2,650. | HFC.846. |

| | | | |
|---|---|---|---|
| C.G.A.GASTIGHT No 12 KYNOCH | C.G.A.WATERPROOF No 12 KYNOCH | C&G 12 12 CRAM | CHAMBERLAIN ANDOVER No 12 |
| Country Gent's Asoc | Country Gent's Asoc | Pla. | Edwin Gnm. |
| GBE/GBE | GBE/GBE | GBE | GBE |
| HFC.847. | HFC.5.433. | HSC.2,651. | HFC.849. |
| CHAMBERLAIN No 12 KYNOCH ANDOVER | CHAMBERLAIN No 12 SALISBURY | CHAMBERS No 12 KYNOCH BRISTOL & CARDIFF | CHAMBERS No 12 CARDIFF |
| Edwin Gnm. | Arthur Gnm. | | |
| GBE/GBE | GBE | GBE-GBW/GBE | GBW |
| HSC.2,652. | HFC.850. | HFC.851. | HFC.2,653. |
| CHAMBERS No 12 CARDIFF | CHAMBERS No 12 DUNSTABLE | CHALLENGER 12 12 CANADA | CHALLENGER 12 12 CANADA |
| | Irm. | | Pla. |
| GBW | GBE | CDN | CDN |
| HSC.2,654. | HFC.852. | HSC.2,661. | HSC.2,662. |
| CHARLES DALY 12 | CHARLES HELLIS & SONS No 12 | CHARLES HELLIS & SONS No 12 | CHARLES HELLIS & SONS No 12 |
| | Loaders. | Loaders. | Loaders. |
| | GBE | GBE | GBE |
| HFC.853. | HSC.5,434. | HFC.854. | HFC.855. |

| | | | |
|---|---|---|---|
| CHARLES HELLIS & SONS No 12 ELEY | CHARLES ROSSON 12 DERBY 12 | CHARLES ROSSON 12 ELEY 12 DERBY | CHARLES No 12 STOURPORT |
| Loaders. | Gnm. | Gnm. | Irm. |
| GBE/GBE | GBE | GBE/GBE | GBE |
| HSC.2,655. | HFC.856. | HFC.857. | HFC.2,656. |
| CHARLES No 12 STOURPORT | CHARLES No 12 WELLS | CHAS. LANCASTER No 12 KYNOCH LONDON | CHAS.E.LANE No 12 PETERCHURCH |
| Irm. | | Gnm. | |
| GBE | GBE | GB/GBE | GBE |
| HSC.2,657. | HSC.2,658. | HFC.858. | HFC.859. |
| C.H.DeROY MALINNES No 12 ELEY | C.H.DeROY No 12 ELEY MALINNES | CHEDDITE 12 | CHEDDITE 12 |
| | | | |
| /GBE | /GBE | I | I |
| HSC.2,2659. | HSC.2,660. | HFC.861. | HFC.860. |
| CHEDDITE 12 12 ITALIA | CHEDDITE 12 12 ITALIA | CHEDDITE 12 12 ITALIA | CHEDDITE AG 12 12 LIESTAL |
| Pla. | | | |
| I | I | I | CH/I |
| HSC.2,663. | HFC.862 | HFC.2,181. | HSC.2,664. |

| | | | |
|---|---|---|---|
| CHEDDITE 12 UNIVERSEL 12 | C.H.MALEHAM No 12 SHEFFIELD | 12 GA C&H PAT PEND OMAHA | C.H.&S. No 12 |
| | Gnm. | | |
| I | GBE | | |
| HFC.863. | HSC.2,665. | HFC.2,182. | HFC.2,183. |
| C.H.SPORCQ 12 12 LIEGE | C.H.TAYLOR&SON.DRIFFIELD No12 ELEY | CHURCHILL 12 12 LONDON | 8.CHURCHILL. ELEY.No12 8 AGAR ST.STRAND |
| | Irm. | Gnm. | Gnm. |
| B | GBE/GBE | GBE | GBE/GBE |
| HFC.864. | HSC.2,666. | HSC.2,667. | HFC.865. |
| CHURCHILL FOREIGN 12 12 MADE CASE LONDON | CHURCHILL FRENCH 12 S*F*M 12 MADE CASE LONDON | CHURCHILL MADE IN FRANCE No 12 8 AGAR ST STRAND | CHURCHILL MADE IN No S*F*M 12 FRANCE LONDON |
| Gnm. | Gnm. | Gnm. | Gnm. |
| GBE/Foreign | GBE/F | GBE/F | GBE/F. |
| HFC.867. | HFC.868. | HFC.866. | HFC.869 |
| CHURCHILL MADE IN No 12 FRANCE LONDON | C&H.WESTON No 12 BRIGHTON | C&H.WESTON.BRIGHTON No12 ELEY | OIC 12 12 OIC |
| Gnm. | Gnm. | Gnm. | Pla. |
| GBE/F | GBE | GBE/GBE | |
| HFC.870. | HSC.2,668/R. | HFC.871. | HSC.2,669. |

| | | | |
|---|---|---|---|
| C-I-L 12 12 CANUCK | C-I-L 12 12 IMPERIAL | C. INGRAM No 12 GLASGOW | C. LANCASTER. LONDON No 12 |
| | | Charles. Gnm. | Gnm. |
| CDN | CDN | GBS | GBE |
| HFC.872. | HFC.873. | HSC.2,670. | HFC.2,671. |
| C. LANCASTER. LONDON No 12 ELEY | C. LANCASTER No 12 ELEY'S EJECTOR | CLARKE No 12 SALISBURY | CLARKE & DYKE No 12 SALISBURY |
| Gnm. | Gnm. | Gnm. | Gnm. |
| GBE/GBE | GBE/GBE | GBE | GBE |
| HFC.874. | HFC.875. | HFC.876. | HFC.877. |
| CLARKE & DYKE No 12 SOUTHAMPTON | CL 12 12 CL | CLEVER 12 12 MIRAGE | CLEVER VERONA 12 |
| Gnm. | Pla. | Manufacturer. | Manufacturer. |
| GBE | | I | I/I |
| HFC.878. | HSC.2,672. | HFC.882. | HFC.884. |
| CLEVER VERONA 12 | CLEVER VERONA 12 | CLEVER VERONA 12 | CLEVER 12 12 VERONA |
| Manufacturer. | Manufacturer. | Manufacturer. | Manufacturer. |
| I/I | I/I | I/I | I/I |
| HFC.883. | HFC.885. | HFC.886. | HFC.887. |

| | | | |
|---|---|---|---|
| CLIMAX SHELL MADE IN U.S.A. 12 12 LOADED IN AUSTRALIA | CLIPPER 12 12 R.H.A.CO. | C.L.LANE 12 12 BRIDGWATER | C.L. 12 12 MADE IN BELGIUM LIEGE |
| | Robin Hood. | Irm. | Manufacturer. |
| AUS/USA | USA | GBE | B |
| HFC.879. | HSC.2,673. | HFC.880. | HSC.2,674. |
| C.L. 12 12 MADE IN BELGIUM LIEGE | CL 12 12 MADE IN BELGIUM LIEGE | C.L. 12 12 MADE IN BELGIUM | C.MOODY.ROMSEY No 12 ELEY |
| Manufacturer. | Manufacturer. | Manufacturer. | Gnm. |
| B | B | B | GBE/GBE |
| HFC.2,675. | HSC.2,676. | HFC.881. | HFC.2,677. |
| C.MOODY.ROMSEY No 12 ELEY | C.MOODY.CHURCH ST.ROMSEY No12 ELEY | C.NAYLOR No 12 SHEFFIELD | C.NAYLOR No 12 SHEFFIELD |
| Gnm. | Gnm. | Gnm. | Gnm. |
| GBE/GBE | GBE/GBE | GBE | GBE |
| HFC.2,678. | HFC.2,679. | HFC.889. | HFC.888. |
| C.NAYLOR No 12 KYNOCH SHEFFIELD | C.O.&C. 12 | C.O.Co No 12 | 12 GGSCHULTZE 12 LONDON |
| Gnm. | | | Manufacturer. |
| GBE/GBE | | | GBE/GBE |
| HFC.890. | HSC.2,680. | HFC.891. | HFC.2,681. |

| | | | |
|---|---|---|---|
| COGSCHULTZE 12 LONDON | COGSCHULTZE 12 LONDON | COGSWELL & HARRISON .12. | COGSWELL & HARRISON No 12 |
| Manufacturer. | Manufacturer. | Gnm. | Gnm. |
| GBE/GBE | GBE/GBE | GBE | GBE |
| HFC.893. | HFC.892. | HFC.894. | HFC.2,682. |
| COGSWELL&HARRISON No 12 | COGSWELL&HARRISON 12 LONDON 12 | COGSWELL & HARRISON 12 LONDON 12 | COGSWELL&HARRISON 12 LONDON 12 |
| Gnm. | Gnm. | Gnm. | Gnm. |
| GBE | GBE | GBE | GBE |
| HFC.2,683. | HSC.2,684. | HFC.900. | HFC.899. |
| COGSWELL&HARRISON 12 LONDON 12 | COGSWELL & HARRISON No12 ELEY | COGSWELL&HARRISON PATENT No 2090 No 12 | COGSWELL&HARRISON LTD KYNOCH'S PATENT GROUSE EJECTOR No 12 |
| Gnm. | Gnm. | Gnm, Ejt. | Gnm, Ejt. |
| GBE | GBE/GBE | GBE/GBE | GBE/GBE |
| HFC.898. | HFC.2,685. | HFC.2,686. | HFC.903. |
| COGSWELL KYNOCH'S No 12 PATENT GROUSE & HARRISON | COGSWELL&HARRISON LTD 12 PARIS 12 | COGSWELL&HARRISON LTD No 12 | COGSWELL&HARRISON LTD No 12 |
| Gnm, Ejt. | Gnm. | Gnm. | Gnm. |
| GBE/GBE | F/ | GBE | GBE |
| HFC.901. | HFC.904. | HFC.2,687. | HFC.895. |

| | | | |
|---|---|---|---|
| (Cogswell & Harrison Ltd 12) | (Cogswell & Harrison Ld No 12 Eley) | (Cogswell & Harrison Ltd No 12 Kynoch Patent Grouse Ejector) | (Cogswell et Harrison *12*) |
| Gnm. | Gnm. | Gnm, Ejt. | Gnm. |
| GBE | GBE/GBE | GBE/GBE | F/ |
| HFC.896. | HFC.897. | HFC.902. | HFC.905. |
| (Cole & Son No 12) | (Cole & Son No 12 Devizes) | (Cole & Son No 12 Kynoch Devizes) | (Cole & Son No 12 Gunmakers) |
| Gnm. | Gnm. | Gnm. | Gnm. |
| GBE | GBE | GBE/GBE | GBE |
| HFC.906. | HFC.907. | HFC.908. | HFC.2,688. |
| (C. Colombia 12 Indumil) | (Colombia Cal 12 Indumil) | (Colonial Ammunition Company, Limited No 12) | (Coltman Foreign 12 12 Made Case Burton) |
|  | Pla. | Manufacturer. | Gnm. |
|  |  | NZ | GBE/Foreign |
| HSC.2,689. | HSC.2,690. | HFC.909. | HFC.910. |
| (Coltman Foreign 12 12 Made Case Burton) | (Coltman Foreign 12 12 Made Case Burton) | (Coltman & Co French No 12 Case Burton) | (12 Comet) |
| Gnm. | Gnm. | Gnm. |  |
| GBE/Foreign | GBE/Foreign | GBE/F |  |
| HFC.911. | HFC.912. | HFC.913. | HFC.2,691. |

| | | | |
|---|---|---|---|
| COMET 12 12 R.H.A.CO. | COMET 12 12 R.H.P.CO. | COMET 12 12 R.H.P.CO. | COMET 12 12 XL |
| Robin Hood. | Robin Hood. | Manufacturer. | |
| USA | USA | USA | CDN |
| HSC.2,692. | HSC.2,693. | HSC.2,694. | HSC.2,695. |
| CONICAL BASE No 12 ST.LOUIS.MO. | CONYERS DRIFFIELD BLANDFORD & POCKLINGTON ELEY No 12 | CONYERS.DRIFFELD ELEY BLANDFORD & POCKLINGTON No 12 | GONZALEZ MARINAX No 12 |
| Williams. | Gnm. | Gnm. | |
| 10. | | | |
| USA | GBE/GGBE | GBE/GBE | I |
| HSC.2,696. | HFC.914. | HSC.2,697. | HSC.2,698. |
| COOPPAL MADE IN BELGIUM 12 | COOPPAL MADE IN BELGIUM 12 | COOPPAL 12 12 MADE IN BELGIUM | COOPPAL 12 12 WETTEREN |
| Manufacturer. | Manufacturer. | Manufacturer. | Manufacturer. Pla. |
| B | B | B | B |
| HSC.2,699. | HSC.2,700. | HFC.915. | HFC.916. |
| COSMI 12 12 ITALY | COX & CLARKE No 12 SOUTHAMPTON | COX & CLARKE No 12 KYNOCH SOUTHAMPTON | COX & McPHERSON 12 12 SOUTHAMPTON |
| Pla. | Gnm. | Gnm. | Gnm. |
| I | GBE | GBE/GBE | GBE |
| HSC.2,701. | HFC.917. | HFC.918. | HFC.2,702. |

| | | | |
|---|---|---|---|
| (Cox & McPherson Southampton No 12) | (Cox & McPherson Southampton No 12) | (Cox & McPherson Southampton Eley No 12) | (Cox & Son Southampton No 12) |
| Gnm. | Gnm. | Gnm. | Gnm. |
| GBE | GBE | GBE/GBE | GBE |
| HFC.2,703. | HSC.2,704. | HFC.2,705. | HFC.2,706. |
| (Cox & Son Southampton No 12) | (Cox & Son Southampton Eley No 12) | (Cox & Son Kynoch Southampton No 12) | (C. Parsons Nuneaton No 12) |
| Gnm. | Gnm. | Gnm. | Hws. |
| GBE | GBE/GBE | GBE/GBE | |
| HFC.2,707. | HFC.2,708. | HFC.919. | HFC.920. |
| (C. Pinder Basingstoke No 12) | (C. Pinder & Co. Basingstoke No 12) | (C. Playfair & Co. Aberdeen No 12) | (C. Playfair & Co. Eley Aberdeen No 12) |
| Irm. | Irm. | Joyce case, Ejt. | |
| GBE | GBE | GBS | GBS/GBE |
| HFC.921. | HFC.922. | HFC.923. | HFC.924. |
| (Cramer & Buchholz *12*) | (Cramer & Buchholz *12*) | (Creber Menheniot 12 12) | (Crescent R.H.A.Co. 12 12) |
| | | | Robin Hood. |
| D | D | /F | USA |
| HSC.2,709. | HSC.2,710. | HSC.2,711. | HSC.2,712. |

| | | | |
|---|---|---|---|
| CRESCENT 12 12 R.H.A.CO. | CROCKART No 12 STIRLING | CROCKHART. STERLING. No 12 ELEY | CROWN BRAND C— |
| Reverse arrows. | Gnm. | Gnm. | 12 gauge. |
| USA | GBS | GBE/GBE | |
| HSC.2,713. | HSC.2,714. | HSC.2,715. | HSC.2,716. |
| CRUZERIO 12 12 CBC | C. SMITH & SONS No 12 NEWARK | C. SMITH & SONS. NEWARK No 2090 No 12 | C. SMITH & SONS. NEWARK KYNOCH'S PATENT GROUSE No 2090 -12- |
| | Gnm. | Gnm, Ejt. | Gnm, Ejt. |
| BR | GBE | GBE/GBE | GBE/GBE |
| HSC.2,717. | HFC.925. | HSC.2,718. | HSC.2,719. |
| C. SMITH & SONS. NEWARK KYNOCH'S PATENT GROUSE No 2090 No 12 | C.T.L. 12 12 SPAIN | CURTIS'S No 12 & HARVEY | CURTIS'S No 12 & HARVEY |
| Gnm, Ejt. | Pla. | Gunpowder makers. | Adv. |
| GBE/GBE | E | GBE | GBE |
| HFC.926. | HSC.2,720. | HSC.2,721. | HSC.2,722. |
| CURTIS'S & HARVEY No 12 LONDON | CURTIS'S & HARVEY No 12 ELEY LONDON | CURTIS'S & HARVEY'S No 12 G.K.& Co LONDON | CURTIS'S & HARVEY LTD No 12 LONDON |
| Gunpowder makers. | Gunpowder makers. | Gunpowder makers. | Gunpowder makers. |
| GBE | GBE/GBE | GBE/GBE | GBE |
| HSC.2,723. | HSC.2,724. | HFC.932. | HFC.928. |

| | | | |
|---|---|---|---|
| Gunpowder makers. | Gunpowder makers. | Gunpowder makers. | Gunpowder makers. |
| GBE | GBE/GBE | GBE/GBE | GBE/GBE |
| HFC.927. | HFC.929. | HSC.2,725. | HSC.2,726. |
| Gunpowder makers. | Gunpowder makers. | Gunsmith. | |
| GBE/GBE | GBE/GBE | IRL | |
| HFC.931. | HFC.930. | HSC.2,727. | HFC.933. |
| Gnm. | Gnm. | Gnm. | 10 gauge. |
| GBE | GBE | GBE/GBE | USA |
| HFC.2,728. | HSC.2,729. | HSC.2,730. | HSC.2,731. |
| 10 gauge. | | | |
| | | 12. | |
| USA | USA | USA | USA |
| HSC.2,732. | HSC.2,733. | HSC.2,734. | HSC.2,735. |

| | | | |
|---|---|---|---|
| C.D.LEET No 10 SPRINGFIELD MASS | C.D.LEET SPRINGFIELD MASS 10 | C.F.C.CO No 10 | CHARLES OSBORNE & CO BIRMINGHAM |
| | | | Gnm. 10 gauge. |
| USA | USA | USA | GBE |
| HSC.2,736/R. | HSC.2,737/R | HSC.2,738. | HFC.2,739. |
| CONICAL BASE No 10 ST. LOUIS. MO. | | | |
| | | | |
| USA | | | |
| HSC.2,740. | | | |

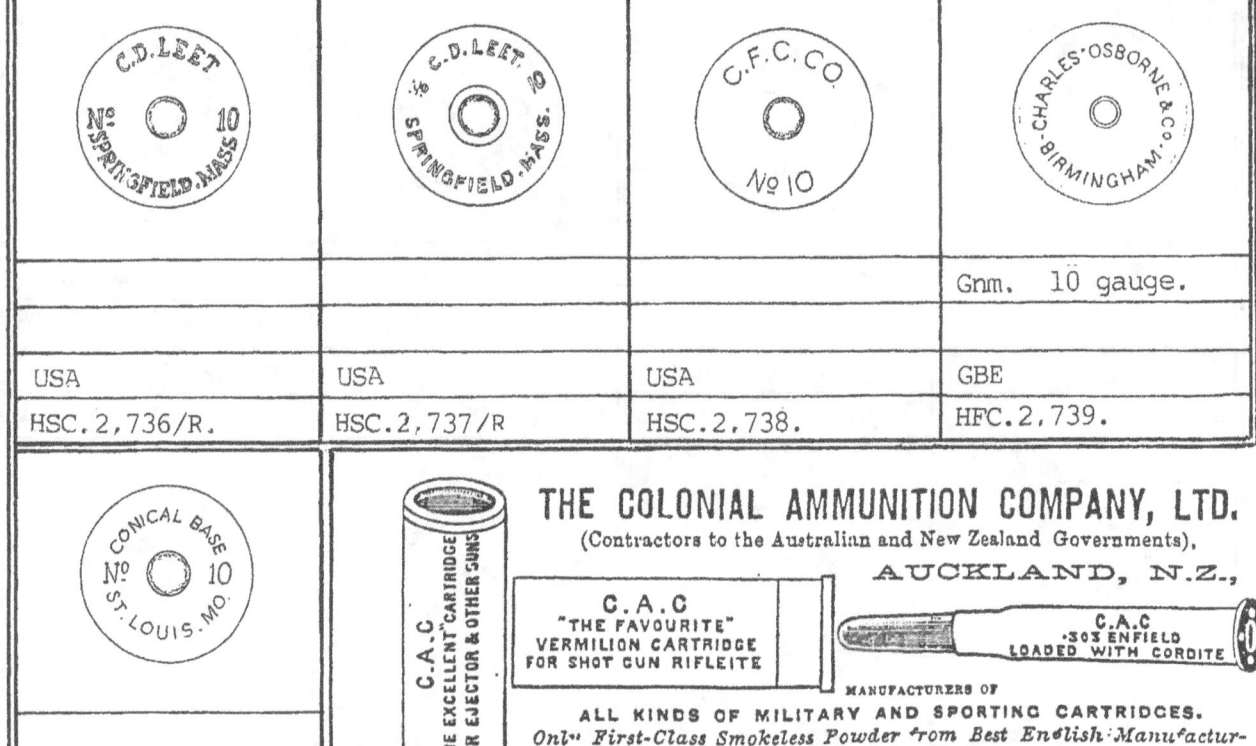

| AUCKLAND WELLINGTON | W. H. TISDALL LTD. | CHRISTCHURCH HAMILTON |
|---|---|---|

Runholders and Station Managers particularly are urged to write for our quotations. We will submit prices for delivery ex our warehouse, or carriage paid to nearest port or railway station, as desired.

NOTE.—Shot sizes. We can supply the majority of our cartridges loaded with a large range of shot sizes. B.B. and No. 1 are used mainly for swan and wallaby shooting; 2, 3, 4, and 5 are popular for rabbit and general game shooting; 6, 7, and 8 are used for live and clay pigeon shooting at the traps; 8 also, is probably the most popular quail shot; and 10 and 12 are used extensively for destroying small bird pests about orchards or farms, and are also in demand for sparrow shooting at the traps.

## Tisdalls "Retriever" Cartridges

**12 GAUGE.**      **2½ INCH.**      **SMOKELESS**

By far our most popular "game" cartridge. Manufactured by the largest ammunition company in the British Empire, "Retriever" cartridges have gained their enviable reputation purely on their merit. They throw splendid patterns with great penetration, and with an absence of the heavy recoil which makes all the difference between enjoyment and discomfort in the course of a day's shooting. Their loading is the outcome of years of experience and exhaustive experiment, and the proportions of powder and shot being admirably balanced, "Retrievers" suit the average "game" gun to perfection.

Buying in huge quantities as we must do to have these cartridges specially manufactured throughout to our specifications, we are enabled to quote them at prices which are most reasonable.

"Retriever" cartridges are supplied at present in **12 gauge only.** They are loaded with the marvellously quick "**Smokeless Diamond**" powder and sizes 2, 3, 4, 5, 6, 7, 8, 10 and 12 **chilled shot.**

For quotations see separate price sheet.

## Tisdalls Long "Retriever" Cartridges
### 2¾ INCH

Owing to the wonderful results achieved by our 2½ in. Retriever cartridges, we have been repeatedly requested by sportsmen requiring a heavier load to supply this favourite cartridge in 2¾ in. shells. We have complied with our clients requests, and this season we are offering for the first time a 2¾ in. Retriever which we have named our "Long Retriever." We have tested these cartridges for pattern and penetration, and are fully confident that they will meet with the requirements of the average sportsman, and we have no hesitation in acclaiming them **the best all round cartridge on the market.**

| | | | |
|---|---|---|---|
| (Dominion Made in Canada .410) | (Dominion .410 Made in Canada) | (Dominion No 32 Made in Canada) | (Dominion No 28 Canada Canuck) |
| .410. | Manufacturer. | 32 gauge. | 28 gauge. |
| | On other gauges. | | |
| CDN | CDN | CDN | CDN |
| HSC.5,435. | HSC.2,741. | HSC.2,742. | HSC.2,743. |
| (D.C.CO. No 20 Sovereign) | (Dickson & Son No 20 Eley Edinburgh) | (Dircks-Beath No 20 Ammo Co.) | (Dominion No 20 Made in Canada) |
| 20 gauge. | Gnm. | Manufacturer. | Manufacturer. |
| | 16, 12. | | |
| USA | GBE/GBE | USA | CDN |
| HSC.2,744. | HSC.2,750. | HSC.2,745. | HSC.2,746. |
| (Dominion No 20 Canada Crown) | (Dominion No 20 Made in Canada Export) | (Dorhout Mees 20) | (Double 20 20 Eagle) |
| Manufacturer. | Manufacturer. | | |
| | | | 12. |
| CDN | CDN | | USA |
| HFC.2,747. | HFC.2,748. | HFC.297. | HSC.2,749. |
| (Diana 18 18 *B*) | (Danarms 16) | (Daws No 16 Patent) | (D.C.CO. No 16 Crown) |
| 18 gauge. | Manufacturer. | Developer, Gnm. | Manufacturer. |
| | | GBE/GBE | USA |
| HFC.424. | HFC.448. | HFC.449/R. | HSC.5,436. |

| | | | |
|---|---|---|---|
| DEFENSOR 16 | DERBY 16 16 | DIANA 16 16 B | DICKSON & SON No 16 ELEY EDINBURGH |
| 16 gauge. | 16 gauge. | | Gnm. |
| | | | 20, 12. |
| RA | D | | GBS/GBE |
| HSC.2,752. | HSC.2,753. | HFC.2,754. | HFC.2,755. |
| DNC ANP 16 ? 16 ALGERIE | DOMINION No 16 | DOMINION No 16 MADE IN CANADA | DOMINION No 16 MADE IN CANADA IMPERIAL |
| | Manufacturer. | Manufacturer. | Manufacturer. |
| | | On other gauges. | 12. |
| DZ | CDN | CDN | CDN |
| HSC.2,756. | HFC.2,757. | HSC.2,758. | HFC.2,759. |
| DOMINION No 16 MADE IN CANADA METEOR | DOMINION No 16 MADE IN CANADA OLD COLONY | DOMINION 16 16 SOVEREIGN | DORHOUT MEES 16 |
| Manufacturer. | Manufacturer. | Manufacturer. | |
| | | | 20, 12. |
| CDN | CDN | CDN | |
| HFC.2,760. | HFC.2,761. | HSC.2,762. | HFC.450. |
| ◇ 12 | DAINTITH No 12 WARRINGTON | DAINTITH KYNOCH PATENT No 12 GROUSE EJECTOR WARRINGTON | DANARMS 12 |
| Delaware C.C. | 12 gauge. Gnm. | Gnm. Ejt. | Manufacturer. |
| 10. | | | |
| USA | GBE | GBE/GBE | |
| HSC.2,763. | HSC.2,764. | HFC.934. | HFC.935. |

| | | | |
|---|---|---|---|
| (DANARMS 12) | (DANIEL FRASER & Co LTD EDINBURGH N°12 ELEY) | (DANIEL FRASER & Co LTD EDINBURGH N°12 ELEY) | (DANIEL FRASER & Co LTD LONDON EDINBURGH ELEY N°12) |
| Manufacturer. | Gnm. | Gnm. | Gnm. |
| | GBS/GBE | GBS/GBE | GBS/GBE |
| HFC.936. | HFC.2,765. | HSC.2,766. | HSC.2,767. |
| (DANIEL FRASER & Co LTD LONDON EDINBURGH ELEY N°12) | (DA 12 12 OTTERUP) | (DAP 12 12 ITALY GF) | (DARLOW N° 12 BEDFORD) |
| Gnm. | | | Gnm. |
| GBS/GBE | DK | I | GBE |
| HFC.2,768. | HSC.2,769. | HFC.937. | HFC.938. |
| (DAUDETEAU ? N° 12) | (DAVIDSON N° 12 WELLS) | (DAVIDSON N° 12 KYNOCH WELLS) | (O.B.CROCKHART PERTH N°12 ELEY) |
| | Loader. | Loader. | Gnm. |
| | GBE | GBE/GBE | GBS/GBE |
| HSC.2,770. | HFC.939. | HFC.940. | HSC.2,771. |
| (D.C.Co. N° 12) | (D.C.Co. N° 12 EMPIRE) | (D.C.Co. N° 12 TRAP) | (D.C.Co. No 12 WIL.DEL) |
| Dominion C C. | Dominion C C. | Dominion C.C. | Delaware C C. |
| | | | 10, 8. |
| CDN | CDN | CDN | USA |
| HSC.2,772. | HSC.2,773. | HSC.2,774. | HSC.2,775. |

| | | | |
|---|---|---|---|
| D.C.Co.LTD No 12 VULCAN | DECATHLON ☆ 12 ☆ | DECATHLON ☆ 12 ☆ | DENDY ELEY No12 SADDLER EASTBOURNE |
| Dominion C C. | | | |
| | | | |
| CDN | | | GBE/GBE |
| HSC.2,776. | HFC.942. | HFC.941. | HFC.2,777. |
| DERBY 12 12 * ᴁB * | D.EVITT.AUCKLAND No12 ELEY | DEXTRA 12 12 * | D.FRASER & Co EDINBURGH No12 ELEY |
| | | | Gnm. |
| D | NZ/GBE | | GBS/GBE |
| HSC.2,778. | HSC.2,779. | HSC.2,780. | HFC.2,781. |
| D.FRASER & Co EDINBURGH No12 ELEY.H | D.GRAY & Co Y. INVERNESS No12 ELEY.SSS | D.GREEN 12 12 DAICEL | DIANE No 12 BRUXELLES |
| Gnm. | Gnm. | Pla. | |
| GBS/GBE | GBS/GBE | | B |
| HFC.2,782. | HFC.943. | HSC.2,783. | HSC.2,784. |
| DICKSON 12 12 EDINBURGH | DICKSON & SON No 12 ELEY EDINBURGH | DICKSON & SON No 12 ELEY EDINBURGH | DIGBY No 12 SHAFTSBURY |
| Gnm. | Gnm. | Gnm. | Sidney W Digby. Irm. |
| GBS | GBS/GBE | GBS/GBE | GBE |
| HFC.944. | HFC.2,185. | HFC.2,786. | HFC.945. |

| | | | |
|---|---|---|---|
| (DIM No 12 MEXICO) | (DIRCKS-BEATH No NOX 12 AMMO CO.) | (DIRCKS-BEATH No 12 AMMO CO.) | (DIRCKS-BEATH No 12 AMMO CO) |
| | Manufacturer. | Manufacturer. | Manufacturer. |
| MEX | USA | USA | USA |
| HSC.2,787. | HSC.2,788. | HSC.2,789. | HFC.946. |
| (DIRCKS-BEATH No MADE IN FRANCE 12 AMMO CO.) | (DIXIE 12 12 S.C.CO.) | (DIXIE 12 12 S.C.CO.) | (DIXIE 12 12 S.C.CO) |
| Manufacturer. | Southern C. Co. | Southern C. Co. | Southern C. Co. |
| USA/F | USA | USA | USA |
| HSC.2,790. | HFC.2,791. | HSC.2,792. | HFC.947. |
| (DIXON & Co No 12 KYNOCH ASTON) | (DIXON & Co No 12 KYNOCH BIRMINGHAM) | (DOBSON & ROSSON DERBY No 12) | (DOMINION No 12 CANADA) |
| Aston, Birmingham. | | Pre Wwl. Gnm. | Manufacturer. |
| GBE/GBE | GBE/GBE | GBE | CDN |
| HFC.948. | HFC.949. | HFC.950. | HSC.2,793. |
| (DOMINION No 12 CANUCK) | (DOMINION MADE IN No 12 CANADA CANUCK) | (DOMINION MADE IN No 12 CANADA EMPTY) | (DOMINION No 12 FALCON) |
| Manufacturer. | Manufacturer. | Manufacturer. | Manufacturer. |
| CDN | CDN | CDN | CDN |
| HSC.2,794. | HSC.2,795. | HSC.2,796. | HSC.2,797. |

| | | | |
|---|---|---|---|
| DOMINION No 12 IMPERIAL | DOMINION No 12 IMPERIAL | DOMINION MADE IN No 12 CANADA IMPERIAL | DOMINION No 12 MADE IN CANADA |
| Manufacturer. | Manufacturer. | Manufacturer. | Manufacturer. |
| CDN | CDN | CDN | CDN |
| HSC.2.798. | HSC.2,799. | HFC.951. | HSC.2,800. |
| DOMINION MADE IN No 12 CANADA MAXUM | DOMINION MADE IN No 12 CANADA MAXUM | DOMINION MADE IN No 12 CANADA METEOR | DOMINION MADE IN No 12 CANADA OLD COLONY |
| Manufacturer. | Manufacturer. | Manufacturer. | Manufacturer. |
| CDN | CDN | CDN | CDN |
| HSC.2,801. | HSC.2,802. | HSC.2,803. | HSC.2,804. |
| DOMINION No 12 REGAL | DOMINION No 12 SETTER | DOMINION MADE IN No 12 CANADA SETTER | DOMINION MADE IN No 12 CANADA SETTER |
| Manufacturer. | Manufacturer. | Manufacturer. | Manufacturer. |
| CDN | CDN | CDN | CDN |
| HSC.2,805. | HSC.2,806. | HSC.2,807. | HFC.2,808. |
| DOMINION No 12 SOVEREIGN | DOMINION 12 12 SOVEREIGN | DORHOUT MEES 12 | DORKAS 12 12 GREECE |
| Manufacturer. | Manufacturer. | | Pla. |
| CDN | CDN | | GR |
| HSC.2,809. | HSC.2,810. | HFC.952. | HSC.2,811. |

96

|  |  |  |  |
|---|---|---|---|
| (DOTT JACO BUCCI-CERCOLA-12-) |  (DOUBLE 12 12 EAGLE) | (DOUGALL Nº 12 GLASGOW) | (DOUGALL Nº 12 GLASGOW) |
|  |  | Gnm. | Gnm. |
|  | 20. |  |  |
|  | USA | GBS | GBS |
| HSC.2,812. | HSC.2,813. | HSC.2,814. | HSC.2,815. |
| (DOUGALL Nº 12 LONDON) | (DOUILLERIE 12 12 FRANCAISE) | (DOUILLERE 12 12 FRANCAISE) | (D.P.I. 12) |
| Gnm. |  |  | Celluloid. |
|  |  |  |  |
| GBE | F | F | DK |
| HFC.2,816. | HFC.954. | HFC.953. | HFC.955. |
| (D.P.I. PAT. ANM.) | (PAT. D.P.I. ANM. 12) | (DUCASSE 12 12 PARIS-BORDEAUX) | (DUPLACH 12 12 RAUCHLOS) |
| 12 gauge. Apc. | Apc. | Pla. |  |
| DK | DK | F | D |
| HSC.2,817. | HSC.2,818. | HSC.2,819. | HSC.2,820. |
| (DUPLACH 12 12 RAUCHLOS) | (Nº 12 DUPONT) | (D.WALES Nº 12 GT.YARMOUTH) | (D.WALES.YARMOUTH Nº12 ELEY) |
|  |  | Derrian Wales. Irm. | Derrian Wales. Irm. |
| D | USA | GBE | GBE/GBE |
| HSC.2,821. | HSC.2,822. | HSC.2,823. | HFC.956. |

97

| | | | |
|---|---|---|---|
| ![headstamp] N⁰ D.WILLIAMSON 12 LONDON | ![headstamp] DYER & ROBSON. H.R.B.L⁰. LON N⁰12 L⁰. | ![headstamp] ◇D◇ 10 | ![headstamp] D.C.Co. N⁰ 10 WIL.DEL |
| Gnm. | London firm. | Delaware C Co. | 10 gauge. |
| | | 12. | 12. |
| GBE | GBE | USA | USA |
| HFC.957. | HFC.958. | HSC.2,824. | HSC.2,825. |
| ![headstamp] D.C.Co. N⁰ 10 TRAP | ![headstamp] DOMINION MADE IN N⁰ 10 CANADA CANUCK | ![headstamp] DOMINION MADE IN N⁰ 10 CANADA CANUCK | ![headstamp] DOMINION 8 GA INDUSTRIAL |
| Delaware C Co. | Manufacturer. | Manufacturer. | 8 gauge. |
| | | | |
| USA | CDN | CDN | CDN |
| HSC.2,826. | HSC.2,827. | HSC.2,828. | HSC.2,829. |

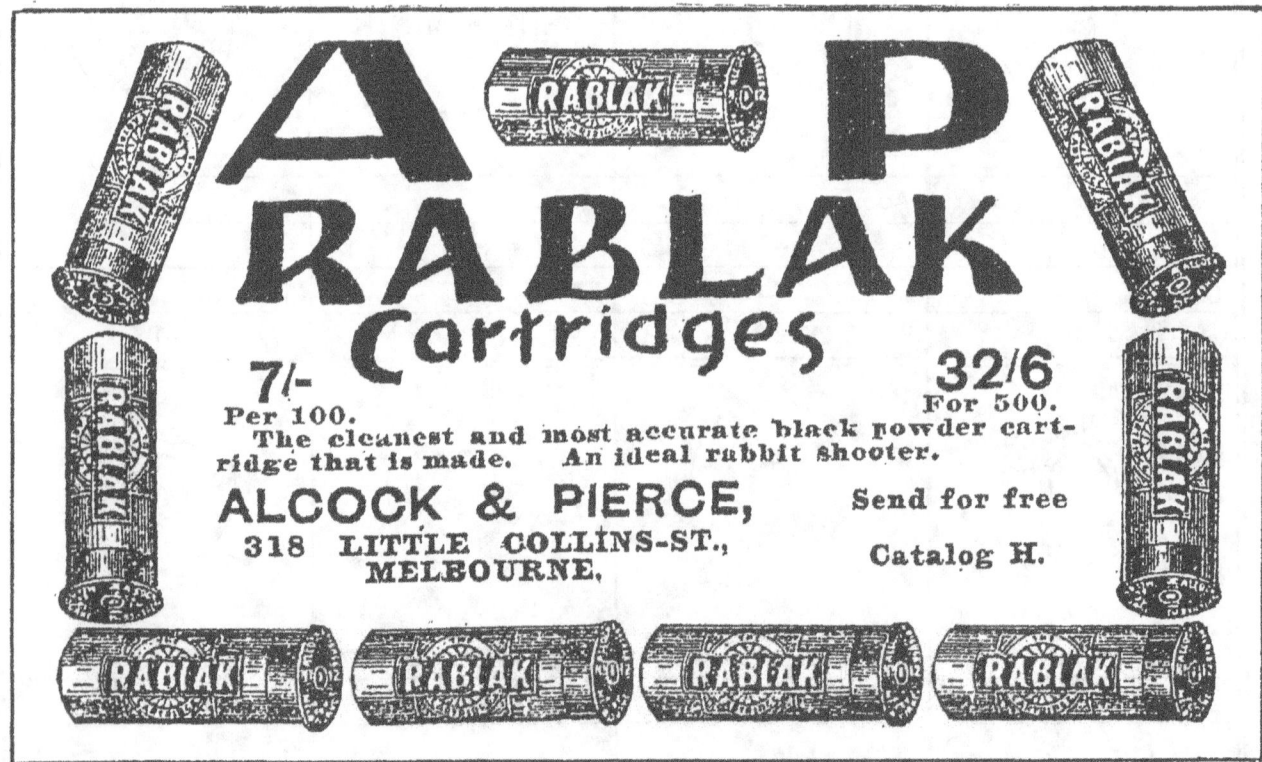

Australian advertisment circa 1910.

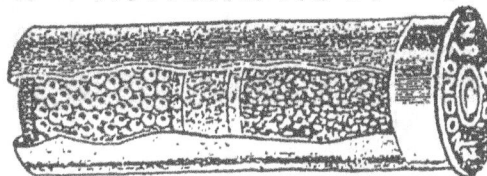

ELEY SHOTGUN CARTRIDGES

The cartridges shown here were taken from a selection of advertisements. I have drawn a few hedstampings from similar advertisements. It is just possible that some may never have been used on a cartridge.

| | | | |
|---|---|---|---|
| 9 mm. Eley | Manufacturer. | ·360, Eley Bros. | Manufacturer. |
| GBE/GBE | GBE/GBE | GBE/GBE | GBE/GBE |
| HSC.2,785. | HSC.2,830. | HFC.2,831. | HSC.2,832. |
| ·360, Eley Bros. | ·410, Eley. | ·410, Eley Kynoch. | Manufacturer. |
| GBE/GBE | GBE/GBE | GBE/GBE | GBE/GBE |
| HFC.215. | HFC.224. | HFC.225. | HFC.226. |
| Eley Bros. | Eley Bros. | ·410 Eley Hawk. | Manufacturer. |
| GBE/GBE | GBE/GBE | GBE/GBE | GBE/GBE |
| HSC.2,833. | HFC.2,834. | HSC.2,835. | HFC.227. |
| Eley Kynoch I.C.I. | Eley Bros. | Eley Bros. 32, 16. | Nobel Industries. |
| GBE/GBE | GBE/GBE | GBE/GBE | GBE/GBE |
| HFC.228. | HFC.229. | HSC.2,836. | HSC.2,837. |

| | | | |
|---|---|---|---|
| 32 gauge. | Nobel Industries, | Manufacturer. | Eley Bros, Ejt. |
| 410, 16. | | On other gauges. | 28, 14, 12, 10, 8. |
| GBE/GBE | GBE/GBE | GBE/GBE | GBE/GBE |
| HSC.2,838. | HFC.2,839. | HSC.2,840. | HSC.2,841. |
| Nobel Industries. | 28 gauge. | Eley Bros. | Pap, Pla. |
| On other gauges. | On other gauges. | On other gauges. | On other gauges. |
| GBE/GBE | GBE/GBE | GBE/GBE | GBE/GBE |
| HSC.2,842. | HFC.249. | HFC.250. | HFC.2,843. |
| Manufacturer. | 28 gauge, | Eley Bros. | Eley Bros. |
| On other gauges. | On other gauges. | On other gauges. | On other gauges. |
| GBE/GBE | GBE/GBE | GBE/GBE | GBE/GBE |
| HFC.251. | HFC.252. | HFC.253. | HFC.254. |
| Nobel Industries. | Manufacturer. | Manufacturer. | Eley Bros, Ejt. |
| On other gauges. | On other gauges. | On other gauges. | On other gauges. |
| GBE/GBE | GBE/GBE | GBE/GBE | GBE/GBE |
| HFC.255. | HFC.2,844. | HFC.2,845. | HFC.2,846. |

| | | | |
|---|---|---|---|
| 24 gauge. | Eley Bros. | Manufacturer. | Eley Bros. |
| On other gauges. | On other gauges. | On other gauges. | On other gauges. |
| GBE/GBE | GBE/GBE | GBE/GBE | GBE/GBE |
| HSC.2,847. | HSC.2,848. | HSC.2,849. | HSC.2,850. |
| Eley Bros. | Nobel Industries. | Manufacturer. | 20 gauge. |
| On other gauges. | On other gauges. | On other gauges. | |
| GBE/GBE | GBE/GBE | GBE/GBE | GBE/GBE |
| HSC.2,851. | HSC.2,852. | HSC.2,853. | HFC.298/R. |
| Gnm. | Robin Hood. | | Eley Bros. |
| On other gauges. | On other gauges. | | On other gauges. |
| GBE/GBE | USA | F/GBE | GBE/GBE |
| HFC.2,854. | HSC.2,855. | HFC.2,856. | HFC.2,857. |
| Eley Bros. | Manufacturer. | Manufacturer. | Manufacturer. |
| | On other gauges. | On other gauges. | On other gauges. |
| GBE/GBE | GBE/GBE | GBE/GBE | GBE/GBE |
| HFC.299. | HFC.2,858/R. | HFC.2,859. | HFC.2,860. |

| | | | |
|---|---|---|---|
| Manufacturer. | Manufacturer. | Eley Bros. | Ejt. |
| On other gauges. | | On other gauges. | |
| GBE/GBE | CDN/CDN | CDN/CDN | GBE/GBE |
| HSC.2,861. | HSC.2,862. | HFC.300. | HSC.2,863. |
| Ejt. | Eley Hawk. | Manufacturer. | Eley Bros. |
| | On other gauges. | Post Ww2. | |
| F/F | GBE/GBE | GBE/GBE | B/GBE |
| HSC.2,864. | HFC.302. | HFC.301. | HSC.2,865. |
| Eley Bros. | Eley Bros. | Manufacturer. | Manufacturer. |
| | On other gauges. | Post Ww2. | Post Ww2. |
| | GBE/GBE | GBE/GBE | GBE/GBE |
| HSC.2,866. | HFC.303. | HFC.304. | HFC.2,867. |
| Irish Metal Ind'. | Aus-NZ | 20 gauge. | E-K I,C.I. |
| 12. | 12. | | On other gauges. |
| IRL/GBE | AUS/AUS | GBE/GBE | GBE/GBE |
| HSC.2,868. | HFC.308. | HFC.2,869. | HFC.306. |

| | | | |
|---|---|---|---|
| Manufacturer. | Eley Rocket. | Manufacturer. | Eley Bros. |
| On other gauges. | 16, 12. | 16, 12. | |
| GBE/GBE | GBE/GBE | AUS/AUS/NZ | GBE/GBE |
| HFC.305. | HFC.307. | HFC.2,142. | HSC.2,870. |
| Eley Bros. | Manufacturer. | Eley Bros. | Eley Bros. |
| 24, 16, 12. | On other gauges. | On other gauges. | On other gauges. |
| GBE/GBE | GBE/GBE | GBE/GBE | GBE/GBE |
| HSC.2,871. | HFC.309. | HFC.310. | HFC.311. |
| Eley Bros. | Eley Bros. | Manufacturer. | Eley Bros. |
| On other gauges. | On other gauges. | On other gauges. | On other gauges. |
| GBE/GBE | GBE/GBE | GBE/GBE | GBE/GBE |
| HSC.2,872. | HFC.312. | HFC.313. | HSC.2,873. |
| Eley Bros. | Eley Bros. | Eley Bros. | Nobel Industries. |
| On other gauges. | On other gauges. | | On other gauges. |
| GBE/GBE | GBE/GBE | GBE/GBE | GBE/GBE |
| HFC.314. | HFC.315. | HFC.2,874. | HFC.316. |

| | | | |
|---|---|---|---|
| Eley Bros. | Manufacturer. | Eley Bros. | Manufacturer. |
|  |  | On other gauges. | On other gauges. |
| GBE/GBE | GBE/GBE | GBE/GBE | GBE/GBE |
| HFC.2,875. | HSC.2,876. | HFC.317. | HFC.318. |
| Nobel Industries. | Nobel Industries. | Manufacturer. | Eley Bros. |
| On other gauges. | On other gauges. | On other gauges. |  |
| GBE/GBE | GBE/GBE | GBE/GBE | GBE/GBE |
| HFC.319. | HFC.320. | HFC.321. | HSC.2,877. |
| Manufacturer. | Eley Bros, Ejt. |  |  |
|  |  |  | On other gauges. |
| GBE | GBE/GBE |  | GBE |
| HSC.2,878. | HFC.332. | HSC.2,879. | HFC.323. |
| 18 gauge. | 16 gauge. | Eley Bros. | Eley Bros. |
|  | On other gauges. | On other gauges. |  |
| D | USA | GBE/GBE | GBE/GBE |
| HSC.2,880. | HFC.2,147. | HFC.452. | HFC.2,881/R. |

| | | | |
|---|---|---|---|
| Eley Bros. | Gnm, | Robin Hood. | Gnm. |
| | On other gauges. | | |
| GBE/GBE | GBE/GBE | USA | GBE |
| HFC.451. | HFC.453. | HSC.2,882. | HFC.2,883. |
| Gnm, | Eley Bros. | Manufacturer. | Manufacturer. |
| | On other gauges. | | |
| GBE | GBE/GBE | GBE/GBE | GBE/GBE |
| HSC.2,884. | HFC.2,885/R. | HFC.2,886. | HFC.2,887. |
| 16 gauge. | Manufacturer. | Eley Bros. | Manufacturer. |
| | | On other gauges. | |
| GBE/GBE | GBE/GBE | CDN/CDN | CDN/CDN |
| HSC.2,888. | HSC.2,889. | HSC.2,890. | HFC.2,891. |
| Eley Bros. | Eley Bros. | Manufacturer. | Eley Bros. |
| CDN/CDN | GBE/GBE | GBE/GBE | GBE/GBE |
| HSC.2,892. | HFC.2,893. | HFC.2,894. | HSC.2,895. |

| | | | |
|---|---|---|---|
| Eley Bros. | Nobel Industries. | Eley Hawk. | Eley Bros. |
| On other gauges. | | On other gauges. | On other gauges. |
| GBE/GBE | GBE/GBE | GBE/GBE | GBE/GBE |
| HSC.2,896. | HSC.2,897. | HFC.454. | HFC.455. |
| IMI (Kynoch) Ltd. | IMI (Kynoch) Ltd. | Irish Metal Ind'. | Manufacturer. |
| On other gauges. | | 12. | On other gauges. |
| GBE/GBE | GBE/GBE | IRL/GBE | GBE/GBE |
| HFC.456. | HFC.2,898. | HSC.2,899. | HFC.457. |
| Eley-Kynoch ICI | Pre Ww2. | Manufacturer. | Manufacturer. |
| On other gauges. | 20, 16. | | |
| GBE/GBE | GBE/GBE | AUS/AUS | AUS/AUS |
| HFC.458. | HFC.459. | HSC.2,900. | HSC.2,901. |
| I.C.I.A.N.Z. | Manufacturer. | Eley Bros. | Eley Bros. |
| On other gauges. | On other gauges. | .410, 32. | |
| AUS-NZ/AUS | AUS-NZ/AUS | GBE/GBE | GBE/GBE |
| HSC.2,902. | HSC.2,903. | HSC.2,904. | HSC.2,905. |

| | | | |
|---|---|---|---|
| Pre Wwl. | Manufacturer. | Eley Bros. | Eley Bros. |
| 24, 20, 12. | On other gauges. | | On other gauges. |
| GBE/GBE | GBE/GBE | GBE/GBE | GBE/GBE |
| HSC.2,906. | HFC.460. | HFC.461. | HFC.462. |
| Eley Bros. | Manufacturer. | Pre Wwl. | Nobel Industries. |
| | | On other gauges. | |
| GBE/GBE | GBE/GBE | GBE/GBE | GBE/GBE |
| HFC.463. | HFC.464. | HFC.465. | HSC.2,907. |
| Post Wwl. | Nobel Industries. | Eley Bros. | Pre Wwl. |
| | | | On other gauges. |
| GBE/GBE | GBE/GBE | GBE/GBE | GBE/GBE |
| HFC.2,908. | HFC.470. | HFC.5,437. | HFC.467. |
| Manufacturer. | Eley Bros. | Nobel Industries. | Post Wwl. |
| On other gauges. | | | |
| GBE/GBE | GBE/GBE | GBE/GBE | GBE/GBE |
| HFC.468. | HFC.469. | HFC.2,909. | HSC.2,910. |

| | | | |
|---|---|---|---|
| (ELEY 16 16 NOBEL) | (ELEY 16 * 16 * NOBEL) | (ELEY 16 16 NOBEL) | (ELEY'S EJECTOR No 16 LONDON) |
| Nobel Industries. | Post Wwl. | Manufacturer. | Pre Wwl. Ejt. |
| On other gauges. | | On other gauges. | |
| GBE/GBE | GBE/GBE | GBE/GBE | GBE/GBE |
| HFC.472. | HSC.2,911. | HFC.473. | HFC.2,912. |
| (ELEY'S EJECTOR No 16 LONDON) | (EL 16 GIGANTE) | (E.M.REILLY & Co No 16) | (E.M.REILLY & Co No 16) |
| Manufacturer. Ejt. | REM-UMC, Export. | Gnm. | Gnm. |
| GBE/GBE | USA | GBE | GBE |
| HFC.471. | HSC.2,913. | HSC.2,914. | HFC.2,915. |
| (E.M.REILLY & Co No 16) | (E.M.REILLY&Co No 16 LONDON) | (E*R No 16 ELEY.LONDON) | (ELEY BROS No 14 LONDON) |
| Gnm. | Gnm. | Eley Bros. | 14 gauge. |
| | | | On other gauges. |
| GBE | GBE | GBE/GBE | GBE/GBE |
| HSC.2,916. | HFC.474/R. | HFC.475. | HFC.612/R. |
| (ELEY BROS No 14 LONDON) | (ELEY No 14 EJECTOR) | (ELEY No 14 LONDON) | (ELEY N.I. No 14 LONDON) |
| 14 gauge. | Pre Wwl. Ejt. | Pre Wwl. | Post Wwl. |
| | On other gauges. | On other gauges. | On other gauges. |
| GBE/GBE | GBE/GBE | GBE/GBE | GBE/GBE |
| HFC.2,153/R. | HSC.2,917. | HFC.613. | HSC.2,918. |

| | | | |
|---|---|---|---|
| (headstamp: E / No 14 / LONDON) | (headstamp: ELEY / No 14 / NOBEL) | (headstamp: ELEY / 14 14 / NOBEL) | (headstamp: ELEY'S No 14 EJECTOR / LONDON) |
| Eley Bros. | Post Wwl. | Nobel Industries. | Eley Bros., Ejt. |
| On other gauges. | On other gauges. | On other gauges. | On other gauges. |
| GBE/GBE | GBE/GBE | GBE/GBE | GBE/GBE |
| HSC.2,919/R. | HSC.2,920. | HFC.614. | HSC.2,921. |
| (headstamp: E/N / 1922) | (headstamp: ELEY / 12 14 / LONDON) | (headstamp: ELEY / 12 14 / LONDON) | (headstamp: crown / No 12 / E) |
| 14 gauge. | 12-14 gauge. | Thin brass case. | 12 gauge. |
| | GBE/GBE | GBE/GBE | |
| HSC.2,922. | HFC.2,923. | HSC.2,924. | HFC.959. |
| (headstamp: E.ADKINS.LEWES / No 12) | (headstamp: Eatonia / 12 12 / Shell) | (headstamp: Eatonia / 12 12 / Shell) | (headstamp: EB / No 12 / LONDON) |
| 12 gauge. | | | Eley Bros. |
| GBE | CDN | CDN | GBE/GBE |
| HSC.5,439. | HSC.5,440. | HFC.960. | HSC.5,438. |
| (headstamp: EB / No 12 / LONDON) | (headstamp: E.B. / No 12 / LONDON) | (headstamp: E.B / No 12 / LONDON) | (headstamp: E.B / No 12 / LONDON) |
| Manufacturer. | Pre Wwl. | Eley Bros. | Eley Bros. |
| GBE/GBE | GBE/GBE | GBE/GBE | GBE/GBE |
| HFC.963/R. | HFC.964. | HFC.2,186. | HSC.2,925. |

| | | | |
|---|---|---|---|
| Eley Bros. | Manufacturer. | Eley Bros. | Pre Wwl. |
| GBE/GBE | GBE/GBE | GBE/GBE | GBE/GBE |
| HFC.2,926. | HFC.2,927. | HFC.962. | HFC.961. |
| Eley Bros. | Manufacturer. | Gnm. | Gnm. |
| GBE/GBE | GBE/GBE | GBE | GBE |
| HFC.2,928. | HSC.2,929. | HFC.2,930. | HFC.965. |
| Pre Wwl. Gnm. On other gauges. | Pre Wwl. | Kynoch case, | |
| GBE/GBE | GBE/GBE | GBE/GBE | |
| HFC.966. | HFC.2,931. | HFC.967. | HFC.968. |
| | | | Robin Hood. |
| | | | USA |
| HFC.2,932. | HSC.2,933. | HFC.969. | HFC.970. |

111

|  |  |  |  |
|---|---|---|---|
| (headstamp: ECO 12 12) | (headstamp: E.C. 12 12 POWDER) | (headstamp: E.C. 12 12 POWDER) | (headstamp: E.C. POWDER No 2 ELEY EJECTOR) |
|  | Powder maker. | Powder maker. | Eley Bros. Ejt. |
|  | GBE | GBE | GBE/GBE |
| HFC.971. | HSC.2,934. | HFC.972. | HFC.973. |
| (headstamp: E.C.T. 12 12 K.K.T.C.) | (headstamp: EDMONDS & WELLDON No 12 RUGBY) | (headstamp: EDWARDS & SON No 12 PLYMOUTH) | (headstamp: EDWARDS & SON PLYMOUTH No 12 ELEY) |
| Pla. |  | Gnm. | Gnm. Pre Wwl. |
|  | GBE | GBE | GBE/GBE |
| HSC.2,935. | HFC.974. | HSC.2,936. | HFC.2,937. |
| (headstamp: EDWARDS & SON No 12 PLYMOUTH BELGIAN MADE SHELL) | (headstamp: EDWARDS & SON No 12 PLYMOUTH FRANCE MADE CASE) | (headstamp: EDWINSON GREEN -12-) | (headstamp: EDWINSON GREEN MADE IN FRANCE CASE No 12) |
| Gnm. | Gnm. | Gnm. | Gnm. |
| GBE/B | GBE/F | GBE | GBE/F |
| HFC.975. | HSC.2,938. | HFC.976. | HSC.2,939. |
| (headstamp: EDWINSON GREEN MADE IN FRANCE CASE No 12) | (headstamp: EDWINSON GREEN MADE IN FRANCE CASE No 12) | (headstamp: EDWINSON GREEN KYNOCH 12) | (headstamp: EDWINSON GREEN KYNOCH -12-) |
| Gnm. | Gnm. | Kynoch case. | Pre Wwl. |
| GBE/F | GBE/F | GBE/GBE | GBE/GBE |
| HFC.2,940. | HFC.2,941. | HFC.978. | HFC.977. |

| | | | |
|---|---|---|---|
| | | | |
| Ernest Fred. Irm. | Gnm, | Gnm. | Gnm. Eley Bros case |
| | | | |
| GBE/GBE | GBE | GBE | GBE/GBE |
| HFC.979. | HFC.980/R. | HSC.2,942. | HSC.2,943. |
| | | | |
| Manufacturer. | | | London Gnm. |
| | | | |
| USA | D | GBE | GBE |
| HSC.2,944. | HFC.981. | HFC.982. | HSC.2,945. |
| | | | |
| London Gnm. | Loader. | | |
| | | | |
| GBE/GBE | AUS | D | D |
| HFC.983. | HSC.2,946. | HSC.2,947. | HSC.2,948. |
| | | | |
| Eley Bros. | Eley Bros. | Pre WW1. | Manufacturer. |
| | | | |
| CDN | GBE/GBE | GBE/GBE | GBE/GBE |
| HSC.2,949. | HSC.2,950. | HFC.2,951. | HSC.2,952. |

113

| | | | |
|---|---|---|---|
| Manufacturer. | Pre Wwl. | Manufacturer. | Manufacturer. |
| On other gauges. | On other gauges. | | On other gauges. |
| GBE/GBE | GBE/GBE | GBE/GBE | GBE/GBE |
| HSC.2,953. | HFC.984/R. | HFC.985/R. | HFC.2,954. |
| Pre Wwl. | Pre Wwl. | Pre Wwl. | Eley Bros. |
| On other gauges. | | | |
| GBE/GBE | GBE/GBE | GBE/GBE | CDN/CDN |
| HFC.2,955. | HSC.2,956. | HSC.2,957. | HSC.2,958. |
| Eley Bros. | Manufacturer. | Manufacturer. | Eley Bros. |
| | 16. | | |
| CDN/CDN | CDN/CDN | F | GBE/GBE |
| HSC.2,959. | HSC.2,960. | HSC.2,961. | HFC.2,962. |
| Manufacturer. | Pre Wwl. | Eley Hawk. | Pap. Pla. |
| On other gauges. | On other gauges. | On other gauges. | On other gauges. |
| GBE/GBE | GBE/GBE | GBE/GBE | GBE/GBE |
| HFC.2,963. | HFC.989. | HFC.988. | HFC.987. |

| | | | |
|---|---|---|---|
| Manufacturer. | Eley Bros. | Pre Ww1. | Eley Bros. |
| On other gauges. | 20. | | On other gauges. |
| GBE/GBE | B/GBE | B/GBE | GBE/GBE |
| HFC.986. | HSC.2,964. | HSC.2,965. | HFC.991. |
| Pre Ww1. | Eley Bros. | IMI (Kynoch) Ltd. | Irish Metal Ind'. |
| On other gauges. | | On other gauges. | 16. |
| GBE/GBE | GBE/GBE | GBE/GBE | IRL/GBE |
| HFC.990. | HFC.992. | HFC.993. | HFC.994. |
| I.C.I.A.N.Z. | Manufacturer. | Pre Ww2. | Eley Rocket. |
| AUS-NZ/AUS | AUS-NZ/AUS | AUS-NZ/AUS | AUS-NZ/AUS |
| HFC.1,006. | HFC.1,007. | HFC.1,008. | HFC.1,009. |
| Pre Ww2. | Eley-Kynoch ICI. | Pre Ww2. | Eley-Kynoch ICI. |
| | On other gauges. | On other gauges. | On other gauges. |
| AUS-NZ/AUS | GBE/GBE | GBE/GBE | GBE/GBE |
| HSC.2,966. | HFC.997. | HFC.999. | HFC.998. |

| | | | |
|---|---|---|---|
| Black powder load. | Eley Rocket. | Explosive star. | Experimental. |
| GBE/GBE | GBE/GBE | GBE/GBE | GBE/GBE |
| HFC.1.001. | HFC.1,002. | HFC.996. | HSC.2,967. |
| Experimental. | Metal case. | Large cap. | Manufacturer. |
| GBE/GBE | GBE/GBE | GBE/GBE | AUS/AUS |
| HSC.2,968. | HFC.1,003. | HFC.995. | HFC.1,000. |
| I.C.I.A.N.Z. | Manufacturer. | Experimental. | Experimental. |
| AUS-NZ-AUS | AUS-NZ/AUS | GBE/GBE | GBE/GBE |
| HFC.1,004. | HFC.1,005. | HSC.2,969. | HFC.2,970. |
| Experimental. | Experimental. | Experimental. | Eley Bros. |
| GBE/GBE | GBE/GBE | GBE/GBE | GBE/GBE |
| HFC.2,971. | HSC.2,972. | HSC.2,973. | HFC.1,010. |

| | | | |
|---|---|---|---|
| (ELEY No 12 LONDON) | (ELEY No 12 LONDON) | (ELEY No 12 LONDON) | (ELEY No 12 LONDON) |
| Eley Bros. | Manufacturer. | Pre Wwl. | Pre Wwl. |
| 24, 16, 10. | On other gauges. | | |
| GBE/GBE | GBE/GBE | GBE/GBE | GBE/GBE |
| HSC.2,974. | HFC.2,975. | HFC.1,011. | HFC.1,013. |
| (ELEY No 12 LONDON) | (ELEY No 12 LONDON) | (ELEY No 12 LONDON) | (ELEY No 12 LONDON) |
| Eley Bros. | Manufacturer. | Pre Wwl. | Eley Bros. |
| On other gauges. | | On other gauges. | |
| GB/GBE | GBE/GBE | GBE/GBE | GBE/GBE |
| HFC.1,012. | HFC.1,014. | HFC.1,015. | HFC.1,016. |
| (ELEY No 12 LONDON) | (ELEY No 12 LONDON) | (ELEY No 12 LONDON) | (ELEY No 12 LONDON) |
| Eley Bros. | Pre Wwl. | Manufacturer. | Pre Wwl. |
| | On other gauges. | | |
| GBE/GBE | GBE/GBE | GBE/GBE | GBE/GBE |
| HFC.1,017. | HFC.1,018. | HFC.1,019. | HFC.1,020. |
| (*ELEY* No 12 LONDON) | (*ELEY* No 12 LONDON) | (*ELEY* No 12 LONDON) | (*ELEY* No 12 LONDON) |
| For New Explosives. | For New Explosives. | For New Explosives. | For New Explosives. |
| | | 20, 16. | |
| GBE/GBE | GBE/GBE | GBE/GBE | GBE/GBE |
| HFC.1,022. | HFC.1,021. | HFC.1,023. | HFC.1,024. |

| | | | |
|---|---|---|---|
| New to me ? | Eley Bros case. | Post Wwl.<br>On other gauges. | Eley Bros.<br>On other gauges. |
| HSC.2,976. | /GBE<br>HFC.1,026. | GBE/GBE<br>HFC.1,025. | GBE/GBE<br>HFC.1,028. |
| Eley Bros. | Manufacturer.<br>On other gauges. | Pre Wwl. | Large cap. |
| GBE/GBE<br>HFC.1,029. | GBE/GBE<br>HFC.1,030. | GBE/GBE<br>HFC.1,031. | GBE/GBE<br>HFC.1,027. |
| Eley Bros. | Eley Bros case. | Eley Bros. | Experimental. |
| GBE/GBE<br>HSC.2,977. | USA/GBE<br>HSC.2,978. | GBE/GBE<br>HFC.1,032. | GBE/GBE<br>HFC.2,979. |
| Nobel Industries. | Manufacturer.<br>On other gauges. | Post Wwl.<br>On other gauges. | Post Wwl. |
| GBE/GBE<br>HFC.1,033. | GBE/GBE<br>HFC.1,037. | GBE/GBE<br>HFC.1,035. | GBE/GBE<br>HFC.2,980. |

| | | | |
|---|---|---|---|
| Nobel Industries. | Manufacturer. | Post Wwl | Nobel Industries. |
| On other gauges. | On other gauges. | | On other gauges. |
| GBE/GBE | GBE/GBE | GBE/GBE | GBE/GBE |
| HFC.1,034. | HFC.1,036. | HSC.2,981. | HFC.1,038. |
| Post Wwl. | Nobel Industries. | Eley Bros. | Pre Wwl. |
| | On other gauges. | | |
| GBE/GBE | GBE/GBE | GBE/GBE | GBE/GBE |
| HSC.2,982. | HFC.1,039. | HFC.1,040. | HFC.1,041. |
| | | | Eley Bros. Ejt. |
| | | | On other gauges. |
| B/ | B/,, | | GBE/GBE |
| HFC.1,042. | HFC.1,043. | HFC.1,044. | HFC.1.045. |
| Manufacturer. Ejt. | Pre Wwl. Ejt. | Pre Wwl. Ejt. | Eley Bros. Ejt. |
| | | | On other gauges. |
| GBE/GBE | GBE/GBE | GBE/GBE | GBE/GBE |
| HSC.2,983. | HSC.2,984. | HSC.2,985. | HFC.1,046. |

| | | | |
|---|---|---|---|
| ELEY'S "GRAND PRIX" 12 | ELEY'S No 12 FOR MULLERITE | ELEY'S SMOKELESS No 12 | 12 12 +ELITE+ |
| Eley Bros. | Manufacturer. | Eley Bros. | |
| GBE/GBE | GBE/GBE | GBE/GBE | GBE/GBE |
| HFC.2,986. | HSC.2,987. | HSC.2,988. | HFC.1,047. |
| ELLICOTT No 12 CARDIFF | ELLICOTT CONED BASE CASE No 12 PATENT No 14918 CARDIFF | ELLICOTT No 12 LAUNCESTON | E No 12 LONDON |
| | | Loader. | Eley Bros. |
| GBW/ | GBW/ | GBE | GBE/GBE |
| HSC.2,989. | HFC.1,048. | HFC.1,049. | HSC.2,990/R. |
| E No 12 LONDON | E No 12 LONDON | E No 12 LONDON | E.M.REILEY & CO ELEY No 12 |
| Eley Bros. | Eley Bros. | Eley Bros. | London Gnm. |
| GBE/GBE | GBE/GBE | GBE/GBE | GBE/GBE |
| HFC.1,051/R. | HFC.1,052/R. | HFC.1,050/R. | HFC.2,991. |
| E.M.REILLY & CO ELEY No 12 | E.P.CARR No 12 KYNOCH NOTTINGHAM | E.REMINGTON 12 | E.RMITAGE 12 12 |
| London Gnm. | Dealer Irm. | | |
| GBE/GBE | GBE/GBE | USA | CH |
| HFC.1,053. | HFC.1,054. | HSC.2,992. | HFC.1,055. |

| | | | |
|---|---|---|---|
| ERNEST MAYOR GENEVE 12 12 | No E.ROBERTS BIRMINGHAM 12 | ERRE 12 12 ITALY | E.R.T. 12 12 ESPANA |
| | Gnm. | | |
| CH | GBE | I | E |
| HSC.2,993. | HSC.2,994. | HFC.1,056. | HFC.1,059. |
| E.R.T. 12 12 ESPANA | E.R.T. 12 12 ESPAÑA | ESTATE 12 GA CARTRIDGE | E·SUMMONTE 12 12 ERCOLANO |
| | | | |
| E | E | | |
| HFC.1,057. | HFC.1,058. | HFC.1,060. | HFC.1,061. |
| EUREKA No 12 | EUROCOMM 12 12 ITALY | EUROPA 12 12 EUROPA | EVANS PATENT GROUSE EJECTOR LONDON |
| | | | Gnm, Ejt. |
| | I | | GBE/GBE |
| HSC.2,995. | HFC.1,062. | HFC.1,063. | HFC.1,064. |
| EVERLASTING No 12 | E.WEST.RETFORD KYNOCH No12 | E.WILSON.NORWICH No 12 ELEY | No E.WOODS 12 LONDON |
| | Elizabeth West, Gnm | Edwin Wilson, Gnm. | Edmund Woods, Gnm. |
| | GBE/GBE | GBE/GBE | GBE |
| HSC.2,996. | HFC.1,065. | HFC.1,066. | HFC.1,067. |

| | | | |
|---|---|---|---|
| EXCELSIOR 12 12 | EXCHEM 12 12 MARK | EXCOPESA 12 12 SPAIN | EXCOPESA 12 12 SPAIN |
| Pla. | Pla. | Pla. | Pla. |
| | | E | E |
| HSC.2,997. | HFC.1,068. | HFC.1,069. | HSC.2,998. |
| 12 EXPRESS | EXPRESS 12 | EXPRESS 12 | EXTRA DEEP 12 12 GASTIGHT |
| Lyavale.  Pla. | Lyavale.  Pla. | Lyavale.  Pla. | |
| GBE/ | GBE/ | GBE/ | |
| HFC.1,070. | HFC.1,072. | HFC.1,071. | HFC.1,073. |
| EXTRA DEEP 12 12 GASTIGHT | EXTRA 12 12 MG | EXTRA No 12 QUALITY | ELEY 10 12 LONDON |
| | | REM-UMC. | 10-12 gauge. E.B. |
| | | USA | GBE/GBE |
| HFC.2,999. | HFC.1,074. | HSC.3,000. | HFC.2,064. |
| E B No 10 LONDON | E B No 10 LONDON | ECLIPSE 10 10 R.H.A.CO. | E.C.MEACHAM & CO. No 10 ST.LOUIS.MO. |
| 10 gauge. | Eley Bros. | Robin Hood. | |
| | 16. 12. | On other gauges. | |
| GBE/GBE | GBE/GBE | USA | USA |
| HFC.3,001/R. | HSC.3,002. | HSC.3,003. | HSC.3,004. |

| | | | |
|---|---|---|---|
| Geo Hart & Co. Abc. | Manufacturer. 12. | Pre Ww1. | Pre Ww1. |
| USA | GBE/GBE | GBE/GBE | GBE/GBE |
| HSC.3,005. | HSC.3,006. | HSC.3,007. | HSC.3,008. |
| Manufacturer. On other gauges. | Pre Ww1. | Eley Bros. 12. | Eley Bros. On other gauges. |
| GBE/GBE | GBE/GBE | CDN/CDN | GBE/GBE |
| HFC.2,073/R. | HSC.3,009. | HFC.2,074. | HFC.3,010. |
| Eley Bros. 12. | Post Ww2. On other gauges. | Pre and post Ww2. On other gauges. | Eley Bros. On other gauges. |
| GBE/GBE | GBE/GBE | GBE/GBE | GBE/GBE |
| HSC.3,011. | HFC.2,076. | HFC.2,077. | HSC.3,012. |
| Manufacturer. On other gauges. | Pre Ww1. On other gauges. | Eley Bros case. 12. | 10 gauge. |
| GBE/GBE | GBE/GBE | USA/GBE | GBE/GBE |
| HSC.3,013. | HFC.2,232. | HFC.2,078. | HFC.2,233. |

| | | | |
|---|---|---|---|
| (ELEY 10 10 NOBEL) | (ELEY N.I. No 10 NOBEL) | (ELEY 10 10 NOBEL) | (ELEY No WATERPROOF "PEGAMOID" 10) |
| Nobel Industries. | Manufacturer. | Pre Ww1. | Eley Bros. |
| On other gauges. | | On other gauges. | On other gauges. |
| GBE/GBE | GBE/GBE | GBE/GBE | GBE/GBE |
| HSC.3,014. | HSC.3,015, | HFC.3,016. | HSC.3,017. |
| (ELEY'S No 10 EJECTOR LONDON) | (ELEY'S "EXPRESS" 10) | (ELEY'S "GRAND PRIX" 10) | (E *** No 10 LONDON) |
| Eley Bros, Ejt. | Eley Bros. | Eley Bros. | Eley Bros. |
| On other gauges. | | 12. | |
| GBE/GBE | GBE/GBE | GBE/GBE | GBE/GBE |
| HSC.3,018. | HFC.2,075. | HSC.3,019. | HFC.2,072/R. |
| (EUREKA No 10) | (EVERLASTING No 10) | (ELEY BROS No 8 LONDON) | (ELEY No 8 GASTIGHT) |
| | Abc. | 8 gauge. | Manufacturer. |
| | | On other gauges. | On other gauges. |
| | | GBE/GBE | GBE/GBE |
| HSC.3,020. | HSC.3,021. | HSC.3,022. | HSC.3,033. |
| (ELEY No 8 GASTIGHT) | (ELEY-KYNOCH 8) | (ELEY-KYNOCH 8 ICI 8) | (ELEY No 8 LONDON) |
| Pre Ww1. | Post Ww2. | Pre and post Ww2. | Eley Bros. |
| On other gauges. | On other gauges. | On other gauges. | On other gauges. |
| GBE/GBE | GBE/GBE | GBE/GBE | GBE/GBE |
| HSC.3,034. | HFC.3,035. | HSC.3,036. | HSC.3,037. |

| | | | |
|---|---|---|---|
| Pre Wwl. | Nobel Industries. | Post Wwl. | Pegamoid Pap. |
| On other gauges. | On other gauges. | On other gauges. | On other gauges. |
| GBE/GBE | GBE/GBE | GBE/GBE | GBE/GBE |
| HFC.2,106. | HSC.3,038. | HSC.3,039. | HSC.3,040. |
| Pre Wwl. | Eley Bros. | Eley Bros, Ejt, | 4 gauge. |
| On other gauges. | On other gauges. | On other gauges. | |
| GBE/GBE | GBE/GBE | GBE/GBE | GBE/GBE |
| HSC.3,041. | HFC.3,042. | HFC.2,107. | HFC.3,043/R. |
| Eley Bros. | Pre Wl. | Manufacturer. | Eley Bros. |
| On other gauges. | On other gauges. | On other gauges. | On other gauges. |
| GBE/GBE | GBE/GBE | GBE/GBE | GBE/GBE |
| HFC.3,045/R. | HFC.2,116. | HFC.2,117. | HFC.3,046. |
| Nobel Industries. | 4 gauge. | Pyrotechnic. | James Pain & Sons. |
| On other gauges. | | | |
| GBE/GBE | GBE/GBE | GBE/GBE | GBE/GBE |
| HSC.3,047. | HFC.2,134. | HSC.3,048. | HFC.3,049. |

| | | | |
|---|---|---|---|
| ELEY 4 4 NOBEL | ELEY 4 4 NOBEL | ELEY 4 4 NOBEL | 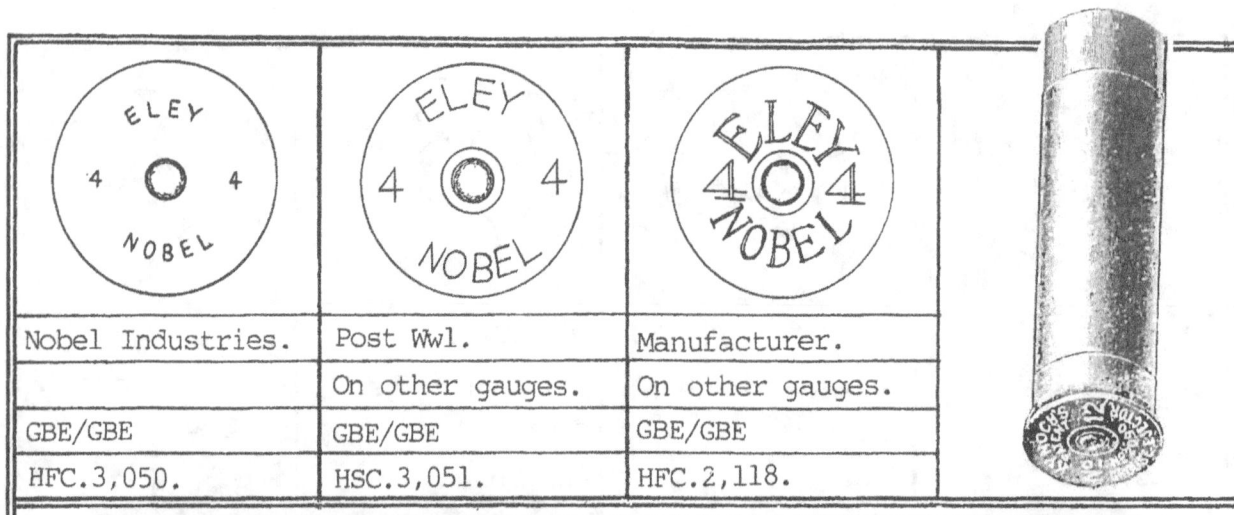 |
| Nobel Industries. | Post Ww1. | Manufacturer. | |
| | On other gauges. | On other gauges. | |
| GBE/GBE | GBE/GBE | GBE/GBE | |
| HFC.3,050. | HSC.3,051. | HFC.2,118. | |

Two of five similar lorries by Kynoch on Win The War Day in 1918.

| | | | |
|---|---|---|---|
| ·360. Fiocchi. | ·360. Pla. | .410. | .410 |
| | | | |
| I/I | I/I | I/I | |
| HFC.217. | HFC.216. | HFC.3,052. | HFC.230. |
| | | | |
| 28 gauge. | Manufacturer. | | |
| | 20, 16, 12. | | |
| USA/USA | USA/USA | I/I | I/I |
| HSC.3,053. | HSC.3,054. | HFC.256. | HFC.257. |
| | | | |
| 20 gauge. | | | |
| | Frankfort Arsenal. | | |
| USA | USA | USA | D |
| HSC.3,055. | HSC.3,056. | HSC.3,057. | HSC.3,058. |
| | | | |
| | | | Manufacturer. |
| | 16, 12. | | 28, 16, 12. |
| | USA/USA | F/GBE | USA/USA |
| HSC.3,059. | HSC.3,060. | HSC.3,061. | HSC.3,062. |

| | | | |
|---|---|---|---|
| (Federal No 20 Reliable) | (Fiocchi 20) | (Fiocchi 20 ? 20 Italy) | (20 Fiocchi 20 Italy) |
| Manufacturer. | Manufacturer. | Manufacturer. | Manufacturer. |
| 16, 12. | 16, 12. | On other gauges. | |
| USA/USA | I/I | I/I | I/I |
| HSC.3,063. | HFC.325. | HSC.3,064. | HFC.5.441. |
| (20 Fiocchi Max 900 Bar) | (FN 20 20 FN) | (FN 20 20 Made in Belgium) | (F.N. 20 20 Made in Belgium Herstal) |
| Manufacturer. | Manufacturer. | Manufacturer. | Manufacturer. |
| | On other gauges. | On other gauges. | On other gauges. |
| I/I | B/B | B/B | B/B |
| HFC.327. | HFC.328. | HSC.3,065. | HSC.3,066. |
| (F.N. 20 20 Made in Belgium Herstal) | (F.T.Baker London 20) | (Farmer No 16 Leighton) | (Favorito 16) |
| Manufacturer. | Gnm. | 16 gauge, Gnm. | 16 gauge, |
| | | | |
| B/B | GBE | GBE | D |
| HSC.3,067. | HFC.329. | HFC.476. | HSC.3,068. |
| (Favorito 16) | (FC 16 GA HL) | (Federal No Hi-Power 16) | (Federal 16 GA Monark) |
| | | Manufacturer. | Manufacturer. |
| | 20, 12. | 12. | 12. |
| D | | USA/USA | USA/USA |
| HSC.3.069. | HSC.3,070. | HFC.477. | HFC.478. |

| | | | |
|---|---|---|---|
| (FEDERAL No 16 RELIABLE) | (FIOCCHI 16) | (FIOCCHI 16 16 ITALY) | (FIOCCHI 16 16 ITALY) |
| Manufacturer. | Pla. | Manufacturer. | |
| 20, 12. | | | |
| USA/USA | I/I | I/I | I/I |
| HSC.3,071. | HFC.3,072. | HFC.479. | HFC.480. |
| (FITCHEW No 16 RAMSGATE) | (F.JOYCE & Co No 16 LONDON) | (FLOBERT PARIS 16) | (FLOBERT PARIS 16) |
| A. T. Fitchew. | Manufacturer. | | |
| 12. | | | |
| GBE | GBE/GBE | F | F |
| HSC.3,073. | HFC.481. | HFC.482. | HFC.483. |
| (FLOBERT 16 16 PARIS) | (FLOBERT 16 16 PARIS) | (FN 16 16 FN) | (FN 16 16 MADE IN BELGIUM) |
| | | Manufacturer. | Manufacturer. |
| 12. | | On other gauges. | On other gauges. |
| F/F | F/F | B/B | B/B |
| HFC.484. | HFC.485. | HFC.486. | HFC.487. |
| (FN 16 16 HERSTAL) | (FORTUNA 16 16 *K*) | (16 16 FRANCE) | (16 16 FREDERIKSVÆRK) |
| Manufacturer. | Pap. | Pla. | H.K. Pap. |
| On other gauges. | | 12. | 12. |
| B/B | | F | DK/DK |
| HFC.3,074. | HSC.3,075. | HFC.3,076. | HFC.488. |

| | | | |
|---|---|---|---|
| (16 FREDERIKSVÆRK 16, crown) | (FULMA 16 ? 16 *MR*) | (F. JOYCE & Co N° 14 LONDON) | (N.F. JOYCE & C° N° 14 LONDON) |
| H.K. Pap. | 16 gauge. | 14 gauge. | Manufacturer. |
| 12. | | | On other gauges. |
| DK/DK | | GBE/GBE | GBE/GBE |
| HFC.489. | HSC.3,077. | HSC.3,078. | HFC.3,079. |
| (FABRICA ROMANA 12 12 BUCURESTI) | (FABRICATION FRANCAISE 12 12) | (FALCON 12 12 PAT No 18308) | (FALKE ☆ ☆ 12) |
| 12 gauge. | | 12 gauge. Apc. | |
| | | | |
| R | F/F | | |
| HSC.3,080. | HFC.1,075. | HSC.3,081. | HFC.1,076. |
| (F.A.M. 12 12 ITALY) | (FANAC N° 12 EQUADOR) | (FARMER N° 12 LEIGHTON) | (FARMERS 12 12 TRADING) |
| Pla. | Pla. | Gnm. | |
| | | 16. | |
| I | EC | GBE | NZ |
| HSC.5,442. | HSC.3,082. | HFC.1,077. | HSC.3,083. |
| (FARMERS 12 12 TRADING) | (FATUB 12 12 PORTO) | (FAVORITO * * 12) | (FC 12 GA PERSONAL DEFENSE) |
| | Pla. | | Spelling ? |
| | | | |
| NZ | P | D | |
| HSC.3,084. | HSC.3,085. | HSC.3,086. | HSC.3,087. |

| | | | |
|---|---|---|---|
| (FC 12 GA HL) | (F.COLE No 12 DEVIZES) | (F.DUMMOND.PARIS ELEY No 12) | (F.E.BOYD PAT FEB 8, 1870) |
| | F. J. Cole, Gnm. | | 12 gauge. |
| | | 20. | |
| USA | GBE | F/GBE | USA |
| HSC.3,088. | HFC.3,089. | HSC.3,090. | HSC.3,091. |
| (F.E.C. 12 12 F.E.C.) | (FEDERAL 12 GA) | (FEDERAL 12 GA CARTRIDGE) | (FEDERAL 12 GA GOLD MEDAL) |
| Pla. | Manufacturer. Pla. | Manufacturer. | Pla. |
| | | | |
| | USA/USA | USA/USA | USA/USA |
| HSC.3,092. | HSC.3,093. | HFC.1,078. | HFC.1,079. |
| (FEDERAL 12 GA HI-POWER) | (FEDERAL No 12 HI-POWER) | (FEDERAL No 12 MONARK) | (FEDERAL No 12 MONARK) |
| Pla. | | Manufacturer. | |
| 16. | | | |
| USA/USA | USA/USA | USA/USA | USA/USA |
| HFC.1,080. | HFC.1,081. | HFC.1,082. | HSC.3,094. |
| (FEDERAL 12 GA MONARK) | (FEDERAL No 12 RELIABLE) | (FEDERAL 12 GA STEEL) | (F.E.STOCKER.St AUSTELL No 12 ELEY) |
| Manufacturer. Pla. | | Manufacturer. | Irm. |
| 16. | 20, 16. | | |
| USA/USA | USA/USA | USA/USA | GBE/GBE |
| HSC.3,095. | HSC.3,096. | HFC.1,083. | HFC.2,187. |

| | | | |
|---|---|---|---|
| (F.E.WALKER No 12 NEWBURY) | (F.H.TIMS No 12 TRURO) | (FIELD) | (FIEM 12 12 ITALY) |
| Gnm. Pre Wwl. | Fred H. Tims. Gnm. | | Pla. |
| GBE | GBE | | I |
| HFC.1,084. | HFC.1,085. | HSC.3,097. | HSC.3,098. |
| (FIOCCHI 12) | (FIOCCHI 12 12 HELLAS) | (FIOCCHI 12 12 HELLAS) | (FIOCCHI 12 12 INNOCENTI) |
| Manufacturer. | | Manufacturer. | Manufacturer. |
| I/I | I/I | I/I | I/I |
| HFC.1,086. | HFC.1,088. | HFC.1,087. | HFC.1,090. |
| (FIOCCHI 12 12 INT.L) | (FIOCCHI 12 12 INT.L) | (FIOCCHI 12 12 ITALY) | (FIOCCHI 12 12 ITALY) |
| Manufacturer. | Pla. | Manufacturer. | |
| | | 16. | 16. |
| I/I | I/I | I/I | I/I |
| HFC.1,091. | HFC.1,089. | HFC.1,092. | HFC.1,095. |
| (FIOCCHI 12 12 ITALY) | (FIOCCHI 12 12 ITALY) | (FIOCCHI 12 12 ITALY) | (FIOCCHI 12 12 U.S.A.) |
| | Manufacturer. | | Pla. |
| 16. | | | |
| I/I | I/I | I/I | USA/USA |
| HFC.1,094. | HFC.1,093. | HFC.1,096. | HFC.1,097. |

| | | | |
|---|---|---|---|
| (FISHER made in GERMANY 12 12 PHILA.PA.) | (FISHER MADE IN GERMANY 12 12 PHILA.PA.) | (FITCHEW Nº 12 RAMSGATE) | (FITZROY 12) |
| | | Excel Cartridge. | |
| USA/D | USA/D | GBE | AUS |
| HSC.3,099. | HSC.3,100. | HFC.1,098. | HSC.3,101. |
| (F.J.COLE 12 12 CIRENCESTER) | (F.JOYCE Nº 12 LONDON) | (F. JOYCE & Cº Nº 12 LONDON) | (F. JOYCE & Cº Nº 12 LONDON) |
| Gnm. | Manufacturer. | | Manufacturer. |
| | | | On other gauges. |
| GBE | GBE/GBE | GBE/GBE | GBE/GBE |
| HSC.3,102. | HSC.3,103. | HSC.3,104. | HFC.3,105. |
| (F.L.B 12×70) | (Fˡˡⁱ SUMMONTE 12 12 ERCOLAND) | (Fˡˡⁱ SUMMONTE 12 12 ERCOLAND) | (Fˡˡⁱ SUMMONTE 12 12 RESINA) |
| Pla. | Pla. | | |
| | | | |
| HSC.3,106. | HFC.3,107. | HSC.3,108. | HSC.1,099. |
| (FLOBERT 12 12 PARIS) | (F.N.C.C. 12 12 VENEZUELA) | (12 FN CF 12) | (12 FN CF 12) |
| | Pla. | Manufacturer. Pla. | Manufacturer. |
| On other gauges. | | | |
| F/F | YV | B/B | B/B |
| HSC.1,100. | HSC.3,109. | HFC.1,101. | HSC.3,110. |

| | | | |
|---|---|---|---|
| (FN 12 12 FN) | (FN 12 12 MADE IN BELGIUM) | (FN 12 12 MADE IN BELGIUM) | (FN 12 12 MADE IN BELGIUM) |
| Manufacturer. | Pla. | Manufacturer. | |
| On other gauges. | | On other gauges. | On other gauges. |
| B/B | B/B | B/B | B/B |
| HFC.1,102. | HFC.1,103. | HFC.1,104. | HFC.1,105. |
| (F.N 12 12 MADE IN BELGIUM HERSTAL) | (12 F.N 12 MADE IN BELGIUM HERSTAL) | (F.N 12 12 HERSTAL) | (FN 12 12 PB) |
| Manufacturer. | | Manufacturer. | Pla. |
| B/B | B/B | B/B | B/B |
| HFC.2,188. | HFC.1,106. | HFC.3,111. | HFC.3,112. |
| (FN 12 12 PROPULSIVE) | (FORT 12 GA DEARBORN) | (FORT 12 GA DEARBORN) | (FORTUNA 12 12 + K +) |
| Manufacturer. Apc. | | | |
| B/B | USA | USA | D |
| HSC.3,113. | HSC.3,114. | HSC.3,115. | HSC.3,116. |
| (FOWLER No 12) | (FOWLER No 12 PLATING CO.) | (12 12 FRANCE) | (12 12 FRANCE) |
| | 10. | | |
| USA | USA | F | F |
| HSC.3,117. | HSC.3,118. | HFC.1,107. | HFC.1,108. |

| | | | |
|---|---|---|---|
| FRANCE.ARMES 12 | FRANCIS No 12 PETERBOROUGH | FRANCIS.PETERBORO No 12 ELEY | FRANK GARRETT No 12 BIRMINGHAM |
| Pla. | Extra large cap. | Charles Francis. Gnm. | Loader. |
| F | GBE | GBE/GBE | GBE |
| HFC.3,119. | HFC.1,109. | HFC.1,110. | HFC.3,120. |
| FRANK GARRETT No 12 BIRMINGHAM | FRANK GARRETT 12 BIRMINGHAM | FRAP 12 12 ITALY | 12 12 FREDERIKSVÆRK |
| Loader. | Loader. | | H.K. |
| | | | 16. |
| GBE | GBE | I | DK/DK |
| HFC.3,121. | HSC.3,122. | HFC.1,111. | HFC.1,112. |
| F.STOCKER.ST.AUSTELL No 12 ELEY | F.T.BAKER.LONDON No 12 | F.T.BAKER.LONDON No 12 | F.T.BAKER LONDON No 12 |
| See No, HFC.2,187. | Gnm. | Gnm. | Gnm. |
| GBE/GBE | GBE | GBE | GBE |
| HSC.3,123. | HSC.3,124. | HFC.1,113. | HFC.1,114. |
| F.T.BAKER.LONDON No 12 ELEY | F.T.BAKER.LONDON No 12 | F.T.BAKER LONDON | F.T.BAKER KYNOCHS PATENT No 12 GROUSE EJECTOR LONDON |
| Gnm. | Gnm. | Gnm. | Gnm, Ejt. |
| GBE/GBE | GBE/F | GBE | GBE/GBE |
| HFC.1,115. | HFC.1,116. | HSC.3,125. | HFC.1,117. |

| | | | |
|---|---|---|---|
| F.TURVEY 12 12 BURY ST. EDMUNDS MADE IN BELGIUM | FURLONG No 12 SAFFRON WALDEN | F.W.LIGHTWOOD No 12 C.H.M.C. BRIGG & GRIMSBY | F.W.LIGHTWOOD No 12 C.H.M.C. BRIGG & GRIMSBY |
| Pre WW2. | | Frank W. Lightwood. | Gunsmith. |
| GBE/B | | GBE/GBE | GBE/GBE |
| HSC.3,126. | HSC.3,127. | HSC.3,128. | HFC.3,129. |
| F.WOOD.SALISBURY No12 ELEY | FOWLER No 10 | FOWLER No 10 PLATING CO. | FOWLER No 10 PLATING CO. |
| | 10 gauge. | 10 gauge. | |
| | 12. | | 12. |
| GBE/GBE | USA | USA | USA |
| HFC.3,130. | HSC.3,131. | HSC.3,132. | HSC.3,133. |
| FIOCCHI 8 8 INDUSTRIALE | FIOCCHI 8 ? 8 KILN | | |
| 8 gauge. | Manufacturer. | | |
| I/I | I/I | | |
| HSC.3,134. | HSC.3,135. | | |

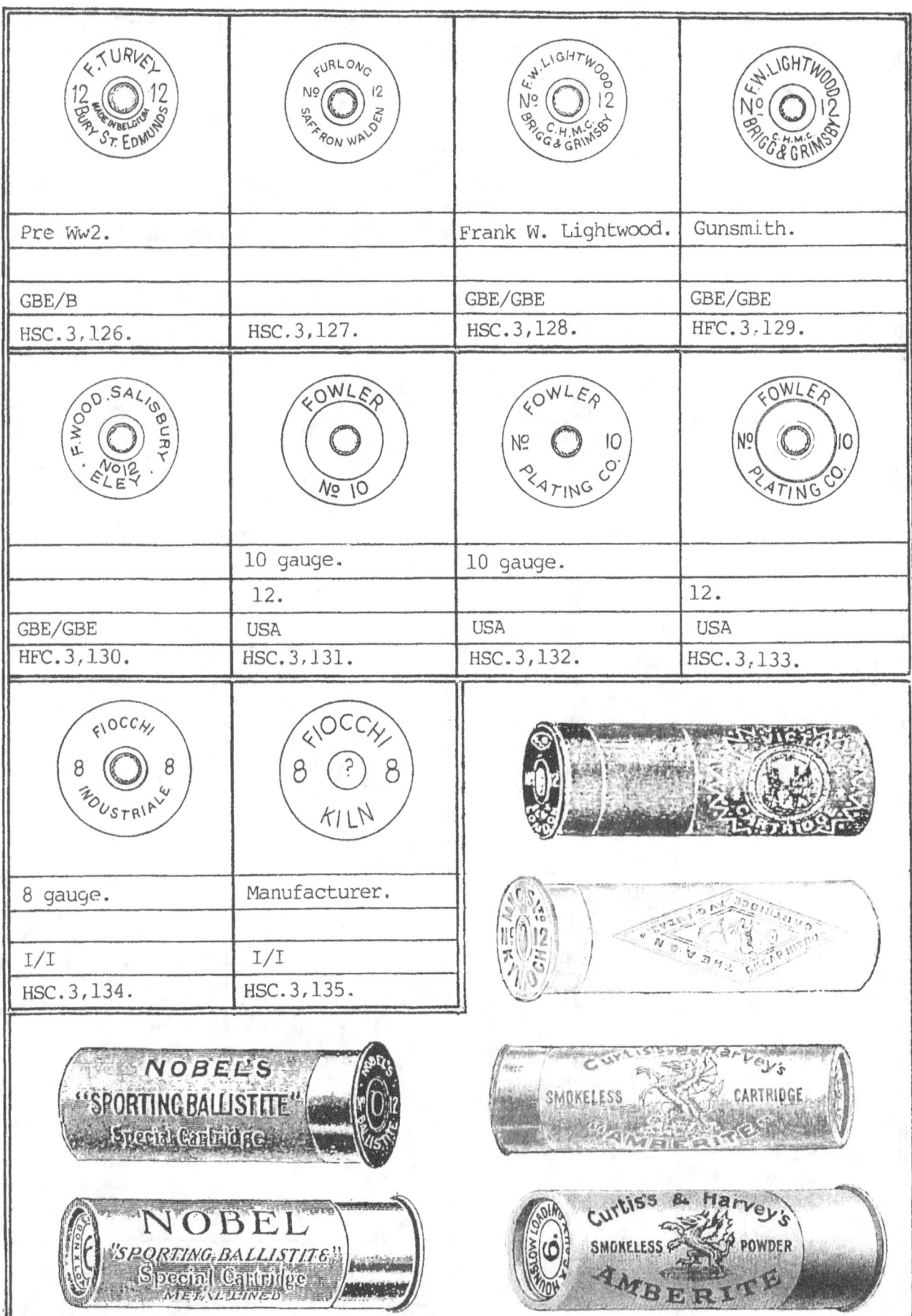

| | | | |
|---|---|---|---|
| .410. | .410. | Pla. | .410 - 12 mm. |
| USA | | I/I | D |
| HSC.3,136. | HFC.231. | HFC.3,137. | HSC.3,138. |
| 14 mm. | 28 gauge. | Manufacturer. | 28 gauge. |
| | | 20, 16, 12. | |
| F/F | CDN/CDN | CDN/CDN | F/F |
| HSC.3,139. | HSC.3,140. | HFC.3,141. | HFC.3,142. |
| Manufacturer. | 20 gauge. | | 20 gauge. |
| | On other gauges. | 16, 12. | |
| I/I | USA/USA | USA | F |
| HFC.258. | HFC.330. | HSC.3,143. | HSC.3,144. |
| 20 gauge. | | | Manufacturer. |
| | | 28, 16, 12. | |
| D | D | CDN/CDN | F/F |
| HSC.3,145. | HSC.3,146. | HFC.331. | HFC.5.443. |

| | | | |
|---|---|---|---|
| GEVELOT 20 20 PARIS | GEVELOT 20 20 PARIS | GEVELOT 20 20 PARIS | GIULIO FIOCCHI LECCO No ? GF 20 |
| Manufacturer. | | Manufacturer. | Manufacturer. |
| On other gauges. | | | |
| F/F | F/F | F/F | I/I |
| HFC.333. | HFC.334. | HFC.335. | HSC.3,147. |
| G.FIOCCHI No 20 LECCO | GIULIO FIOCCHI LECCO ? 20 GF 20 | GREEN CHELTENHAM No 20 | GYTTORP 20 20 GYTTORP |
| Manufacturer. | | Gnm. | Manufacturer. |
| | | | On other gauges. |
| I/I | I/I | GBE/GBE | S/S |
| HSC.3,148. | HSC.3,149. | HFC.336. | HFC.337. |
| GYTTORP 20 20 MADE IN SWEDEN | GARANTIE 18 18 B | GARANTIE 18 18 D | 16 GA HUNTSMAN |
| Manufacturer. | 18 gauge. | 18 gauge. | 16 gauge. |
| | | | 12. |
| S/S | D | D | MEX |
| HFC.338. | HSC.3,150. | HSC.3,151. | HSC.3,152. |
| 16 GA MADE IN U.S.A. | GAMBLES No 16 ACE | GARANTIE * * 16 | GARANTIE 16 16 B |
| 16 gauge. | | | |
| On other gauges. | 20, 12. | | |
| USA | USA | D | D |
| HFC.490. | HSC.3,153. | HSC.3,154. | HSC.3,155. |

| | | | |
|---|---|---|---|
| (16 GAUGE BROWNING) | (16 GAUGE BROWNING) | (16 ☆ 16 G.C.C.) | (16 ☆ 16 G.C.C.) |
| Manufacturer. | Post Ww2. | | |
| 28, 20, 12. | | | |
| CDN/CDN | CDN/CDN | AUS | AUS |
| HSC.3,156. | HSC.3,157. | HSC.3,158. | HSC.3,159. |
| (G.E.BOND No 16 THETFORD) | (GENSCHOW 16 16 NORMAL) | (GERMANIA 16) | (GERMANIA C.16) |
| Gnm. | Manufacturer. | | |
| | | | |
| GBE | D/D | | |
| HSC.3.160. | HFC.491. | HSC.3,161. | HSC.3,162. |
| (GEVELOT 16 16 LONDON) | (GEVELOT 16 16 PARIS) | (G.H.DAW No 16 LONDON) | (GIVLIO FIOCCHI LECCO 16 GF) |
| Abc. | Manufacturer. | Gnm. Developer. | Manufacturer. |
| | | | |
| F/GBE | F/F | GBE/GBE | I/I |
| HFC.492. | HFC.493. | HFC.3,163/R. | HFC.3,164. |
| (GONZALEZ MARINA Y CA No 16) | (GOSSELIN 16 16 SANS DEPERDITION) | (G.R. No 16 ELEY.LONDON) | (GUSTAV GENSCHOW&CO 16 16 DURLACH) |
| Havana. | | | |
| | | 20. | |
| C | F | GBE/GBE | D/D |
| HSC.3,165. | HSC.3,166. | HSC.3,167. | HFC.3,168. |

| | | | |
|---|---|---|---|
| (GARANTIE 14) | (GEO.G.BUSSEY&Co LONDON 14) | (G.K No 14 LONDON) | (G.K No 14 LONDON) |
| 14 gauge. | 14 gauge. Ejt. | May have been George Kynoch. | |
| D | GBE | GBE | GBE |
| HSC.3.169. | HFC.615. | HFC.616. | HFC.3,170. |
| (GRENFELL&ACCLES BIRMINGHAM 14) | (12 12 G) | (12 GA. BLACK POWDER PAT PEND C.A.I.) | (12 CAL 12 GA) |
| Manufacturer. | 12 gauge. | 12 gauge. | 12 gauge. |
| GBE/GBE | SU | USA | |
| HFC.617. | HSC.3,171. | HSC.3,172. | HFC.1,118. |
| (12 CAL 12 GA) | (GAFAB 12 12 GAFAB) | (12 GA 12 GA) | (12 GA G&H OMAHA 12 GA PAT PEND) |
| | | | Pla. |
| | | | USA |
| HFC.1,119. | HFC.1,120. | HSC.3,173. | HSC.3,174. |
| (12 GA. GOLD MEDAL) | (12 GA HUNTSMAN) | (GALLYON MADE IN BELGIUM 12 CAMBRIDGE) | (GALLYON&SONS.CAMBRIDGE No12 ELEY) |
| Manufacturer. | | Gnm. | Gnm. |
| On other gauges. | 16. | | |
| USA | MEX | GBE/B | GBE/GBE |
| HFC.1,121. | HSC.3,175. | HFC.1,122. | HSC.3,176. |

| | | | |
|---|---|---|---|
| A.W.Gamage Ltd. | Stores Inc. | Stores Inc. | |
| GBE/GBE | USA | USA | |
| HSC.3,177. | HSC.3,178. | HSC.3,179. | HSC.3,180. |
| | | | Gnm, Post Ww2. |
| USA | USA | USA | GBE |
| HFC.3,181. | HFC.1,124. | HFC.1,123. | HFC.1,125. |
| Gnm, Post Ww2. | | | William, Gnm. |
| GBE | D | D | GBS/GBE |
| HFC.1,126. | HSC.3,182. | HSC.3,183. | HSC.3,184. |
| William. Gnm. | Adv. | Gevelot. | Manufacturer. |
| GBE | B | F/F | GBE/GBE |
| HFC.1,127. | HSC.3,185. | HSC.3,186. | HFC.3,187. |

| | | | |
|---|---|---|---|
| (12 GASTINNE RENETTE 12) | (12 GAUGE) | (12 Gauge) | (◇ 12 GAUGE 12) |
| | | | Manufacturer. |
| | | | NZ/NZ |
| HSC.3,188. | HFC.1,128. | HFC.2.189. | HFC.1,129. |
| (12 GAUGE BROWNING) | (GAUGE 12 12 GAUGE) | (GAUPILLAT 12 12 SUPERIOR) | (G.BATES No 12 EASTBOURNE) |
| | | Gnm. | George Bates. |
| | | F | GBE |
| HFC.824. | HFC.1,130. | HFC.3,189. | HSC.3,190. |
| (G B B 12 12 ITALY) | (GBB 12 Jg2 ITALY) | (G.B.B. 12 12 MADE IN ITALY) | (G B 12 12 G B) |
| | | Pla. | Post Ww2. |
| I | I | I | E |
| HFC.1,131. | HSC.3,191. | HSC.3,192. | HSC.3,193. |
| (G B 12 12 G B) | (G B 12 12 G B) | (G B 12 12 G B) | (G B 12 12 SPAIN) |
| | | | |
| E | E | E | E |
| HFC.1,132. | HFC.1,133. | HFC.1,134. | HFC.1,135. |

| | | | |
|---|---|---|---|
| G.B 12 12 SPAIN | 12 ☀ 12 G.C.C. | 12 ☀ 12 G.C.C. | G.COONEY Nº 12 KELLS |
| | | | George Cooney. Hws. |
| E | AUS | AUS | IRL |
| HFC.1,136. | HSC.3,194. | HSC.3,195. | HFC.1,137. |
| G.E.BOND Nº 12 THETFORD | G.E.BOND Nº 12 THETFORD | G.E.BOND Nº 12 THETFORD | G.E.BOND THETFORD KYNOCH PATENT GROUSE Nº2090 Nº12 |
| Gnm. | Gnm. | Gnm. | Gnm, Ejt. |
| GBE | GBE | GBE | GBE/GBE |
| HSC.3,196. | HSC.3,197. | HFC.2,190. | HSC.3,198. |
| G.E.BOND KYNOCH'S PATENT GROUSE Nº2090 Nº12 THETFORD | GENTRY 12 12 | Geo F. HART 12 A | Nº GEO.G.BUSSEY&Cº 12 LONDON |
| Gnm, Ejt. | Pla. | | |
| GBE/GBE | | USA | GBE |
| HFC.1,138. | HSC.3,199. | HSC.3,200. | HFC.1,139. |
| GEORGE BARNITT&Cº Nº 12 KYNOCH YORK | GEORGE BATES Nº 12 EASTBOURNE | GEORGE GIBBS, BRISTOL & LONDON 12 | GEORGE GIBBS LTD, BRISTOL & LONDON Nº12 |
| | Gnm. | Gnm. | Gnm. |
| GBE/GBE | GBE | GBE | GBE |
| HFC.1,140. | HSC.3,201. | HSC.3,202. | HFC.1,142. |

| | | | |
|---|---|---|---|
| (George Gibbs Ltd Bristol & London No 12) | (Germania 12) | (Gey Chedd Universel 12) | (Gevelot 12) |
| Gnm. | | | Manufacturer. |
| GBE | D | | F/F |
| HFC.1,141. | HSC.3,203. | HFC.1,143. | HFC.1,144. |
| (Gevelot 12) | (Gevelot 12) | (Gevelot Canada 12) | (Gevelot Canada 12) |
| Manufacturer. Pla. | | Manufacturer. | |
| F/F | F/F | CDN/ | CDN/ |
| HSC.3,204. | HSC.3,205. | HSC.3,206. | HFC.1,145. |
| (Gev Lot Cyprus 12) | (Gevelot Paris 12) | (Gevelot Paris 12) | (Gevelot Paris 12) |
| Manufacturer, Pla. | Manufacturer. | | Manufacturer. |
| CY/ | F/F | F/F | F/F |
| HSC.3,207. | HFC.3,208. | HFC.1,149. | HFC.1,148. |
| (Gevelot Paris 12) | (Gevelot Paris 12) | (Gevelot Paris 12) | (Gevelot Paris 12) |
| | Manufacturer. | | Manufacturer. |
| On other gauges. | | On other gauges. | On other gauges. |
| F/F | F/F | F/F | F/F |
| HFC.1,147. | HFC.1,146. | HFC.1,150. | HFC.5,444. |

| | | | |
|---|---|---|---|
| G.FIOCCHI N. ? 12 LECCO | G.FIOCCHI No 12 LECCO | G.FORMULE 12 12 LE ROE ULX | G F 12 12 USA |
| Manufacturer. | Manufacturer. | | Pla. |
| I/I | I/I | | USA |
| HSC.3,209. | HFC.1,152. | HSC.3,210. | HFC.3,211. |
| G.H.DAW'S No 12 PATENT | G.H.DAW'S No 12 PATENT | G.HINTON.TAUNTON No12 ELEY | G.HINTON.TAUNTON No12 ELEY |
| Gnnm, Developer. | Gnm, Developer. | Gnm. | Gnm. |
| GBE/GBE | GBE/GBE | GBE/GBE | GBE/GBE |
| HFC.1,153. | HFC.2,191. | HFC.3,212. | HSC.3,213. |
| G&H.OMAHA.12 GA. PAT.PEND.12 GA. | GIBBS.BRISTOL No12 ELEY | GIBBS.BRISTOL No12 ELEY | No GIBBS 12 BRISTOL & LONDON |
| Apc. | Gnm. | Gnm. | |
| USA | GBE/GBE | GBE/GBE | GBE |
| HFC.1,154. | HFC.3,214. | HSC.3,215. | HFC.1,155. |
| GIBBS BRISTOL&LONDON No12 ELEY | No GIBBS 12 KYNOCH BRISTOL&LONDON | 12 GI-ESSE 12 ITALY | 12 GIESSE 12 LAMEZIA-T |
| Gnm. | Gnm. | Pla. | |
| GBE/GBE | GBE/GBE | I | I |
| HFC.2,192. | HFC.1,156. | HSC.3,216. | HFC.1,157. |

| | | | |
|---|---|---|---|
| (Giulio Fiocchi Lecco ? No 12) | (Giulio Fiocchi Lecco 12 12 GF) | (Giulio Fiocchi Lecco 12 12 GF) | (Giulio Fiocchi Lecco No 12 GF) |
| Manufacturer. | | Manufacturer. Pla. | |
| | | | 16. |
| I/I | I/I | I/I | I/I |
| HSC.3,217. | HFC.1,158. | HSC.3,218. | HFC.1,159. |
| (Giulio-Fiocchi-Lecco No 12 GF) | (Giulio-Fiocchi-Lecco 12 12 GF) | (Giulio Fiocchi Lecco No 12 Ejector) | (Giulio Fiocchi 12 12 Made in Italy) |
| Manufacturer. | Pla. | Manufacturer | Pla. |
| 20. | | | |
| I/I | I/I | I/I | I/I |
| HFC.1,160. | HSC.3,219. | HSC.3,220. | HSC.3,221. |
| (Giulio Fiocchi 12 12 Made in Italy) | (G.K No 12 London) | (G&L 12 12 Calibers) | (G&L 12 12 Cyprus) |
| Manufacturer. | Possibly G. Kynoch | | |
| | 14. | | |
| I/I | GBE | CY | CY |
| HFC.1,161. | HSC.3,222. | HFC.1,162. | HFC.1,163. |
| (12 Global Shot.com) | (Gloria 12 12) | (G.L. Woods 12 12 Norfolk) | (G.L. Woods 12 12 Norfolk) |
| | | Loader. | Loader. |
| | | | |
| | | GBE | GBE |
| HFC.1,164. | HFC.1,165. | HFC.1,167. | HFC.1,166. |

| | | | |
|---|---|---|---|
| (G.L.WOODS & SONS 12 12 IMPORTED CASE) | (G.L. WOODS & SONS NORFOLK 12) | (G M G 12 12 CYPRUS) | (G.NEWNHAM No 12 KYNOCH LANDPORT) |
| Loaders. | Loaders. | | George Newnham. |
| GBE / | GBE | CY | GBE/GBE |
| HFC.1,168. | HFC.1,169. | HFC.1,170. | HFC.1,171. |
| (G. NEWNHAM KYNOCH'S PATENT GROUSE EJECTOR No2090 LANDPORT 12) | (GOLDEN. HUDDERSFIELD No 12 ELEY) | (GOLD TOP 12 12 CHINA) | (GORDON 12 SYSTEM 12) |
| Gnm, Ejt. Pre Wwl. | William Golden. Irm | | Pla. |
| GBE/GBE | GBE/GBE | RC | |
| HFC.1,172. | HSC.3,223. | HSC.3,224. | HFC.1,173. |
| (GRAHAM COCKERMOUTH No 12) | (GRANT & SON No 12 LONDON) | (GRANT & SON No 12 LONDON) | (GREEN CHELTENHAM & GLOUCESTER KYNOCH No 12) |
| Gnm. | Gnm. | Gnm. | Gnm. Pre Wwl. |
| GBE | GBE | GBE | GBE/GBE |
| HFC.1,174. | HFC.3,225. | HFC.3,226. | HFC.3,227. |
| (GREENER KYNOCH PATNT No 12 GROUSE EJECTOR LONDON & BIRMINGHAM) | (GREENERS No 12 PAT. APD.FOR) | (GRENFELL & ACCLES 12 BIRMINGHAM) | (GREENFIELD. STORRINGTON No 12 ELEY) |
| Gnm, Ejt. Pre Wwl. | Gnm. | Manufacturer. | |
| GBE/GBE | GBE | GBE/GBE | GBE/GBE |
| HFC.1,175. | HFC.1,176. | HSC.3,228. | HFC.1,177. |

| | | | |
|---|---|---|---|
| GUNMARK 12 | GUSTAV GENSCHOW&CO AKTIENGESELLSCHAFT 12 DURLACH 12 | GUSTAV GENSCHOW&CO AKTIENGESELLSCHAFT 12 DURLACH 12 | GUSTAV GENSCHOW&CO AKTIENGESELLSCHAFT 12 KARLSRUHE·DURLACH 12 |
| Gnm. Pla.Post Ww2. | | Manufacturer. | |
| GBE | D/D | D/D | D/D |
| HFC.1,178. | HSC.3,229. | HFC.1,179. | HFC.1,180. |
| G.W.BALES No 12 IPSWICH | G.WREN.HUNGERFORD No.12. ELEY. | GYTTORP 12 | GYTTORP 12 |
| George William. Gnm | Gnm & saddler. | Manufacturer. | Pla. |
| GBE | GBE/GBE | S/S | S/S |
| HFC.1,181/R. | HFC.1,182. | HFC.1,183. | HSC.3,230. |
| GYTTORP 12 | GYTTORP 12 | GYTTORP 12 | GYTTORP * * 12 |
| Knurled rim. | Manufacturer. | Pla. | Manufacturer. |
| S/S | S/S | S/S | S/S |
| HSC.3,231. | HFC.1,184. | HSC.3,232. | HFC.1,185. |
| GYTTORP 12 12 AMF AB | GYTTORP 12 12 GYTTORP | GYTTORP 12 12 GYTTORP | GYTTORP 12 12 MADE IN SWEDEN |
| Pla. | Manufacturer. | Pla. | Manufacturer. |
| | | 20. | 20. |
| S/S | S/S | S/S | S/S |
| HFC.1,186. | HFC.3,233. | HFC.1,187. | HFC.1,188. |

| | | | |
|---|---|---|---|
| (GYTTORP 12 12 MADE IN SWEDEN) | (GYTTORP 12 12 MADE IN SWEDEN) | (GYTTORP 12 12 MADE IN SWEDEN) | (GAVARD & CO 10 PARIS) |
| Manufacturer. | | 12 gauge. | 10 gauge. |
| S/S | S/S | | F |
| HFC.3,234. | HFC.3,235. | HFC.1,189. | HSC.3,236. |

| | | | |
|---|---|---|---|
| (G.E. HART'S PAT. NEWARK N.J. 10) | (GEO. E. HART. PAT'D SEP.23.73 NEWARK N.J.) | (GIULIO FIOCCHI LECCO No ? 10 GF) | (GEVELOT 4 4 PARIS) |
| Abc. 10 gauge. | Abc. 10 gauge. | Manufacturer. | 4 gauge. |
| | | | On other gauges. |
| USA/USA | USA/USA | I/I | F/F |
| HSC.3,237. | HSC.3,238. | HSC.3,239. | HFC.2,119. |

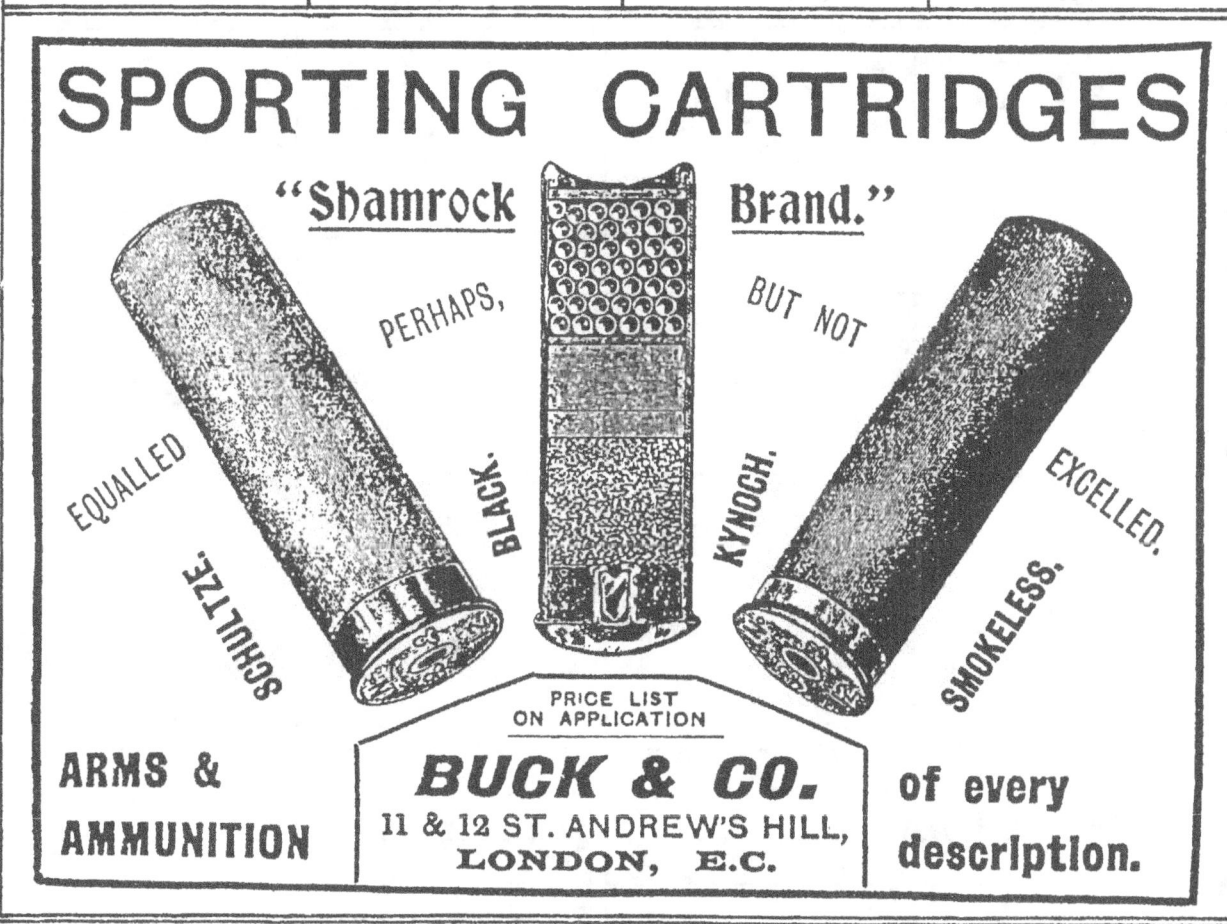

| | | | |
|---|---|---|---|
| 12 mm, .410. 28. | 28 gauge. .410. | Gnm. 20 gauge. On other gauges. GBE | Montgomery Ward Co. 16, 12. USA |
| HSC.3,240. | HSC.3,241. | HFC.3,242. | HSC.3,3243. |
| Montgomery Ward Co. 16. 12. USA | Gambles Stores Inc. 16, 12. USA | 16, 12. USA | Loaders. GBE/B |
| HSC.3,244. | HSC.3,245. | HSC.3,246. | HSC.3,247. |
| Loaders. GBE/B | Gnm. B/GBE | Gnm. On other gauges. GBE | |
| HFC.3,248. | HSC.3,249. | HFC.339. | HFC.340. |
| Loaders. On other gauges. | | 18 gauge. On other gauges. D/D | |
| HFC.341. | HFC.2.143. | HSC.3,250. | HSC.3,251. |

| | | | |
|---|---|---|---|
| HAMMOND BROS No 16 WINCHESTER | HAREN 16 16 LONDON | HASLOCH 16 16 | HASLOCH 16 16 NORMAL |
| Gnm. | | | |
| On other gauges. | | | |
| GBE | GBE | D | D |
| HFC.3,252. | HFC.494. | HSC.3,253. | HFC.496. |
| H.ATKIN PATENT No 16 2 JERMYN STREET SW | HAWTHORNE No 16 LONG RANGE | HAWTHORNE No 16 RELIANCE | H.B. No 16 FISHER |
| Gnm, Ejt. | Montgomery Ward Co. | Montgomery Ward Co. | |
| | 20, 12. | 20, 12. | 12. |
| GBE/GBE | USA | USA | USA |
| HFC.495. | HSC.3,254. | HSC.3,255. | HFC.497. |
| H.CLARKE No 16 LEICESTER | H.CLARKE & SONS LEICESTER No 16 | H.CLARKE & SONS LEICESTER EXPRESS CARTRIDGE No 16 | HENRITE EXPLOSIVES 16 16 LONDON |
| Gnm. | Gnm. | Gnm. | Powder Mills. |
| GBE | GBE | GBE | GBE |
| HFC.499. | HFC.498. | HFC.3,256. | HSC.3,257. |
| HENRITE EXPLOSIVES 16 16 LONDON | HIAWATHA No 16 ACE | HIAWATHA No 16 AIRWAY | HIRTENBERG G 16 G |
| Explosives. | Gambles Stores Inc. | Gambles Stores Inc. | |
| | 20, 12. | 20, 12. | |
| GBE | USA | USA | |
| HSC.3,258. | HSC.3,259. | HSC.3,260. | HSC.3,261. |

|  |  |  |  |
|---|---|---|---|
|  | London Gnm. | Manufacturer. | London Gnm. |
|  |  | On other gauges. | On other gauges. |
|  | GBE/GBE | DK/DK | GBE |
| HFC.501. | HSC.3,262. | HFC.3,263. | HFC.503. |
|  |  |  |  |
| London Gnm. | Gnm. | Loaders. | Snap cap. |
| On other gauges. |  | On other gauges. |  |
| GBE/GBE | GBS/GBE | GBE/I | USA |
| HFC.504. | HSC.3,264. | HFC.505. | HSC.3,265. |
|  |  | 16 gauge. | 12 gauge. |
| 20, 12, 10. |  |  |  |
| USA | D | D |  |
| HFC.2,150. | HSC.3,266. | HFC.506. | HSC.3,267. |
|  |  | 12 gauge. | Gnm. |
| 12 gauge. |  |  |  |
| IND/GBE | GBE | SU | GBE |
| HFC.1,190. | HFC.1,191. | HSC.3,268. | HFC.1,192. |

| | | | |
|---|---|---|---|
| (Hammond Bros No 12 Winchester) | (Hammond Bros No 12 Winchester) | (Hammond Bros No 12 Winchester) | (Hammond Bros 12 12 Winchester) |
| Gnm. | Gnm. | Gnm. | Gnm. |
| On other gauges. | | | |
| GBE | GBE | GBE | GBE |
| HFC.3,269. | HFC.3,270. | HFC.3,271. | HFC.3,272. |
| (Hammond Bros Winchester No 12 Eley) | (Hammond Bros Foreign 12 12 Made Case Winchester) | (Hammond Bros Kynoch's Patent No 12 Grouse Ejector Winchester) | (Hanson No 12 Lincoln) |
| Gnm. | Gnm. | Gnm, Ejt. | Gnm. |
| | | | |
| GBE/GBE | GBE/ | GBE/GBE | GBE |
| HFC.1,193. | HFC.1,194. | HFC.1,195. | HSC.3,273. |
| (Hardy Bros Ltd No 12 Kynoch Alnwick) | (Hardy Bros Kynoch's Patent No 12 Grouse Ejector Alnwick) | (Harkom & Son No 12 Edinburgh) | (Harrison Bros Carlisle No 12 Eley) |
| Gnm. | Gnm, Ejt. | Joseph & Son. Gnm. | |
| GBE/GBE | GBE/GBE | GBE | GBE/GBE |
| HFC.1,197. | HFC.1,196. | HSC.3,274. | HSC.3,275. |
| (Harrod's Ltd No 12 Eley London) | (Harry Williams No 12 Newport I.O.W.) | (Hartforth No 12 Eley) | (Hart's Pat. Nov 9.75 A 12 Newark N.J.) |
| Dps. | Irm. | | 12 gauge. |
| GBE/GBE | GBE | /GBE | USA/USA |
| HFC.3,276. | HFC.1,198. | HSC.3,277. | HSC.3,278. |

| | | | |
|---|---|---|---|
| HART'S PAT.NOV.9.75 NEWARK.N.J. 12 | HARTSPORT SHELL MADE IN GERMANY SPECIAL 12 12 | HASLOCH 12 12 | H.ATKIN PATENT No 2090 2.JERMYN ST.S.W. No 12 |
| | Hws. | | Gnm, Ejt. |
| USA/USA | AUS/D | D | GBE/GBE |
| HSC.3,279. | HSC.3,280. | HSC.3,281. | HFC.1,199. |
| H.ATKIN 18 OXENDON STREET.W. No 12 | HAWK BEST 12 12 | HAWK BEST 12 12 | HAWK BEST 12 12 |
| London Gnm. | Manufacturer. | Pla. Post Ww2. | Manufacturer. |
| GBE | GBE/GBE | GBE/GBE | GBE/GBE |
| HFC.1,200. | HFC.1,202. | HFC.1,201. | HFC.1,203. |
| HAWTHORNE LONG RANGE No 12 | HAWTHORNE RELIANCE No 12 | HAYMAN WEYMOUTH No 12 | HAYMAN WEYMOUTH AND DORCHESTER No 12 |
| Montgomery Ward Co. | | | |
| 20, 16. | 20, 16. | | |
| USA | USA | GBE | GBE |
| HSC.3,282. | HSC.3,283. | HFC.3,284. | HSC.3,285. |
| HAZEL.DORCHESTER ELEY No12 | H.BARHAM.HITCHIN ELEY No12 | H.B. FISHER No 12 | H.B.FISHER MADE IN GERMANY PHILA.PA. 12 12 |
| R.Hazel. Irm. | Gnm. | | |
| | | 16. | |
| GBE/GBE | GBE/GBE | USA | USA/D |
| HSC.3,286. | HFC.1,204. | HSC.3,287. | HSC.3,288. |

| | | | |
|---|---|---|---|
| H.C.ELLIOT DARTFORD 12 12 | H.C.ELLIOTT CASE MADE IN BELGIUM DARTFORD 12 12 | H.CLARKE&SONS.LEICESTER. No 12 H.ELEY | H.CLARKE&SONS EXPRESS No 12 CARTRIDGE LEICESTER |
| Gnm. | Gnm. | Gnm. | Gnm. |
| GBE | GBE/B | GBE/GBE | GBE |
| HFC.1,205. | HFC.1,206. | HFC.3,289. | HFC.1,208. |
| H.CLARKE&SONS EXPRESS No 12 CARTRIDGE LEICESTER | H.E.KERRIDGE No 12 YARMOUTH | 12 HELIKON 12 ESPAÑA | HELLIS 12 12 LONDON.ENGD |
| Gnm. | Gunsmith, Irm. | Pla. | Loaders. |
| GBE | GBE | E | GBE |
| HFC.1,207. | HSC.3,290. | HSC.3,291. | HSC.3,292. |
| 12 HELLIS 12 LONDON.ENGLAND | HELLIS 12 12 LONDON ENGLAND | HELLIS & SONS.LONDON 12 | HELLIS & SONS-LONDON MADE IN BELGIUM 12 |
| Experts. | Loaders. | Experts. | Loaders. |
| GBE | GBE | GBE | GBE/B |
| HFC.3,293. | HFC.1,209. | HSC.3,294. | HFC.1,211. |
| HELLIS & SONS-LONDON MADE IN BELGIUM 12 | HELLIS&SONS-LONDON MADE IN BELGIUM 12 | HELLIS & SONS KYNOCH PATENT No 12 GROUSE EJECTOR LONDON | HELSON No 12 KYNOCH EXETER |
| Experts. | Loaders. | Experts, Ejt. | J. Helson. |
| GBE/B | GBE/B | GBE/GBE | GBE/GBE |
| HFC.1,213. | HFC.1,212. | HFC.1,210. | HFC.1,214. |

| | | | |
|---|---|---|---|
| (Henderson Dundee No 12) | (Henrite No 12 Eley London) | (Henrite Explosives 12 London 12) | (Henrite Explosives 12 London 12) |
| | Explosives. | Manufacturer. | Explosives. |
| GBS | GBE/GBE | GBE | GBE |
| HFC.1,215. | HFC.3,295. | HFC.1,216. | HFC.1,217. |
| (Henrite 12 London 12) | (Henry Atkin No 12 Kynoch London) | (Henry Atkin No 12 London N) | (Henry Atkin No 12 London) |
| Manufacturer. | Kynoch case. Gnm, | Nobel case. Gnm, | London Gnm. |
| GBE | GBE/GBE | GBE/GBE | GBE |
| HSC.3,296. | HSC.3,297. | HFC.2,193. | HFC.1,220. |
| (Henry Atkin Ltd No 12 London) | (Henry Atkin Ltd No 12 London N) | (Henry Atkin Ltd No 12 London) | (Henry Atkin Ltd No 12 London) |
| London Gnm. | Nobel case, Pre Wwl. | Joyce case. | Abc. Gnm. |
| GBE | GBE/GBE | GBE/GBE | GBE/GBE |
| HFC.1,219. | HFC.1,222. | HFC.3,298. | HFC.3,299. |
| (Henry Atkin Ltd No 12 London K) | (Henry Atkin Ltd No 12 Kynoch London) | (Henry Atkin 2 Jermyn Street Kynoch's Patent No 2080 12) | (Henry Atkin Ltd Kynoch Patent No 12 Grouse Ejector London) |
| Kynoch case. | London Gnm. | Gnm, Ejt. | Gnm, Ejt. Pre Wwl. |
| GBE/GBE | GBE/GBE | GBE/GBE | GBE/GBE |
| HFC.1,221. | HFC.1,223. | HFC.1,218. | HFC.1,224. |

| | | | |
|---|---|---|---|
| HERTER'S 12 12 PAT | HERTER'S INC 12 12 PAT. PEND | HIAWATHA 12 GA ACE | HIAWATHA 12 GA AIRWAY |
| | | Gambles Stores, Inc. | |
| | | 20, 16. | 20, 16. |
| | | USA | USA |
| HFC.1,225. | HSC.3,300. | HFC.1,227. | HFC.1,228. |
| HIGHAM.OSWESTRY N°12 ELEY | HIGHAM FRENCH N° 12 MADE CASE OSWESTRY | HIGHAM N°12 OSWESTRY & WELSHPOOL | HILL & SON N° 12 HORNCASTLE |
| George G. Higham, Gnm. | | Adv, Gnm. | Gnm. |
| GBE/GBE | GBE/F | GBE/GBW/ | GBE |
| HFC.1,229. | HFC.3,301. | HFC.3,302. | HFC.1,230. |
| HILL & SON 12 12 HORNCASTLE | HIRTENBERG * * | HIRTENBERG * 12 * | HIRTENBERG * 12 * |
| Gnm. | 12 gauge, Pla. | | |
| | | | On other gauges. |
| GBE | | | |
| HFC.3,304. | HSC.3,305. | HFC.1,231. | HFC.1,232. |
| HIRTENBERG * 12 * | HIRTENBERGER ✯ 12 ✯ | HIRTENBERGER ✯ 12 ✯ | H.JONES.WREXHAM N°12 ELEY |
| | | | Terminated 1927. Gnm. |
| | | | GBE/GBE |
| HFC.1,233. | HFC.1,234. | HFC.1,235. | HFC.1,236. |

| | | | |
|---|---|---|---|
| (HK 12 FREDERIKSVÆRK 12) | (HK 12 FREDERIKSVÆRK 12) | (H.LUTHY 12 12 NEUCHÂTEL) | (H.LUTHY 12 12 NEUCHÂTEL) |
| Manufacturer. | Manufacturer. On other gauges. | | |
| DK/DK | DK/DK | CH | CH |
| HFC.1.238. | HFC.1,237. | HSC.3,306. | HFC.1,239. |
| (H.MAHILLON.BRUXELLES No12 ELEY) | (H.M.JULIAN No 12 BASINGSTOKE) | (HOBSON.LEAMINGTON No12 ELEY) | (HOBSON No 12 KYNOCH LEAMINGTON) |
| | Gunsmith Irm. | J.Hobson, Gnm. | Gnm. |
| B/GBE | GBE | GBE/GBE | GBE/GBE |
| HSC.3,307. | HFC.1,240. | HSC.3,308. | HFC.1,241. |
| (HOBSON No12 KYNOCH'S PATENT GROUSE No 2080 LEAMINGTON) | (HODGSON No 12 RIPON) | (H.HODGSON CASE MADE 12 12 IN FRANCE IPSWICH & BURY ST EDMUNDS) | (HODGSON.RIPON No12 ELEY) |
| J. Hobson. Ejt. | R. C. Hodgson. | Henry Hodgson, Gnm. | Gnm. |
| GBE/GBE | GBE | GBE/F | GBE/GBE |
| HFC.1,242. | HSC.3,309. | HFC.1,244. | HFC.1,243. |
| (HOLDRON.ASHBY No12 ELEY) | (Holiday 12 12 GAUGE) | (HOLLAND No 12 CIRENCESTER) | (HOLLAND & HOLLAND 12) |
| John Holdron, Irm. | Post Ww2. | Gnm. | Gnm. Post Ww2. 20, 16. |
| GBE/GBE | | GBE | GBE |
| HSC.3,310. | HFC.1,245. | HFC.1,246. | HFC.1,248. |

| | | | |
|---|---|---|---|
| HOLLAND & HOLLAND 12 | HOLLAND & HOLLAND No 12 | HOLLAND & HOLLAND No 12 | HOLLAND & HOLLAND No 12 ELEY |
| London Gnm. | London Gnm. | London Gnm. | London Gnm. |
| | | | On other gauges. |
| GBE | GBE | GBE | GBE/GBE |
| HFC.1,247. | HFC.3,311. | HFC.1,249. | HFC.1,251. |
| HOLLAND & HOLLAND ELEY No 12 NITRO PARADOX | HOLLAND & HOLLAND ELEY No 12 H&H PARADOX | HOLLAND & HOLLAND KYNOCH No 12 | HOLLAND No 12 LONDON |
| Gnm, Ejt. | Gnm, Ejt. | London Gnm. | Gnm. |
| GBE/GBE | GBE/GBE | GBE/GBE | GBE |
| HFC.1,253. | HSC.3,312. | HFC.1,252. | HFC.1,250/R. |
| HON. G. KEPPEL KYNOCH'S PATENT GROUSE EJECTOR No 12 | HOOTON & JONES No 12 LIVERPOOL | HOOTON & JONES No 12 LIVERPOOL | HOOTON & JONES No 12 ELEY LIVERPOOL |
| Private shell, Ejt. | Gnm. | Gnm. | Gnm. |
| GBE/GBE | GBE | GBE | GBE/GBE |
| HFC.1,254. | HFC.1,256. | HFC.5,445. | HFC.1,257. |
| HOOTON & JONES. LIVERPOOL No 12 ELEY | HOOTON & JONES No 12 KYNOCH LIVERPOOL | HORNE No 12 READING | HORSLEY 12 12 YORK |
| Gnm. | Gnm. | | Tom Horsley. Gnm. |
| GBE/GBE | GBE/GBE | GBE | GBE |
| HSC.3,313. | HFC.1,258. | HFC.1,259/R. | HFC.1,260. |

| | | | |
|---|---|---|---|
| (HORTON·N°12·MOG / HOH·GLASGOW) | (HORTON N°12 GLASGOW) | (HORTON, GLASGOW N°12 ELEY) | (HP 2mm 12/70) |
| Gnm. | Gnm. | Gnm. | Pla. |
| | | | |
| GBS | GBS | GBE/GBE | |
| HFC.1,261. | HFC.3,314. | HFC.1,262. | HSC.3,315. |
| ('H' 12 12 RAUCHLOS) | (H.S.B.& CO. 12 G AJAX) | (H.SEARS & CO. N°12) | (HUDSON'S BAY N° 12 COMPANY) |
| | | | |
| | | | |
| D | USA | USA | CDN |
| HSC.3,316. | HSC.3,317. | HSC.3,318. | HFC.1,263. |
| (HULL 12 12 CARTRIDGE) | (HULL CARTRIDGE CO. 12) | (HULL CARTRIDGE Co. 12) | (HULL CARTRIDGE Co. Ld. 12) |
| Loaders, Post Ww2. | Apc. | Apc. | Post Ww2. |
| GBE/I | GBE | GBE | GBE |
| HFC.1,264. | HFC.1,265. | HFC.3,319. | HFC.3,320. |
| (HUNTER 12) | (HUNTER N°12) | (HUNTER N°12 ONE TRIGGER) | (HUNTER & SON BELGIAN 12 12 MADE SHELL BELFAST) |
| | | Snap cap. | Gnm. |
| | | 20,16,10. | |
| | USA | USA | GBI/B |
| HFC.1,266. | HSC.3,321. | HSC.3,322. | HSC.3,323. |

| | | | |
|---|---|---|---|
| HUNTER & SON BELGIAN No 12 SHELL BELFAST | HUNTER & SON CASE MADE 12 12 IN FRANCE BELFAST | HUNTER & SON CASE MADE 12 12 IN FRANCE BELFAST | HUNTER & SON CASE MADE 12 12 IN FRANCE BELFAST |
| Gnm. | Gnm. | Gnm. | Gnm. |
| GBI/B | GBI/F | GBI/F | GBI/ F |
| HSC.3,324. | HSC.3,325. | HFC.3,326. | HSC.3,327. |
| HUNTER & SON.BELFAST No12 H. ELEY | HUNTER & SON FRENCH No 12 CASE BELFAST | 12 — GA ? HUNTSMAN | HURLSTONE No 12 WARMINSTER |
| Gnm. | Gnm. | | William. Irm. |
| GBI/GBE | GBI/F | MEX | GBE |
| HSC.3,328. | HSC.3,329. | HSC.3,330. | HFC.1,267. |
| HUSSA ☆ ☆ 12 | HUSSA ☆ ☆ 12 | HUSSA 12 12 *C.&B.* | HUSSEY. L⁰. NEW BOND STREET 81. N⁰12. ELEY |
| | | | Gnm, Eley case. |
| D | D | D | GBE/GBE |
| HFC.1,269. | HSC.3,331. | HSC.3,332. | HSC.3,333. |
| HUSSEY LTD.81 NEW BOND ST.W. N⁰12 JOYCE | HUSSEY.LTD.58 JERMYN ST.S.W. N⁰12 ELEY | HUTENDORFFER 12 12 NURNBERG | H.W.ROBERTS & C⁰ N⁰ 12 KYNOCH RHYL |
| Gnm, Joyce case. | London Gnm. | | Kynoch case. |
| GBE/GBE | GBE/GBE | D | GBE/GBE |
| HFC.1.268. | HFC.3,334. | HSC.3,335. | HFC.1,270. |

| | | | |
|---|---|---|---|
| 12 gauge. | 10 gauge. | Abc. 10 gauge. | London Gnm. |
| | | USA | GBE |
| HFC.1,271. | HSC.3,336. | HSC.3,337. | HSC.3,338. |
| Gnm, 10 gauge. | 12. | Raised centre. | |
| GBE | USA | USA | USA |
| HSC.3,339. | HSC.3,340. | HSC.3,341. | HSC.3,342. |
| Snap cap. On other gauges. | Snap cap. 20, 16, 12. | 8 gauge. | 8 gauge. |
| USA/USA | USA/USA | USA | USA |
| HSC.3,343. | HSC.3,344. | HSC.3,345. | HSC.3,346. |
| London Gnm, Ejt. | Gnm, Ejt. | | 8 gauge. |
| GBE/GBE | GBE/GBE | D | D |
| HFC.2,108. | HSC.3,347. | HSC.3,348. | HSC.3,349. |

| | | | |
|---|---|---|---|
| H ☆ ☆ ☆ | H & H 4 ○ 4 REWA | HOLLAND & HOLLAND K LTD 27 |  |
| 4 gauge. | Holland & Hollad. | 4 gauge. | |
| | GBE | GBE | |
| HSC.3,350. | HSC.3,351. | HSC.3,352. | |

1915.]  SALISBURY ADVERTISEMENTS.

## CHAMBERLAIN'S GUNS,

**REVOLVERS, RIFLES.**

*Ejector, Hammerless and Hammer Guns at Moderate Low Prices.*

SPORTING REQUISITES OF EVERY DESCRIPTION.

Guns built to order to any Length, Bend and Weight.

REPAIRS of all kinds executed with care and despatch

THE "SARUM" CARTRIDGES.

The greatest attention given to loading with Nitro Powders.

**FISHING TACKLE** of every description kept in stock.

Sole Address: **A. CHAMBERLAIN,** Practical Gunmaker and Cartridge Manufacturer,

Telegrams: Chamberlain, Salisbury.   MARKET PLACE, SALISBURY.

---

## CHAMBERLAIN'S GUNS,

**REVOLVERS, RIFLES.**

*Ejector, Hammerless and Hammer Guns at Moderate Low Prices.*

SPORTING REQUISITES OF EVERY DESCRIPTION.

Guns built to order to any Length, Bend and Weight.

REPAIRS of all kinds executed with care and dispatch.

THE "SARUM" CARTRIDGES.

The greatest attention given to loading with Nitro Powders.

**FISHING TACKLE** of every description kept in stock.

Sole Address: **A. CHAMBERLAIN,** Practical Gunmaker and Cartridge Manufacturer,

TELEGRAMS: CHAMBERLAIN, SALISBURY.   MARKET PLACE, SALISBURY.

| | | | |
|---|---|---|---|
| 14mm 32 gauge. | 20 gauge. | 20 gauge. | Manufacturer. |
|  | 16, 12. | On other gauges. |  |
| P | USA | CDN/CDN | CDN/CDN |
| HSC.3,353. | HSC.3,354. | HSC.3,355. | HSC.3,356. |
| 16 gauge. | Manufacturer. | 16 gauge. | Robin Hood. |
| 20, 12. | 12. |  | 12. |
| USA | GBE/GBE |  | USA/USA |
| HSC.3,357. | HFC.3,358. | HFC.3,359. | HSC.3,360. |
| Robin Hood. |  |  | 16 gauge. |
| 12. | 12. |  |  |
| USA/USA | P | P |  |
| HSC.3,361. | HSC.3,362. | HSC.3,363. | HSC.3,364. |
| 16 gauge. | 12 gauge. | Manufacturer. | 12 gauge. |
|  | 12 gauge only. | 12 gauge only. | 12 gauge only. |
| CDN/CDN | USA/USA | USA/USA | USA/USA |
| HFC.3,365. | HSC.3,366. | HSC.3,367. | HSC.3,368. |

| | | | |
|---|---|---|---|
| Zinc, no pocket. | Manufacturer. | | Believed 12 gauge. |
| GBE/GBE | AUS-NZ/AUS | | GBE/GBE |
| HSC.3,369. | HSC.3,370. | HFC.1,273. | HFC.1,272. |
| | | | Manufacturer. |
| | | 20, 16. | 16. |
| AUS-NZ | AUS-NZ | USA | AUS |
| HSC.3,371. | HSC.3,372. | HSC.3,373. | HFC.3,374. |
| | Pla. | Pla. | Manufacturer. On other gauges. |
| AUS | | | CDN/CDN |
| HFC.1,274. | HFC.1,275. | HSC.3,375. | HFC.1,277. |
| | Manufacturer. | | Manufacturer. |
| CDN/CDN | USA | | USA/USA |
| HFC.1,276. | HFC.1,279. | HSC.3,376. | HSC.3,377. |

| | | | |
|---|---|---|---|
| INDIAN 12 12 R.H.A.CO. | INDIAN 12 12 R.H.P.CO. | INMAN MORROW & CO KYNOCH LEEDS No 12 | IN. PA. 12 12 ITALY |
| Robin Hood. | Manufacturer. | Gnm, Kynoch case. | |
| 16. | 16. | | |
| USA/USA | USA/USA | GBE/GBE | I |
| HSC.3,378. | HSC.3,379. | HFC.1,280. | HFC.1,283. |
| INSULINED ☆ ☆ 12 | INTERNATIONAL No 12 REPEATER | INTERSTATE 12 12 ENGLAND | INT.PAT. A.E.1301 |
| | | Pla.   Post Ww2. | Believed 12 gauge. |
| | | GBE | |
| HSC.3,380. | HFC.1,281. | HFC.1,282. | HFC.1,284. |
| I.P.M. 12 12 I.P.M. | I.P.M. 12 12 PORTUGAL | (IPM) 12 12 (PORTUGAL) | IRIS 12 12 IRIS |
| Pla. | | Pla. | Pla. |
| | 16. | | |
| P | P | P | |
| HFC.1,285. | HSC.3,381. | HSC.3,382. | HSC.3,383. |
| IRLEC 12 | IVI 12 12 IMPERIAL | IXI No 12 | I.F.S. No 10 |
| Pla. | 12 gauge. | 12 gauge. | 10 gauge. |
| | CDN/CDN | USA | USA |
| HSC.3,384. | HFC.1,278. | HSC.3,385. | HSC.3,386. |

| | | | |
|---|---|---|---|
| INDIAN 10 10 R.H.P.CO. | I X L №10 | I.X.L. №10 | I.X.L. №10 |
| Powder company. | 10 gauge. | | 10 gauge. |
| On other gauges. | | | |
| USA/USA | USA | USA | USA |
| HSC.3,387. | HFC.3,388. | HSC.3,389. | HFC.2,079. |

| | | | |
|---|---|---|---|
| (JOYCE LONDON .410) | (JACK RABBIT No 20 A.A.Co) | (J.A.&R.WATSON&Co 20 20 LONDON) | (JENVEY & TITE No 20 GRANTHAM) |
| .410 | 20 gauge. | | |
| | 16, 12. | On other gauges. | |
| GBE/GBE | USA/USA | GBE | GBE |
| HSC.3,390. | HFC.5,446. | HFC.343. | HSC.3,391. |
| (JOYCE·LONDON No 20) | (JOYCE·LONDON No 20) | (JOYCE·LONDON No 20) | (JOYCE No 20 LONDON) |
| Manufacturer. | Pre Wwl. | Manufacturer. | Pre Wwl. |
| | On other gauges. | | |
| GBE/GBE | GBE/GBE | GBE/GBE | GBE/GBE |
| HSC.3,392. | HFC.3,393. | HSC.3,394. | HSC.3,395. |
| (JOYCE No 20 LONDON) | (JOYCE No 20 LONDON) | (JOYCE&CO No 20 LONDON) | (J.W.ROSIER No 20 MELBOURNE) |
| Manufacturer. | Pre Wwl. | Pre 1908. | Estb, 1850. |
| On other gauges. | | | |
| GBE/GBE | GBE/GBE | GBE/GBE | AUS |
| HFC.344. | HFC.345. | HSC.3,396. | HSC.3,397. |
| (JAGD 18 18 B) | (JACK RABBIT No 16 A.A.Co.) | (JACK RABBIT No 16 A.A.Co) | (JAGD 16 16 B) |
| 18 gauge. | 16 gauge. | | 16 gauge. |
| 16. | | On other gauges. | 18. |
| D | USA/USA | USA/USA | D |
| HSC.3,398. | HSC.3,399. | HFC.508. | HSC.3,400. |

| | | | |
|---|---|---|---|
| (JAGD 16 16 B) | (JAS.R.WATSON&Co CASE MADE IN BELGIUM 16 C.F. PARIS 16 LONDON) | (JAS.R.WATSON&Co 16 16 LONDON) | (J.BURROW No 16 PRESTON) |
| 16 gauge. | 16 gauge. | Ammo dealers. | James Burrow. |
| | 12. | 12. | |
| D | GBE/B | GBE | GBE |
| HSC.3,401. | HFC.3,402. | HSC.3,403. | HFC.509. |
| (J.DEUSSEN 16 16 BRUXELLES) | (J.GRAHAM&Co No 16 ELEY INVERNESS) | (J.L.GALFF GERMANY NEW-YORK) | (JOHNSON&WRIGHT NORTHAMPTON No 16) |
| | Gnm. | Cig lighter. | Irm. |
| | | | |
| B | GBS/GBE | USA/D | GBE |
| HSC.3,404. | HSC.3,405. | HSC.3,406. | HFC.510. |
| (JOYCE&Co.LONDON BAILEYS PATENT No 16) | (JOYCE LONDON BAILEYS PATENT GAS CHECK No 16) | (JOYCE&Co No BAILEYS PATENT 16 LONDON) | (JOYCE LONDON No 16) |
| Pre Ww1. | Manufacturer. | Pre 1908. | Manufacturer. |
| GBE/GBE | GBE/GBE | GBE/GBE | GBE/GBE |
| HSC.3,407. | HSC.3,408. | HFC.513. | HFC.3,409. |
| (JOYCE.LONDON No 16) | (JOYCE No 16 LONDON) | (JOYCE No 16 LONDON) | (J.PURDEY&SONS No 16 ELEY EJECTOR) |
| Pre 1908. | Manufacturer. | Pre 1908. | London Gnm. Ejt. |
| On other gauges. | | On other gauges. | |
| GBE/GBE | GBE/GBE | GBE/GBE | GBE/GBE |
| HSC.3,410. | HFC.511. | HFC.512. | HSC.3,411. |

| | | | |
|---|---|---|---|
| (J. Purdey & Sons, No 16, Eley London) | (J. Swinfen, Maidstone, No 16, Eley) | (Joyce & Co London, No 14) | (Joyce & Co London, No 14) |
| London Gnm. On other gauges. | Gnm, 16 gauge. | 14 gauge. | Manufacturer. |
| GBE/GBE | GBE/GBE | GBE/GBE | GBE/GBE |
| HFC.3,412. | HFC.514. | HFC.3,413. | HFC.3,414. |
| (Jack Rabbit, No 12, A.A.Co.) | (Jack Rabbit, No 12, A.A.Co.) | (Jackson, No 12, Bungay Halesworth) | (Jackson, Nottingham, No 12, Eley) |
| 12 gauge. | 12 gauge. | Irm, gunsmith. | Samuel Jackson. |
| USA | USA | GBE | GBE/GBE |
| HSC.3,415. | HFC.1,286. | HSC.3,416. | HSC.3,417. |
| (Jackson, Nottingham, No 12) | (J.A. Davidson Special, No 12, Gastight, Wells Next Sea) | (James B. Warrilow, Trade Mark, No 12, Accurate, Chippenham) | (James B. Warrilow, Trade Mark, No 12, Accurate, Chippenham England) |
| Gnm. | Wines, loader. | Gunsmith. | Gunsmith. |
| GBE | GBE | GBE | GBE |
| HSC.3,418. | HSC.3,419. | HFC.2,194. | HFC.1,287. |
| (James Kirk, No 12, Ayr) | (James Kirk, Ayr, No 12, Eley) | (James Kirk, No 12, K, Ayr) | (Jarry, 12 12, Angouleme) |
| Gnm. | Gnm. | Gnm. | |
| GBE | GBE/GBE | GBE/GBE | F |
| HFC.3,420. | HSC.3,421. | HFC.1,288. | HFC.1,289. |

| | | | |
|---|---|---|---|
| (headstamp) | (headstamp) | (headstamp) | (headstamp) |
| Ammo dealers. | | Ammo dealers. | |
| | 16. | 20. | |
| GBE | GBE | GBE | GBE/B |
| HFC.1,291. | HSC.3,422. | HFC.1,290. | HFC.1,292. |
| (headstamp) | (headstamp) | (headstamp) | (headstamp) |
| Ammo dealers. | | Ammo dealers. | |
| | | 16. | |
| GBE/B | GBE/B | GBE/B | GBE/B |
| HFC.3,423. | HFC.3,424. | HFC.3,425. | HFC.3,426. |
| (headstamp) | (headstamp) | (headstamp) | (headstamp) |
| Ammo dealers. | Irm. | Gnm. | Gnm, Ejt. |
| GBE/B | GBE | GBE/GBE | GBE/GBE |
| HFC.1,294. | HFC.2,195. | HFC.1,296. | HFC.1,297. |
| (headstamp) | (headstamp) | (headstamp) | (headstamp) |
| Gnm, Ejt. | Kynoch case, Ejt. | James Burrow. | |
| GBE/GBE | GBE/GBE | GBE/GBE | |
| HFC.1,298. | HFC.1,308. | HFC.1,309. | HFC.1,295. |

| | | | |
|---|---|---|---|
| (J.B.WARRILOW TRADE MARK No 12 ACCURATE CHIPPENHAM) | (J.B.WARRILOW TRADE MARK No 12 ACCURATE CHIPPENHAM) | (J.B.WARRILOW KYNOCH'S PATENT GROUSE No 2090 CHIPPENHAM 12) | (J.CALVERT.WALSDEN No 12 ELEY) |
| James Bakewell Warrilow. Gunsmith. | | Kynoch case, Ejt. | Eley Bros cse. |
| | | | |
| GBE | GBE | GBE/GBE | GBE/GBE |
| HFC.3,427. | HFC.1,320. | HFC.3,428. | HSC.3,429. |
| (J.C.HIGGINS 12 12 CANADA) | (JC 12 12 JC) | (J.CONYERS & SONS No 12 KYNOCH DRIFFIELD) | (J.COSTAS 12 12 BARCELONA) |
| | | Gnm, Kynoch case. | Pla. |
| CDN | | GBE/GBE | E |
| HSC.3,430. | HFC.1,299. | HFC.1,300. | HFC.1,301. |
| (J.DEUSSEN 12 12 BRUXELLES) | (J.D.DOUGALL No 12 LONDON) | (J.D.DOUGALL & SONS.GLASGOW. No 12 ELEY.) | (J.E.COOKE No 12 BROMYARD) |
| | Gnm. | Gnm. | |
| B | GBE | GBE/GBE | GBE |
| HFC.3,431. | HFC.3,432/R. | HFC.1,302. | HFC.1,303. |
| (JEFFERY No 12 DORCHESTER) | (JEFFERY No 12 ELEY DORCHESTER) | (JEFFERY No 12 GUILDFORD) | (JEFFERY.GUILDFORD No 12 ELEY) |
| Charles Jeffery, Gnm. | | Samuel R. Jeffery, Gnm. | |
| GBE | GBE/GBE | GBE | GBE/GBE |
| HFC.3,434. | HFC.3,435. | HFC.1,304. | HFC.3,436. |

| | | | |
|---|---|---|---|
| JEFFERY&SON 12 12 GUILDFORD | JEFFERY No 12 PLYMOUTH | JEFFERY.PLYMOUTH No 12 ELEY | JEFFRIES.NORWICH No 12 ELEY |
| Gnm. | Gnm. | Gnm. Pre Wwl. | Eley Bros case. |
| GBE | GBE | GBE/GBE | GBE/GBE |
| HSC.3,437. | HFC.1,305. | HFC.3,438. | HFC.3,439. |
| JENVEY&TITE No 12 GRANTHAM | JESSE.P.HODGSON No 12 KYNOCH LOUTH | JEWSON.HALIFAX No 12 ELEY | J.F.LAYCOCK.WISETON No 12 ELEY |
| | Gnm. Kynoch case. | Gnm. Pre Wwl. | Pre Wwl. |
| GBE | GBE/GBE | GBE/GBE | GBE/GBE |
| HFC.1,306. | HFC.1,307. | HSC.3,433. | HFC.1,310. |
| J.F.MASON.EYNSHAM HALL No 12 ELEY | J.GRAYHAM&Co No 12 ELEY INVERNESS | J.T.COOK&Co.CIRENCESTER No 12 ELEY | J.H.MARTIN&Co.ST JOHNS No 12 ELEY |
| Private. Pre Wwl. | Gnm. Pre Wwl. | | |
| GBE/GBE | GBS/GBE | GBE/GBE | /GBE |
| HFC.1,311. | HFC.1,312. | HFC.1,313. | HFC.1,314. |
| J.HOBSON No 12 LEAMINGTON | J.HOBSON No 12 KYNOCH LEAMINGTON | J.H.P 12 12 FRANCE | JIALING 12 12 CHINA |
| Gnm. | Gnm. Pre Wwl. | | |
| GBE | GBE/GBE | F | RC |
| HFC.1,315. | HFC.1,316. | HFC.1,317. | HFC.1,318. |

| | | | |
|---|---|---|---|
| J.LANG & SON No 12 KYNOCH LONDON | J.LANG & SON KYNOCH PATENT No 12 GROUSE EJECTOR LONDON | J.L.WOOD No 12 STAMFORD | J.McCRIRICK & SONS No 12 AYR |
| Gnm. Pre Wwl. | Gnm, Ejt. | Gnm. | Gnm. |
| GBE/GBE | GBE/GBE | GBE | GBS |
| HFC.1,321. | HFC.1,322. | HFC.1,323. | HFC.1,324. |
| JMP 12 | J.MUES 12 12 MELBOURNE | J.MUES 12 12 MADE IN BELGIUM MELBOURNE | J.MUES SHELL 12 12 MADE IN BELGIUM MELBOURNE |
| | Loader. | Loader. | Loader. |
| | AUS | AUS/B | AUS/B |
| HFC.1,325. | HFC.1,326. | HSC.3,440. | HFC.1,327. |
| JOHN BARNES 12 12 CASE MADE IN BELGIUM AYR | JOHN FRASER No 12 ELEY EDINBURGH | JOHN FRY No 12 DERBY | JOHN REYNOLDS FRENCH No 12 MADE CASE CULLOMPTON |
| Gnm. | Gnm. | Gnm. | |
| GBS/B | GBS/GBE | GBE | GBE/F |
| HSC.3,441. | HFC.1,328. | HFC.1,329. | HFC.3,442. |
| JOHN RIGBY & Co. DUBLIN No.12. | JOHNSON 12 GA INTERNATIONAL | JOHNSON & REID. DARLINGTON No 12 ELEY | JOHNSON & REID DARLINGTON No 12 ELEY |
| Gnm. | | Irm. | Irm. |
| IRL | | GBE/GBE | GBE/GBE |
| HSC.3,443. | HSC.3,444. | HFC.1,330. | HFC.1,331. |

| | | | |
|---|---|---|---|
| (JOHNSON & WRIGHT NORTHAMPTON No 12) | (JOHNSON & WRIGHT NORTHAMPTON No 12) | (JOHNSON & WRIGHT KYNOCH LTD NORTHAMPTON No 12) | (JOHN WARRICK READING No 12) |
| Irm. | Irm. | Irm.    Pre Wwl. | Cycles, motors. |
| GBE | GBE | GBE/GBE | GBE |
| HSC.3,445. | HFC.3,446. | HFC.1,332. | HFC.1,333. |
| (JOSLINS LTD. COLCHESTER No 12 ELEY) | (JOYCE LONDON No 12) | (JOYCE No 12 LONDON) | (JOYCE No 12 LONDON) |
| Eley Bros case. | Pre Wwl. On other gauges. | Manufacturer. | Prior 1908. |
| GBE/GBE | GBE/GBE | GBE/GBE | GBE/GBE |
| HSC.3,447. | HFC.3,448. | HFC.3,449/R. | HFC.3,450/R. |
| (JOYCE No 12 LONDON) | (JOYCE No 12 LONDON) | (JOYCE No 12 LONDON) | (JOYCE No 12 LONDON) |
| Manufacturer. | | Pre Wwl. | Manufacturer. |
| GBE/GBE | GBE/GBE | GBE/GBE | GBE/GBE |
| HFC.1,338. | HFC.1,340. | HFC.1,341. | HFC.1,342. |
| (JOYCE No 12 LONDON) | (JOYCE No 12 LONDON) | (JOYCE No 12 LONDON) | (JOYCE No 12 LONDON) |
| | Manufacturer. | | Pre Wwl. |
| On other gauges. | | | |
| GBE/GBE | GBE/GBE | GBE/GBE | GBE/GBE |
| HFC.1,335. | HFC.1,337. | HFC.1,336. | HFC.1,334. |

| | | | |
|---|---|---|---|
| (JOYCE.LONDON No.12) | (JOYCE & Co LONDON BAILEY'S PATENT GASTIGHT No.12) | (JOYCE & Co LONDON BAILEY'S PATENT GAS CHECK No.12) | (JOYCE.LONDON.GASTIGHT No.12) |
| Manufacturer. | | Pre Wwl. | |
| | | | |
| HSC.3,451. | HFC.3,452. | HFC..1,347. | HSC.3,453. |
| (JOYCE LONDON No.12 GASTIGHT) | (JOYCE.LONDON No.12 GASTIGHT) | (JOYCE.LONDON No.12 GASTIGHT) | (JOYCE.LONDON No.12 GASTIGHT) |
| | Manufacturer. | | Pre Wwl. |
| | | | |
| HFC.3,454. | HSC.3,455. | HFC.3,456. | HFC.3,457. |
| (JOYCE & Co. LONDON No.12) | (JOYCE & Co. No.12 LONDON) | (JOYCE & Co No.12 LONDON) | (JOYCE & Co No.12 LONDON) |
| | Manufacturer. | | Pre Wwl. |
| | | | |
| HFC.3,458. | HFC.3,459/R. | HSC.3,460. | HSC.3,461. |
| (JOYCE & Co No.12 LONDON) | (JOYCE Ltd No.12 LONDON) | (JOYCE Ltd No.12 LONDON) | (JOYCE Ltd No.12 LONDON) |
| Manufacturer. | | Pre Wwl. | |
| | | | |
| HSC.3,462. | HFC.3,463. | HFC.3,464. | HFC.3,465. |

| | | | |
|---|---|---|---|
| (JOYCE LTD No 12 LONDON) | (JOYCE LTD No 12 LONDON) | (JOYCE LIMITED No 12 EJECTOR LONDON) | (JOYCE LIMITED No 12 GASTIGHT LONDON) |
| Manufacturer. | | Pre Wwl. Ejt. | |
| GBE/GBE | GBE | GBE/GBE | GBE/GBE |
| HSC.3,466. | HSC.3,467. | HFC.1,343. | HFC.1,344. |
| (JOYCE LIMITED No 12 GASTIGHT LONDON) | (JOYCE LIMITED No 12 GASTIGHT LONDON) | (WRIGHT·JOYCE·JOHNSON No 12) | (J. PARKINSON No 12 DUBLIN) |
| Manufacturer. | Pre Wwl. | Northants Irm. | |
| GBE/GBE | GBE/GBE | GBE/GBE | IRL |
| HFC.1,345. | HFC.1,346. | HFC.3,468. | HSC.3,469. |
| (J. PARKINSON No 12 ELEY DUBLIN) | (J.P. LOWER & SON No 12 DENVER.COL.) | (J. PURDEY & SONS No 12 ELEY LONDON) | (J. PURDEY & SONS No 12 ELEY EJECTOR) |
| Eley Bros case. | | Gnm. Pre Wwl. | Pre Wwl. Ejt. |
| IRL/GBE | USA/USA | GBE/GBE | GBE/GBE |
| HSC.3,470. | HSC.3,471. | HFC.3,472. | HFC.2,196. |
| (J. PURDEY & SONS No 12 ELEY EJECTOR) | (J. PURDEY & SONS No 12 ELEY'S EJECTOR) | (J. RIGBY & Co. No 12 KYNOCH LONDON) | (Canceled Rigby) |
| Gnm. Ejt. | Gnm. Ejt. | Gnm. Pre Wwl. | Canceled Rigby. |
| GBE/GBE | GBE/GBE | GBE/GBE | GBE/GBE |
| HFC.1,349. | HFC.1,348. | HFC.1,350. | HFC.1,351. |

| | | | |
|---|---|---|---|
| (Rigby & Co London, Kynochs Patent Grouse, No 2090, No 12) | (J.R.Watson & Co, No 12, London) | (J.R.Watson & Co, No 12, London) | (J.R.Watson & Co London, Made in Belgium, 12) |
| Gnm, Ejt. | Gun and ammunition dealers. | | |
| GBE/GBE | GBE | GBE | GBE/B |
| HFC.1,352. | HSC.3,473. | HFC.3,474. | HFC.1,293. |
| (JSS 12 GAUGE) | (J.S.Williams, No 12, Pontypridd) | (JULIAD 12 12 * *) | (JULIAN No 12 Basingstoke) |
| | Irm, explosives. | | H. Julian, Irm. |
| | GBW | | GBE |
| HFC.1,354. | HFC.1,355. | HSC.3,475. | HFC.1,356. |
| (JULIAN No 12 Basingstoke) | (Julian.Basingstoke. No 12 Eley) | (J.Van Maele Bruxelles No 12 Eley) | (J.Venables & Son Foreign Made Case No ? 12 Oxford) |
| Irm and gunsmiths. | Pre Wwl. | Eley Bros case. | Gnm. |
| GBE | GBE/GBE | B/GBE | GBE |
| HFC.1,357. | HFC.1,358. | HSC.3,476. | HSC.3,477. |
| (J.Venables & Son French Made Case No 12 Oxford) | (J.V.Needham * 12 *) | (J.V.Needham * 12 *) | (J.Woodward & Sons No 12) |
| Gnm. | Gnm. | Gnm. | London Gnm. |
| GBE/F | GBE | GBE | GBE |
| HFC.3,478. | HSC.3,479. | HFC.1,359. | HSC.3,480/R. |

| | | | |
|---|---|---|---|
| London Gnm. | Eley Bros case. | Kynoch case. | James Woodward |
| GBE | GBE/GBE | GBE/GBE | GBE/GBE |
| HFC.1.361. | HFC.1,362. | HFC.1,363. | HFC.1,364. |
| Gnm. Ejt. Pre Wwl. | Gnm, Ejt. | | |
| GBE/GBE | GBE/GBE | | AUS |
| HFC.1,365. | HFC.3,481. | HFC.1,366. | HFC.3,482. |
| | Joseph W. Irm. | 10 gauge. | 10 gauge. |
| AUS | GBE/GBE | GBE/GBE | GBE/GBE |
| HSC.3,483. | HFC.1,360. | HSC.3,484/R. | HSC.3,485. |
| Manufacturer. | 4 gauge. | James Pain & Sons, Salisbury. Pyrotechnics. | |
| GBE/GBE | GBE | GBE | GBE |
| HFC.2,080. | HFC.3,486. | HSC.3,487. | HFC.3,488. |

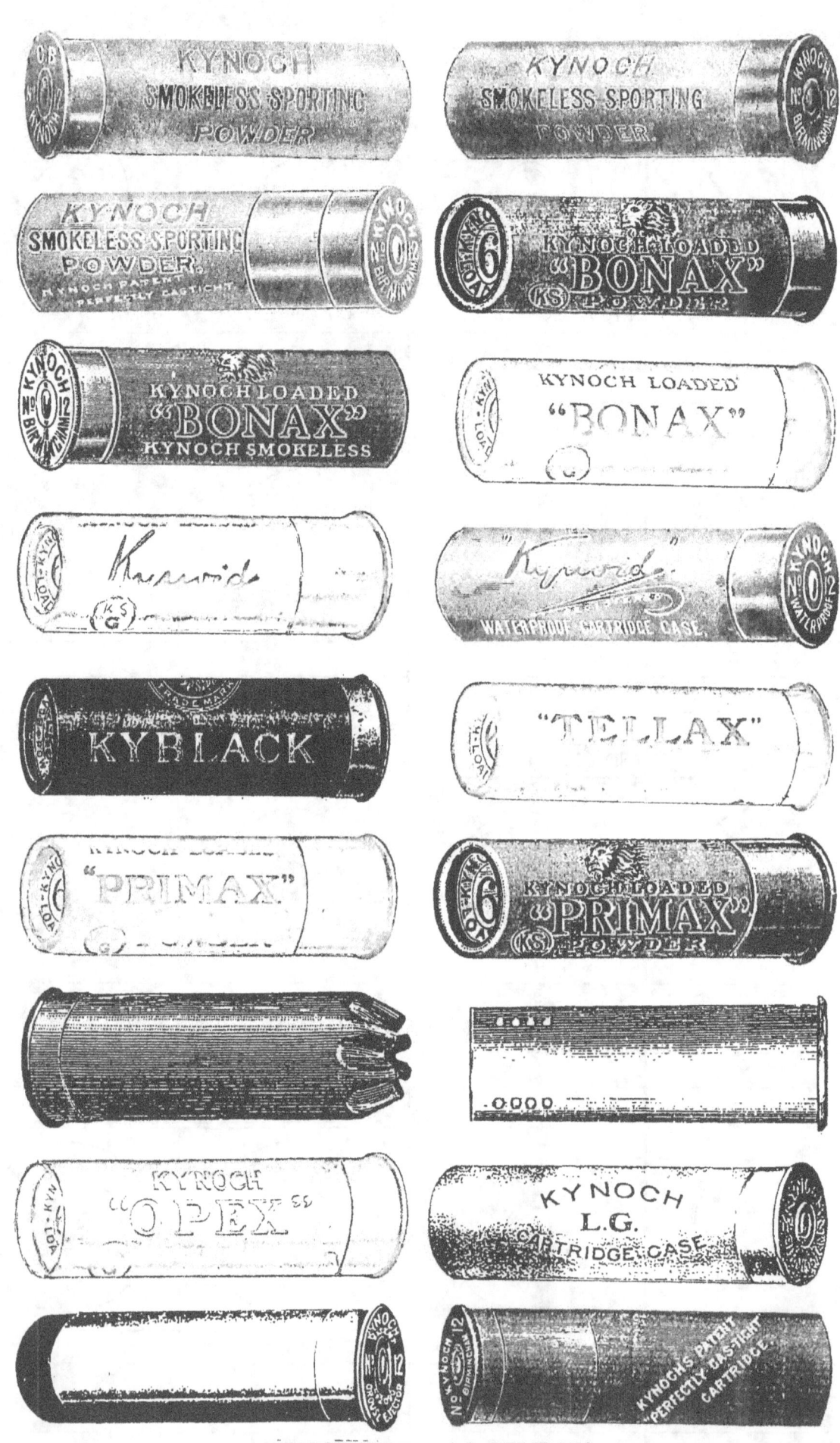

KYNOCH SHOTGUN CARTRIDGES

A selection from the many old Kynoch brands that were once manufactured at the old Lion Works at Witton, Birmingham, England. These illustrations have been taken from off of bygone adverisments.

| | | | |
|---|---|---|---|
| Manufacturer. | .360. | .410. | .410. |
| GBE/GBE | GBE/GBE | GBE/GBE | GBE/GBE |
| HFC.3,489. | HFC.3,490. | HFC.232. | HFC.233. |
| Manufacturer. | .410, Pre Wwl. | .410. Pre Wwl. | 12 mm - .410. |
| GBE/GBE | GBE/GBE | GBE/GBE | GBE/GBE |
| HFC.2,139. | HFC.234. | HSC.3,491. | HSC.3,492. |
| 12 mm - .410. | 14 mm - 32 gauge. | 14 mm - 32 gauge. | 32 gauge. |
| GBE/GBE | GBE/GBE | GBE/GBE | GBE/GBE |
| HSC.3,493. | HSC.3,494. | HFC.241. | HFC.243. |
| Manufacturer. | On other gauges. | 28 gauge, Ejt. | 28 gauge, Ejt. On other gauges. |
| GBE/GBE | GBE/GBE | GBE/GBE | GBE/GBE |
| HFC.259. | HSC.3,495. | HFC.260. | HSC.3,496. |

| | | | |
|---|---|---|---|
| 28 gauge. Pre Wwl. | 28 gauge. Abc. | Manufacturer. | 28 gauge. |
| GBE/GBE | GBE/GBE | GBE/GBE | GBE/GBE |
| HFC.263. | HFC.261. | HSC.3,497. | HFC.262. |
| 24 gauge. | Manufacturer. | Pre Wwl. | Pre. Wwl. On other gauges. |
| GBE/GBE | GBE/GBE | GBE/GBE | GBE/GBE |
| HFC.3,498. | HSC.3,499. | HFC.3,500. | HSC.3,501. |
| 24 gauge. Ejt. | 20 gauge, Gmn. | Manufacturer. | Pre Wwl. |
| GBE/GBE | IRL | GBE/GBE | GBE/GBE |
| HFC.271. | HFC.346. | HFC.347. | HFC.348. |
| 20 gauge. 16. | Manufacturer. On other gauges. | Pre Wwl. On other gauges. | Nobel Industries. On other gauges. |
| GBE/GBE | GBE/GBE | GBE/GBE | GBE/GBE |
| HSC.3,502. | HFC.349. | HFC.350. | HFC.351. |

| | | | |
|---|---|---|---|
| Nobel Industries | Black powder. | Explosive Trades | Manufacturer. |
| | 16, 14, 12, 10. | 16, 12. | On other gauges. |
| GBE/GBE | GBE/GBE | GBE/GBE | GBE/GBE |
| HFC.3,503. | HSC.3,504. | HFC.352. | HFC.353. |
| Ejt. | Ejt. | Nobel Industries. | Pre Ww1. |
| On other gauges. | | On other gauges. | |
| GBE/GBE | GBE/GBE | GBE/GBE | GBE/GBE |
| HFC.354. | HFC.357. | HSC.3,505. | HSC.3,506. |
| Manufacturer. | Exported case. | Thin brass case. | Ejt. |
| On other gauges. | On other gauges. | | |
| GBE/GBE | USA/GBE | GBE/GBE | GBE/GBE |
| HFC.3,507. | HFC.358. | HFC.3,508. | HFC.355. |
| 20 gauge, Ejt. | 18 gauge.  Abc. | 16 gauge. | 16 gauge. |
| | On other gauges. | | |
| GBE/GBE | GBE/GBE | | |
| HFC.356. | HFC.425. | HFC.515. | HFC.3,509. |

183

| | | | |
|---|---|---|---|
| KIRK 16 16 AYR | KONDOR 16 16 D | KRIEGSPATRONE 16 | KRIEGSPATRONE 16 |
| 16 gauge, Gnm. | | | |
| GBS | D | | |
| HSC.3,510. | HSC.3,511. | HSC.3,512. | HFC.516. |
| "KRUSIK" 16 16 "KPYUNK" | "KRUSIK" 16 ? 16 "Крушик" | KYNOCH * * 16 | KYNOCH * * 16 |
| Cyrillic alphabet, 16 gauge. | | Manufacturer. | Pre. Wwl. |
| | | GBE/GBE | GBE/GBE |
| HSC.3,513. | HSC.3,514. | HSC.3,515. | HFC.5,447. |
| KYNOCH ✦ ✦ 16 | KYNOCH No 16 BIRMINGHAM | KYNOCH. BIRMINGHAM. No 16 | KYNOCH No 16 BIRMINGHAM |
| Abc. | 16 gauge. | Manufacturer. | Pre Wwl. |
| | 20. | 12. | On other gauges. |
| GBE/GBE | GBE/GBE | GBE/GBE | GBE/GBE |
| HFC.517. | HFC.3,516. | HSC.3,517. | HFC.519. |
| No KYNOCH 16 BIRMINGHAM | KYNOCH N. 16 16 BIRMINGHAM | KYNOCH No 16 BLACK | KYNOCH E.T.L. 16 16 BONAX |
| Pre Wwl. | Nobel Industries. | Black powder. | Explosives Trades. |
| On other gauges. | On other gauges. | On other gauges. | 20, 12. |
| GBE/GBE | GBE/GBE | GBE/GBE | GBE/GBE |
| HFC.520. | HFC.521. | HFC.518. | HSC.3,518. |

| | | | |
|---|---|---|---|
| *KYNOCH No 16 GROUSE* | *KYNOCH PATENT No 16 GROUSE EJECTOR No 2090* | *KYNOCH No 16 LONDON* | *KYNOCH 16 16 NOBEL* |
| 16 gauge, Ejt. | Ejt, Pre Wwl. | Pre Wwl. | Nobel Industries. |
| 20, 12. | On other gauges. | | On other gauges. |
| GBE/GBE | GBE/GBE | GBE/GBE | GBE/GBE |
| HSC.3,519. | HSC.3,520. | HSC.3,521. | HSC.3,522. |
| *KYNOCH 16 16 NOBEL* | *KYNOCH No 16 PATENT* | *KYNOCH No "PERFECT" 16* | *KYNOCH'S No 16 PATENT* |
| Post Wwl. | Manufacturer. | Pre Wwl. | Thin brass case. |
| On other gauges. | 20, 12, 10. | | 20. |
| GBE/GBE | GBE/GBE | GBE/GBE | GBE/GBE |
| HFC.522. | HSC.3,523. | HFC.526. | HFC.3,524. |
| *KYNOCH'S No 16 PATENT* | *KYNOCH'S No 16 PATENT* | *KYNOCH'S PATENT No 16 No 2090 PATENT* | *KYNOCH'S W.BITTER No 16 M.COELN PATENT* |
| Abc. | Manufacturer. | Ejt, Pre Wwl. | Kynoch case. |
| On other gauges. | | | |
| GBE/GBE | GBE/GBE | GBE/GBE | D/GBE |
| HFC.523. | HFC.3,525. | HSC.3,526. | HFC.525. |
| *KYNOCH'S W.BITTER No 16 COELN PATENT* | *KYNOCH'S PATENT No 16 EXPERT SHELL SQUIRES.N.Y.* | *KYNOCH No 14 BIRMINGHAM* | *KYNOCH No 14 BLACK* |
| Kynoch case. | 16 gauge. | 14 gauge. | 14 gauge. |
| 12, | | On other gauges. | 20,16,12,10. |
| D/GBE | USA/GBE | GBE/GBE | GBE/GBE |
| HSC.3,527. | HFC.524. | HFC.618. | HSC.3,528. |

| | | | |
|---|---|---|---|
| KYNOCH PATENT No 2090 GROUSE EJECTOR No 14 | KYNOCH'S "GROUSE" PATENT No 2090 No 14 | KYNOCH'S PATENT No 14 | KYNOCH'S PATENT No 14 |
| 14 gauge, Ejt. 20,16,12. | Ejt. | Abc. On other gauges. | 14 gauge. Abc. On other gauges. |
| GBE/GBE | GBE/GBE | GBE/GBE | GBE/GBE |
| HSC.3,529. | HFC.619. | HFC.620. | HFC.621. |
| KALCO 12 12 EUROPE | KAVANAGH & SON No 12 DUBLIN | KAVANAGH & SON No 12 DUBLIN | KAVANAGH & SON No 12 DUBLIN |
| | William & Son. | Gnm. | Gnm. |
| | IRL | IRL | IRL |
| HFC.1,368. | HSC.3,530. | HSC.3,531. | HFC.1,369. |
| KAVANAGH & SON No 12 ELEY DUBLIN | KAVANAGH & SON No 12 ELEY DUBLIN | KAWAGUCHYA 12 12 (KFC) | K.D.RADCLIFFE No 12 COLCHESTER |
| Gnm. Pre. Wwl. | Pre Wwl, Gnm, | Pla. | Gnm. |
| IRL/GBE | IRL/GBE | | GBE |
| HFC.3,532. | HSC.3,533. | HSC.3,534. | HFC.1,370. |
| KELLY & SON. DUBLIN No 12 ELEY | KELSEY No 12 PAT. APL FOR | KENT 12 12 KENT | KENT 12 12 KENT |
| Pre Wwl. | | Loader. | Loader. |
| IRL/GBE | | GBE | GBE |
| HSC.3,535. | HFC.3,536. | HFC.1,372. | HFC.1,371. |

| | | | |
|---|---|---|---|
| (KENT No 12 WANTAGE) | (KENT & SON No 12 WANTAGE) | (KENT & SON No 12 WANTAGE) | (KENT & SON WANTAGE No 12 ELEY) |
| Irm, Pre Wwl. | Gunsmith Irm. | Irm, Pre Wwl. | Eley Bros case. |
| | | | |
| GBE | GBE | GBE | GBE/GBE |
| HFC.1,373. | HFC.1,375. | HFC.1,374. | HFC.1,376. |
| (KERRIDGE 12 12 YARMOUTH) | (KETTERING 12 GA INTERNATIONAL) | (KETTERING 12 GA INTER-NATION) | (KEYSTONE 12) |
| Gunsmith, Irm. | | | |
| | | | |
| GBE | GBE | GBE | USA |
| HFC.1,377. | HSC.3,537. | HSC.3,538. | HFC.3,539. |
| (KEYSTONE No12) | (KEYSTONE No 12) | (K.F. 12 12 SPECIAL) | (KILBY 12A) |
| 10. | | | |
| USA | USA | | |
| HSC.3,540. | HSC.3,541. | HFC.1,378. | HSC.3,542. |
| (KINGDON No 12 BASINGSTOKE) | (KINGDON BASINGSTOKE No 12 ELEY) | (KINGDON No 12 KYNOCH BASINGSTOKE) | (KING No 12 M.F.C.) |
| Irm. Pre Wwl. | Eley Bros case. | Kynoch case, | |
| | | | |
| GBE | GBE/GBE | GBE/GBE | J |
| HFC.1,379. | HFC.1,380. | HFC.1,381. | HSC.3,543. |

| | | | |
|---|---|---|---|
| KIRK 12 12 AYR | K-K 12 12 K-K | KOLN-ROTTWEIL 12 12 AKTIENGESELLSCHAFT | KOLN-ROTTWEIL 12 12 AKTIENGESELLSCHAFT |
| Gnm. 16. | | Manufacturer. | Manufacturer. |
| GBS | | D/D | D/D |
| HSC.3,544. | HSC.3,545. | HFC.1,383. | HFC.1,382. |
| KONDOR 12 12 D | K.RIDER.PHILA. No.12 ELEY | KROMSON 12 12 ESPAÑA | KYNOCH 12 |
| | Eley Bros case. | | Manufacturer. |
| D | USA/GBE. | E | GBE/GBE |
| HSC.3,546. | HFC.1,384. | HSC.3,547. | HFC.1,386. |
| KYNOCH *12* | KYNOCH No12 BALL | KYNOCH.BIRMINGHAM No12 | KYNOCH.BIRMINGHAM No.12 |
| Pre. Wwl. | Ball load. | Manufacturer. | Abc, Pre Wwl. |
| GBE/GBE | GBE/GBE | GBE/GBE | GBE/GBE |
| HSC.3,548. | HFC.1,387. | HFC.1,388. | HFC.1,389. |
| KYNOCH No 12 BIRMINGHAM | KYNOCH No 12 BIRMINGHAM | KYNOCH No 12 BIRMINGHAM | KYNOCH No 12 BIRMINGHAM |
| Abc, Pre Wwl. | Manufacturer. | Pre Wwl. On other gauges. | Manufacturer. |
| GBE/GBE | GBE/GBE | GBE/GBE | GBE/GBE |
| HFC.1,396. | HFC.3,549. | HFC.1,391. | HFC.1,395. |

| | | | |
|---|---|---|---|
| Much used. | Manufacturer. | Pre Ww1. | Manufacturer. |
| On other gauges. | | On other gauges. | |
| GBE/GBE | GBE/GBE | GBE/GBE | GBE/GBE |
| HFC.1,393. | HFC.1,394. | HFC.5,448. | HFC.1,392. |
| Large cap. | Explosives Trades. | Nobel Industries. | Kynoch case. |
| | 20,16. | On other gauges. | |
| GBE/GBE | GBE/GBE | GBE/GBE | IND/GBE |
| HFC.1,390. | HFC.3,550. | HFC.1,398. | HFC.1,399. |
| Exported case. | Brown Pap. | Black powder. | Explosives Trades. |
| | | 20,16. | 20,16. |
| GBE/GBE | GBE/GBE | GBE/GBE | GBE/GBE |
| HFC.1,400. | HFC.1,401. | HFC.1,402. | HFC.1,403. |
| Manufacturer. | Pre Ww1. | Pre Ww1. | Pre Ww1. |
| | | On other gauges. | On other gauges. |
| GBE/GBE | GBE/GBE | GBE/GBE | GBE/GBE |
| HFC.1,404. | HFC.1,406. | HFC.1,405. | HFC.1,407. |

| | | | |
|---|---|---|---|
| KYNOCH No 12 GROUSE | KYNOCH PATENT No 2090 12 GROUSE EJECTOR | KYNOCH 12 12 NITRO BALL | KYNOCH 12 12 NITRO-BALL |
| Ejt, Pre Wwl. | Ejt. | Kynoch ball load. | Ball load. |
| | On other gauges. | | |
| GBE/GBE | GBE/GBE | GBE/GBE | GBE/GBE |
| HFC.1,408. | HFC.1,409. | HFC.1,410. | HFC.1,411. |
| KYNOCH N.I. 12 12 NITRO-BALL | KYNOCH 12 12 NOBEL | KYNOCH 12 12 NOBEL | KYNOCH 12 12 NOBEL |
| Nobel Industries. | Nobel Industries. | Post Wwl. | Post Wwl. |
| | On other gauges. | | On other gauges. |
| GBE/GBE | GBE/GBE | GBE/GBE | GBE/GBE |
| HSC.3,551. | HFC.1,413. | HFC.3,552. | HFC.1,412. |
| KYNOCH 12 12 NOBEL | KYNOCH PATENT No 12 "OPEX" | KYNOCH PATENT No 12 "OPEX" | KYNOCH 12 12 PARADOX |
| Post Wwl. | Kynoch Ejt. | Kynoch Ejt. | Kynoch Ejt. |
| On other gauges. | | | |
| GBE/GBE | GBE/GBE | GBE/GBE | GBE/GBE |
| HFC.1,414. | HFC.1,416. | HFC.1,415. | HFC.1,417. |
| KYNOCH No 12 PATENT | KYNOCH W.BITTER No COELN 12 PATENT | KYNOCH No 12 PERFECT | KYNOCH E.T.L 12 12 PRIMAX |
| Thin brass. | | Thin brass. | No tube print. |
| On other gauges. | | On other gauges. | |
| GBE/GBE | D/GBE | GBE/GBE | GBE/GBE |
| HFC.3,553. | HFC.1,429. | HFC.3,554. | HFC.3,555. |

| | | | |
|---|---|---|---|
| (headstamp) | (headstamp) | (headstamp) | (headstamp) |
| Pap. | Pap. | Brown Pap. | Manufacturer. |
| GBE/GBE | GBE/GBE | GBE/GBE | GBE/GBE |
| HFC.1,420. | HFC.1,421. | HSC.3,556. | HSC.3,557. |
| (headstamp) | (headstamp) | (headstamp) | (headstamp) |
| Pre Wwl. | Abc. Recessed. | 12 gauge, recess. | Kynoch case, Ejt. |
| GBE/GBE | GBE/GBE | GBE/GBE | GBE/GBE |
| HFC.3,558/R. | HFC.1,423/R. | HFC.1,422/R. | HFC.1,432. |
| (headstamp) | (headstamp) | (headstamp) | (headstamp) |
| Kynoch case, Ejt. | Kynoch case, Ejt. | Manufacturer. | Abc. |
| GBE/GBE | GBE/GBE | GBE/GBE | B/GBE |
| HFC.3,559. | HFC.3,560. | HFC.5,449. | HFC.1,425. |
| (headstamp) | (headstamp) | (headstamp) | (headstamp) |
| Pre Wwl. | Pre Wwl. | Pre Wwl. | Manufacturer. |
| 10. | | | |
| CDN/GBE | IRL/GBE | GBE/GBE | GBE/GBE |
| HFC.1,426. | HFC.1,428. | HFC.3,561. | HSC.3,562. |

| | | | |
|---|---|---|---|
| KYNOCH'S S.D.&G. No 12 PATENT | KYNOCH'S PATENT No 12 EXPERT LOAD SQUIRES N.Y. | KYNOCH'S PATENT No 12 EXPERT SHELL SQUIRES N.Y. | KYNOCH'S No W.W.GREENER BIRMINGHAM 12 PATENT |
| New York, NY. | New York, NY. | New York, NY. | Gnm, Kynoch case. |
| USA/GBE | USA/GBE | USA/GBE | GBE/GBE |
| HFC.1,427. | HFC.3,563. | HFC.1,431. | HFC.1,430. |
| KYNOCH'S PATENT PERFECTLY GAS TIGHT LONDON No 12 | KELSEY No 10 | KEYSTONE No 10 | KEYSTONE No 10 |
| 12 gauge Ejt. | 10 gauge only. | 10 gauge. | |
| GBE/GBE | USA | USA/USA | USA/USA |
| HFC.1,433. | HSC.3,564. | HSC.3,565. | HSC.3,566. |
| KYNOCH 10 | KYNOCH L10 | KYNOCH No 10 BIRMINGHAM | KYNOCH No 10 BIRMINGHAM |
| 10 gauge, Pap. | Manufacturer. | Pre Wwl. On other gauges. | Abc. |
| GBE/GBE | GBE/GBE | GBE/GBE | GBE/GBE |
| HFC.2,081. | HFC.2,082. | HSC.3,567. | HFC.2,084. |
| KYNOCH No 10 BIRMINGHAM | KYNOCH WITTON No 10 CARTRIDGE BIRMINGHAM | KYNOCH No 10 BLACK | KYNOCH No 10 PATENT |
| Manufacturer. | Pre Wwl. | Black powder. 20,16,14,12. | 10 gauge. On other gauges. |
| GBE/GBE | GBE/GBE | GBE/GBE | GBE/GBE |
| HFC.2,085. | HFC.2,087. | HSC.3,568. | HSC.3,569. |

| | | | |
|---|---|---|---|
| 10 gauge. | Recessed. Abc, | Manufacturer. | Pre. Wwl. |
| 16,12,8. | 12. | | 12. |
| GBE/GBE | GBE/GBE | GBE/GBE | GBE/GBE |
| HSC.3,570. | HFC.2,083/R. | HFC.2,086. | HSC.3,571. |
| Pre Wwl. | Pre Wwl. | New York. | 10 gauge. |
| 12. | 20,16,14,12,8. | 16,12. | |
| CDN/GBE | GBE/GBE | USA/GBE | USA/GBE |
| HSC.3,572. | HSC.3,573. | HSC.3,574. | HSC.3,575. |
| 8 gauge. | Manufacturer. | Much used. | Pre Wwl. |
| | On other gauges. | On other gauges. | On other gauges. |
| GBE/GBE | GBE/GBE | GBE/GBE | GBE/GBE |
| HFC.2,109. | HFC.3,576. | HFC.3,577. | HSC.3,578. |
| Thin brass. | Gnm. 8 gauge. | Abc. 4 gauge Kynoch | 4 gauge. |
| 16,12,10. | 12. | | |
| GBE/GBE | GBE/GBE | GBE/GBE | GBE/GBE |
| HSC.3,579. | HSC.3,580. | HFC.2,120. | HFC.2,121. |

| | | | |
|---|---|---|---|
|  KYNOCH No. 4 BIRMINGHAM |  KYNOCH No. 4 BIRMINGHAM |  KYNOCH No. 4 BIRMINGHAM |  KYNOCH PATENT No. 4 PERFECT BIRMINGHAM |
| Pre. Wwl. | Ejt, Green Pap. | Manufacturer. On other gauges. | 4 gauge. On other gauges. |
| GBE/GBE | GBE/GBE | GBE/GBE | GBE/GBE |
| HSC.3,581. | HFC.3,582. | HFC.2,123. | HFC.2,125. |
| KYNOCH PATENT No. 4 PERFECT BIRMINGHAM | KYNOCH 4 4 NOBEL | KYNOCH & Co. No. 4 BIRMINGHAM | F.N. All-Metal STAR Cartridge light load. From a 1933 advert. Also made with heavy load and ordinary turnover. |
| Manufacturer. | Nobel Industries. On other gauges. | Pre Wwl, 4 gauge. 12. | |
| GBE/GBE | GBE/GBE | GBE/GBE | |
| HFC.2,124. | HFC.2,126. | HFC.2,122/R. | |

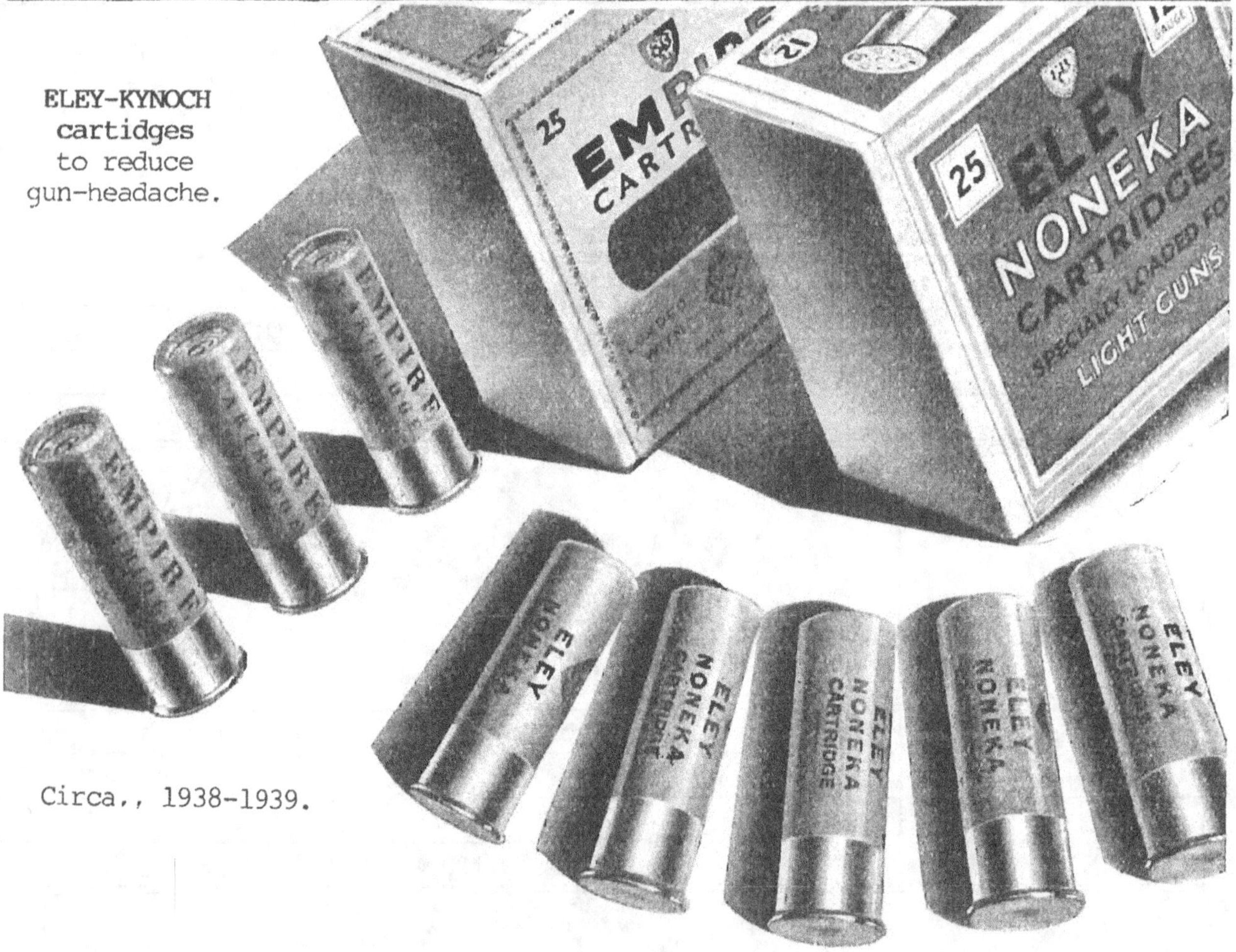

**ELEY-KYNOCH** cartridges to reduce gun-headache.

Circa,, 1938-1939.

| | | | |
|---|---|---|---|
| .410. | Gnm. 20 gauge. | Gnm. | Gnm. 20 gauge. |
| | | | 16. |
| | GBE/GBE | GBE/GBE | BGE/F |
| HSC.3,583. | HSC.3,584. | HFC.3,585. | HFC.3,586. |
| Leon Beaux. | | | 20 gauge. |
| | | | |
| I/I | B/GBE | USA | I/I |
| HFC.359. | HSC.3,587. | HSC.3,588. | HSC.3,589. |
| 20 gauge. | 20 gauge. | 18 gauge. | Gnm, 16 gauge. |
| | 16,14,12,10,8. | | |
| D | USA | A | GBE/B |
| HFC.360. | HFC.3,590. | HSC.3,591. | HSC.3,592. |
| Gnm, 16 gauge. | Leon Beaux. | Winchester. | Union Metalic. |
| 20. | | On other gauges. | 12,10. |
| GBE/F | I/I | USA/USA | USA/USA |
| HFC.3,593. | HSC.3,594. | HSC.3,595. | HSC.3,596. |

| | | | |
|---|---|---|---|
| 16 gauge. | Hws, London. | Hws, London. | 16 gauge. |
| | | | |
| D | GBE/D | GBE/D | B |
| HSC.3,597. | HFC.441. | HSC.3,598. | HSC.3,599. |
| 16 gauge. | 14 gauge. | 14 gauge. | 14 gauge. |
| 14,12,10,8. | | | 20,16,12,10,8. |
| USA/USA | I/I | I/I | USA/USA |
| HFC.3,600. | HSC.3,601. | HFC.622. | HSC.3,602. |
| 12 gauge. | 12 gauge. | Pla. | 12 gauge. |
| | | | |
| B | F | F | I |
| HFC.1,434. | HFC.1,435. | HSC.3,603. | HFC.1,436. |
| | Gnm. | Gnm. | London Gnm. |
| | | | |
| I | GBE/GBE | GBE/GBE | GBE |
| HFC.1,437. | HFC.1,438. | HFC.3,604. | HSC.3,605. |

| | | | |
|---|---|---|---|
| Joseph H. Lang. | Gnm, Joyce case. | London Gnm. | James J. Langley. |
| GBE/GBE | GBE/GBE | GBE | GBE |
| HFC.1,442. | HSC.3,606. | HSC.3,607. | HFC.1,439. |
| Eley Bros case. | Gnm. | Gnm. | Gnm. Large cap. |
| GBE/GBE | GBE/F | GBE/F | GBE/F |
| HFC.3,608. | HSC.3,609. | HFC.3,610. | HSC.3,611. |
| Gnm. | Gnm. | Gnm. | Gnm, Kynoch case. |
| GBE/F | GBE/F | GBE | |
| HFC.3,612. | HFC.3,613. | HFC.2,197. | HFC.1,440. |
| Gnm, Pre Wwl. | Gnm. | Gnm, Large cap. | Gnm. |
| GBE/GBE | GBE/B | GBE/B | GBE/F |
| HFC.3,614. | HFC.3,615. | HSC.3,616. | HFC.1,441. |

| | | | |
|---|---|---|---|
| LAPITENA 12 12 BEZIERS | LAPORTE 12 12 INT'L | LAPUA 12 12 | LAPUA 12 |
| 12 gauge, Pla. | | | 12 gauge. |
| F | | | |
| HSC.3,617. | HFC.1,443. | HSC.3,618. | HSC.3,619. |
| LAPUA 12 | LATENIT 12 12 FRANCE | LATENIT 12 12 ITALY | 12 LB |
| 12 gauge. | Pla. | Pla. | Leon Beaux. |
| | F | I | I/I |
| HFC.2,198. | HFC.1,444. | HSC.3,620. | HSC.3,621. |
| 12 LB | LB 12 | L.BACHMANN 12 12 BREVETE | L.C.SMITH 12 A |
| Large cap. | Leon Beaux. | | |
| I/I | I/I | | USA |
| HFC.3,622. | HFC.3,623. | HFC.2,199. | HSC.2,200. |
| 1901 No W 12 LEADER | 1901 No 12 LEADER | 1901 No 12 LEADER | LEATHAM 12 12 DURHAM |
| Winchester. | W.R.A. | W.R.A. On other gauges. | |
| USA/USA | USA/USA | USA/USA | GBE |
| HSC.3,624. | HFC.1,445. | HSC.3,625. | HFC.1,466. |

| | | | |
|---|---|---|---|
| LEECH & SONS CHELMSFORD No. 12 | LEECH & SONS CHELMSFORD No 12 | LEECH & SONS 12 12 CHELMSFORD | LEECH & SONS CASE MADE IN FRANCE No 12 CHELMSFORD |
| Gnm. | Gnm. | Gnm. | Gnm. |
| GBE | GBE | GBE | GBE/F |
| HSC.3,626. | HFC.1,447. | HSC.3,627. | HSC.3,628. |
| LEECH & SONS No 12 KYNOCH CHELMSFORD | LEECH & SON CHELMSFORD KYNOCH'S PATENT GROUSE No 2090 No 12 | LEIGH & JACKSON WITNEY No 12 ELEY | LEON BEAUX & C 12 MILANO 12 |
| Gnm. Kynoch case. | Gnm, Ejt. | Irm. Pre. Wwl. | |
| GBE/GBE | GBE/GBE | GBE/GBE | I/I |
| HFC.1,448. | HFC.1,449. | HSC.3,629. | HFC.1,453. |
| LEON BEAUX & C 12 MILANO 12 | LEON BEAUX & C 12 MILANO 12 | LEON BEAUX 12 12 MILANO | LEON BEAUX & C 12 MILANO 12 |
| | | | Large cap. |
| I/I | I/I | I/I | I/I |
| HFC.1,454. | HFC.1,451. | HFC.1,450. | HFC.1,452. |
| LEPUS 12 | L-EXPRESS 12 | L.L.FREARSON.SKIPTON No 12 ELEY | LIBERTY No 12 BULK |
| | Pla. Lyavle. | Eley Bros case. | Liberty Car'ge Co. |
| | GBE | GBE/GBE | USA |
| HFC.5,450. | HFC.1,455. | HFC.3,630. | HSC.3,631. |

| | | | |
|---|---|---|---|
| LIBERTY No 12 BULK | LIBERTY No 12 CARTRIDGE CO | LIGHTFIELD 12 | LIGHTNING No 12 U.M.C.CO. |
| Liberty Crtridge Company. | | | Union Metalic. |
| USA | USA | | USA/USA |
| HFC.1,456. | HSC.3,632. | HSC.3,633. | HFC.1,457. |
| LIGHTNING R No W A 12 W CO. V.L.&D. | LIGHTNING No 12 V.L.&D. | LIGNOSE 12 | LIGNOSE SPRENGSTOFF GMBH 12 BERLIN 12 |
| W,R.A. case. | | | |
| USA/USA | USA | D | D |
| HSC.3,634. | HSC.3,635. | HSC.3,636. | HSC.3,637. |
| LINE'S GUN CO CASE MADE 12 IN FRANCE 12 BRIGG | LINNINGTON NEWPORT I.W. No12 ELEY | LINSLEY BROS LEEDS No12 | LINSLEY BROS LEEDS No12 |
| Gnm. | Diisplay round. | Gnm. | Gnm. |
| GBE/F | GBE/GBE | GBE | GBE |
| HFC.3,638. | HFC.1,458. | HFC.3,639. | HSC.3,640. |
| LINSLEY BROS LEEDS No12 ELEY | LINSLEY BROS No 12 KYNOCH LEEDS | No LINSLEY BROS 12 LEEDS&BRADFORD | LINSLEY BROS LEEDS&BRADFORD ELEY No 12 |
| Gnm, Pre Wwl. | Gnm, Kynoch Case. | Gnm. | Gnm, Pre Wwl. |
| GBE/GBE | GBE/GBE | GBE | GBE |
| HSC.3,641. | HFC.1,459. | HFC.1,460. | HFC.1,461. |

| | | | |
|---|---|---|---|
| (Linsley Bros headstamp) | (Lisle Derby headstamp) | (Lisle Derby headstamp) | (Lisle Derby headstamp) |
| Gnm, Kynoch Ejt. | Gnm. | Gnm. | Gnm. |
| GBE/GBE | GBE | GBE/F | GBE/F |
| HFC.1,462. | HFC.1,463. | HFC.1,464. | HFC.1,465. |
| (Littleford headstamp) | (L. Keegan Dublin headstamp) | (L. Keegan Dublin headstamp) | (L-L Auckland headstamp) |
| Irm, gunsmith. | Gnm. | Gnm. | |
| GBE/GBE | IRL | IRL | NZ |
| HFC.5,451. | HSC.3,642. | HFC.1,467. | HSC.3,646. |
| (Lloyd Lewes headstamp) | (Lloyd-Lewes headstamp) | (Lloyds Champion Lewes headstamp) | (Lloyd & Son Lewes headstamp) |
| Gnm. | Gnm. | Gnm. | Gnm. |
| GBE/D | GBE/D | GBE | GBE |
| HFC.1,468. | HSC.3,644. | HSC.3,645. | HSC.3,643. |
| (Lloyd & Son Eley Lewes headstamp) | (Lloyd & Sons Champion Lewes headstamp) | (Lloyd & Sons Champion Lewes headstamp) | (Lloyd & Sons Champion Lewes headstamp) |
| Eley Bros case. | Gnm. | Gnm. | Gnm. |
| GBE/GBE | GBE | GBE | GBE |
| HSC.3,647. | HSC.3,648. | HFC.1,469. | HSC.3,649. |

| | | | |
|---|---|---|---|
| Eley Bros case. | Gnm.    Pre WwI. | Pla. | |
| GBE/GBE | GBE/GBE | | AUS/D |
| HSC.3.650. | HSC.3,651. | HFC.1,470. | HSC.3,652. |
| | London Hws. | Manufacturer. | Manufacturer. |
| AUS/D | GBE/D | AUS | AUS |
| HFC.1,471. | HFC.1,472. | HFC.1,473. | HFC.1,474. |
| | | | |
| GBE | GBE/GBE | GBE/GBE | GBE |
| HFC.3,653/R. | HFC.3,654. | HFC.2,201. | HSC.3,655. |
| Possibly by Joyce. | | 10. | |
| GBE | F | USA | USA |
| HFC.1,475. | HSC.3,656. | HSC.3,657. | HSC.3,658. |

| | | | |
|---|---|---|---|
| LOWELL No 12 U.S.C.CO | LOWRANCE&SON No 12 BARNSLEY | L P 12 12 ITALY | L.P.M. 12 12 PORTUGAL |
| 12 gauge. | | Pla. | 12 gauge. |
| 20,16,14,10,8. | | | |
| USA/USA | GBE | I | P |
| HSC.3,659. | HFC.1,476. | HSC.3,660. | HFC.1,477. |
| L P 12 12 SPAIN | LUCK'S EXPLOSIVES 12 12 LONDON | LUPERINI 12 12 ARMI | LUX * * 12 |
| Pla. | | Pla. | |
| E | GBE | | D |
| HSC.3,661. | HFC.1,478. | HSC.3,662. | HFC.1,479. |
| LUX 12 12 D | LYALVALE 12 | LYALVALE ★ ☆ 12 | LYON&LYON No 12 CALCUTTA |
| 12 gauge. | Pla. | Pla. | 12 gauge. |
| | GBE | GBE | IND |
| HSC.3,663. | HFC.1,480. | HFC.1,481. | HFC.2,202. |
| LYON&LYON LTD MADE IN 12 12 GERMANY CALCUTTA | L.C.SMITH No 10 | L.C.SMITH 10 A | L.D.F. No 10 |
| 12 gauge. | 10 gauge. | Hunter Arms Co. | 10 gauge. |
| IND/D | USA | USA/USA | USA |
| HFC.1,482. | HSC.3,664. | HSC.3,665. | HSC.3,666. |

| | | | |
|---|---|---|---|
| 1901 №W 10 LEADER | 1901 № 10 LEADER | 1901 № 10 LEADER | LIDDLE & KEADING 10 A |
| 10 gauge. W.R.A.Co. | W.R.A.Co. | W.R.A.Co. | 10 gauge. |
| USA/USA | USA/USA | USA/USA | USA |
| HSC.3,667. | HFC.2,088. | HFC.2,089. | HSC.3,668. |
| LIDDLE & 10 A KEADING | LIDDLE & N° 10 KEADING | LIDDLE & N° 10 KEADING | L.M N° 10 |
| | 10 gauge only. | 10 gauge. | Elm City Manuf' Co. |
| USA/USA | USA | USA | USA |
| HSC.3,669. | HSC.3,670. | HSC.3,671. | HSC.3,672. |
| LOWELL N° 10 EXTRA | LOWELL N° 10 U.S.C.CO. | 1901 N° W 8 LEADER | 1901 N° W 8 LEADER |
| 10 gauge. | 10 gauge. | 8 gauge. | 8 gauge. W.R.A.Co. |
| 12. | 20,16,14,12,8. | | |
| USA | USA | USA/USA | USA/USA |
| HSC.3,673. | HSC.3,674. | HSC.3,675. | HSC.3,676. |
| LOWELL N° 8 U.S.C.CO. | 1901 N° W 4 LEADER | | |
| W.R.A.Co. | 4 gauge, W.R.A.Co. | | |
| On other gauges. | On other gauges. | | |
| USA/USA | USA/USA | | |
| HSC.3,677. | HSC.3,678. | | |

| | | | |
|---|---|---|---|
| .410. Large cap. | H.S.B.& Co. .410. | 32 gauge. | 32 gauge. |
| B/B | USA/USA | B/B | I/I |
| HFC.235. | HSC.3,679. | HFC.244. | HSC.3,680. |

| | | | |
|---|---|---|---|
| 14mm - 32 gauge. | 28 gauge. Gnm. | 20, 12. | 28 gauge. On other gauges. |
| F/F | GBS/GBE | IND | B/B |
| HFC.242. | HFC.3,681. | HSC.3,682. | HSC.3,683. |

| | | | |
|---|---|---|---|
| 28 gauge. Pla. | 28 gauge. | 24 gauge. | 24 gauge. |
| I/I | B/B | J | B/B |
| HFC.3,684. | HSC.3,685. | HSC.3,686. | HSC.3,687. |

| | | | |
|---|---|---|---|
| Aluminium case. On other gauges. | 24 gauge. | 24 gauge. | 20 gauge. Pre Ww1. |
| B/B | F/F | I/I | GBS/GBE |
| HFC.3,688. | HSC.3,689. | HSC.3,690. | HSC,3,691. |

| | | | |
|---|---|---|---|
| MAIONCHI 20 20 ITALY | MAIONCHI 20 20 L.M.I. | MALLARD 20 20 C.C.Co. | MANTON No 20 CALCUTTA |
| 20 gauge. | Pla. | | Gnm. 20 gauge. |
| | On other gauges. | On other gauges. | On other gauges. |
| I/I | I/I | USA/USA | IND |
| HFC.361. | HFC.362. | HFC.3,692. | HFC.363. |
| MARTIGNONI 20 20 GENOVA | METEOR 20 20 CANADA | M<sup>re</sup> F<sup>que</sup> D'ARMES 20 DE ST ETIENNE | MARQUE 18 AU LION |
| 20 gauge. | | 20 gauge. | 18 gauge. |
| | | 16,12,4. | |
| I/I | CDN | F | B/B |
| HFC.364. | HSC.3,693. | HSC.3,694. | HSC.3,695. |
| MACPHERSON No 16 KYNOCH INVERNESS | 16 16 MADE IN HOLLAND | Made in Hungary 16 | MAIONCHI L.M 16 |
| Gnm. 16 gauge. | 16 gauge. | | 16 gauge. |
| On other gauges. | On other gauges. | On other gauges. | |
| GBS/GBE | NL/NL | H/H | I/I |
| HFC.527. | HFC.528. | HFC.529. | HFC.530. |
| MAIONCHI L.M.I. 16 | MAIONCHI 16 16 L.M.I. | MALLARD 16 16 C.C.Co. | MARKE 16 16 FASAN |
| 16 gauge. | Manufacturer. | Manufacturer. | 16 gauge. |
| 12. | On other gauges. | | |
| I/I | I/I | USA/USA | D |
| HFC.531. | HFC.532. | HFC.533. | HSC.3,696. |

| | | | |
|---|---|---|---|
| MARTIGNONI 16 GENOVA | METAL GEVELOT CAL 16 N°7 BREVETE S.G.D.G | METAL GEVELOT CAL 16 N°7 BREVETE S.G.D.G | METROPOLE 16 |
| 16 gauge. | Manufacturer. | Aluminium case. | 16 gauge. |
| 12. | | 12. | |
| I/I | F/F | F/F | |
| HFC.534. | HSC.3,697. | HSC.3,698. | HFC.535. |
| M.F. D'ARMES 91 D'ST ETIENNE ? | M.F.se D'ARMES & CYCLES ST ETIENNE 91 | MIDLAND GUN C° CASE MADE N° 16 IN FRANCE BIRMINGHAM | MILBURN & SON N° 16 BRAMPTON |
| 16 gauge. | | Gnm. | Gnm. |
| 20,12,4. | | | |
| F | F | GBE/F | GBE |
| HSC.3,699. | HFC.3,700. | HSC.3,701. | HFC.536. |
| MKEK 16 16 TURKEY | MONK-CHESTER N°16 ELEY | MORRIS N° 16 HEREFORD | MUNITIONS 16 16 MGM |
| 16 gauge. | Gnm. 16 gauge. | Irm, gunsmiths. | Manufacturer. |
| | 12. | | |
| TR/TR | GBE/GBE | GBE | F/F |
| HSC.3,702. | HFC.3,703. | HFC.3,704. | HSC.3,705. |
| MUNITIONSWERKE SCHOENEBECK 16 | M.A.C.C. 12 12 P.te NOIRE | MACNAUGHTON EDINBURGH 12 | N° MACNAUGHTON 12 ELEY EDINBURGH |
| 16 gauge. | 12 gauge, Pla. | Gnm. | Gnm, 12 gauge. |
| | | | 28. |
| D | | GBS | GBS/GBE |
| HFC.537. | HSC.3,706. | HFC.2,203. | HSC.3,707. |

| | | | |
|---|---|---|---|
| (MACNAUGHTON KYNOCH EDINBURGH No 12) | (MACNAUGHTON PERTH No12 ELEY) | (MACPHERSON INVERNESS No 12) | (MACPHERSON INVERNESS No 12) |
| Gnm, Kynoch case. | Gnm, Pre Ww1. | Gnm. | Gnm. |
| GBS/GBE | GBS/GBE | GBS | GBS |
| HFC.1,483. | HFC.3,708. | HFC.1,485. | HFC.1,484. |
| (MADD 12) | (MADD FRANCE 12 12) | (MADD 12 12 MADD) | (12 12 MADE HOLLAND) |
| Post Ww2. | | 12 gauge. | |
| F/F | F/F | F/F | NL/NL |
| HFC.1,486. | HFC.1,488. | HFC.1,487. | HFC.1,497. |
| (12 MADE IN BELGIUM) | (12 MADE IN BELGIUM) | (MADE IN BELGIUM 12 12) | (MADE IN BELGIUM 12 12) |
| On other gauges. | | | |
| B/B | B/B | B/B | B/B |
| HSC.3,709. | HSC.3,710. | HFC.1,489. | HSC.5,452. |
| (MADE IN ENGLAND 12 12) | (MADE IN ENGLAND 12 12) | (MADE IN ENGLAND 12 12) | (MADE IN FRANCE 12) |
| | | | |
| GBE/GBE | GBE/GBE | GBE/GBE | F/F |
| HFC.1,490. | HFC.1,491. | HFC.2,204. | HSC.3,711. |

| | | | |
|---|---|---|---|
| Large cap, Pre WwI. | | | |
| GBE/F | D/D | GBE/GBE | GBE/GBE |
| HFC.1,492. | HFC.1,493. | HFC.2,205. | HFC.1,494. |
| | Grenwood & Batley. | | On other gauges. |
| GBE/GBE | GBE/GBE | GBE/GBE | H/H |
| HFC.3,712. | HFC.1,496. | HFC.1,495. | HFC.1,498. |
| | 12 gauge. | Length 65mm. | Year 1969. |
| H/H | J/J | SU/SU | SU/SU |
| HFC.1,499. | HFC.2,206. | HFC.1,500. | HSC.3,713. |
| Manufacturer. | Year 1970. | Length 65mm. | Year 1970. |
| SU/SU | SU/SU | SU/SU | SU/SU |
| HFC.1,502. | HFC.1,501. | HFC.1,503. | HSC.3,714. |

| | | | |
|---|---|---|---|
| Pap. | Pla. | Manufacturer. | Pla. |
| SU/SU | I/I | I/I | I/I |
| HFC.1,504. | HFC.1,505. | HFC.1,506. | HFC.1,507. |
| | Manufacturer. | Pla. | Pla. |
| | | 16. | |
| I/I | I/I | I/I | I/I |
| HFC.1,508. | HFC.1,509. | HFC.1,513. | HFC.1,510. |
| Post Ww2. | | Pla. | Kynoch case, Ejt. |
| On other gauges. | On other gauges. | | |
| I/I | I/I | I/I | GBS/GBE |
| HFC.1,512. | HFC.1,511. | HSC.3,715. | HFC.1,514. |
| 12 gauge. | Large cap. | Auctioneers. | Gnm. Pre Ww1. |
| | | GBI | GBE/GBE |
| HSC.3,716. | HFC.1,515. | HFC.1,516. | HFC.1,517. |

| | | | |
|---|---|---|---|
| (MALEHAMS N°12 FIELD CARTRIDGE) | (MALEHAMS SHEFFIELD N°12 ELEY) | (MALLARD 12 12 C.C.Co.) | (MALLARD 12 GA C.C.Co.) |
| Gnm. | Gnm. Eley Bros case. | | Manufacturer. |
| | | On other gauges. | |
| GBE | GBE/GBE | USA/USA | USA/USA |
| HSC.3,717. | HSC.3,718. | HFC.1,519. | HFC.1,518. |
| (MALLARD 12 12 SMOKELESS) | (MALLARD 12 12 SMOKELESS) | (MALLARD 12 12 S.R.&Co.) | (MANTON N° 12 CALCUTTA) |
| | | | Gnm. |
| | | | On other gauges. |
| USA | USA | | IND |
| HSC.3,719. | HSC.3,720. | HSC.3,721. | HFC.2,207. |
| (MANTON MADE IN N° 12 BARVARIA CALCUTTA) | (MANTON MADE IN N° 12 BARVARIA CALCUTTA) | (MANTON MADE IN USA N° 12 CALCUTTA) | (MANTON & Co. 12 12 CALCUTTA) |
| Gnm. | Gnm. | Gnm. | Gnm. |
| | | | |
| IND/D | IND/D | IND/USA | IND |
| HSC.3,722. | HSC.3,723. | HSC.3,724. | HSC.3,725. |
| (MANTON & CO. CALCUTTA N°12 ELEY) | (M.A.P. 12 12 SCAFATI-SA) | (MANUFRANCE 12 12 SAINT-ETIENNE) | (MARATHON 12 12 FRANCE) |
| Gnm. Pre Wwl. | | Pla. | |
| IND/GBE | | F | F |
| HSC.3,726. | HSC.3,727. | HFC.1,520. | HSC.3,728. |

| | | | |
|---|---|---|---|
| MARCEL GAUPILLAT & Cie | MARCEL GAUPILLAT & Cie PARIS 12 12 | MARCO 12 12 | MARK AITKEN & SONS MADE IN FRANCE 12 12 CRIEFF |
| | | 12 gauge. | Gnm. |
| F/F | F/F | | GBS/F |
| HFC.1,521. | HSC.3,729. | HSC.3,730. | HFC.3,731. |
| MARRIAGE & Co No 12 REIGATE | MARTIGNONI 12 12 GENOVA | MARTIGNONI 12 12 GENOVA | MARTIGNONI 12 12 GENOVA |
| | Pla. | | Manufacturer. |
| GBE | I/I | I/I | I/I |
| HFC.1,522. | HFC.1,525. | HFC.1,524. | HFC.1,523. |
| MARTIN. GLASGOW & ABERDEEN No12 ELEY | MARTIN. GLASGOW & ABERDEEN No12 ELEY | No MARTIN 12 GLASGOW, EDINBURGH & ABERDEEN | MARY-ARM 12 |
| Gnm. | Gnm.    Pre, Wwl. | Gnm. | |
| GBS/GBE | GBS/GBE | GBS | F |
| HFC.1,528. | HFC.1,527. | HFC.1,529. | HFC.1,530. |
| MARY 12 12 Bergerac | MASTER 12 | MASTER 12 | 12 * ? * MATCH |
| | | Pla. | |
| F | | | |
| HFC.1,531. | HFC.1,532. | HSC.3,732. | HFC.3,733. |

| | | | |
|---|---|---|---|
| (MATTHEWS BROS. AXMINSTER. ELEY. No 12) | (MATTHEWS BROS. ELEY. HONITON & AXMINSTER No 12) | (No MATTHEWS BROS. HONITON 12) | (MAVRULIS HELLAS 12 12) |
| Irm.    Pre Ww1. | Irm. | Irm. | Pla. |
| GBE/GBE | GBE/GBE | GBE | |
| HSC.3,734. | HSC.3,735. | HSC.3,736. | HFC.1,533. |
| (MAXUM 12 12 CANADA) | (MAXUM 12 12 CANADA) | (M B 12 12 ITALY) | (M B R No ? 12 A) |
| | | | |
| CDN | CDN | I | |
| HFC.3,737. | HFC.3,738. | HFC.1,534. | HSC.3,739. |
| (MB-SA 12 12 MEXICO) | (M&C 12 12 CA) | (M&C 12 12 C.A.) | (McLOUGHLIN No 12 CIRENCESTER) |
| Pla. | | | 12 gauge. |
| MEX | B | B | GBE |
| HSC.3,740. | HFC.3,741. | HSC.3,742. | HFC.3,743. |
| (ME.CA 12 12 ITALY) | (MECC 12 12 LEBANON) | (melior 12 12 JIC) | (MELIOR 12 12 MELIOR) |
| | Pla. | Pla. | Post Ww2. |
| I | RL | | |
| HFC.1,535. | HSC.3,744. | HFC.1,536. | HFC.1,537. |

| | | | |
|---|---|---|---|
| METAL GEVELOT 12 12 | METAL BREVETE GEVELOT CAL 12 N° 6 | 1901 N° 12 METAL LINED | METEOR 12 |
| 12 gauge. | Manufacturer. 16. | W.R.A.Co. Pre Ww1. | 12 gauge. |
| F/F | F/F | USA/USA | |
| HSC.3,745. | HFC.1,538. | HSC.3,746. | HFC.1,539. |
| METEOR 12 12 CANADA | METIN 12 12 **** | M<sup>F</sup>D'ARMES 12 12 DE S<sup>t</sup> ETIENNE | M.GAUPILLAT 12 12 PARIS |
| | Pla. | 12 gauge. 20,16,4. | |
| CDN | | F | F/F |
| HSC.3,747. | HSC.3,748. | HSC.3,749. | HFC.1,540. |
| M G C ? 12 | M.G. 12 12 ESPAÑA | M.G.M. 12 12 MUNITIONS | MGM 12 12 VALENCE |
| | Pla. | Pla. | |
| | E | F/F | F/F |
| HSC.3,750. | HSC.3,751. | HSC.3,752. | HFC.1,541. |
| M.HALPIN.SHEPPERTON N°12 ELEY | M H 12 12 INC | MICRO MADE IN USA 12 12 HUNTER | MIDLAND 12 12 CARTRIDGE |
| Eley Bros case. | | | Post Ww2. Pap. |
| GBE/GBE | | USA/USA | GBE |
| HSC.3,753. | HSC.3,754. | HSC.3,755. | HFC.1,542. |

| | | | |
|---|---|---|---|
| MIDLAND GUN Co 12 12 BHAM | MIDLAND GUN Co No 12 BIRMINGHAM | MIDLAND GUN Co CASE MADE No 12 IN FRANCE BIRMINGHAM | MIDLAND GUN Co CASE MADE No 12 IN FRANCE BIRMINGHAM |
| Gnm. | Gnm. | Gnm. | Gnm. |
| GBE | GBE | GBE/F | GBE/F |
| HSC.3,756. | HFC.1,543. | HFC.3,757. | HFC.3,758. |
| MIDLAND GUN Co CASE MADE No 12 IN FRANCE BIRMINGHAM | MIDLAND GUN Co No 12 KYNOCH BRIGG | MILBURN No 12 BRAMPTON | MILBURN, BRAMPTON No 12 ELEY |
| Gnm. | Gnm, Kynoch case. | Gnm. | Gnm.    Pre Wwl. |
| GBE/F | GBE/GBE | GBE | GBE/GBE |
| HFC.3,759. | HFC.1,544. | HFC.2.208. | HFC.3,760. |
| MILBURN KYNOCH'S PATENT No 12 CROSSE EJECTOR BRAMPTON | MILBURN & SON No 12 KYNOCH BRAMPTON | MILBURN & SON No 12 KYNOCH BRAMPTON | MIRITA 12 12 C |
| Kynoch case, Ejt. | Gnm.  Kynoch case. | Gnm.    Pre Wwl. | |
| GBE/GBE | GBE/GBE | GBE/GBE | |
| HFC.1,546. | HFC.1,545. | HFC.3,761. | HFC.1,547. |
| MIRY-FIOCCHI 12 12 GFF | MKE 12 12 TURKEY | M.M.STEYTLER & Co No 12 ELEY | MOHAWK 12 GA BY REMINGTON |
| Manufacturer. | Pla. | | |
| I/I | TR | ?/GBE | USA/USA |
| HSC.3,762. | HSC.3,763. | HSC.3,764. | HFC.1,548. |

| | | | |
|---|---|---|---|
| Eley Bros case. | Gnm. | Taken off box. | Gnm. |
| GBE/GBE | GBE/GBE | USA/USA | GBE |
| HFC.1,549. | HFC.1,550. | HSC.3,765. | HSC.3,766. |
| Gnm. | Gnm. | Eley Bros case. 16. | Gnm. Pre. Wwl. |
| GBE | GBE | GBE/GBE | GBE/GBE |
| HSC.3,767. | HSC.3,768. | HSC.3,769. | HFC.1,551. |
| Gnm. Kynoch case. | Kynoch case, Ejt. | Apc. | Apc. |
| GBE/GBE | GBE/GBE | USA | USA/USA |
| HFC.1,552. | HFC.1,553. | HSC.3,770. | HSC.3,771. |
| Gnm. | Gnm. | Gnm. | |
| GBE/GBE | GBE/GBE | GBS | |
| HSC.3,772. | HSC.3,773. | HFC.1,554. | HSC.3,774. |

| | | | |
|---|---|---|---|
| (Mfres d'Armes & de Cycles St Etienne) | (MULLERITE 12) | (MUNICAR 12 12 FRANCE) | (MUNICAR-O 12 12 FRANCE) |
| 12 gauge. | | Pla. | 12 gauge. Pla. |
| F | B/B | F | F |
| HFC.2,029. | HFC.1,555. | HFC.1,556. | HSC.3,775. |
| (MUNICAR 12 12 ITALY) | (MUNICAR 12 12 VIERZON) | (MUNICAR 12 12 VIERZON) | (MUNICAR 12 12 VIERZON) |
| Pla. | | | |
| I | F | F | F |
| HSC.3,776. | HFC.1,560. | HFC.1,558. | HFC.1,559. |
| (MUNICOES DE MOCAMBIQUE LDA 12) | (MUNITIONS 12 12 M.G.M) | (MUNITIONS 12 12 MGM) | (MUNITIONS 12 12 MGM) |
| | Manufacturer. | | |
| MOZ | F/F | F/F | F/F |
| HFC.1,561. | HFC.3,777. | HFC.1,562. | HFC.3,778. |
| (MUNITIONS 12 12 MGM) | (MUNITIONSWERKE 12 12 SCHOENEBECK) | (MUNIZIONI ... ITALY 12) | (MUNYSUR 12 12 ESPANA) |
| Manufacturer. | | Pla. | 12 gauge. |
| F/F | D | I | E |
| HFC.1,563. | HSC.3,779. | HFC.1,564. | HFC.1,565. |

217

| | | | |
|---|---|---|---|
| MURRAY & Co. CAWNDORE No 12 ELEY | 10 GA MADE IN U.S.A. | 10 G MAG | MANTON No 10 CALCUTTA |
| 12 gauge. | 10 gauge. | 10 gauge. | Gnm. |
| | | | On other gauges. |
| ?/GBE | USA/USA | GBE | IND |
| HSC.3,780. | HFC.2,090. | HSC.3,781. | HFC.2,091. |
| MANU FRANCE 10 SAINT-ETIENNE | M. GAUPILLAT 10 PARIS | 1901 No W 8 METAL LINED | 1901 No W 4 METAL LINED |
| Manufacturer. | 10 gauge. | 8 gauge. W.R.A.Co. | 4 gauge. W.R.A.Co. |
| | | 12,10,4. | 12,10,8. |
| F/F | F/F | USA/USA | USA/USA |
| HSC.3,782. | HFC.3,783. | HSC.3,784. | HSC.3,785. |

| | |
|---|---|
| 4 M"F" DARMES DE ST ETIENNE | |
| 4 gauge. | |
| | |
| F/F | |
| HSC.3,786. | |

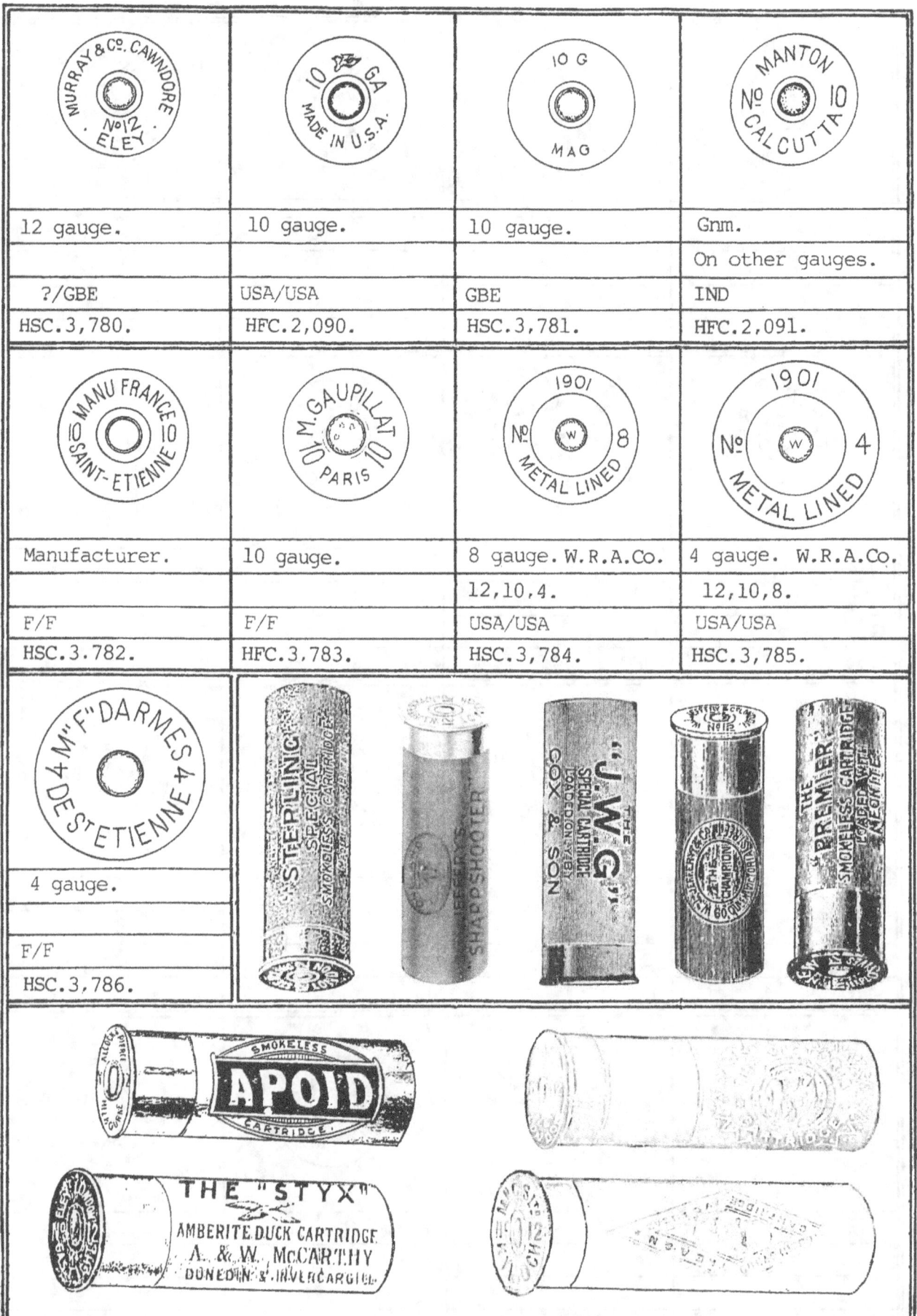

| | | | |
|---|---|---|---|
| 410 | Explosives Co. | Pre Wwl. | 410 |
| GBS | GBS | GBS | GBS |
| HFC.3,787. | HFC.3,788. | HFC.3,789. | HFC.3,790. |
| 410 | 28 gauge. | Pre Wwl. | 28 gauge. |
| GBS | GBS/GBE | GBS/GBE | GBS/GBE |
| HSC.3,791. | HFC.264. | HFC.265. | HSC.3,792. |
| 28 gauge. | 24 gauge. | 20 gauge. | 20 gauge. |
| | 20,16,12. | | |
| GBS/GBE | J | USA/USA | |
| HSC.3,793. | HSC.3,794. | HFC.365. | HFC.366. |
| 20 gauge. | Explosives Co. | Ballistite load. | 20 gauge. |
| On other gauges. | On other gauges. | | |
| GBS/GBE | GBS/GBE | GBS/GBE | GBS/GBE |
| HFC.367. | HFC.368. | HFC.369. | HFC.3,795. |

| | | | |
|---|---|---|---|
| 20 gauge. | Eley Bros shield. | Eley Bros case. | Pre Ww1, 20 gauge. |
|  | 12. |  | 12. |
| GBS/GBE | GBS/GBE | GBS/GBE | GBS/GBE |
| HSC.3,796. | HFC.3,797. | HSC.3,798. | HSC.3,799. |
| Explosives Co. | Empire powder. |  | 20 gauge. |
|  |  | 12. | On other gauges. |
| GBS/GBE | GBS/GBE | GBS/GBE | GBE/B |
| HSC.3,800. | HSC.3,801. | HSC.3,802. | HSC.3,803. |
| Powder Co. | W.R.A.Co.. | 20 gauge. | 16 gauge. |
| 12. | 12. | 16,12. | 12. |
| GBE/B | USA/USA | J | GBE/GBE |
| HSC.3,804. | HSC.3,805. | HSC.3,806. | HSC.3,807. |
| Arms & Ammo. | W.R.A.Co. |  | 16 gauge. Pre Ww1. |
| 12. | On other gauges. |  | On other gauges. |
| GBE/GBE | USA/USA | D | GBS/GBE |
| HSC.3,808. | HFC.538. | HSC.3,809. | HFC.539. |

| | | | |
|---|---|---|---|
| NOBEL No 16 GLASGOW | NOBEL N.I. No 16 GLASGOW | NOBEL-GLASGOW 16 16 N | NOBEL'S No 16 ELEY BALLISTITE |
| 16 gauge. | Nobel Industries. | Nobel Explosives. | 16 gauge. |
| On other gauges. | | On other gauges. | On other gauges. |
| GBS/GBE | GBS/GBE | GBS/GBE | GBS/GBE |
| HFC.3,810. | HSC.3,811. | HFC.540. | HFC.3,812. |
| NOBEL'S EMPIRE No 16 ELEY | NORMAL 16 | NORMAL 16 16 | NORMAL MADE IN No 16 BELGIUM HENDON |
| Empire powder. | 16 gauge. | | Powder Co. |
| | | | On other gauges. |
| GBS/GBE | | GBE | GBE/B |
| HSC.3,813. | HSC.3,814. | HFC.3,815. | HSC.3,816. |
| NORMAL 16 16 HENDON | NORMAL No 16 NIMROD | NORMAL No 16 NIMROD | NORMAL KYNOCH'S PATENT No 16 GROUSE EJECTOR POWDER |
| Powder Co. | 16 gauge. | | Hendon, London. |
| | | | |
| GBE/D | GBE | USA/USA | GBE/GBE |
| HSC.3,817. | HSC.3,818. | HSC.3,819. | HSC.3,820. |
| NORMAL KYNOCH'S PATENT No 16 GROUSE EJECTOR POWDER Co | N.P.K. BEST SHOT No 16 | N.P.K. No 16 SUPER | N.A & A. Co No 14 PATENT |
| Kynoch Ejt case. | | 16 gauge. | 14 gauge. |
| | | 20,12. | 16,12. |
| GBE/GBE | J | J | GBE |
| HFC.541. | HSC.3,821. | HSC.3,822. | HSC.3,823. |

| | | | |
|---|---|---|---|
| 14 gauge. | Manufacturer. | Gnm. | 14 gauge. |
| | On other gauges. | | On other gauges. |
| GBE | B/B | GBE | GBE/GBE |
| HSC.3,824. | HFC.623. | HSC.3,825. | HFC.624. |
| 12 gauge. | 12 gauge. | National Arms & Ammunition Co. | |
| | | | 16. |
| IND | | GBE/GBE | GBE/GBE |
| HSC.3.826. | HFC.3,827. | HFC.3,828. | HSC.3,829. |
| National Arms & Ammunition Co. | | | Post Ww2. |
| | 16. | | |
| GBE/GBE | GBE/GBE | GBE/GBE | I |
| HFC.3.830. | HSC.3,831. | HSC.3,832. | HFC.1.566. |
| 12 gauge, Pla. | Pla. | | 12 gauge. |
| I | I | GBE | GBE |
| HSC.3,833. | HSC.3,834. | HSC.3,835. | HSC.3,836. |

| | | | |
|---|---|---|---|
| NEWLAND & STIDOLPH Nº12 ELEY | NEWMAN & SON Nº 12 HAVERHILL | NEWNHAM Nº 12 LANDPORT | 1901 Nº W 12 NEW RIVAL |
| Irm, Stratford. | | Gnm. | W.R.A.Co. 12 gauge. |
| | | | 20,16,14,10. |
| GBE/GBE | GBE | GBE | USA/USA |
| HFC.1,567. | HFC.1,568. | HFC.1,569. | HSC.3,837. |
| 1901 Nº 12 NEW RIVAL | NEWTON. MANCHESTER. Nº 12 ELEY | NEW ZEALAND LOAN & M.A.Co. LTD. SHELL MADE IN GERMANY 12 | NIKA ? 12 |
| W.R.A.Co. | Gnm. Eley Bros case | | |
| On other gauges. | | | |
| USA/USA | GBE/GBE | NZ/D | NL |
| HFC.1,570. | HFC.1,571. | HSC.3,838. | HSC.3,839. |
| NIKA 12 | NIMROD 12 | NIMROD SB 12 | NIMROD 12 12 NIMROD |
| | | | |
| NL | | | USA |
| HSC.3,840. | HFC.1,572. | HSC.3,841. | HSC.3,842. |
| NIMROD MADE IN USA 12 12 NIMROD | NITEDAL 12 | NITEDALS 12 12 KRUDTVÆRK | NITEDALS 12 12 KRUDTVÆRK |
| | | Pla. | |
| USA/USA | | | |
| HSC.3,843. | HFC.1,573. | HFC.1,574. | HFC.1,575. |

223

| | | | |
|---|---|---|---|
| NITRO 12 GA EXPRESS | NITROKOL No 12 LONDON | NITROX 12 12 SWEDEN | N M T No 12 |
| 12 gauge. | | Pla. | Joyce Ejt case. |
| USA/USA | GBE | S | GBE |
| HFC.1,576. | HFC.1,577. | HSC.3,844. | HFC.1,578. |
| NOBBS 12 12 MADE IN BELGIUM LINCOLN | NOBEL No 12 GLASGOW | NOBEL No 12 GLASGOW | NOBEL No 12 GLASGOW |
| Irm, taxidermist. | Ejt. | Manufacturer. | |
| GBE/B | GBS/GBE | GBS/GBE | GBS/GBE |
| HFC.1,579. | HFC.1,580. | HFC.1,583. | HFC.1,582. |
| NOBEL No 12 GLASGOW | NOBEL No 12 ELEY GLASGOW | NOBEL GLASGOW No N 12 | NOBEL N.I. No 12 GLASGOW |
| 12 gauge. | | | Nobel Industries. |
| GBS/GBE | GBS/GBE | GBS/GBE | GBE/GBE |
| HFC.1,581. | HFC.3,845. | HSC.3,846. | HFC.3,847. |
| NOBEL N.I. No 12 GLASGOW | NOBEL No 12 MADE IN CANADA GLASGOW | NOBEL No 12 MADE IN ENGLAND GLASGOW | NOBEL 12 12 GLASGOW |
| Post Wwl. | | Manufacturer. | 12 gauge. |
| GBE/GBE | GBS/CDN | GBS/GBE | GBS/GBE |
| HFC.5,453. | HFC.3,848. | HSC.3,849. | HFC.1,585. |

| | | | |
|---|---|---|---|
| (NOBEL GLASGOW 12 12) | (NOBEL-EJECTOR 12 12 N) | (NOBEL-GLASGOW 12 12 N) | (NOBEL No 12 LONDON) |
| 12 gauge. | Ejt. | Much used. | Circa 1907. Rare. |
| | | On other gauges. | |
| AUS | GBS/GBE | GBS/GBE | GBS/GBE |
| HSC.3,850. | HSC.3,851. | HFC.1,586. | HFC.1,587. |
| (NOBEL REY 12 12 FRANCE) | (NOBEL 12 12 SPORT) | (NOBEL'S No 12 BALLISTITE) | (NOBEL'S No 12 BALLISTITE) |
| Post Ww2. | Post Ww2. | | Manufacturer. |
| | | | |
| F | | GBS/ | GBS/GBE |
| HFC.1,588. | HFC.1,589. | HSC.3,852. | HFC.3,853. |
| (NOBEL'S No 12 BALLISTITE) | (NOBEL'S BALLISTITE No 12 EB) | (NOBEL'S BALLISTITE No 12 EB) | (NOBEL'S BALLISTITE No 12) |
| | | Manufacturer. | |
| | On other gauges. | | |
| GBS/GBE | GBS/GBE | GBS/GBE | GBS/GBE |
| HFC.3,854. | HFC.3,855. | HSC.3,856. | HSC.3,857. |
| (NOBEL'S No 12 ELEY BALLISTITE) | (NOBEL'S No 12 ELEY BALLISTITE) | (NOBEL'S No 12 ELEY BALLISTITE) | (NOBEL'S No 12 ELEY BALLISTITE) |
| 12 gauge. | | | Manufacturer. |
| On other gauges. | | | |
| GBS/GBE | GBS/GBE | GBS/GBE | GBS/GBE |
| HFC.1,590. | HFC.1,592. | HFC.1,591. | HSC.3,858. |

| | | | |
|---|---|---|---|
| 12 gauge. | Manufacturer. | | Much used. |
| | | | On other gauges. |
| GBS | USA | USA | GBS/GBE |
| HFC.1,593. | HFC.1,594. | HFC.1,595. | HFC.1,596. |
| | | | |
| | | | |
| GBS | GBS/GBE | GBS/GBE | GBS/B |
| HFC.1,597. | HFC.1,598. | HSC.3,859. | HSC.3,860. |
| | | | |
| Manufacturer. | | | Post Ww2. |
| GBS/GBE | GBS | | GBE |
| HFC.3,861. | HSC.3,862. | HFC.1,600. | HFC.1,601. |
| | | | |
| 12 gauge. | | Powder Co. | 12 gauge. |
| | | GBE/F | GBE |
| HFC.1,611. | HSC.3,863. | HFC.1,604. | HFC.1,602. |

| | | | |
|---|---|---|---|
| (NORMAL HENDON MADE IN BELGIUM 12) | (NORMAL HENDON MADE IN FRANCE 12 12) | (NORMAL LONDON No 12) | (NORMAL NIMROD No 12) |
| 12 gauge. | Powder Co. | | W.R.A.Co. |
| | | | On other gauges. |
| GBE/B | GBE/F | GBE | USA/USA |
| HFC.1,603. | HSC.3,864. | HFC.1,605. | HFC.1,606. |
| (NORMAL NMFS 12 12) | (NORMAL POWDER No 12) | (NORMAL KYNOCH'S PATENT GROUSE EJECTOR POWDER Co No 12) | (NORMAL WATERPROOF No 12) |
| | | Kynoch Ejt case. | W.R.A.Co. |
| | | | |
| | GBE | GBE/GBE | USA/USA |
| HSC.3,865. | HFC.1,607. | HFC.1,608. | HFC.1,609. |
| (NORMAL W.R.A.CO No 12) | (NORMA NITEDAL 12 12) | (NORWESTERN NOX 12) | (N.P.K. JAPAN 12 12) |
| Winchester. | | | |
| | | | |
| USA/USA | | | J |
| HFC.1,610. | HSC.3,866. | HFC.1,612. | HSC.3,867. |
| (N.P.K. SUPER No 12) | (N.P.K. SUPER No 12) | (N.S.DAL.. CHICHESTER No 12 ELEY) | (N.S.W. AUST A.D.I. P/V 12 12) |
| 12 gauge. | | Eley Bros case. | 12 gauge.  Pla. |
| 24,20,16. | | | |
| J | J | GBE/GBE | |
| HSC.3,868. | HFC.3,869. | HFC.3,870. | HFC.1,613. |

| | | | |
|---|---|---|---|
| 12 gauge. | | A.L.Howard & Co. | New York. |
| | 10. | | 10. |
| | | USA/USA | USA/USA |
| HSC.3,871. | HSC.3,872. | HSC.3,873. | HSC.3,874. |
| 12 gauge. | 10 gauge, Pre Wwl. | Nobel Explosives. | New York. 10 gauge. |
| | | On other gauges. | 12. |
| USA | USA/USA | GBS/GBE | USA/USA |
| HSC.3,875. | HFC.2,092. | HSC.3,876. | HSC.3,877. |
| No - in number. | 10 gauge. | 8 gauge. | |
| | 12. | | |
| USA/USA | USA/USA | GBS/GBE | |
| HSC.3,878. | HSC.3,879. | HFC.2,110. | |

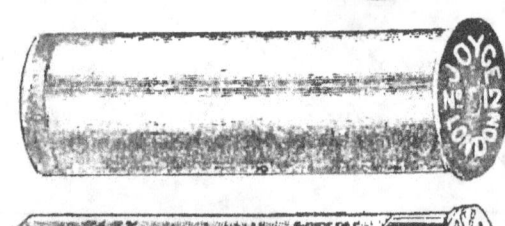
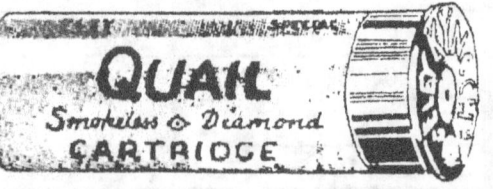

| | | | |
|---|---|---|---|
| ORBEA VITORIA 24 24 | ORBEA VITORIA 20 20 | ORBEA CAL.16 ? | 12 65 70 |
| 24 gauge. | 20 gauge. | 16 gauge. | 12 gauge, Pla. |
| E/E | E/E | E/E | |
| HSC.3,880. | HFC.370. | HSC.3,881. | HSC.3,882. |
| OJP 12 12 KRAMSACH | Olin 12 GA 100 YEARS | ORBEA CAL.12 | ORBEA CAL.12 |
| 12 gauge. | | Pla. | |
| | | E/E | E/E |
| HSC.3,883. | HFC.1,614. | HSC.3,884. | HSC.3,885. |
| ORBEA 12 12 SPAIN | ORBEA 12 12 VITORIA | ORBEA 12 12 VITORIA | ORIGINALE NOBEL'S N° 12 |
| Manufacturer. | Post Ww2. | | Eley Bros case. |
| E/E | E/E | | /GBE |
| HFC.1,615. | HFC.1,616. | HFC.1,617. | HSC.3,886. |
| ORIGINALE NOBEL'S N° 12 O.N. | OZTAY 12 12 **** | OWEN N° 4 REWA NITRO | |
| 12 gauge. | 12 gauge. | 4 gauge. | |
| | | IND | |
| HFC.1,618. | HSC.3,887. | HSC.3,888. | |

229

| | | | |
|---|---|---|---|
| .410. | Manufacturer. | | .410. |
| USA/USA | USA/USA | USA/USA | USA/USA |
| HSC.3,889. | HSC.3,890. | HSC.3,891. | HSC.3,892. |
| High Velocity .410. | 28 gauge. | Manufacturer. On other gauges. | On other gauges. |
| USA/USA | USA/USA | USA/USA | USA/USA |
| HSC.3,893. | HSC.3,894. | HSC.3,895. | HSC.3,896. |
| Manufacturer. On other gauges. | On other gauges. | 28 gauge. On other gauges. | Clinton Cartridge. 20,16,12,10. |
| USA/USA | USA/USA | USA/USA | USA/USA |
| HSC.3,897. | HSC.3,898. | HSC.3899. | HSC.3,900. |
| 20 ga, Peters C.C. 16,12,10. | Manufacturer. 16,12. | High Velocity. 28,16,12,10. | 20 gauge. On other gauges. |
| USA/USA | USA/USA | USA/USA | USA/USA |
| HSC.3,901. | HSC.3,902. | HSC.3,903. | HFC.371. |

| | | | |
|---|---|---|---|
| PETERS IDEAL | PETERS LEAGUE | PETERS LEAGUE | PETERS PREMIER |
| Manufacturer. | | | 20 gauge. |
| 16,12,10. | 16,12,10. | 16,12,10. | 16,12,10. |
| USA/USA | USA/USA | USA/USA | USA/USA |
| HSC.3,904. | HSC.3,905. | HSC.3,906. | HSC.3,907. |
| PETERS REFEREE | PETERS REFEREE | PETERS SKEETLOAD | PETERS TARGET |
| 20 gauge. | | | Manufacturer. |
| 16,12,10. | 28,16,12. | 16. | 28,16,12,10. |
| USA/USA | USA/USA | USA/USA | USA/USA |
| HSC.3,908. | HSC.3,909. | HSC.3,910. | HSC.3,911. |
| PETERS VICTOR | PETERS VICTOR | PHOENIX AA SUPER | POINTER C.C.Co. |
| Manufacturer. | | | Clinton Cartridge. |
| 16,12. | | 12. | On other gauges. |
| USA/USA | USA/USA | USA | USA |
| HSC.3,912. | HFC.372. | HSC.3,913. | HFC.3,914. |
| POINTER S.R.&Co. | ORR & SONS MADRAS & RANGOON No.20 P.ELEY | PURDEY & SONS LONDON No.20 | PURDEY & SONS LONDON No.20 |
| Sears Roebuck & Co. | | Gnm. | Gnm, 20 gauge. |
| 16,12. | | | |
| USA | IND/GBE | GBE | GBE |
| HSC.3,915. | HSC.3,916. | HSC.3,917. | HFC.375. |

| | | | |
|---|---|---|---|
| 20 gauge. | 20 gauge. | 16 ga, snap-cap. | 16 gauge. |
| | 16,12. | | |
| B/B | CDN | GBE/GBE | |
| HFC.373. | HFC.374. | HSC.3,918. | HSC.3,919. |
| Post Ww2. | Post Ww2. | Peters C.Co. | Manufacturer. |
| | On other gauges. | | 12,10. |
| PL/PL | PL/PL | USA/USA | USA/USA |
| HSC.3,920. | HFC.542. | HSC.3,921. | HSC.3,922. |
| Manufacturer. | Peters C.Co. | | Peters C.Co. |
| | 12,10. | 12,10. | |
| USA/USA | USA/USA | USA/USA | USA/USA |
| HSC.3,923. | HSC.3,924. | HSC.3,925. | HSC.3,926. |
| 16 gauge. | | Manufacturer. | 16 gauge. |
| | 20,12. | 12,10. | 28,20,12,10. |
| A | USA/USA | USA/USA | USA/USA |
| HFC.545. | HSC.3,927. | HSC.3,928. | HSC.3,929. |

| | | | |
|---|---|---|---|
| High Velocity. | Manufacturer. | | 16 gauge. |
| On other gauges. | On other gauges. | | |
| USA/USA | USA/USA | USA/USA | USA/USA |
| HSC.3,930. | HSC.3,931 | HFC.543. | HFC.544. |
| | | Manufacturer. | |
| 12,10. | 12,10. | 12,10. | 20,12,10. |
| USA/USA | USA/USA | USA/USA | USA/USA |
| HSC.3,932. | HSC.3,933. | HSC.3,934. | HSC.3,935. |
| 16 gauge. | | | Manufacturer. |
| | 12,10. | 20,12,10. | 10. |
| USA/USA | USA/USA | USA/USA | USA/USA |
| HSC.3,936. | HSC.3,937. | HSC.3,938. | HSC.3,939. |
| 16 gauge. | | Manufacturer. | 16 gauge. |
| 12,10. | On other gauges. | | On other gauges. |
| USA/USA | USA/USA | USA/USA | USA/USA |
| HSC.3,940. | HSC.3,941. | HSC.3,942. | HSC.3,943. |

| | | | |
|---|---|---|---|
| 16 gauge. | Manufacturer. | | 16 gauge. |
| | 20.12 | 28,20,12,10. | |
| USA/USA | USA/USA | USA/USA | PL |
| HSC.3,944. | HSC.3,945. | HSC.3,946. | HSC.3,947. |
| Clinton C. Co. | Clinton C. Co. | | Adv. |
| On other gauges. | | 12,10. | |
| USA/USA | USA/USA | USA | USA |
| HFC.546. | HFC.3,948. | HFC.3,949. | HSC.3,950. |
| | Proof shell. | 16 gauge. | |
| | | 20.12. | |
| B/B | B/B | CDN | D |
| HSC.3,951. | HSC.3,952. | HSC.3,953. | HSC.3,954. |
| 16 gauge. | London Gnm, Ejt. | | 16 gauge. |
| | On other gauges. | | |
| D | GBE/GBE | YU | YU |
| HFC.547. | HFC.548. | HSC.3,955. | HSC.3,956. |

| | | | |
|---|---|---|---|
| (Pachmayr Los Angeles 15 Calif.) | (Page Wood Bath 12) | (Page Wood Bristol No 12) | (Palmer. Sittingbourne No 12 Eley) |
| 12 gauge cruet set. | Gnm. | Gnm. | W.G. Palmer, Gnm. |
| USA/USA | GBE | GBE | GBE/GBE |
| HFC.1,619. | HFC.1,620. | HFC.1,621. | HSC.3,957. |
| (Pape Newcastle & Sunderland Kynoch No 12) | (Star with 12s, P, S) | (Parker Bros Meriden Ct. 12 A) | (Parker Bros W. Meriden Ct. No 12) |
| Gnm. Kynoch case. | Paris. 12 gauge. | | |
| | On other gauges. | | 10. |
| GBE/GBE | F/F | USA | USA |
| HFC.1,622. | HFC.1,623. | HSC.3,958. | HSC.3,959. |
| (Parker Bro's West Meriden Ct. 12 A) | (Parker Bro's West Meriden Ct. 12 A) | (Parker Bro's West Meriden Ct. 12 A) | (Parker Bro's West Meriden Ct. 12 B) |
| | | | |
| USA | USA | USA | USA |
| HSC.3,960. | HSC.3,961. | HSC.3,962. | HSC.3,963. |
| (Parker-Hale Made in England 12 G) | (Parkinson Ulverston No 12) | (Parsons Nuneaton No 12) | (Parsons, Sherwin & Co. Nuneaton No 12) |
| 12 ga, Snap-cap. | Tom Parkinson. | Agricultural and Hws. | |
| GBE/GBE | GBE | GBE | GBE |
| HSC,3.964. | HFC,1,624. | HFC.1.625. | HFC.1.626. |

235

| | | | |
|---|---|---|---|
| 12 gauge. | Post Ww2. | Manufacturer. | 12 gauge. |
| I/I | I/I | I/I | I/I |
| HFC.1,627. | HFC.1,628. | HFC.1,629. | HFC.1,630. |
| Apc. | Apc. | Gnm. | Gnm. |
| | | GBE | GBE |
| HSC.3,965. | HFC.3,966. | HFC.3,967. | HFC.3,968. |
| Gnm. | Eley Bros case. | Apc. | Manufacturer. |
| | | | On other gauges. |
| GBE/F | GBE/GBE | USA/USA | PL/PL |
| HFC.3,969. | HFC.1,631. | HSC.3,970. | HFC.1,632. |
| 12 gauge. | Post Ww2. Pla. | Beretta. | 12 gauge. Pla. |
| On other gauges. | | | |
| PL/PL | | | |
| HFC.1,633. | HFC.1,636. | HFC.1,635. | HFC.1,634. |

| | | | |
|---|---|---|---|
| (P.C.Co. 12 G FIELD) | (P.C.C. No 12 LEAGUE) | (P.C.C. No 12 LEAGUE) | (P.C.C. No 12 LEAGUE) |
| 12 gauge. | Peters Cartridge Company. | | Manufacturer. |
|  | 20,16,10. | 16. | 16,10. |
| USA/USA | USA/USA | USA/USA | USA/USA |
| HSC.3,971. | HFC.1,637. | HSC.3,972. | HSC.3,973. |
| (P.C.C. 12 G LEAGUE) | (P.C.C. No 12 LEAGUE) | (P.C.Co. 12 G PRIZE) | (P.C.Co. 12 G QUICK SHOT) |
| Peters Cartridge Company. | | Manufacturer. | 12 gauge. |
| 16,10. | 16,10, | 10. |  |
| USA/USA | USA/USA | USA/USA | USA/USA |
| HSC.3,974. | HSC.3,975. | HSC.3,976. | HSC.3,977. |
| (P.C.Co. 12 G VICTOR) | (PENGUIN 12 GA FLARE) | (PERAZZI 12 12 BRESCIA) | (PERRINS & SON. WORCESTER. No 12. ELEY) |
| Manufacturer. |  |  | Eley Bros case. |
|  |  |  |  |
| USA/USA | GBE | I | GBE/GBE |
| HSC.3,978. | HSC.3,979. | HFC.1,638. | HSC.3,980. |
| (PETERS MADE IN 12 GA USA DELUXE TARGET) | (PETERS No 12 HIGH GUN) | (PETERS No 12 HIGH GUN) | (PETERS No 12 H.V.) |
| 12 gauge. | Manufacturer. |  | High Velocity. |
| 20,16. | 16,10. | 20,16,10. | 28,20,16,10. |
| USA/USA | USA/USA | USA/USA | USA/USA |
| HSC.3,981. | HSC.3,982. | HSC.3,983. | HSC.3,984. |

| | | | |
|---|---|---|---|
| 12 gauge. | Peters Cartridge Company. | | 12 gauge. |
| USA/USA | USA/USA | USA/USA | USA/USA |
| HFC.1,641. | HFC.1,639. | HSC.3,985. | HSC.3,986. |
| | Peters Cartridge Company. | | Manufacturer. |
| 20,16,10. | | 20,16,10. | 20,16,10. |
| USA/USA | USA/USA | USA/USA | USA/USA |
| HSC 3,987. | HFC.1,640. | HSC.3,988. | HSC.3,989. |
| Manufacturer. | Peters Cartridge Company. | | |
| | 16,10. | | 16,10. |
| USA/USA | USA/USA | USA/USA | USA/USA |
| HSC.3,990. | HSC.3,991. | HSC.3,992. | HSC.3,993. |
| 12 gauge. | Peters Cartridge Company. | | 12 gauge. |
| 16,10. | 20,16,10. | 16,10. | 20,16,10. |
| USA/USA | USA/USA | USA/USA | USA/USA |
| HSC.3,994. | HSC.3,995. | HSC.3,996. | HSC.3,997. |

| | | | |
|---|---|---|---|
| 12 gauge. | Peters Cartridge Company. | | Manufacturer. |
| 16,10. | 28,20,16,10. | 10. | |
| USA/USA | USA/USA | USA/USA | USA/USA |
| HSC.3,998. | HSC.3,999. | HSC.4,000. | HFC.2,210. |
| | Peters Cartridge Company. | | |
| | 28,20,16,10. | 28,20,16,10. | |
| USA/USA | USA/USA | USA/USA | USA/USA |
| HSC.4,001. | HSC.4,002. | HSC.4,003. | HSC.4,004. |
| Manufacturer. | | Peters Cartridge Company. | |
| | | | |
| USA/USA | USA/USA | USA/USA | USA/USA |
| HSC.4,005. | HSC.4,006. | HSC.4,007. | HFC.1,642. |
| Irm. | | | 12 gauge. |
| | | 20. | |
| GBE | USA | USA | USA |
| HFC.1,643. | HSC.4,008. | HSC.4,009. | HSC.4,010. |

| | | | |
|---|---|---|---|
| (1901 No 12 PIGEON) | (P.J.CLARKE No 12 BOURNE) | (P.KNIGHT.NOTTINGHAM No12 ELEY) | (P.KNIGHT.NOTTINGHAM No12 ELEY) |
| W.R.A.Co. | | Gnm. Eley Bros. | Gnm. Eley Bros. |
| 10. | | | |
| USA/USA | GBE | GBE/GBE | GBE/GBE |
| HSC.4,011. | HFC.1,645. | HFC.4,012. | HSC.4,013. |
| (PLUMBERS Ld 12 12 Gt YARMOUTH) | (P.MORRIS&SON No 12 KYNOCH HEREFORD) | (PNEUMATIC 12 12 EDINBURGH) | (PNEUMATIC CARTRIDGE Co EDINBURGH Ltd No 12) |
| Gun dealers. | Gunsmiths Irm. | Manufacturer. | |
| GBE | GBE/GBE | GBS. | GBS. |
| HFC.1,646. | HFC.1,647. | HSC.4,014. | HFC.1,648. |
| (PNEUMATIC CARTRIDGE Co LTD EDINBURGH ELEY No 12) | (PNEUMATIC CARTRIDGE Co LTD ELEY No 12) | (POINTER 12 12 C.C.Co) | (POINTER 12 12 M.F.A.Co) |
| Eley Bros case. | Eley Bros case. | Clinton C. Co. | Meridan Fwk. |
| | | 28,20.16,10. | 10. |
| GBS/GBE | GBS/GBE | USA | USA |
| HFC.1,649. | HFC.1,650. | HFC.5,455. | HSC.4,015. |
| (POINTER 12 12 M.F.A.Co) | (POINTER 12 12 S.R.&Co) | (POINTER 12 12 S.R.&Co) | (POLYEX 12 12 MADE IN RUSSIA) |
| Meridan Fwk. | Sears-Roebuck & Company. | | Pla. |
| | | 20,16. | |
| USA | USA | USA | SU/SU |
| HSC.4,016. | HSC.4,017. | HSC.4,018. | HSC.4,019. |

| | | | |
|---|---|---|---|
| POLY-SHOT 12 70 AUSTRIA | PONTON COLLINGWOOD No 12 ELEY | No P.ORR & SONS LTD 12 RANGOON | P. POULSEN No KYNOCH PATENT CROSS EJECTOR 12 KJØBENHAVN |
| Circa 1970. | | | Kynoch Ejt case. |
| A | ?/GBE | BUR | ?/GBE |
| HSC.4,020. | HSC.4,021. | HSC.4,022. | HFC.1,651. |
| PRINCE of WALES 12 | PROUT No 12 LANSTON | PRUNO 12 12 ESPAÑA | PULVERFABRIK 12 PH 12 HASLOCH A/MAIN |
| | Launceston. | Pla. | |
| 20,16. | | | |
| CDN | GBE | E | D |
| HSC.4,023. | HSC.4,024. | HSC.4,025. | HSC.4,026. |
| PULVERFABRIK 12 D D 12 HASLOCH A/MAIN | PULVERFABRIK 12 12 HASLOCH A/MAIN | PURDEY 12 | PURDEY No 12 |
| | | Gnm. Pre Wwl. | Gnm. Pre Wwl. |
| D | D | GBE | GBE |
| HFC.4,027. | HSC.4,028. | HSC.4,029/R. | HFC.1,652/R. |
| PURDEY No 12 | PURDEY + + No 12 | PURDEY & SONS No 12 LONDON | PURDEY & SONS No 12 LONDON |
| Gnm. Pre Wwl. | Gnm. Pre Wwl. | Gnm. | Gnm. |
| GBE | GBE | GBE | GBE |
| HFC.1,653/R. | HSC.4,030/R. | HFC.4,031. | HFC.1,654. |

| | | | |
|---|---|---|---|
| Gnm. 12 gauge. | Eley Bros case. | Kynoch Ejt case. | R.S.Purdey, Irm. |
| GBE/GBE | GBE/GBE | GBE/GBE | GBE |
| HFC.4,032. | HFC.4,033. | HFC.1,655. | HFC.1,656. |
| 12 gauge. | 12 gauge. | 10 gauge. | 10 gauge. |
| YU | YU | | |
| HSC.4,034. | HSC.4,035. | HSC.4,036. | HSC.4,037. |
| 10 gauge. | | | 10 gauge. |
| | 12. | | |
| USA | USA | USA | USA |
| HSC.4,038. | HSC.4,039. | HSC.4,040. | HSC.4,041. |
| 10 gauge. | Peters Cartridge Company. | | |
| | 20,16,12. | 16,12. | |
| USA | USA/USA | USA/USA | USA |
| HSC.4,042. | HSC.4,043. | HSC.4,044. | HFC.2,093. |

| | | | |
|---|---|---|---|
| P.C.C. LEAGUE No 10 | P.C.Co. 10 NITRO G | P.C.Co. 10 PRIZE G | P.C.Co. 10 QUICK SHOT G |
| 10 gauge. | Peters Cartridge Company. | | Manufacturer. |
| 16,12. | 12. | 12. | |
| USA/USA | USA/USA | USA/USA | USA/USA |
| HSC.4,045. | HSC.4,046. | HSC.4,047. | HSC.4,048. |
| P.C.Co. 10 QUICK SHOT G | P.C.Co. 10 VICTOR G | PETERS No 10 CTG'E CO | PETERS No 10 HIGH GUN |
| | Peters Cartridge Company. | | |
| 16,12. | | | 16,12. |
| USA/USA | USA/USA | USA/USA | USA/USA |
| HSC.4,049. | HSC.4,050. | HSC.4,051. | HSC.4,052. |
| PETERS No 10 HIGHGUN | PETERS No 10 H.V. | PETERS MADE IN U.S.A. No 10 H.V. | PETERS No 10 IDEAL |
| | Peters Cartridge Company. | | |
| 20,16,12. | 28,20,16,12. | 28,20,16,12. | |
| USA/USA | USA/USA | USA/USA | USA/USA |
| HSC.4,053. | HSC.4,054. | HSC.4,055. | HSC.4,056. |
| PETERS No 10 IDEAL | PETERS No 10 LEAGUE | PETERS No 10 LEAGUE | PETERS No 10 NEW VICTOR |
| Manufacturer. | Peters Cartridge Company. | | 10 gauge. |
| 20,16,12. | 20,16,12. | 20,16,12. | 16,12. |
| USA/USA | USA/USA | USA/USA | USA/USA |
| HSC.4,057. | HSC.4,058. | HSC.4,059. | HSC.4,060. |

| | | | |
|---|---|---|---|
| PETERS 10 G NEW VICTOR | PETERS No 10 PREMIER | No PETERS 10 PREMIER | PETERS No 10 QUICK SHOT |
| 10 gauge. | Peters Cartridge Company. | | Manufacturer. |
| 16,12. | 16,12. | 20,16,12. | |
| USA/USA | USA/USA | USA/USA | USA/USA |
| HSC.4,061. | HFC.4,062. | HSC.4,063. | HSC.4,064. |
| PETERS 10 G QUICK SHOT | PETERS No 10 REFEREE | PETERS No 10 REFEREE | PETERS No 10 REFEREE |
| | Peters Cartridge Company. | | 10 gauge. |
| | 20,16.12. | 16. | 16,12. |
| USA/USA | USA/USA | USA/USA | USA/USA |
| HSC.4,065. | HSC.4,066. | HSC.4,067. | HSC.4,068. |
| No PETERS 10 REFEREE | MADE IN U.S.A. PETERS 10 REFEREE | PETERS 10 G REINFORCED | PETERS No 10 TARGET |
| Manufacturer. | Peters Cartridge Company. | | |
| 28,20,16,12. | | 12. | |
| USA/USA | USA/USA | USA/USA | USA/USA |
| HSC.4,069. | HSC.4,070. | HSC.4,071. | HFC.2,234. |
| No PETERS 10 TARGET | MADE IN U.S.A. PETERS 10 TARGET | MADE IN U.S.A. PETERS 10 VICTOR | 1901 No 10 PIGEON |
| 10 gauge. | Peters Cartridge Company. | | W.R.A.Co. 10 gauge. |
| 28,20,16,12. | | 28,20,16,12. | 12. |
| USA/USA | USA/USA | USA/USA | USA/USA |
| HSC.4,072. | HSC.4,073. | HSC.4,074. | HSC.4,075. |

| | | | |
|---|---|---|---|
| 10 gauge. W.R.A.Co. | Clinton Cartridge. | Meridan Fwk. | 10 gauge. |
| 12. | 28, 20, 16, 12. |  | 12. |
| USA/USA | USA | USA | USA |
| HSC.4.076. | HSC.4.077. | HSC.4.078. | HSC.4.079. |

| |
|---|
| Sears-Roebuck. |
|  |
| USA |
| HSC.4.080. |

J. W. & E. SOWMAN, Ltd., OLNEY.   Telephone 13

# ELEY Always Reliable

Specially Loaded for

J. W. & E. SOWMAN, Ltd.

BY

ELEY BROTHERS, Ltd.

Market Place,

OLNEY.

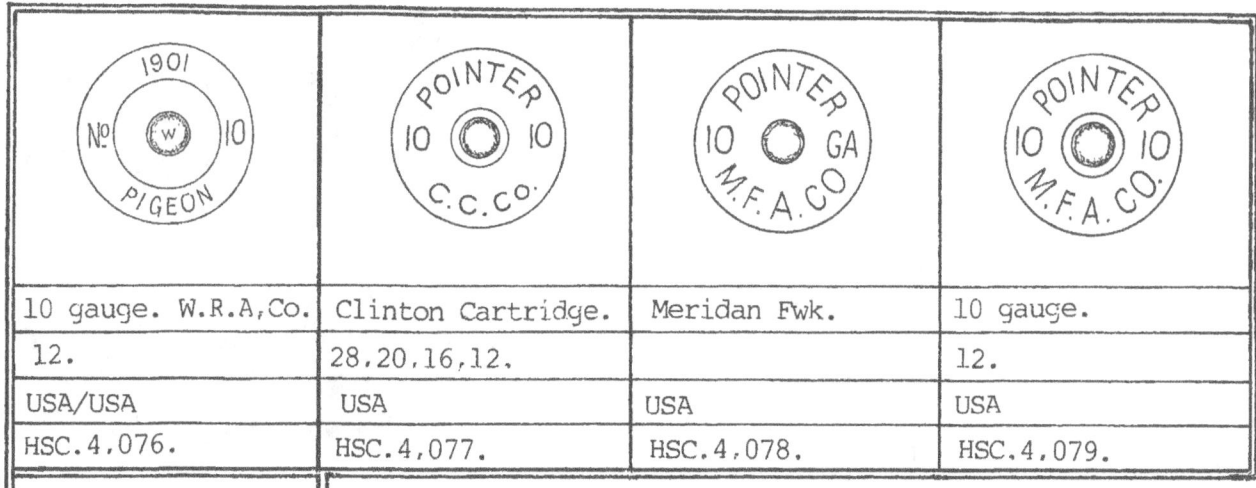

### PROPRIETARY

7/- per 100

7/6 per 100

8/6 per 100

9/6 per 100

5/6 per 100

### THE HARE

A Deep-shell Crimson Case loaded with Improved E.C. Powder.

9/6 per 100.   Cash price.

### THE PHEASANT

A Gastight Case loaded with Improved E.C. Powder.

10/6 per 100.   Cash price.

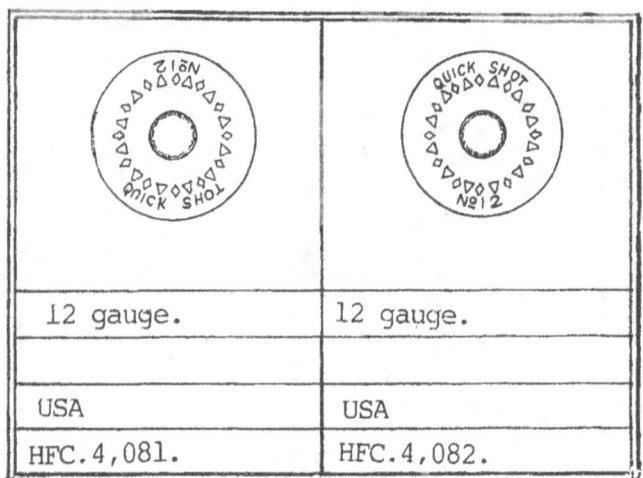

### Nobel's "Primrose Ballistite"
#### 12 GAUGE.

Primrose coloured, metal lined, cone based cases loaded with "Sporting Ballistite" powder. These cartridges have enjoyed wide popularity in the past, and they still have many friends in spite of the increasing tendency to turn to the more recent productions such as "Ajax Heavies." Stocked in a limited range of shot sizes only.

# ELEY CARTRIDGES

| | | | |
|---|---|---|---|
| .360, Remington. | .410. | Manufacturer. | .410. |
| USA/USA | USA/USA | USA/USA | USA/USA |
| HFC.4,083. | HSC.4,084. | HSC.4,085. | HFC.4,086. |
| Manufacturer. | .410/12mm. | | .410. |
| USA/USA | USA/USA | USA/USA | ZA |
| HSC.4,087. | HSC.4,088. | HSC.4,089. | HSC.4,090. |
| 32 gauge. | | Manufacturer. | 32 gauge. |
| | | | On other gauges. |
| USA/USA | USA/USA | USA/USA | USA/USA |
| HSC.4,091. | HSC.4,092. | HSC.4,093. | HSC.4,094 |
| 28 gauge. | Manufacturer. | | 28 gauge. |
| | | | 24,20,16.12.10. |
| D | USA/USA | USA/USA | USA/USA |
| HSC.4,095. | HFC.4,096. | HSC.4,097. | HSC.4,098. |

| | | | |
|---|---|---|---|
| (ROTTWEIL 28) | (RAUCHLOS 24 24) | (REMINGTON UMC No 24 NITRO CLUB) | (REM-UMC 24 BEST) |
| 28 gauge. | 24 gauge. | Manufacturer. | 24 gauge. |
|  |  | 28,20,16,12,10. |  |
| D/D | D | USA/USA | USA/USA |
| HSC.4,099. | HSC.4,100. | HSC.4,101. | HSC.4,102. |
| (ROTTWEIL 24) | (R.W.S. 24 24 NURNBERG) | (RAUCHLOS 20 20) | (R.B.RODDA&Co 20 20 CALCUTTA) |
| Manufacturer. | 24 gauge. |  | 20 gauge. |
|  |  |  |  |
| D/D | D/D | D | IND |
| HSC.4,103. | HSC.4,104. | HSC.4,105. | HSC.4,106. |
| (R.B.RODDA&Co No 20 KYNOCH CALCUTTA) | (R C 20 20 ITALY) | (R C 20 20 ITALY) | (REDHEAD 20 GA) |
| Kynoch made case. | Post Ww2. | Post Ww2. | 20 gauge. |
| IND/GBE | I/I | I/I | USA/USA |
| HFC.376. | HFC.377. | HFC.378. | HSC.4,107. |
| (REDHEAD No 20 D.N.OVAL) | (REDHEAD No 20 LONG RANGE) | (REDHEAD No 20 RELIANCE) | (REMINGTON UMC No. 20 ARROW) |
| | Montomery Ward Company. | | 20 gauge. |
| 16,12. | 16,12. | 16,12. |  |
| USA/USA | USA/USA | USA/USA | USA/USA |
| HSC.4,108. | HSC.4,110. | HSC.4.111. | HSC.4,112. |

| | | | |
|---|---|---|---|
| (Remington Express 20 GA) | (Remington UMC New Club 20) | (Remington UMC Nitro Club 20) | (Remington Peters 20 GA) |
| 20 gauge. | Manufacturer. | | 20 gauge. Post Ww2. |
| | | | On other gauges. |
| USA/USA | USA/USA | USA/USA | USA/USA |
| HSC.4,113. | HFC.4,114. | HSC.4,115. | HFC.379. |
| (Rem-UMC Arrow 20) | (Rem-UMC Best 20) | (Rem-UMC Nitro Club 20) | (Rem-UMC Case Made Nitro Club 20) |
| Remington Union Metallic Cartridge Company. | | | |
| On other gauges. | On other gauges. | On other gauges. | On other gauges. |
| USA/USA | USA/USA | USA/USA | USA/USA |
| HSC.4,116. | HFC.4,117. | HFC.2,144. | HFC.2,145. |
| (Rem-UMC Remington 20) | (Rem-UMC Shurshot 20 GA) | (Rem-UMC Shurshot 20) | (1901 Repeater 20) |
| Remington Union Metallic Cartridge Company. | | | W.R.A.Co. Pre Ww1. |
| On other gauges. | On other gauges. | 16,12. | |
| USA/USA | USA/USA | USA/USA | USA/USA |
| HFC.380. | HSC.4,118. | HSC.4,119. | HFC.381. |
| (R.M.C. ? 20 20) | (Rocket Brasil 20 20) | (Rosson Derby Eley 20 Norwich) | (Rottweil 20) |
| 20 gauge. | | Gnm. | 20 gauge. |
| 12. | | | |
| ZA | BR | GBE/GBE | D/D |
| HSC.4,120. | HSC.4,121. | HFC.382. | HSC.4122. |

| | | | |
|---|---|---|---|
| 20 gauge. | Manufcturer. | 20 gauge. | 18 gauge. |
| 16,12. | On other gauges. | | |
| GBE | D/D | D/D | D/D |
| HFC.385. | HFC.384. | HFC.383. | HSC.4,123. |
| 18 gauge. | 16 gauge. | | 16 gauge. |
| On other gauges. | | | |
| USA/USA | D | D | D |
| HFC.4,124. | HSC.4,109. | HSC.4,125. | HSC.4,126. |
| | | | |
| N/N | N/N | N/N | USA/USA |
| HSC.4,127. | HSC.4,128. | HSC.4,129. | HFC.549. |
| | Montgomery Ward Company. | | 16 gauge. |
| | 20,12. | 20,12. | |
| USA/USA | USA/USA | USA/USA | USA/USA |
| HSC.4,130. | HSC.4,131. | HSC.4,132. | HSC.4,133. |

| | | | |
|---|---|---|---|
| REDHEAD No.16 RELIANCE | REDHEAD No.16 TRIUMPH | REMINGTON 16-B | REMINGTON 16 16 CAMPO |
| 16 gauge. Montgomery Ward Co. | | Manufacturer. | |
| 20,12. | 12. | 14,12,10. | |
| USA/USA | USA/USA | USA/USA | MEX |
| HSC.4,134. | HSC.4,135. | HSC.4,136. | HSC.4,137. |
| REMINGTON 16 GA EXPRESS | REMINGTON UMC No.16 NEW CLUB | REMINGTON UMC No.16 NITRO CLUB | REMINGTON UMC No.16 NITRO CLUB |
| Remington Union Metallic Cartridge Company. | | | |
| | 12. | | 28,20,14,12,10. |
| USA/USA | USA/USA | USA/USA | USA/USA |
| HSC.4,138. | HFC.4,139. | HFC.4,140. | HSC.4,141. |
| REMINGTON UMC No.16 REMILION | REMINGTON 16 GA PETERS | REM-UMC No.16 ARROW | REM-UMC No.16 NEW CLUB |
| 16 gauge. | Manufacturer. | | |
| | | 20,12,10,8. | |
| USA/USA | USA/USA | USA/USA | USA/USA |
| HSC.4,142. | HFC.550. | HSC.4,143. | HSC.4,144. |
| REM-UMC No.16 NEW CLUB | REM-UMC No.16 NEW CLUB | REM-UMC No.16 NITRO CLUB | REM-UMC No.16 Remington |
| Remington Union Metallic Cartridge Company. | | | 16 gauge. |
| | | | |
| USA/USA | USA/USA | USA/USA | USA/USA |
| HSC.4,145. | HSC.4,146. | HSC.4,147. | HSC.4,148. |

| | | | |
|---|---|---|---|
| (REM-UMC CASE MADE IN USA Remington No 16) | (REM-UMC SHURSHOT No 16) | (1901 REPEATER No 16) | (REVELATION No 16 W.A.) |
| 16 gauge. | | W.R.A.Co. | |
| 20,12. | 20,12. | | 12. |
| USA/USA | USA/USA | USA/USA | USA |
| HFC.551. | HSC.4,149. | HSC.552. | HSC.4,150. |
| (REY FRERES NIMES 16) | (R.HOWSE FRENCH MADE CASE SOUTH HILL FAIRFORD 16 16) | (ROBIN HOOD No 16 1903) | (ROBIN HOOD 16 16 R.H.P.CO.) |
| | | | Powder Company. |
| | | | |
| F | GBE/F | USA/USA | USA/USA |
| HFC.4,151. | HFC.553. | HSC.4,152. | HSC.4,153. |
| (ROBIN HOOD 16 16 R.H.P.CO.) | (ROTTWEIL 16) | (ROTTWEIL 16) | (ROTTWEIL 16 16 NORMAL) |
| Reversed arrows. | | Manufacturer. | |
| USA/USA | D/D | D/D | D |
| HSC.4,154. | HSC.4,155. | HSC.4,156. | HSC.4,157. |
| (ROTTWEIL 16 16 NORMAL) | (RUSTLESS 16) | (R.W.S. 16 16 GASDICHT) | (RWS/GECO 16 16 ROTTWEIL) |
| | Frank Dyke. | Manufacturer. | 16 gauge. |
| | 20,12. | | |
| D | GBE | D/D | D |
| HFC.554 | HFC.555. | HFC.4,158. | HFC.557. |

| | | | |
|---|---|---|---|
| (RWS/GECO 16 16 ROTTWEIL) | (RWS 16 16 NURNBERG) | (RAUCHLOS 14 14) | (RAUFOSS 14) |
| 16 gauge. | 16 gauge. | 14 gauge. | 14 gauge. |
| D | D | D | D |
| HFC.556. | HFC.4,159. | HSC.4,160. | HFC.625. |
| (REMINGTON 14-A) | (REMINGTON UMC No 14 NITRO CLUB) | (RAKER 12 12 RAKER) | (RAMSBOTTOM MANCHESTER No12 ELEY) |
| 14 gauge. | 14 gauge. | 12 gauge. Post Ww2. | Gnm. 12 gauge. |
| 16,12,10. | On other gauges. | | |
| USA/USA | USA/USA | GBE | GBE/GBE |
| HSC.4,161. | HSC.4,162. | HFC.1,657. | HFC.1,658. |
| (RANDELL'S FOREIGN 12 12 MADE CASE SPECIAL SMOKELESS) | (RAPID FRENCH 12 12 MADE SHELL L.B.L.) | (R A 12 GA TRACER) | (RAUCHLOS *12*) |
| Irm. 12 gauge. | | Pap. | |
| GBE/? | ?/F | ?/USA | D |
| HFC.1,659. | HSC.4,163. | HFC.1,660. | HSC.4,164. |
| (RAUCHLOS 12 12) | (RAUCHLOS 12 12 ROSTFREI) | (RAUFOSS SINOX 12) | (RAUFOSS 12) |
| 12 gauge. | | | 12 gauge. |
| On other gauges. | | | |
| D | D | N/N | N/N |
| HSC.4,165. | HSC.4,166. | HSC.4,167. | HSC.4,168. |

| | | | |
|---|---|---|---|
| RAUFOSS 12 | RAUFOSS 12 12 MADE IN NORWAY | NºR.B.RODDA & Cº ? 12 CALCUTTA | R.B.RODDA & Cº 12 12 CALCUTTA |
| 12 gauge. | | | |
| | | | 20. |
| N/N | N/N | IND | IND |
| HSC.4,169. | HSC.4,170. | HSC.4,171. | HSC.4,172. |
| NºR.CAMPBELL&SONS 12 KYNOCH LEYBURN | R C 12 12 ITALY | *R C* 12 12 ITALY | R D 12 12 R D |
| Kynoch made case. | Post Ww2. | Manufacturer, Pla. | Pla. |
| GBE/GBE | I/I | I/I | |
| HFC.1,662. | HFC.1,661. | HSC.4,173. | HSC.4,174. |
| RED Nº 12 DEVIL | RED Nº 12 DEVIL | RED Nº 12 DEVIL | RED DEVIL'S Nº 12 A.A.Cº |
| 12 gauge. | Montgomery Ward Company. | | |
| USA/USA | USA/USA | USA/USA | USA/USA |
| HFC.1,664. | HFC.2,211. | HFC.1,663. | HSC.4,175. |
| REDHEAD 12 GA | REDHEAD Nº 12 D.N. | REDHEAD Nº 12 D.N.OVAL | REDHEAD Nº 12 LONG RANGE |
| Montgomery Ward Company. | | | 12 gauge. |
| | | 10. | 20,16. |
| USA/USA | USA/USA | USA/USA | USA/USA |
| HSC.4,176. | HSC.4,177. | HSC.4,178. | HSC.4,179. |

| | | | |
|---|---|---|---|
| (REDHEAD 12 GA MW) | (REDHEAD No 12 RELIANCE) | (REDHEAD No 12 TRIUMPH) | (REDHEAD 12 GA TRIUMPH) |
| 12 gauge. | Montgomery Ward Company. | | Adv, 12 gauge. |
| | 20.16. | 16. | |
| USA/USA | USA/USA | USA/USA | USA |
| HSC.4,180. | HSC.4,181. | HSC.4,182. | HSC.4,183. |
| (R&E.J.BELL No 12 MARKET HARBORO) | (REMINGTON 12) | (REMINGTON 12) | (REMINGTON 12 GA) |
| Edmd Jsph Bell, Irm. | | Pla. | |
| | 16B,14A.10. | | |
| GBE | USA/USA | I/I | USA/USA |
| HFC.4,184. | HSC.4,185. | HSC.4,186. | HFC.1,665. |
| (REMINGTON 12 GA) | (REMINGTON UMC No 12 ARROW) | (REMINGTON UMC No 12 CLUB) | (Remington 12 GA MADE IN USA DUPONT) |
| Remington Union Metallic Cartridge Company. | | | |
| | | | |
| | USA/USA | USA/USA | USA/USA |
| HFC.1,666. | HFC.1,672. | HFC.1,673. | HFC.2,212. |
| (REMINGTON 12 GA EXPRESS) | (REMINGTON EXPRESS 12 GA MADE IN USA 3¾-1¼-6) | (REMINGTON UMC No 12 LIGHTNING) | (REMINGTON UMC No 12 NEW CLUB) |
| Remington Union Metallic Cartridge Company. | | | |
| | | | 16. |
| USA/USA | USA/USA | USA/USA | USA/USA |
| HFC.1,667. | HFC.2,213. | HFC.1,675. | HFC.4,187. |

| | | | |
|---|---|---|---|
| (NEW CLUB No 12) | (NITROCLUB No 12) | (REMILION No 12) | (REMILION No 12) |
| 12 gauge. | Remington Union Metallic Cartridge Company. | | |
| USA/USA | USA/USA | USA/USA | USA/USA |
| HSC.4,188. | HFC.1,676. | HFC.1,678. | HFC.1,677. |
| (REMINGTON 12 GA R X P) | (REMINGTON 12 GA PETERS) | (REMINGTON 12 GA PETERS) | (REMINGTON 12 GA PETERS) |
| Manufacturer. | Pla. | Manufacturer. | Pla. |
| USA/USA | USA/USA | USA/USA | USA/USA |
| HFC.1,671. | HFC.1,668. | HFC.1,669. | HFC.1,670. |
| (REMINGTON 12 U GA PETERS) | (REMINGTON'S 12) | (REM-UMC No 12 ARROW) | (REM-UMC No 12 ARROW) |
| M.15 Smoke shell. | Remington Union Metallic Cartridge Company. | | |
| | 10. | | |
| USA/USA | USA/USA | USA/USA | USA/USA |
| HSC.4,189. | HSC.4,208. | HSC.4,190. | HFC.1,679. |
| (REM-UMC CASE MADE IN USA No 12 ARROW) | (REM-UMC MADE IN U.S.A. No 12 ARROW) | (REM-UMC No 12 BEST) | (REM-UMC 3 No 12 3 BEST) |
| 12 gauge. | | Ejt. | Ejt. |
| On other gauges. | On other gauges. | | |
| USA/USA | USA/USA | USA/USA | USA/USA |
| HFC.1,680. | HSC.4,191. | HFC.1,681. | HFC.4,192. |

| | | | |
|---|---|---|---|
| 12 gauge. | Remington Union Metallic Cartridge Company. | | |
| USA/USA | USA/USA | USA/USA | USA/USA |
| HSC.4,193. | HFC.1,684. | HSC.4,194. | HFC.1,685. |
| | | | |
| Remington Union Metallic Cartridge Company. | | | |
| 16. | | | |
| USA/USA | USA/USA | USA/USA | USA/USA |
| HSC.4,195. | HFC.1,686. | HSC.4,196. | HFC.4,197. |
| | | | |
| | Manufacturer. | | Dished head. |
| | | | 20, 16. |
| USA/USA | USA/USA | USA/USA | USA/USA |
| HSC.4,198. | HSC.4,199. | HFC.1,687. | HSC.4,200. |
| | | | |
| Remington Union Metallic Cartridge Company. | | | 12 gauge. |
| | | | On other gauges. |
| USA/USA | USA/USA | USA/USA | USA/USA |
| HFC.1,688. | HSC.4,201. | HFC.1,689. | HFC.1,682. |

| | | | |
|---|---|---|---|
| 12 gauge. | Remington Union Metallic Cartridge Company. | | |
| USA/USA | USA/USA | USA/USA | USA/USA |
| HFC.1,683. | HFC.4,202. | HSC.4,203. | HFC.1,690. |
| | Winchester Repeating Ams Company. | | |
| | | | 16. |
| USA/USA | USA/USA | USA/USA | USA |
| HSC.4,204. | HSC.4,205. | HFC.1,691. | HSC.4,206. |
| | | Post Ww2, Pla. | Alu. |
| F | F | F | |
| HFC.1,693. | HFC.1,692. | HSC.4,207. | HSC.4,209. |
| Apc. | Gnm. E.B.L. case. | J.Rigby & Co. (Believd canceled) | Pla, 12 gauge. |
| USA | GBE/GBE | GBE/GBE | RA/RA |
| HFC.4,210 | HFC.4,211. | HFC.1,694. | HSC.4,212. |

| | | | |
|---|---|---|---|
| RILA CAL.12 | RINGER No 12 | RIVAL No 12 MADE IN CANADA | RL No 12 |
| 12 gauge. Pla. | Possibly AUS. | | 12 gauge. |
| | | /CDN. | USA |
| HSC.4,213. | HSC.4,214. | HSC.4,215. | HSC.4,216. |
| R.L.CAPELL 12 12 NORTHAMPTON | R✱M✱C 12 12 | R.METCALFE No 12 ELEY RICHMOND | R.M 12 12 ROMA |
| Richard Lovat. Irm. | | Gnm, E.B.L. case. | |
| | 20. | | |
| GBE | ZA | GBE/GBE | I/I |
| HFC.1,695. | HFC.1,697. | HSC.4,217. | HFC.1,696. |
| ROBERTSON & SON.WICK No12 ELEY | ROBIN HOOD No 12 | ROBIN HOOD No 12 | ROBIN HOOD No 12 |
| Alx' Robertson. Irm | | | |
| | | | |
| GBE/GBE | USA | USA | USA |
| HFC.1,698. | HSC.4,218. | HSC.4,219. | HSC.4,220. |
| ROBIN HOOD No 12 | ROBINHOOD No 12 | No ROBIN HOOD 12 1903 | ROBINHOOD W.R.A.Co No 12 CHAMPION |
| 12 gauge. | | | Case by W.R.A.Co. |
| | | | 10. |
| USA | USA | USA | USA/USA |
| HSC.4,221. | HSC.4,222. | HFC.1,699. | HSC.4,223. |

| | | | |
|---|---|---|---|
| ROBIN HOOD No 12 COMET | ROBIN HOOD No 12 COMET | ROBIN HOOD No 12 COMET | ROBIN HOOD 12 12 R.H.A.CO. |
| 12 gauge. | Ammunition Co. | | Ammunition Co. |
| USA | USA | USA | USA |
| HSC.4,224. | HSC.4,225. | HSC.4,226. | HSC.4,227. |
| ROBIN HOOD 12 12 R.H.P.CO. | ROBIN HOOD 12 12 R.H.P.CO. | ROBIN HOOD No 12 SMOKELESS | ROBINSON No 12 HULL |
| Powder Co. 16,10. | Reversed arrows. 16. | | Rob't Robinson. Gnm |
| USA | USA | USA | GBE |
| HFC.1,700. | HSC.4,228. | HSC.4,229. | HFC.1,701. |
| ROB'JN 12 | ROB'JN 12 | ROBUN 12 | ROCKET 12 12 BRASIL |
| | | Apc. | |
| NL | NL | NL | BR |
| HSC.4,230. | HSC.4,231. | HSC.4,232. | HSC.4,233. |
| ROCKET 12 12 BRASIL | ROMANA C.S 12 12 ROMA | ROSKELLEY.LOSTWITHIEL No12 ELEY | ROSSON DERBY No12 ELEY |
| Pla. | Pla. | Irm, optician, etc. | 12 gauge. Gnm. |
| BR | I | GBE/GBE | GBE/GBE |
| HSC.4,234. | HSC.4,235. | HSC.4,236. | HFC.1,702. |

| | | | |
|---|---|---|---|
| 12 gauge. Gnm. Ejt. | Gnm. | Case by Eley Bros. | E.B.L. case. Gnm. |
| GBE/GBE | GBE | GBE/GBE | GBE/GBE |
| HFC.1,704. | HSC.4,237. | HFC.1,703. | HFC.1,705. |
| Gnm. | Gnm. | Gnm. | Manufacturer. |
| GBE | GBE | GBE | D/D |
| HSC.4,238. | HFC.4,239. | HFC.4,240. | HSC.4,241. |
| | Alu. | Alu. Black print. | |
| D/D | D/D | D/D | D/D |
| HFC.1,707. | HSC.4,242. | HFC.1,706. | HFC.1,708. |
| Manufacturer. | John Rowlatt, Guns. | | 12 gauge. |
| D/D | GBE | MEX | MEX |
| HFC.1,709. | HFC.1,710. | HSC.4,243. | HFC.1,711. |

| | | | |
|---|---|---|---|
| R.PINTO 12 12 COMO | R.PINTO 12 12 ESTE | R.PINTO 12 12 ESTE | R.PINTO.12 VERONA.12 |
| 12 gauge. Apc. | | | Apc, Post Ww2. |
| I | I | I | I |
| HSC.4,244. | HFC.1,713. | HFC.1,712. | HSC.4,245. |
| R.RAINE.CARLISLE No12 ELEY | R.RAINE No 12 ELEY CARLISLE | R.RAINE.CARLISLE KYNOCH No12 | R 12 12 RAUCHLOS |
| Rob't Raine. Gnm. | E.B.L. cases. | Case by Kynoch. | |
| GBE/GBE | GBE/GBE | GBE/GBE | D |
| HSC.4,246. | HSC.4,247. | HFC.1,714. | HSC.4,248. |
| R.ROBINSON No 12 KYNOCH HULL | R.ROBINSON No 12 KYNOCH HULL | R.STREET TETBURY No12 ELEY | R.T.HODGSON No 12 KYNOCH HARROGATE |
| Robert Robinson, | Gnm. Kynoch cases. | Rob't Street. Irm. | Gnm. Kynoch case. |
| GBE/GBE | GBE/GBE | GBE/GBE | GBE/GBE |
| HFC.4,249. | HFC.1,715. | HSC.4,250. | HFC.1,716. |
| RUDD No 12 NORWICH | RUSTLESS 12 | RUSTLESS 12 12 WATERPROOF | RWA 12 |
| Arthur J. Rudd. Gnm | Frank Dyke. | | 12 gauge. |
| | 20,16. | | |
| GBE | GBE | | |
| HFC.1,717. | HFC.1,718. | HFC.1,719. | HSC.4,251. |

| | | | |
|---|---|---|---|
| (headstamp: R.WISE.KIDDERMINSTER.No.12) | (headstamp: RWS 12) | (headstamp: RWS 12 NURNBERG 12) | (headstamp: RWS 12 NURNBERG 12) |
| Rich'd Wise. Irm. | Rheinische Westfalische Springstoff. | | 12 gauge. |
| GBE | D/D | D/D | D/D |
| HFC.1,720. | HSC.4,252. | HSC.4,253. | HFC.1,722. |
| (headstamp: R.W.S. 12 NURNBERG 12) | (headstamp: RWS 12 RAUCHLOS 12) | (headstamp: RWS/GECO 12 ROTTWEIL 12) | (headstamp: RWS/GECO 12 ROTTWEIL 12) |
| | RWS Smokeless. | | |
| D/D | D/D | D/D | D/D |
| HFC.1,721. | HFC.1,723. | HFC.1,724. | HFC.4,254. |
| (headstamp: RWS/GECO 12 ROTTWEIL 12) | (headstamp: RWS/GECO 12 ROTTWEIL 12) | (headstamp: RWS/GECO 12/65 ROTTWEIL 12/65) | (headstamp: RAUCHLOS 10 10) |
| Rheinische Westfalische Springstoff. | | 12 gauge, Apc. | Smokeless. 10 gauge |
| | | | On other gauges. |
| D/D | D/D | D/D | D |
| HFC.1,726. | HFC.1,725. | HSC.4,255. | HSC.4,256. |
| (headstamp: REMINGTON'S 10) | (headstamp: REMINGTON 10) | (headstamp: REMINGTON EXPRESS 10 GA) | (headstamp: REMINGTON UMC No 10 NITRO CLUB) |
| 10 gauge. | Remington Arms Company. | | 10 gauge. |
| | 16,14,12. | On other gauges. | |
| USA/USA | USA/USA | USA/USA | USA/USA |
| HSC.4,257. | HSC.4,258. | HFC.4,259. | HSC.4,260. |

| | | | |
|---|---|---|---|
| (Remington Peters 10 GA) | (Remington's 10) | (Rem-UMC No 10 Arrow) | (Rem-UMC No 10 New Club) |
| Manufacturer. | | | 10 gauge. |
| | 12. | 20,16,12,8. | |
| USA/USA | USA/USA | USA/USA | USA/USA |
| HFC.2,094. | HSC.4,261. | HSC.4,262. | HSC.4,263. |
| (Rem-UMC No 10 Nitro Club) | (Rem-UMC No 10 Nitro Club) | (Rem-UMC No 10 Remington) | (1901 No 10 Repeater) |
| Remington Union Metallic Cartridge Company. | | | W.R.A.Co. |
| On other gauges. | | Much used. | On other gauges. |
| USA/USA | USA/USA | USA/USA | USA/USA |
| HSC.4,264. | HSC.4,265. | HSC.4,266. | HSC.4,267. |
| (R.F. No 10) | (R.G.&Mfg.Co. Limited) | (R.G.&M.F.C.Co Limited) | (R L No 10) |
| | Rawbone Gun & Manufacturing Co Ltd. | | |
| | | | |
| USA | CDN/CDN | CDN/CDN | USA |
| HSC.4,268. | HFC.2,095. | HFC.2,235. | HC.4,269. |
| (R L No 10) | (Robin Hood No 10) | (Robin Hood No.10) | (Robin Hood W.R.A.Co. No 10 Champion) |
| 10 gauge. | Robin Hood Ammunition Co. | | Case by W.R.A.Co. |
| | | | |
| USA | USA | USA | USA/USA |
| HSC.4,270. | HSC.4,271. | HSC.4,272. | HSC.4,273. |

| | | | |
|---|---|---|---|
| ROBIN HOOD W.R.A.Co N°10 NEW RIVAL | ROBIN HOOD 10 10 R.H.P.CO. | ROBIN HOOD 10 10 R.H.P.CO. | ROYAL N°10 L.B.&Co. |
| 10 gauge. | Robin Hood Powder Company. | | Lewis Bros & Co. |
| | On other gauges. | | |
| USA/USA | USA/USA | USA/USA | CDN |
| HSC.4,274. | HSC.4,275. | HSC.4,276. | HSC.4,277. |

| | | | |
|---|---|---|---|
| REMINGTON UMC N°8 ARROW | REM-UMC N°8 ARROW | Remington CEMENT GUN | |
| 8 gauge. | | 8 gauge. | |
| 20,16,12,10. | 20,16,12,10. | | |
| USA/USA | USA/USA | USA/USA | |
| HSC.4,278. | HSC.4,279. | HFC.4,280. | |

| | |
|---|---|
| REMINGTON INDUSTRIAL | RG/4/63 |
| 4 gauge. | 4 gauge. |
| | |
| USA/USA | |
| HSC.4,281. | HSC.4,282. |

| | | | |
|---|---|---|---|
| .410. | .410. | | Sears Roebuck. |
| D/D | D/D | | USA/USA |
| HSC.4,283. | HSC.4,284. | HSC.4,285. | HSC.4,286. |
| | .410. | Smith & Wesson .410. | 28 gauge. |
| USA/USA | USA/USA | USA | /D |
| HSC.4,287. | HSC.4,288. | HSC.4,289. | HFC.268. |
| 24 gauge. | 20 gauge, Post Ww2. | | Sellier & Bellot. 16, 12. |
| CS/CS | E/E | | CS/CS |
| HFC.272. | HFC.386. | HFC.387. | HFC.388. |
| Powder Co. 12. | Manufacturer. | On other gauges. | 20 gauge. |
| GBE | CS/CS | CS/CS | F/F |
| HSC.4290. | HFC.389. | HFC.390. | HSC.4,291. |

| | | | |
|---|---|---|---|
| (S&G No 20 GAMBLES) | (SMI 20 NOC 20 MADE IN ITALY) | (SMI 20 20 MADE IN ITALY) | (SMOKELESS 20 20) |
| 20 gauge. | Societa Metallurgica Italiana. | | 20 gauge. |
| 16,12. | | | |
| USA | I/I | I/I | |
| HSC.4,292. | HSC.4,293. | HFC.391. | HFC.392. |
| (SMOKELESS 20 20) | (SMOKELESS 20 20 GASTIGHT) | (SMOKELESS 20 20 GASTIGHT) | (SNIABPD 20 20 ITALY) |
| Gevelot. | | Foreign case. | |
| 16. | | On other gauges. | |
| F/F | | | I |
| HSC.4,294. | HFC.393. | HFC.394. | HFC.395. |
| (SPECIAL 20 20 SMOKELESS) | (SPECIAL 20 20 SMOKELESS) | (SPECIAL 20 20 SMOKELESS) | (SPECIAL 20 20 SMOKELESS) |
| Post Ww2. | | Much used. | 20 gauge. |
| 16,12. | | 16,12. | |
| /I | | /I | |
| HFC.400. | HFC.398. | HFC.401. | HFC.399. |
| (SPECIAL 20 20 GASTIGHT) | (SPECIAL 20 20 GASTIGHT) | (SPECIAL FOREIGN 20 20 MADE CASE SMOKELESS) | (SPORTLOAD 20 20 S.R.&CO.) |
| 20 gauge. | Much used. | | Sears Roebuck & Co. |
| | | | 16.12. |
| | | | |
| HFC.396. | HFC.397. | HFC.4,295. | HSC.4,296. |

| | | | |
|---|---|---|---|
| 20 gauge, Adv. | | H.S.B.& Co. | Extra large cap. |
| | | 16,12. | |
| D | | USA/USA | F/F |
| HSC.4,297. | HFC.4,298. | HSC.4,299. | HFC.4,300. |
| | Smith & Wesson. | 20 gauge. | 18 gauge. |
| 16. | On other gauges. | | |
| GBE | USA | USA | CS/CS |
| HFC.402. | HFC.403. | HFC.404. | HSC.4,301. |
| 18 gauge. | 16 gauge. | Sellier & Bellot. | |
| | | 20,12. | |
| CS/CS | USA | CS/CS | CS/CS |
| HFC.426. | HSC.4,302. | HFC.558. | HFC.559. |
| 16 gauge. | | Powder Co. | 16 gauge. |
| F | D | GBE/? | |
| HSC.4,303. | HSC.4,304. | HSC.4,305. | HFC.560. |

| | | | |
|---|---|---|---|
| SEARS 16 GA XTRA·RANGE | SELLIER & BELLOT 16 | SELLIER & BELLOT SCHOENEBECK 16 NORMAL 16 | SELLIER & BELLOT SCHOENEBECK 16 NORMAL 16 |
| 16 gauge. | | | 16 gauge. |
| 12. | On other gauges. | | |
| USA | CS/CS | D/D | D/D |
| HSC.4,306. | HFC.561. | HFC.4,307. | HSC.4,308. |
| SELLIER&BELLOT 16 16 SCHOENEBECK | SELLIER&BELLOT 16 MADE IN GERMANY 16 SCHOENEBECK | SEQUOIA 16 16 SAN FRANCISCO | SEVRAN 16 16 LIVRY |
| | | Cig' lighter. | |
| | 12. | | |
| D/D | D/D | USA | |
| HSC.4,309. | HSC.4,310. | HSC.4,311. | HSC.4,312. |
| S.F.M 16 GEVELOT 16 | S.F 16 16 PARIS | S & G No 16 GAMBLES | SILVANUS RAUCHLOS 16 |
| Society Francaise des Munitions. | | | 16 gauge. |
| | | 20,12. | |
| | | USA | D |
| HFC.562. | HSC.4,313. | HSC.4,314. | HSC.4,315. |
| SMITH No 16 NEWARK | SMOKELESS 16 16 | SMOKELESS 16 16 MADE IN ENGLAND | SMOKELESS 16 16 GASTIGHT |
| Gnm. | Gevelot. | | Much used. |
| | 20. | | On other gauges. |
| GBE | F | GBE/GBE | |
| HFC.4,316. | HSC.4,317. | HFC.568. | HFC.565. |

| | | | |
|---|---|---|---|
| 16 gauge. | | Extra large cap. | 16 gauge. |
| On other gauges. | | On other gauges. | |
| | | | |
| HFC.566. | HFC.564. | HFC.563. | HFC.567. |
| | | | |
| | | | |
| D/D | I | I | |
| HFC.569. | HFC.570. | HFC.571. | HFC.4,318. |
| | | | |
| | | | |
| S | | | |
| HSC.4,319. | HFC.572. | HFC.573. | HFC.574. |
| | | | |
| 16 gauge. | Much used. | | 16 gauge. |
| 20,12. | On other gauges. | 20,12. | |
| /I | | /I | ?/D |
| HFC.576. | HFC.578. | HFC.577. | HFC.579. |

| | | | |
|---|---|---|---|
| (Special Foreign Made Case Smokeless 16) | (Sportload 16 S.R.&Co.) | (Stahl 16) | (Standard No 16) |
| 16 gauge. | | | A.C. Howard & Co. |
| On other gauges. | 20,12. | | |
| | USA | D | USA/USA |
| HFC.580. | HSC.4,320. | HSC.4,321. | HSC.4,322. |
| (Standard 16 Type Championnat) | (Star Brand Made in USA 16) | (Ste Fse Des Munitions Paris SFM 16) | (Ste Fse Des Munitions Paris 16) |
| Asc. | H.S.B & Co. | | |
| 12. | 20,12. | | |
| F/F | USA | F/F | F/F |
| HFC.581. | HSC.4,323. | HSC.4,324. | HSC.4,325. |
| (Ste Fse Des Munitions Paris 16) | (Stephen Grant London) | (Stephen Grant London No 16) | (Stephen Grant London No 16) |
| | Gnm. | Gnm. | Gnm. |
| | 12. | | |
| F/F | GBE | GBE | GBE |
| HSC.4,326. | HSC.4,327/R. | HSC.4,328. | HSC.4,329. |
| (Stephen Grant London No 16) | (Stephen Grant London No) | (Sterling London No 16) | (GWF 16 USA) |
| 16 gauge. Gnm. | Gnm. | | Pla. 16 gauge. |
| | | 20. | |
| GBE | GBE | GBE | USA |
| HSC.4,330. | HSC.4,331. | HSC.4,332. | HFC.4,333. |

271

| | | | |
|---|---|---|---|
| 14 gauge. | 14 gauge. | 12 gauge, Pla. | 12 gauge, Pla. |
| F/F | F/F | | E/E |
| HFC.4,334. | HSC.4,335. | HSC.4,336. | HFC.1,727. |
| Post Ww2, Pla. | | | Pla. |
| E/E | E/E | E/E | |
| HFC.1,728. | HFC.1,730. | HFC.1,729. | HSC.4,337. |
| Post Ww2. | | | |
| HFC.1,731. | HFC.1,732. | HSC.4,338. | HSC.4,339. |
| 12 gauge. | | | 12 gauge. |
| /B | /B | CH | GBE |
| HSC.4,340. | HSC.4,341. | HSC.4,342. | HSC.4,343. |

| | | | |
|---|---|---|---|
| (Sarson's Aylesbury No 12) | (Savage Hi-Power No 12) | (Savage Superior No 12) | (Savage Superior No 12) |
| 12 gauge. | Post WW2. | | 12 gauge. |
| GBE | | | |
| HFC.1,733. | HFC.1,734. | HFC.1,736. | HFC.1,735. |
| (12 SB 12 Granada) | (SBP 12 12 Made in Czechoslovakia) | (SBP 12 12 Made in Czechoslovakia) | (SBP 12 12 Made in Czechoslovakia) |
| Pla. | | Sellier & Bellot. | |
| | | 20,16. | |
| E | CS/CS | CS/CS | CS/CS |
| HSC.4,344. | HFC.1,738. | HFC.1,737. | HFC.1,739. |
| (S.C.Co. No 12) | (S.C.Co. x x No 12) | (S.C.Co. No 12 Rocket) | (S.C.Co. No 12 Star) |
| Strong Cartridge Company. | | | |
| 10. | 10. | 12 gauge only. | 12 gauge only. |
| USA | USA | USA | USA |
| HFC.4,345. | HSC.4,346. | HSC.4,347. | HFC.1,740. |
| (Schaefer 12) | (Schönebeck 12) | (Schönebeck 12) | (Schultze No 12) |
| 12 gauge. | Pla. | | Powder Co. |
| 12 gauge only. | | | |
| USA | D | D | GBE |
| HSC.4,348. | HFC.1,741. | HFC.1,742. | HFC.1,743. |

| | | | |
|---|---|---|---|
| SCHULTZE No 12 LONDON | SCHULTZE No 12 C.H.M.C LONDON | SCHULTZE No 12 E.B. LONDON | SCHULTZE No 12 E.B. LONDON |
| Schultze Gunpowder Co, Ltd. | | Eley Bros case. | Pre Ww1. |
| GBE | GBE/GBE | GBE/GBE | GBE/GBE |
| HFC.2,214. | HFC.1,744. | HSC.4,349. | HSC.4,350. |
| 12 12 SCHUTZMARKE | SCORPIO 12 | SCOTCHER No 12 BURY ST EDMUNDS | SCOTCHER INVINCIBLE No 12 CARTRIDGE BURY ST EDMUNDS |
| | Post Ww2. | Gnm. | Gnm. |
| | AUS | GBE | GBE |
| HSC.4,351. | HFC.1,745. | HFC.1,746. | HSC.4,352. |
| SCOTCHER & SON No 12 KYNOCH BURY ST EDMUNDS | SEAM 12 12 MADRED | SEARS 12 GA | SEARS 12 GA SPORTLOAD |
| Gnm, Kynoch case. | | Post Ww2. | Post Ww2. |
| GBE | E | USA/USA | USA/USA |
| HFC.1,747. | HSC.4,353. | HFC.1,748. | HFC.1,749. |
| SEARS 12 GA TED WILLIAMS | SEARS 12 12 XTRA-RANGE | SEARS 12 GA XTRA-RANGE | SECOND No 12 QUALITY |
| 12 gauge, Pla. | | Post Ww2. | Worcester Ct'ge Co. |
| USA/USA | USA/USA | USA/USA | USA |
| HFC.1,750. | HSC.4,354. | HFC.1,751. | HSC.4,355. |

| | | | |
|---|---|---|---|
| 12 gauge. | Pla. | Case by W.R.A.Co. | 12 gauge. |
| | | | On other gauges. |
| | I | USA/USA | CS/CS |
| HFC.1,752. | HSC.4,356. | HFC.1,753. | HFC.1,754. |
| | | Post Ww2. | |
| On other gauges. | 16. | | |
| CS/CS | CS/CS | CS/CS | CS/CS |
| HFC.1,755. | HFC.1,756. | HFC.1,758. | HFC.1,757. |
| Post Ww2. | | | |
| | 16. | | |
| CS/CS | D/D | D/D | |
| HFC.4,357. | HFC.1,759. | HFC.4,358. | HSC.4,359. |
| 12 gauge, Pla. | Societe Francaise des Munitions. | | |
| | F/F | F/F | F/F |
| HSC.4,360. | HFC.1,760. | HFC.4,361. | HSC.4,362. |

| | | | |
|---|---|---|---|
| (SGCo No 12 E.B. YEOMAN) | (SGCo No 12 J YEOMAN) | (S&G No 12 GAMBLES) | (S.GRANT No 12 LONDON) |
| 12 gauge. Schultze Gunpowder Co. | | Gambles Stores. | Stephn Grant, Gnm. |
| | | 20,16. | |
| GBE/GBE | GBE/GBE | USA | GBE |
| HSC.1,761. | HFC.2,215. | HSC.4,363. | HFC.1,762. |
| (S.GRANT & SONS LONDON No12 ELEY) | (S.GRANT & SONS No 12 KYNOCH LONDON) | (Canceled mark) | (S.GRANT & SON KYNOCHS PATENT No 12 GROUSE EJECTOR LONDON) |
| Gnm. Eley Bros case. | Gnm, Kynoch case. | Canceled mark. | Kynoch Ejt case. |
| | | | |
| GBE/GBE | GBE/GBE | GBE/GBE | GBE/GBE |
| HFC.1,764. | HFC.1,765. | HFC.1,766. | HFC.1,763. |
| (SHELL 12 12 MADE IN BELGIUM) | (SHELL 12 12 MADE IN BELGIUM) | (SHELL 12 12 MADE IN BELGIUM) | (S.I.C.O. No 12 ROCKET) |
| | | | |
| B/B | B/B | B/B | USA |
| HSC.4,364. | HSC.4,365. | HSC.4,366. | HSC.4,367. |
| (S.I.C.Co No 12 ROCKET) | (S.I.C.Co No 12 ROCKET) | (S.I.C.Co No 12 STAR) | (S.I.C.Co No 12 STAR) |
| Sportsman International Cartridge Co. | | | Dished. 12 gauge, |
| 12 gauge only. | Dished. | 12 gauge only. | |
| USA | USA | USA | USA |
| HSC.4,368. | HSC.4,369. | HSC.4,370. | HSC.4,371. |

| | | | |
|---|---|---|---|
| (S.JACKSON KYNOCH NOTTINGHAM No 12) | (S.K.D ☆ ☆ 12) | (S.K.D ☆ ☆ 12) | (S.K.D 12 12 BLITZ) |
| Samuel Jackson, Gnm | | | 12 gauge. |
| GBE/GBE | AUS | AUS | AUS |
| HFC.1,767. | HSC.4,372. | HSC.4,373. | HSC.4,374. |
| (S.K.D 12 12 BLITZ) | (SKELTONS.L°.WARRINGTON. No 12. ELEY) | (SLINGSBY BROS No 12 BOSTON) | (SMALL No 12 NEWCASTLE) |
| | Eley Bros case. | Gnm. | P.Small. |
| AUS | GBE/GBE | GBE | GBE |
| HSC.4,375. | HFC.1,768. | HFC.1,769. | HSC.4,376. |
| (SMALL No 12 KYNOCH NEWCASTLE) | (SMALL KYNOCH'S PATENT No 12 GROUSE EJECTOR NEWCASTLE) | (SMALLWOOD.SHREWSBURY N°12) | (SMI 12 12 ITALY) |
| | Kynoch Ejt case. | Samuel. Gnm. | Post Ww2. |
| GBE/GBE | GBE/GBE | GBE | I/I |
| HFC.1,770. | HFC.1,771. | HFC.1,772. | HFC.1,774. |
| (SMI 12 12 ITALY) | (SMI 12 NOC 12 MADE IN ITALY) | (SMI 12 12 MADE IN ITALY) | (SMITH & SONS.NEWARK N°12) |
| 12 gauge. | Societa Metallurgica Italiana. | Post Ww2. | Gnm. 12 gauge. |
| I/I | I/I | I/I | GBE |
| HFC.1,773. | HSC.4,377. | HFC.1,775. | HFC.4,378. |

| | | | |
|---|---|---|---|
| (Smith & Sons Newark No.12) | (Smith & Sons Newark No.12) | (Smith & Sons Newark No.12) | (Smith & Sons Newark Kynoch No.12) |
| 12 gauge. Gnm. | | Gnm. | 12 gauge. Gnm. |
| GBE | GBE | GBE | GBE/GBE |
| HSC.4,379. | HFC.4,380. | HFC.1,776. | HFC.1,777. |
| (Smokeless 12) | (Smokeless No.12) | (12 Smokeless 12) | (Smokeless No.12) |
| Pla. | | | Gevlot. |
| | | | /F |
| HFC.1,788. | HSC.4,381. | HSC.4,382. | HFC.4,383. |
| (Smokeless No.12) | (Smokeless *12*) | (Smokeless *12*) | (Smokeless ☆12☆) |
| Gevelot. | | | 12 gauge. |
| /F | | | |
| HFC.1,784. | HFC.1,779. | HFC.1,780. | HFC.1,782. |
| (Smokeless ☆12☆) | (Smoke *12*) | (Smokeless No.12 Cartridge) | (Smokeless 12 Gastight 12) |
| 12 gauge. | Over stamped. | | Much used. |
| HFC.1,781 | HFC.1,783. | HFC.4,384. | HFC.1,778. |

| | | | |
|---|---|---|---|
| 12 gauge. | Much used. | | 12 gauge. |
| | | | |
| HFC.1,785. | HFC.1,787. | HFC.1,786. | HFC.4,385. |
| | | | |
| | /D | /D | CH |
| HFC.1,789. | HFC.1,797. | HFC.1,791. | HSC.4,386. |
| | | | |
| GBE/GBE | GBE/GBE | | |
| HFC.1,792. | HFC.1,793. | HFC.1,795. | HFC.1,794. |
| 12 ga' Kynoch case. | J.F.Smythe Ltd. Gnm. | | Gnm. 12 gauge. |
| GBE/GBE | GBE/GBE | GBE/GBE | GBE |
| HFC.1,796. | HFC.4,387. | HFC.1,799. | HFC.1,798. |

| | | | |
|---|---|---|---|
| Gnm. Kynoch Ejt. | Pla. | Post Ww2. | Post Ww2. |
| GBE/GBE | I/I | I/I | I/I |
| HFC.1,800. | HFC.1,801. | HFC.1,802. | HSC.4,388. |
| Southern Ct'ge Co. 12 gauge only. | Pla. | Post Ww2. Pla. | |
| USA | I/I | I/I | |
| HSC.4,389. | HFC.1,803. | HFC.1,804. | HFC.1,805. |
| Pla. | Pla. | | |
| ZA | ZA | ZA | ZA |
| HSC.4,390. | HFC.1,806. | HSC.4,391. | HFC.4,392. |
| Smokeless Powder & Ammunition Company. | | | Post Ww2. Pla. |
| GBE | (Eley Bros case). | | |
|  | GBE/GBE | GBE | F |
| HFC.1,807. | HFC.1,808. | HSC.4,393. | HFC.1,809. |

| | | | |
|---|---|---|---|
| (12 SPEC 12 HUNTING) | (SPECIAL 12) | (SPECIAL ☆ 12 ☆) | (SPECIAL No 12) |
| 12 gauge. Pla. | | | 12 gauge. |
| | | | 10. |
| | D | D | USA |
| HFC.4,394. | HSC.4,395. | HSC.4,396. | HSC.4,397. |
| (SPECIAL No.12) | (SPECIAL 12 GASTIGHT 12) | (SPECIAL 12 GASTIGHT 12) | (SPECIAL 12 GASTIGHT 12) |
| Standard Ct'ge Co. | | | |
| 10. | | | |
| USA | | | |
| HSC.4,398. | HFC.1,811. | HFC.1,812. | HFC.1,813. |
| (SPECIAL 12 GASTIGHT 12) | (SPECIAL IGNITION No 12 ELEY LONDON) | (SPECIAL No 12 LONG RANGE) | (SPECIAL 12 RUSTLESS 12) |
| | Eley Bros ct'ge. | | |
| | | | |
| | GBE/GBE | | |
| HFC.1,814. | HSC.4399. | HFC.4,400. | HSC.4,401. |
| (SPECIAL 12 RUSTLESS 12) | (SPECIAL 12 SMOKELESS 12) | (SPECIAL 12 SMOKELESS 12) | (SPECIAL 12 SMOKELESS 12) |
| Post Ww2. | | Much used. | 12 gauge. |
| | | | |
| | | | |
| HSC.4,402. | HFC.1,815. | HFC.1,820. | HFC.1,818. |

| | | | |
|---|---|---|---|
| 12 gauge. | | Extra large cap. | 12 gauge. |
| | | | |
| HFC.1,821. | HFC.1,816. | HFC.1,817. | HFC.1,825. |
| | | | Post Ww2. Pla. |
| | 10. | | |
| HFC.1,824. | HFC.4,403. | HFC.1,810. | HFC.1,826. |
| Fred P.Spencer. Irm. | | | |
| | | 20,16. | 10. |
| GBE/GBE | CDN. | USA | USA |
| HFC.1,827. | HFC.4,404. | HSC.4,405. | HSC.4,406. |
| 12 gauge. | | Post Ww2. Pla. | 12 gauge. |
| USA | USA | | USA |
| HFC.1,828. | HSC.4,407. | HFC.1,829. | HSC.4,408. |

| | | | |
|---|---|---|---|
| STAHL 12 | STANDARD 12 | STANDARD No 12 | STANDARD No 12 |
| 12 gauge. | | | 12 gauge. |
| D | USA | USA | |
| HSC.4,409. | HSC.4,410. | HSC.4,411. | HFC.4,412. |
| STANDARD No 12 BLACK PRINCE | STANDARD C 12 B | STANDARD 12 12 TYPE CHAMPIONHAT | STANDARD 12 12 CRB |
| | | Asc. | |
| | | 16. | |
| USA | | F/F | |
| HSC.4,413. | HSC.4,414. | HFC.1,830. | HSC.4,415. |
| STANDARD 12 12 PAT'D NOV '75 | STANGER.HULL No 12 ELEY | STANLEY 12 GA STANLEY | STAR MADE IN USA 12 BRAND |
| | Case by Eley Bros. | Pla. | H.S.B.& Co. |
| | | | 20,16. |
| | GBE/GBE | | USA |
| HSC.4,416. | HSC.4,417. | HSC.4,418. | HFC.1,831. |
| STAR 12 12 S.C.Co. | STAR 12 12 SHOT | STEEL 12 GA LINED | STEEL 12 GA LINED |
| Southern Ct'ge Co. | Pla. | | 12 gauge. |
| USA | USA | USA | USA |
| HFC.1,832. | HFC.1,833, | HFC.1,834. | HFC.1,835. |

| | | | |
|---|---|---|---|
| STEEL N°12 LINED | STEEL N°12 NITRO | STEEL N°12 SPECIAL | Ste Franc.se des MUNITIONS 12 12 |
| Chicago Cartridge Company. | | | 12 gauge. |
| USA | USA | USA | F/F |
| HSC.4,419. | HSC.4,420. | HSC.4,421. | HSC.4,422. |
| STE FSE DES MUNITIONS PARIS 12 12 | STE FSE DES MUNITIONS PARIS 12 12 | STEINBOCK 12 | STE L.CAFFORT MADE IN 12 12 BELGIUM SAIGON |
| | | Extra large cap. | |
| F/F | F/F | D | VN/B |
| HFC.2,216. | HFC.1,836. | HSC.4,423. | HSC.4,424. |
| STENSBY MANCHESTER N°12 ELEY | STENSBY MANCHESTER N°12 ELEY | N° STEPHEN·GRANT 12 LONDON | STEPHEN GRANT.LONDON N°12 |
| Gnm. Pre Wwl. | Gnm. | Gnm. | Gnm. Pre Wwl. |
| HFC.1,837. | HFC.1,838. | HFC.4,425/R. | HFC.4,426. |
| STEPHENS N°12 HORSHAM | STEPHENSON·STOKESLEY·N°12· | STERLING N°12 | STERLING 12 12 LONDON |
| H.Stephns. Irm. | North Yorkshire. | | 12 gauge. |
| GBE | GBE | GBE | GBE |
| HFC.1,839. | HSC.4,427. | HSC.4,428. | HSC.4,429. |

| | | | |
|---|---|---|---|
| (S.THORNLEY LTD No 12 BIRMINGHAM) | (STOEGER 12 12 NEW YORK) | (STOVIN No 12 GRANTHAM) | (SUPER 12 12 ALL METAL) |
| Ammo dealers. | | William Stovin.Gnm. | Alu.   12 gauge. |
| | 12 gauge only. | | |
| GBE | USA | GBE | AUS/AUS |
| HSC.4,430. | HSC.4,431. | HFC.1,840. | HFC.1,841. |
| (SUPER 12 12 EXPRESS) | (SUPER 12 12 EXPRESS) | (SUPER DD 12 12 MADE IN HOLAND) | (SUPERIOR 12 12 CANADA) |
| | Pla. | Alu. | Pla. |
| | | | |
| AUS/AUS | | NL/NL | CDN |
| HSC.4,432. | HSC.4,433. | HFC.1,842. | HSC.4,434. |
| (SUPERIOR No 12 GUARANTEED) | (SUPERIOR No 12 GUARANTEED) | (SUPERIOR No 12 MOGUL) | (SUPER 12 12 STAR) |
| | | | Pla. |
| | | | |
| HSC.4,435. | HFC.1,847. | HFC.1,848. | HFC.1,843. |
| (SUPER STAR 12 12 SWEDEN) | (SUPER 12 12 SUPER) | (SUPER 12 12 SUPER) | (SUPERTUNET 12) |
| Pla. 12 gauge. | Alu. | Alu. | Pla. 12 gauge. |
| | | | |
| S/S | AUS/AUS | AUS/AUS | |
| HFC.1,844. | HFC.1,846. | HFC.1,845. | HFC.1,850. |

| | | | |
|---|---|---|---|
| SUPERTUNET 12 | SUPER XL 12 12 | SUPREME 12 12 SPC | SWARTKLIP 12 |
| 12 gauge. Pla. | | Pla. | 12 gauge. Pla. |
| | CDN | | ZA |
| HFC.1,849. | HSC.4,436. | HSC.4,437. | HFC.1,852. |
| SWEET HOME CART CO. No 12 SWEET HOME.OR. | S W F 12 12 USA | S & W-F 12 12 USA | S.W.SILVER & Co No 12 LONDON |
| Rare when new. | Post Ww2. | | Remains found in IND |
| USA | USA | USA | GBE |
| HSC.4,438. | HFC.1,853. | HSC.4,439. | HSC.4,440. |
| S & W 12 12 USA | SYKES & SONS No 12 OLDHAM | SYKES & SONS No 12 OLDHAM | S.C.CO No 10 |
| Smith & Wesson. | Robert Sykes & Sons | 12 gauge. | 10 gauge. |
| On other gauges. | | | 12. |
| USA | GBE | GBE | USA |
| HFC.1,851. | HFC.1,854. | HFC.1,855. | HSC.4,441. |
| S.C.CO x x No 10 | No SELBY ELECTRIC 10 W W.R.A.CO. | S.G No 10 | SPECIAL No. 10 |
| Southern Ct'ge Co. | Case by W.R.A.Co. | 10 gauge. | Standard Ct'ge Co. |
| 12. | 12. | | 12. |
| USA | USA | | USA |
| HSC.4,442. | HSC.4,443. | HSC.4,444. | HSC.4,445. |

| | | | |
|---|---|---|---|
| SQ № 10 | ST № 10 | STANDARD 10 | STANDARD № 10 |
| Winchester. | 10 gauge. | A.L. Howard & Co. | 10 gauge. |
| 12. | | | |
| | USA | USA | USA |
| HSC.4,446. | HSC.4,447. | HFC.4,448. | HSC.4,449. |
| STANDARD 10 PAT'D NOV '75 A | STANDARD 10 PAT'D NOV '75 A | SK * * 8 | SWARTKLIP 8 8 KILN |
| 10 gauge. | 10 gauge. | 8 gauge. | 8 gauge. |
| | | | |
| | USA | | ZA |
| HSC.4,450. | HSC.4,451. | HSC.4,452. | HSC.4,453. |

| |
|---|
| Soe Fse des MUNITIONS 4 4 |
| 4 gauge. |
| |
| F/F |
| HSC.4,454. |

287

| | | | |
|---|---|---|---|
| 28 gauge. Gnm. | 20 gauge. Gnm. | | Ammunition Co. |
| | 16. | 16. | 16. |
| GBE/F | GBE | | USA |
| HFC.4,455. | HFC.405. | HSC.4,456. | HSC.4,457. |
| 20 gauge. Adv. | 20 gauge. Gnm. | 16 gauge. Gnm. | 16 gauge. |
| 16. | | 20. | |
| D | GBE/GBE | GBE | |
| HFC.4,458. | HFC.406. | HFC.582. | HSC.4,459. |
| 16 gauge. | | | |
| 12. | 12. | 12. | |
| | D | D | AUS |
| HFC.583. | HSC.4,460. | HSC.4,461. | HSC.4,462. |
| 16 gauge. | | | 16 gauge. Adv. |
| | | | 12. |
| AUS | USA | | D |
| HSC.4,463. | HSC.4,464. | HFC.584. | HSC.4,465. |

| | | | |
|---|---|---|---|
| (TRENT 16 16 TRENT-GRIMSBY) | (TURNER CASE MADE 16 16 IN FRANCE READING) | (TURNER.READING&NEWBURY N°16 ELEY) | (TURNER&SONS.READING N°16 ELEY) |
| Ct'ge loadings. | 16 gauge. Gnm. | Gnm. Pre Ww1. | Gnm. Pre Ww1. |
| 12. | 14.12. | 12. | |
| GBE/? | GBE/F | GBE/GBE | GBE/GBE |
| HFC.585. | HFC.4,466. | HFC.586. | HSC.4,467. |
| (T.W.MURRAY&Co ESTABLISHED 1828 N° 16 CORK) | (T.Y.K. TOKYO 16 16 PHEASANT) | (TURNER.READING&NEWBURY N°14) | (TURNER CASE MADE 14 14 IN FRANCE READING) |
| 16 gauge. Gnm. | 16 gauge. | 14 gauge. Gnm. | 14 gauge. Gnm. |
| 12. | | | 16,12. |
| IRL | J/J | GBE | GBE/F |
| HSC.4,468. | HSC.4,469. | HFC.4,470. | HFC.626. |
| (TAITAL SUDAN 12) | (TARDY 12 12 BEAUREPAIRE) | (TARGET 12.G. 12.G. N.Z.) | (TARRANT N° 12 CAMBRIDGE) |
| 12 ga'. Post Ww2. | Pla. | Post Ww2. | Elijah Tarrant. |
| | | | |
| SUD | F | NZ | GBE |
| HFC.1,856. | HSC.4,471. | HFC.1,857. | HFC.1,858. |
| (TAYLOR.LANCASTER&Co MELBOURNE N°12 ELEY) | (TAYLOR&SONS N°12 PENZANCE) | (T.BLAND&SONS.LONDON N°12) | (T.DAINTITH N°12 ELEY WARRINGTON) |
| 12 gauge. | S.R.Taylor & Sons. | Gnm. | Gnm. 12 gauge. |
| | | | |
| GBE/GBE | GBE | GBE | GBE/GBE |
| HSC.4,472. | HFC.1,859. | HFC.1,860. | HFC.1,861. |

| | | | |
|---|---|---|---|
| TEC ☆ ☆ 12 | TEC ☆ ☆ CAL 12 | TEC 12 12 TEC | "TELL" 12 12 DURLACH |
| 12 gauge. | | Pla. | 12 gauge. |
| | | 16. | 16. |
| | | | D |
| HSC.4,473. | HSC.4,475. | HSC.4,476. | HSC.4,477. |
| TEMA 12 12 TEMA | TEMA 12 12 TEMA | TEMPLE & Co No 12 BASINGSTOKE | TEUTONIA 12 12 M.W.S. |
| Pla. | Pla. | Irm, Pre Wwl. | |
| | | | 16. |
| | | GBE | D |
| HFC.1,862. | HFC.1,863. | HFC.1,864. | HSC.4,478. |
| T.HEATHMAN No 12 CREDITON | THE BOOMERANG 12 | THE BOOMERANG 12 | THE CLUB No 12 CARTRIDGE |
| Gun shop. | | | |
| | | | |
| GBE | AUS | AUS | GBE |
| HFC.1,865. | HSC.4,479. | HSC.4,480. | HFC.1,866. |
| THE CLUB No 12 SPECIAL | THE COLONIAL AMUNITION Co Ld EB No 12 | THE NORMAL POWDER SYNDICATE ELEY No 12 | T.HEPPLESTONE KYNOCH'S PATENT No 12 GROUSE EJECTOR MANCHESTER |
| 12 gauge. | Eley Bros case. | Eley Bros case. | Gnm, Kynoch Ejt. |
| | | | |
| NZ | NZ/GBE | GBE/GBE | |
| HSC.4,481. | HSC.4,482. | HSC.4,483. | HFC.1,867. |

| | | | |
|---|---|---|---|
| Garnet, Herts. | Joyce cartridge. | No gauge size. | W.H.C.Thurman.Irm. |
| | | | |
| GBE/GBE | GBE | GBE | GBE |
| HFC.1,868. | HFC.4,484. | HFC.1,869/R. | HFC.4,485. |
| | | | |
| Pre Wwl. | Robin Hood. Ammo. | | |
| | | | |
| GBE/GBE | | GBE | GBE/GBE |
| HFC.4,486. | HSC.4,487. | HFC.1,870. | HFC.1,871. |
| | | | |
| 12 gauge. | | | Gnm. |
| | | GBW | GBE |
| HSC.4,488. | HSC.4,489. | HFC.1,872. | HSC.4,490. |
| | | | |
| Thomas & Son.Gnm. | Thomas J. Gnm. | Irm. Pre Wwl. | 12 gauge. |
| | | | |
| GBE/GBE | GBE | GBE/GBE | D |
| HSC.4,491. | HFC.4,492. | HFC.4,493. | HSC.4,494. |

291

| | | | |
|---|---|---|---|
| T.PAGE-WOOD No12 BRISTOL | T.PAGE-WOOD. BRISTOL. No12 ELEY | T.PAGE WOOD & Co. BRISTOL. No12 | T.P.WOOD & Co. BRISTOL & CARDIFF No12 |
| 12 gauge, Gnm. | Gnm. | Gnm. | 12 gauge, Gnm. |
| GBE | GBE/GBE | GBE | GBE and GBW |
| HFC.1,873. | HSC.4,495. | HSC.4,496. | HFC.1,874. |
| T.POWELL & Co Ld No12 SALISBURY | T.POWELL & Co Ld No12 ELEY SALISBURY | TREFF 12 12 JB | TRENT MADE IN BELGIUM 12 12 FAIRFIELD-GRIMSBY |
| Explosives merchants at Bemerton. | | Adv. 16. | 12 gauge. |
| GBE | GBE/GBE | D | GB/B |
| HFC.2,217. | HFC.4,497. | HSC.4,498. | HFC.1,880. |
| TRENT 12 12 GRIMSBY | TRENT 12 12 GRIMSBY | TRENT 12 12 GRIMSBY | TRENT 12 12 GRIMSBY |
| | Trent Gun & Cartridge Works. | | |
| GBE | GBE | GBE | GBE |
| HFC.1,877. | HFC.1,876. | HFC.1,875. | HFC.4,499. |
| TRENT MADE 12 12 IN ENGLAND | TRENT 12 12 MADE IN ENGLAND | TRENT FOREIGN MADE 12 12 TRENT-GRIMSBY | TRENT FOREIGN MADE 12 12 TRENT-GRIMSBY |
| 12 gauge. | Trent Gun & Cartridge Works. | | 12 gauge. |
| GBE/GBE | GBE/GBE | GBE/? | GBE/? |
| HFC.1,878. | HFC.1,879. | HFC.1,882. | HFC.1,881. |

| | | | |
|---|---|---|---|
| (TRENT FOREIGN MADE 12 12 LOADED IN ENGLAND TRENT-GRIMSBY) | (TRENT FOREIGN MADE 12 12 LOADED IN ENGLAND TRENT-GRIMSBY) | (TRENT MADE IN 12 12 BELGIUM TRENT-GRIMSBY) | (TREPCA 12 12 YU) |
| 12 gauge. | Trent Gun & Cartridge Works. | | 12 gauge. |
| | 16. | | |
| GBE/? | GBE/? | GBE/B | |
| HFC.1,883. | HFC.1,884. | HFC.1,885. | HFC.1,886. |
| (TRI-TEST PAT 12 PEND) | (TROISDORF 12) | (TROPICAL 12 12 C.B.C.) | (TRULOCK & HARRIS, DUBLIN ·12·) |
| Apc. | | | Gnm. |
| | | BR | IRL |
| HSC.4,500. | HFC.4,501. | HSC.4,502. | HSC.4,503. |
| (TRULOCK & HARRIS, DUBLIN No 12) | (TRULOCK & HARRIS, DUBLIN No 12) | (TRULOCK & HARRIS, DUBLIN No 12) | (TRULOCK & HARRIS, DUBLIN KYNOCH No 12) |
| Gnm. | Gnm. | Gnm. | Gnm, Kynoch case. |
| IRL | IRL | IRL | IRL/GBE |
| HFC.1,887. | HFC.4,504. | HFC.4,505. | HFC.1,888. |
| (TRULOCK & HARRIS, DUBLIN KYNOCH PATENT GROUSE EJECTOR No 12) | (TRUST 12 12 EIBAR) | (TRUST CAL 12 EIBAR) | (T. TURNER & SONS No 12 READING) |
| Gnm. Kynoch Ejt. | Post Ww2. | Pla. | Gnm. Pre Ww1. |
| IRL/GBE | E | E | GBE |
| HFC.1,889. | HSC.4,506. | HFC.1,890. | HSC.4,507. |

| | | | |
|---|---|---|---|
| TUNET 12 | TUNET 12 12 | TUNET 12 12 TUNET | TURNBULL No 12 BRIDGNORTH |
| Post Ww2. | Pla. | Pla. | 12 gauge. |
| | | | GBE |
| HFC.1,891. | HFC.1,893. | HFC.1,892. | HSC.4,508. |
| TURNBULL No 12 JOYCE BRIDGNORTH | TURNER CASE MADE 12 12 IN FRANCE READING | TURNER CASE MADE 12 12 IN FRANCE READING | TURNER. READING & NEWBURY No12 |
| Case by F.Joyce. | Thos Turner. Gnm. 16,14. | Wonder ct'ge. | Gnm. |
| GBE/GBE | GBE/F | GBE/F | GBE |
| HSC.4,509. | HFC.1,894. | HFC.1,895. | HFC.1,896. |
| TURNER READING & NEWBURY No12 | TURNER. READING & NEWBURY ELEY No12 | TURNER.READING& NEWBURY No12 T.ELEY | TURNER. READING & NEWBURY No12 T.ELEY |
| Gnm. | Thomas Turner. Gnm. | Gnm. | Gnm. |
| GBE | GBE/GBE | GBE/GBE | GBE/GBE |
| HFC.1,897. | HSC.4,510. | HFC.1,899. | HFC.1,898. |
| TURNER READING & NEWBURY KYNOCH No.12 | TURNER.READING& NEWBURY KYNOCH'S PATENT GROUSE No 2090 No.12 | T. TURNER & SONS No 12 READING | TURNER & SONS. READING No.12 |
| Gnm. Kynoch case. | Gnm. Kynoch Ejt. | Gnm. Prior 1890. | Gnm. 12 gauge. |
| GBE/GBE | GBE/GBE | GBE | GBE |
| HFC.1,900. | HFC.1,901. | HFC.4,511/R. | HSC.4,512. |

| | | | |
|---|---|---|---|
| (Turner & Sons Reading No 12 Eley) | (T. Warnock 12 12 Benalla) | (T.W. Murray & Co No 12 Cork) | (T.W. Murray & Co 12 12 Cork) |
| Thos Turner & Sons. | Private shell. | Gnm. | Gnm. |
| 16. | | | |
| GBE/GBE | AUS | IRL | IRL |
| HSC.4,513. | HFC.1,902. | HSC.4,514. | HSC.4,515. |
| (T.W. Murray & Co Established 1828 No 12 Cork) | (T.W. Murray & Co Established 1828 12 12 Cork) | (T.Y.K. Tokyo 12 12 Gastight) | (TYK 12 12 TYK) |
| Gnm. | Gnm. | | 12 gauge. |
| 16. | | | |
| IRL | IRL | J/J | J/J |
| HFC.1,903. | HFC.1,904. | HSC.4,516. | HSC.4,517. |
| (T.Y.K. 12 12 T.Y.K.) | (Tyler No 12 Highbridge) | (Taylor No 10 Chicago) | (T.E.I. No 10) |
| 12 gauge. | Gun dealer. | 10 gauge. | 10 gauge. |
| | | 10 gauge only. | |
| J/J | GBE | USA | USA |
| HSC.4,518. | HFC.1,905. | HSC.4,519. | HSC.4,520. |

295

| | | | |
|---|---|---|---|
| ·410. | United States Cartridge Company. | | 32 gauge. |
| | 32. | | ·410. |
| USA/USA | USA/USA | USA/USA | USA/USA |
| HSC.4,521. | HSC.4,522. | HSC.4,523. | HSC.4,524. |
| 28 gauge. | 24 gauge. | 24 gauge. | 20 gauge. |
| 24,20.16,12,10. | 20,16,12,10. | 28,20,16,12,10. | |
| USA/USA | USA/USA | USA/USA | E |
| HSC.4,525. | HSC.4,526. | HSC.4,527. | HFC.407. |
| 20 gauge. | Union Metallic Cartridge Company. | | |
| 16,14,12,10, 8, 2. | | | 16,14,12,10. |
| USA/USA | USA/USA | USA/USA | USA/USA |
| HSC.4,528. | HSC.4,529. | HSC.4,530. | HSC.4,531. |
| 20 gauge. | Union Metallic Cartridge Company. | | 20 gauge. |
| | 16,12,10. | | |
| USA/USA | USA/USA | USA/USA | USA/USA |
| HSC.4,532. | HSC.4,533. | HSC.4,534. | HSC.4,535. |

| | | | |
|---|---|---|---|
| 20 gauge. | Union Metallic Cartridge Company. | | 20 gauge. |
| 24,16,12,10. | On other gauges. | 16,12,10. | |
| USA/USA | USA/USA | USA/USA | USA/USA |
| HSC.4.536. | HFC.4,537. | HSC.4,538. | HSC.4,539. |
| | United States Cartridge Company. | | Dished. |
| | 16,12. | | |
| USA/USA | USA/USA | USA/USA | USA/USA |
| HSC.4,540. | HSC.4,541. | HSC.4,542. | HSC.4,543. |
| | United States Cartridge Company. | | |
| 28,16,12. | | 16,12,10. | 16,12,10,8. |
| USA/USA | USA/USA | USA/USA | USA/USA |
| HSC.4.544. | HFC.408. | HSC.4,546. | HFC.4,547. |
| 20 gauge, | United States Cartridge Company. | 20 gauge. | 18 gauge. |
| | 16,12. | 16,14,12,10. | On other gauges. |
| USA/USA | USA/USA | USA/USA | USA/USA |
| HFC.4,548. | HSC.4,549. | HFC.4,550. | HFC.2.146. |

| | | | |
|---|---|---|---|
| (U.M.C.Co. No. 16) | (U.M.C.Co. No.16.) | (U.M.C.Co. No 16 BLACK CLUB) | (U.M.C.Co. No 16 CHALLENGE) |
| 16 gauge. | Union Metallic Cartridge Company. | | 16 gauge. |
| 20,14,12,10,8,2. | | 20,14,12,10. | |
| USA/USA | USA/USA | USA/USA | USA/USA |
| HSC.4,551. | HSC.4,552. | HSC.4,553. | HSC.4,555. |
| (U.M.C.Co. No 16 HIGH-BASE) | (U.M.C.Co. No 16 MAGIC) | (U.M.C.Co. No 16 MAJESTIC) | (U.M.C.Co. No 16 MAJESTIC) |
| | Union Metallic Cartridge Company. | | |
| 12. | 12,10,8. | 12,10. | 20,12,10. |
| USA/USA | USA/USA | USA/USA | USA/USA |
| HFC.587. | HFC.588. | HSC.4,556. | HSC.4,557. |
| (U.M.C.Co. No 16 NEW CLUB) | (U.M.C.Co. No 16 NITRO) | (U.M.C.Co. No 16 NITRO CLUB) | (U.M.C.Co. No 16 NITRO CLUB) |
| | Union Metallic Cartridge Company. | | |
| | 20,12,10. | 24,20,12,10. | 28,24,20,12,10. |
| USA/USA | USA/USA | USA/USA | USA/USA |
| HFC.589. | HFC.590. | HSC.4,558. | HSC.4,559. |
| (U.M.C.Co. No 16 PRIMROSE CLUB) | (U.M.C.Co. No 16 UNION) | (U.M.C.Co. No 16 WALSRODE) | (No.16 U S AJAX) |
| 16 gauge. | Union Metallic Cartridge Company. | | 16 gauge. |
| 20,12,10. | | 12,10. | 20,12,14. |
| USA/USA | USA/USA | USA/USA | USA/USA |
| HSC.4,560. | HFC.591. | HSC.4,561. | HSC.4,562. |

| | | | |
|---|---|---|---|
| 16 gauge. | United States Cartridge Co. | | 16 gauge. |
| 20,12. | | | 12,10. |
| USA/USA | USA/USA | USA/USA | USA/USA |
| HSC.4,563. | HSC.4,564. | HSC.4,565. | HSC.4,566. |
| | United States Cartridge Company. | | |
| 12,10. | 20,12,10. | 20,12,10,8. | 12,10. |
| USA/USA | USA/USA | USA/USA | USA/USA |
| HSC.4,567. | HSC.4,568. | HFC.4,569. | HSC.4,570. |
| 16 gauge. | 16 gauge. | 14 gauge. | 14 gauge. |
| 20,14,12,10. | 12,10. | 20,16,12,10,8,2. | |
| USA/USA | USA/USA | USA/USA | USA/USA |
| HFC.4,571. | HSC.4,572. | HSC.4,573. | HSC.4,574. |
| 14 gauge. | Union Metallic Cartridge Co. | | 14 gauge. |
| 20,16,12,10. | 12. | | |
| USA/USA | USA/USA | USA/USA | USA/USA |
| HSC.4,575. | HSC.4,576. | HSC.4,577. | HSC.4,578. |

| | | | |
|---|---|---|---|
| 14 gauge. | | 14 gauge. | 13B gauge. |
| | 20,16,12,10. | 12. | |
| USA/USA | USA/USA | USA/USA | USA/USA |
| HSC.4,579. | HFC.4,580. | HSC.4,581. | HFC.628. |
| 12 gauge. | Post Ww2. | Manufacturer. | 12 gauge. |
| | | | |
| E/E | E/E | E/E | E/E |
| HFC.1,906. | HFC.1,907. | HSC.4,582. | HSC.4,583. |
| John Uglow. Gnm. | Union Metallic Cartridge Company. | | |
| | 20,16,14,10,8,2. | | |
| GBE | USA/USA | USA/USA | USA/USA |
| HFC.1,908. | HSC.4,584. | HSC.4,585. | HSC.4,586. |
| 12 gauge. | Manufacturer. | | 12 gauge. |
| | | | |
| USA/USA | USA/USA | USA/USA | USA/USA |
| HFC.1,909. | HFC.1,910. | HFC.1,911. | HSC.4,587. |

|  |  |  |  |
|---|---|---|---|
|  | 12 gauge. | Union Metallic Cartridge Company. |  | 12 gauge. |
| USA/USA | USA/USA | USA/USA | USA/USA |
| HSC.4,588. | HSC.4,589. | HFC.1,912. | HFC.1,914. |
|  |  |  |  |
|  | Steel head. | Manufacturer. |  |
| USA/USA | USA/USA | USA/USA | USA/USA |
| HFC.1,913. | HFC.4,590. | HSC.4,591. | HFC.2,219. |
|  |  |  |  |
|  | Union Metallic Cartridge Company. |  |  |
| USA/USA | USA/USA | USA/USA | USA/USA |
| HSC.4,592. | HFC.1,915. | HFC.1,916. | HFC.1,917. |
|  |  |  |  |
| 12 gauge. |  | Manufacturer. | 12 gauge. |
|  |  |  | 20,24,16,14,10. |
| USA/USA | USA/USA | USA/USA | USA/USA |
| HFC.1,918. | HFC.1,919. | HFC.1,920. | HFC.1,921. |

| | | | |
|---|---|---|---|
| NITRO CLUB | NITRO CLUB | NITRO CLUB | NORMAL NIMROD |
| 12 gauge. | Union Metallic Cartridge Company. | | 12 gauge. |
| 24,20,16,10. | | 16,10. | |
| USA/USA | USA/USA | USA/USA | USA/USA |
| HFC.4,593. | HFC.1,922. | HSC.4,594. | HSC.4,595. |
| NORMAL NIMROD | PRIMROSE CLUB | SEIBOLD'S PATENT | S.G. |
| | Manufacturer. | | |
| 12 gauge only. | | | 10. |
| USA/USA | USA/USA | USA/USA | USA/USA |
| HSC.4,596. | HFC.1,923. | HSC.4,957. | HSC.4,598. |
| SMOKELESS | SMOKELESS | STAR | STAR |
| | Union Metallic Cartridge Company. | | |
| USA/USA | USA/USA | USA/USA | USA/USA |
| HFC.1,924. | HSC.4,599. | HSC.4,600. | HSC.4,601. |
| TRAP | UNION | UNION | V.L.&D. |
| 12 gauge. | | Manufacturer. | 12 gauge. |
| 10,8. | | | 10. |
| USA/USA | USA/USA | USA/USA | USA/USA |
| HSC.4,602. | HFC.1,925. | HFC.2,220 | HSC.4,603. |

| | | | |
|---|---|---|---|
| U.M.C.Co. No 12 WALSRODE | UNIFRANCE 12 | UNIFRANCE 12 12 CHEDDITE | UNION EXTRA 12 12 MEXICO |
| 12 gauge. | Post Ww2, Pla. | Post Ww2. | 12 gauge, Pla. |
| 16,10. | | | |
| USA/USA | F | F | MEX |
| HSC.4,604. | HFC.4,605. | HFC.1,926. | HSC.4,606. |
| UNION EXTRA 12+2 12+2 MEXICO | UNION 12 12 MEXICO | No.12 U S AJAX | No.12 U S AJAX |
| | Pla. | United States | Cartridge Co. |
| | | 20,16.10. | |
| MEX | MEX | USA/USA | USA/USA |
| HSC.4,607. | HSC.4,608. | HSC.4,609. | HFC.1,927. |
| No.12 MADE IN USA U S AJAX | No.12 U S CLIMAX | No.12 U S CLIMAX | No.12 U S CLIMAX |
| | Manufacturer. | | |
| 20,16. | | | |
| USA/USA | USA/USA | USA/USA | USA/USA |
| HSC.4,610. | HFC.1,928. | HFC.1,929. | HFC.1,930. |
| No.12.S U CONICAL CLIMAX | No.12 MADE IN USA U S CLIMAX | No.12 U S DEFIANCE | No.12 U S DEFIANCE |
| 12 gauge. | United States | Cartridge Co. | 12 gauge. |
| 10. | 28,20,16. | 16,10. | |
| USA/USA | USA/USA | USA/USA | USA/USA |
| HSC.4,611. | HSC.4,612. | HSC.4,613. | HFC.4,614. |

| | | | |
|---|---|---|---|
| 12 gauge. | United States Cartridge Company. | | 12 gauge. |
| | | | 12 gauge only. |
| USA/USA | USA/USA | USA/USA | USA/USA |
| HFC.2,221 | HFC.2,222. | HSC.4,615. | HSC.4,616. |
| | Manufacturer. | | |
| 16,10. | | 20,16,10. | |
| USA/USA | USA/USA | USA/USA | USA/USA |
| HSC.4,617. | HSC.4,618. | HSC.4,619. | HFC.1,931. |
| Walsrode powder. | United States Cartridge Company. | | |
| | | 20,16,10,8. | |
| USA/USA | USA/USA | USA/USA | USA/USA |
| HFC.4,620. | HSC.4,621. | HFC.4,622. | HFC.4,623. |
| 12 gauge. | | Manufacturer. | 12 gauge. |
| 10. | 14. | 10. | 10. |
| USA/USA | USA/USA | USA/USA | USA/USA |
| HFC.4,624. | HSC.4,625. | HSC.4,626. | HSC.4,627. |

| | | | |
|---|---|---|---|
| U.S.C.Co. No 12 STAR | U.S.SECOND No 12 QUALITY | UZ 2 12 ? 12 OR STALIN | U F No 10 |
| 12 gauge. | | 12 gauge. | 10 gauge. |
| | | | |
| USA/USA | USA/USA | | USA |
| HFC.4,628. | HSC.4,629. | HSC.4,630. | HSC.4,631. |
| U.M.C.Co. No 10 | UMC No 10 | U.M.C.Co. No 10 A | U.M.C.Co. No 10 ACME |
| Union Metallic Cartridge Company. ||||
| 20,16,14,12,8,2. | | | 20,12. |
| USA/USA | USA/USA | USA/USA | USA/USA |
| HSC.4,632. | HSC.4,633. | HFC.2,099. | HSC.4,634. |
| U.M.C.Co. No 10 BLACK CLUB | U.M.C.Co. BRIDGEPORT.CONN 10 A | U.M.C.Co. No 10 BRIDGEPORT.CONN | U.M.C.Co. BRIDGEPORT.CONN 10 A |
| | | Manufacturer. | |
| 20,16,14,12. | | | |
| USA/USA | USA/USA | USA/USA | USA/USA |
| HSC.4,635. | HSC.4,636. | HSC.4,637. | HSC.4,638. |
| U.M.C.Co. No 10 BRIDGEPORT.CT. | UMC No 10 CLUB | U.M.C.Co. No 10 CLUB | U.M.C.Co. No 10 FIELD |
| 10 gauge. | Manufacturer. | | 10 gauge. |
| | | 12. | 10 gauge only. |
| USA/USA | USA/USA | USA/USA | USA/USA |
| HSC.4,639. | HSC.4,640. | HSC.4,641. | HSC.4,642. |

| | | | |
|---|---|---|---|
| U.M.C.CO. No 10 HIGH BASE | U.M.C.CO. No 10 MAGIC | U.M.C.CO. No 10 MAGIC | U.M.C.CO. No 10 MAJESTIC |
| 10 gauge. | Union Metallic Cartridge Company. | | 10 gauge. |
| | | | 20,16,12. |
| USA/USA | USA/USA | USA/USA | USA/USA |
| HSC.4,643. | HSC.4,644. | HSC.4,645. | HSC.4,646. |
| U.M.C.CO. No 10 NEW CLUB | U.M.C.CO. No 10 NEW CLUB SS | U.M.C.CO. No 10 NEW CLUB SS | U.M.C.CO. No 10 NITRO |
| | | Manufacturer. | |
| 12. | | | |
| USA/USA | USA/USA | USA/USA | USA/USA |
| HSC.4,647. | HSC.4,648. | HSC.4,649. | HSC.4,650. |
| U.M.C.CO. No 10 NITRO | U.M.C.CO. No 10 NITRO CLUB | U.M.C.CO. No 10 NITRO CLUB | U.M.C.CO. No 10 NITRO CLUB |
| | Union Metallic Cartridge Company. | | |
| | 24,20,16,12. | 28,24,20,16,12. | 16,12. |
| USA/USA | USA/USA | USA/USA | USA/USA |
| HSC.4,651. | HSC.4,652. | HSC.4,653. | HSC.4,654. |
| U.M.C.CO. No 10 PRIMROSE CLUB | U.M.C. No 10 SEIBOLDS PATENT | U.M.C.CO. No 10 SMOKELESS | U.M.C. No 10 STAR |
| 10 gauge. | Manufacturer. | | 10 gauge. |
| 20,16,12. | | | 12. |
| USA/USA | USA/USA | USA/USA | USA/USA |
| HSC.4,655. | HSC.4,656. | HFC.2,100. | HSC.4,657. |

| | | | |
|---|---|---|---|
| (TRAP) | (UNION) | (V.L.&D.) | (WALSRODE) |
| 10 gauge. | Union Metallic Cartridge Company. | | 10 gauge. |
| 12,8. | | 12. | 16,12. |
| USA/USA | USA/USA | USA/USA | USA/USA |
| HSC.4,658. | HFC.2,101. | HSC.4,659. | HSC.4,660. |
| (U.M.C.Co. No.10 XX) | (U.M.C. X X 10) | (U.M.C. No.10 XX) | (AJAX) |
| | Manufacturer. | | |
| | | | 20,16,12. |
| USA/USA | USA/USA | USA/USA | USA/USA |
| HSC.4,661. | HSC.4,662. | HSC.4,663. | HSC.4,664. |
| (CLIMAX) | (CLIMAX) | (CONICAL CLIMAX) | (DEFIANCE) |
| | United States Cartridge Company. | | |
| | | 12. | 16,12. |
| USA/USA | USA/USA | USA/USA | USA/USA |
| HSC.4,665. | HSC.4,666. | HSC.4,667. | HSC.4,668. |
| (NEWMAX) | (NEW RAPID) | (ROMAX) | (U.S.C.Co. NO.10) |
| 10 gauge. | Manufacturer. | | 10 gauge. |
| 16,12. | | 20,16,12. | 20,16,12,8. |
| USA/USA | USA/USA | USA/USA | USA/USA |
| HSC.4,669. | HSC.4,670. | HSC.4,671. | HSC.4,672. |

| | | | |
|---|---|---|---|
| (CLIMAX headstamp) | (FIRST headstamp) | (LOWELL headstamp) | (LOWELL headstamp) |
| 10 gauge. | United States Cartridge Company. | | 10 gauge. |
| 20,16,14,12. | 12. | 14,12. | |
| USA/USA | USA/USA | USA/USA | USA/USA |
| HFC.4,673. | HSC.4,674. | HSC.4,675. | HFC.4,676. |
| (SECOND headstamp) | (STAR headstamp) | (STAR headstamp) | (XX headstamp) |
| | Manufacturer. | | |
| 12. | | 12. | 12. |
| USA/USA | USA/USA | USA/USA | USA/USA |
| HSC.4,677. | HFC.4,678. | HFC.4,679. | HSC.4,680. |
| (USE BERDAN PRIMER No1 10A headstamp) | (USA BERDAN PRIMER No1 10A headstamp) | (U.S.CARTRIDGE CO. LOWELL MASS 10A headstamp) | (U.S.CARTRIDGE CO. XOX LOWELL MASS 10A headstamp) |
| | | Manufacturer. | |
| | | | |
| USA/USA | USA/USA | USA/USA | USA/USA |
| HFC.2,102. | HSC.4,681. | HSC.4,682. | HSC.4,683. |
| (U.S. SECOND QUALITY No 10 headstamp) | (U.M.C.Co. No 8 headstamp) | (U.M.C.Co. No 8 headstamp) | (U.M.C.Co. No.8A headstamp) |
| 10 gauge. | 8 gauge. | | 8 gauge. |
| | On other gauges. | | |
| USA/USA | USA/USA | USA/USA | USA/USA |
| HSC.4,684. | HSC.4,685. | HSC.4,686. | HSC.4,687. |

| | | | |
|---|---|---|---|
| U.M.C.Co. No 8 MAGIC | U.M.C.Co. No 8 TRAP | U.S.C.Co. NO.8. | U.M.C.Co. No 4 |
| 8 gauge. | Manufacturer. | 8 gauge. | 4 gauge. |
| | 12,10. | 20,16,12,10. | |
| USA/USA | USA/USA | USA/USA | USA/USA |
| HSC.4,688. | HSC.4,689. | HSC.4,690. | HSC.4,691. |

Two of the many ironmongers shops that once sold cartridges.
Top photo. DALE & CO. 134-135 High Street, Marlborough, Wilts.
Bottom photo. F. G. WOODROW, High Street, Brandon, Suffolk.
At one time James Woodrow was in the High Street and Fred G. Woodrow was in the London Road.  Circa; Top 1916. Bottom 1905.

| | | | |
|---|---|---|---|
| 20 gauge. | 16 gauge. | | 16 gauge. |
| On other gauges. | | On other gauges. | |
| D/D | D/D | D/D | USA/USA |
| HSC.4,692. | HSC.4,693. | HSC.4,694. | HSC.4,695. |
| 16 gauge. | 12 gauge. | | 12 gauge. |
| | GBE | USA | USA/USA |
| HSC.4,696. | HSC.4,697. | HSC.4,698. | HSC.4,699. |
| | | Gnm. | Gnm. |
| D | BR | GBE | GBE/F |
| HSC.4,700. | HSC.4,701. | HFC.1,932. | HFC.1,933. |
| 12 gauge. Gnm. | Gnm. | Kynoch made case. | 12 gauge. Gnm. |
| GBE/GBE | GBE/? | GBE/GBE | GBE/F |
| HFC.4,702. | HSC.4,703. | HFC.1,934. | HSC.4,704. |

| | | | |
|---|---|---|---|
| (VERAPLAST 12) | (VEREINIGTE KÖLN-ROTTWEIL PULVERFABRIKEN) | (VEREINIGTE KÖLN-ROTTWEILER PULVEREABRIKEN) | (VERNEY-CARRON 12) |
| 12 gauge, Pla. | | | 12 gauge. Pla. |
| | On other gauges. | On other gauges. | |
| | D | D | |
| HSC.4,705. | HSC.4,706. | HFC.1,935. | HSC.4,707. |
| (C.V.F.M&C. 12 L) | (tv 12 12 VICENZA) | (VICTORY 12 12) | (VIHTAVUORI -12-) |
| | | Post Ww2. Pla. | Post Ww2, Pla. |
| F | | CY/CY | |
| HSC.4,708. | HSC.4,709. | HFC.1,936. | HFC.1,938. |
| (VIHTAVUORI 12) | (VIKING 12 12 HUNTER) | (VIRI 12 12 CAL.12) | (VIRI 12 12 FRANCE) |
| Post Ww2., Pla. | Post Ww2, Pla. | Post Ww2. | Post Ww2, Pla. |
| | | F | F |
| HFC.1,937. | HFC.1,939. | HFC.1,940. | HFC.1,941. |
| (VON LENGERKE 12 12 DETMOLD) | (& VON LENGERKE W.R.A.CO. W No 12 DETMOLD) | (VOUZELAUD 12 12 BROU) | (VOUZELAUD 12 12 BROU) |
| 12 gauge. | | Post Ww2. | 12 gauge, Pla. |
| D | USA/USA | F | F |
| HSC.4,710. | HSC.4,711. | HSC.4,712. | HFC.1,942. |

| | | | |
|---|---|---|---|
| VOUZELAUD 12 12 BROU | VOUZELAUD 12 12 BROU | VULCAN 12 12 ESPAÑA | VULKAN 12 12 G.G.&Cº |
| 12 gauge, Pla. | Post Ww2. | Pla. | 12 gauge. |
| F | F | E | |
| HFC.1,944. | HFC.1,943. | HSC.4,713. | HFC.1,945. |
| V.F.M. Nº 10 | VICTOR Nº 10 L.B.&Cº | VICTOR Nº 10 L.B.&Cº | V.L&A. Nº 10 CHICAGO |
| Vitale Fwk Manu'f. | Lewis Brothers & Company. | | 10 gauge. |
| USA | CDN | CDN | USA/USA |
| HSC.4,714. | HSC.4,715. | HSC.4,716. | HSC.4,717. |
| V.L&D. Nº 10 KYNOCH | V.L&D. NEW YORK Nº 10 KYNOCH | VON LENGERKE W.R.A.CO. W Nº 10 & DETMOLD | V.L&D. NEWYORK Nº 8 KYNOCH |
| 10 gauge. | Von Lengerke & Detmold. | 10 gauge. | 8 gauge. |
| | | 10 gauge only. | |
| USA/GBE | USA/GBE | USA/USA | USA/GBE |
| HSC.4,718. | HFC.2,103. | HSC.4,719. | HFC.2,111. |

  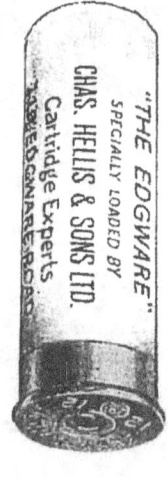  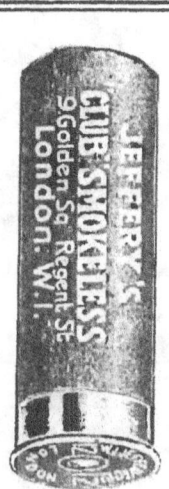  

| | | | |
|---|---|---|---|
| | | | |
| .410. | Western Cartridge Company. | | .410. |
| USA/USA | USA/USA | USA/USA | USA/USA |
| HSC.4,720. | HSC.4,721. | HFC.238. | HSC.4,722. |
| | | | |
| Western Cartridge Company. | | | Manufacturer. |
| USA/USA | USA/USA | USA/USA | USA/USA |
| HSC.4,723. | HSC.4,724. | HSC.4,725. | HSC.4,726. |
| | | | |
| Winchester Repeating Arms Company. | | | |
| USA/USA | USA/USA | USA/USA | USA/USA |
| HSC.4,727. | HSC.4,728. | HSC.4,729. | HSC.4,730. |
| | | | |
| .410. | Manufacturer. | .410. | Gnm. 32 gauge. |
| USA/USA | USA/USA | USA/USA | GBE |
| HSC.4,731. | HSC.4,732. | HFC.239. | HFC.245. |

| | | | |
|---|---|---|---|
| 28 gauge. | Western Cartridge Company. | | 28 gauge. |
| 20,16,12,10. | 20,16,12,10. | 20,16,12,10. | |
| USA/USA | USA/USA | USA/USA | USA/USA |
| HSC.4,735. | HSC.4,734. | HSC.4,733. | HSC.4,736. |
| 28 gauge, Pla. | Winchester Repeating Arms Co. | | 28 gauge, Pla. |
| USA/USA | USA/USA | USA/USA | USA/USA |
| HSC.4,737. | HSC.4,738. | HSC.4,739. | HFC.4.740. |
| 24 gauge. | Winchester Repeating Arms Co. | | Gnm, 24 gauge. |
| | | | On other gauges. |
| USA/USA | USA/USA | USA/USA | GBE |
| HSC.4,741. | HSC.4,742. | HSC.4,743. | HFC.273. |
| 20 gauge. | Apc. | Gnm. | 20 gauge. |
| | | | 28,16,12,10. |
| D | USA/USA | GBE | USA/USA |
| HSC.4,744. | HFC.4,745. | HFC.409. | HSC.4,746. |

| | | | |
|---|---|---|---|
| (Western Record No 20) | (Western Record Made in USA No 20) | (Western Super X Made in USA No 20) | (Western Xpert Made in USA No 20) |
| 20 gauge. | Western Cartridge Company. | | 20 gauge. |
| 16,12,10. | 16,12,10. | 28,16,12,10. | 28,16,12,10. |
| USA/USA | USA/USA | USA/USA | USA/USA |
| HSC.4,747. | HSC.4,748. | HSC.4,749. | HSC.4,750. |
| (Western Xpert Made in USA No 20) | (Westley Richards & Co Eley) | (Westley Richards Fauneta No 20) | (Westley Richards Knoch Patent Grouse Ejector London No 20) |
| Manufacturer. | Gnm. | Bullet load. | Gnm, Ejt. |
| 28,16,12,10. | On other gauges. | | |
| USA/USA | GBE/GBE | GBE/GBE | GBE/GBE |
| HFC.410. | HFC.411. | HSC.4,751. | HSC.4,752. |
| (W.H.Tisdall Ltd No 20 Wellington & Christchurch) | (W.H.Tisdall No 20 Wellington) | (Winchester No 20) | (Winchester 20 GA) |
| | | | Manufacturer. |
| | | 16,14,12,10,8,4. | On other gauges. |
| NZ | NZ | USA/USA | USA/USA |
| HSC.4,753. | HSC.4,754. | HSC.4,755. | HFC.413. |
| (Winchester No 20) | (Winchester Leader 20 GA) | (Winchester Nublack No 20) | (Winchester Nublack 20 GA) |
| 20 gauge. | Winchester Repeating Arms Company. | | 20 gauge. |
| On other gauges. | | 16,12,10. | 16,12,10. |
| USA/USA | USA/USA | USA/USA | USA/USA |
| HFC.412. | HSC.4,756. | HSC.4,757. | HSC.4,758. |

| | | | |
|---|---|---|---|
| (Winchester Ranger No 20) | (Winchester Ranger No 20) | (Winchester Ranger No 20) | (Winchester Repeater No 20) |
| 20 gauge. | Winchester Repeating Arms Company. | | 20 gauge. |
| USA/USA | USA/USA | USA/USA | USA/USA |
| HSC.4,759. | HSC.4,760. | HFC.4,761. | HSC.4,762. |
| (Winchester Super-Speed No 20 Made in Italy) | (Winchester Super Speed No 20 Made in U.S.A.) | (Winchester Western 20 GA) | (Winchester 20 20) |
| Pla. | | Manufacturer. | |
| | | | On other gauges. |
| I/I | USA/USA | USA/USA | USA/USA |
| HFC.414. | HFC.415. | HFC.416. | HFC.417. |
| (Winchester Yellow Rival No W 20) | (W.J.Jeffery & Co London No 20) | (W.J.Jeffery & Co No 20 E London) | (W.J.Jeffery & Co London Made in Belgium) |
| | Gnm. | Gnm. | Gnm. |
| 16,14,12,10. | | | |
| USA/USA | GBE | GBE/GBE | GBE/B |
| HSC.4,763. | HFC.418. | HSC.4,764. | HFC.4,765. |
| (W.Kavanagh & Son No 20 Kynoch Dublin) | (* 20 20 W.M.C.) | (Wolff & Co 20 20 Walsrode) | (W.R.A.Co No 20 XX) |
| 20 gauge, Gnm. | | | 20 gauge. |
| | | | 16,12,10. |
| IRL/GBE | | D | USA/USA |
| HSC.4,766. | HSC.4,767. | HSC.4,768. | HSC.4,769. |

| | | | |
|---|---|---|---|
| (W.R. PAPE No 20 NEWCASTLE) | (W.R. PAPE No 20 NEWCASTLE) | (W-W 20 GA AA) | (W-W 20 GAUGE) |
| 20 gauge, Gnm. | Gnm. | Manufacturer. | 20 gauge. |
| GBE | GBE | USA/USA | USA/USA |
| HFC.4,770. | HSC.4,771. | HFC.419. | HFC.420. |
| (W.W. GREENER No 20) | (WM 18 18 B) | (WM 18 18 AB) | (WALSRODE 16 SINOX 16 NORMAL) |
| 20 gauge, Gnm. | 18 gauge. | 18 gauge. | 16 gauge. |
| GBE | D | D | D/D |
| HSC.4,772. | HSC.4,773. | HSC.4,774. | HFC.592. |
| (WASAG 16 16 NORMAL) | (W.C.CO No 16 NEW CHIEF) | (W.DARLOW No 16 BEDFORD) | (W.E.EKINS.ADELAIDE No 16 ELEY) |
| | | Gnm. | |
| | USA/USA | GBE | AUS/GBE |
| HSC.4,775. | HSC.4,776. | HFC.593. | HFC.4,777. |
| (WESTERN No 16 FIELD) | (WESTERN No 16 MARVEL) | (WESTERN MADE IN U.S.A. No 16 RECORD) | (WESTERN No 16 CANADA SUPER-X) |
| 16 gauge. | | | 16 gauge. |
| On other gauges. | 12. | 20,12,10. | |
| USA/USA | USA/USA | USA/USA | CDN |
| HFC.594. | HSC.4,778. | HSC.4,779. | HSC.4,780. |

| | | | |
|---|---|---|---|
| (WESTERN SUPER-X No 16) | (WESTERN XPERT No 16) | (WESTERN XPERT No 16) | (WESTLEY RICHARDS & Co No 16 ELEY) |
| 16 gauge, | Western Cartridge Co. | | Gnm.   16 gauge. |
| On other gauges. | On other gauges. | 28,20,12,10. | |
| USA/USA | USA/USA | USA/USA | GBE/GBE |
| HFC.595. | HFC.4,781. | HSC.4,782 | HSC.4,783. |
| (W.GUTTLER PULVERFABRIKEN 16 16 REICHENSTEIN) | (WHITEHOUSE.OAKHAM No 16 ELEY) | (W.H.TISDALL No 16 WELLINGTON) | (W.H.TISDALL Ltd No 16 WELLINGTON & CHRISTCHURCH) |
| | Gnm. | | |
| D | GBE/GBE | NZ | NZ |
| HSC.4,784. | HSC.4,785. | HSC.4,786. | HSC.4,787. |
| (WILLIAMS & POWELL L'POOL No 16) | (WINCHESTER No.16) | (WINCHESTER No 16) | (WINCHESTER No 16) |
| Joyce made case. | Winchester Repeating Arms Co. | | |
| | | 20,14,12,10,8,4. | |
| GBE/GBE | USA/USA | USA/USA | USA/USA |
| HSC.4,788. | HSC.4,789. | HSC.4,790. | HSC.4,791. |
| (WINCHESTER No W 16 BLUE RIVAL) | (WINCHESTER No W 16 LEADER) | (WINCHESTER No 16 NEW RIVAL) | (WINCHESTER 16 GA NEW RIVAL) |
| 16 gauge. | Extra large cap. | Manufacturer. | 16 gauge. |
| USA/USA | USA/USA | USA/USA | USA/USA |
| HSC.4,792. | HSC.4,793. | HSC.4,794. | HSC.4,795. |

| | | | |
|---|---|---|---|
| (Winchester Nublack) | (Winchester Nublack) | (Winchester Repeater) | (Winchester Super-Speed) |
| 16 gauge. | Winchester Repeating Arms Company. | | 16 gauge. |
| 20,12,10. | 20,12,10. | | |
| USA/USA | USA/USA | USA/USA | I/I |
| HSC.4,796. | HSC.4,797. | HSC.4,798. | HFC.599. |
| (Winchester Western) | (Winchester Winchester) | (Winchester Wonder) | (Winchester Wonder) |
| | | Manufacturer. | |
| | | | 12. |
| USA/USA | USA/USA | USA/USA | USA/USA |
| HFC.598. | HFC.600. | HSC.4,799. | HSC.4,800. |
| (Winchester Yellow Rival) | (W.J. Jeffery & Co London) | (W.J. Jeffery & Co Ltd London) | (W.J. Jeffery & Co Ltd London) |
| | Case by Eley Bros. | Kynoch made case. | Gnm. |
| 20,14,12,10. | | | |
| USA/USA | GBE/GBE | GBE/GBE | GBE/? |
| HSC.4,801. | HFC.4,802. | HSC.4,803. | HFC.601. |
| (W. Locke & Co. Calcutta Eley) | (WM) | (Wm Richards Preston) | (Wolff & Co Walsrode) |
| 16 gauge. | | Gnm. | 16 gauge. |
| | 18. | | On other gauges. |
| IND/GBE | D | GBE | D |
| HSC.4,804. | HSC.4,805. | HFC.602. | HSC.4,806. |

| | | | |
|---|---|---|---|
| (Wolff & Co 16 16 Walsrode) | (Wolff & Co 16 16 Walsrode) | (Weston Brighton & Hailsham Kynoch No.16) | (W.R.A.Co No 16 XX) |
| 16 gauge. | | Gnm. | 16 gauge. |
| On other gauges. | On other gauges. | | 20,12,10. |
| D/D | D/D | GBE/GBE | USA/USA |
| HSC.4,807. | HSC.4,808. | HFC.597. | HSC.4,809. |
| (W.Richards Preston No 16 Eley) | (W.R.Pape No 16 Newcastle) | (W.R.Pape Newcastle No 16 Eley) | (W-W 16 Gauge) |
| Gnm. | Gnm. | Gnm. | Pla. |
| | | | On other gauges. |
| GBE/GBE | GBE | GBE/GBE | USA/USA |
| HSC.4,810. | HFC.604. | HFC.4,811. | HFC.605. |
| (W.W.Greener No 16) | (W.W.Greener No 16 London) | (W.W.Greener No 16 London) | (W.W.Greener No 16 London & Birmingham) |
| Gnm. | Gnm, Abc. | William Wellington Greener. Gnm. | |
| | | | On other gauges. |
| GBE | GBE | GBE | GBE |
| HFC.606. | HFC.4,812. | HSC.4,813. | HFC.607. |
| (Weston Brighton & Hailsham Kynoch No.16) | (Western No 14 Xpert) | (Winchester No 14) | (Winchester No 14) |
| 16 gauge. | Smaller diam 14 ga. | 14 gauge. | 14 gauge. |
| On other gauges. | | | 20,16,12,10,8,4. |
| GBE/GBE | USA/USA | USA/USA | USA/USA |
| HFC.596. | HFC.627. | HSC.4,814. | HSC.4,815. |

| | | | |
|---|---|---|---|
| WINCHESTER MADE IN USA 14 GAUGE | No WINCHESTER W 14 YELLOW RIVAL | W-A 12 (?) GA 8-1980 | No 12 |
| 14 gauge. | 14 gauge. | 12 gauge. | 12 gauge. |
| | 20,16,12,10. | | |
| USA/USA | USA/USA | AUS | |
| HSC.4,816. | HSC.4,817. | HSC.4,818. | HFC.4,819. |
| No BAILEY'S PATENT CASE & CHECK W | WAGNER 12 GA | WALSHE No 12 KIMBERLEY | WALLEY & WINDOWS No 12 KYNOCH DORCHESTER |
| | | | Irm, Circa 1911. |
| | | ZA | |
| HSC.4,820. | HSC.4,821. | HSC.4,822. | HFC.4,823. |
| WALLIS BROS No 12 LINCOLN | WALLIS BROS. LINCOLN No 12 ELEY | WALNO 12 12 IMW | WALSRODE 12 |
| Kynoch made case. | Gnm, etc. | | |
| GBE/GBE | GBE/GBE | | |
| HSC.4,824. | HFC.1,946. | HSC.4,825. | HFC.1,947. |
| WALSRODE 12 | WALTER COTON No 12 COVENTRY | WALTER LOCKE & Co LTD No 12 CALCUTTA | PAT. WANDA PEND. 12 |
| 12 gauge, Pla. | Gunsmith. | | Apc. |
| | | | 16. |
| | GBE | IND | USA/USA |
| HSC.4,826. | HSC.4,827. | HSC.4,828. | HFC.1,948/R. |

| | | | |
|---|---|---|---|
| (Wanless Sunderland No 12) | (Wanless Sunderland No 12 Eley) | (Ward & Son Kynoch Patent No 12 Grouse Ejector Worcester) | (Ward Thompson 12 Stockton 12) |
| 12 gauge. Gnm. | Gnm. | J. Ward & Son. Irm. | 12 gauge. Gnm. |
| GBE | GBE/GBE | GBE/GBE | GBE |
| HFC.1,949. | HFC.1,950. | HFC.1,952. | HFC.1,953. |
| (Watkins No 12 Banbury) | (Watkins No 12 Banbury) | (Watkins No 12 Eley Banbury) | (Watkins & Co. Banbury No 12 Eley) |
| Thomas J. Watkins. Gnm. High Street. | | | Gnm. |
| GBE | GBE | GBE/GBE | GBE/GBE |
| HSC.4,829. | HFC.4,830. | HSC.4,831. | HFC.1,954. |
| (Watson Bros No 12 Old Bond St) | (Watson Bros No 12 Old Bond Street) | (Watson Bros No 12 Old Bond Street) | (Watson Bros No 12 29 Old Bond St) |
| Watson Brothers. Gnm. 29 Old Bond Street. Also at Pall Mall, London. | | | |
| GBE | GBE | GBE | GBE |
| HSC.4,832. | HSC.4,833. | HFC.1,955. | HFC.4,834. |
| (Watson Bros Old Bond Street No 12 Kynoch) | (Watson Bros Old Bond Street Kynochs Patent Grouse Ejector No 12) | (Watson Bros Old Bond Street Kynochs Patent Grouse Ejector No 12) | (Watson Bros Patent No 2080 No 12 Pall Mall) |
| Gnm. 12 gauge. | Gnm. Ejt. | Gnm, Ejt. | Kynoch Ejt case. |
| GBE/GBE | GBE/GBE | GBE/GBE | GBE/GBE |
| HSC.4,835. | HFC.1,956. | HFC.1,957. | HSC.4,836. |

| | | | |
|---|---|---|---|
| W.CAMERON KYNOCH BALLYMENA No 12 | W.C.CO. No 12 ESSEX | W.C.CO. No 12 ESSEX | W.C.CO. No 12 ESSEX |
| William, gundealer. | Western Cartridge Company. | | 12 gauge. |
| GBI/GBE | USA/USA | USA/USA | USA/USA |
| HFC.1,958. | HSC.4,837. | HSC.4,838. | HSC.4,839. |
| W.C.CO. No 12 ESSEX | W.C.CO. No 12 FIELD | W.C.CO. No 12 FIELD | W.C.CO. No 12 HIGHGRADE |
| | Western Cartridge Company. | | Manufacturer. |
| USA/USA | USA/USA | USA/USA | USA/USA |
| HSC.4,840. | HSC.4,841. | HSC.4,842. | HSC.4,843. |
| W.C.CO. No 12 MARVEL | W.C.CO. No 12 NEW CHIEF | W.C.CO. No 12 PEERLESS | W.C.CO. No 12 RECORD |
| Manufacturer. | Western Cartridge Company. | | |
| USA/USA | USA/USA | USA/USA | USA/USA |
| HSC.4,844. | HSC.4,845. | HSC.4,846. | HSC.4,847. |
| W.C.CO. No 12 RECORD | W.C.CO. No 12 RECORD | W.C.CO. No 12 SURE SHOT | W.C.CO. No 12 SURE SHOT |
| 12 gauge. | Western Cartridge Company. | | 12 gauge. |
| USA/USA | USA/USA | USA/USA | USA/USA |
| HSC.4,848. | HSC.4,849. | HFC.1,959. | HSC.4,850. |

| | | | |
|---|---|---|---|
| (W.C.Co. No 12 VELOX) | (W.COOMBS No 12 FROME) | (W.COOMBS No 12 FROME) | (W.COTON No 12 KYNOCH COVENTRY) |
| Western C. C. | William Coombs. Irm Frome and Devenport. | | Gunsmith. |
| USA/USA | GBE | GBE | GBE/GBE |
| HSC.4,851. | HFC.4,852. | HFC.1,960. | HFC.1,961. |
| (W.COULTAS No 12 GRANTHAM) | (W.DARLOW No 12 BEDFORD) | (W.E.BAKER No 12 TAVISTOCK) | (WEBB-HULL No 12 ELEY) |
| Irm. | Gnm. | Irm. | Pre Wwl. |
| GBE | GBE | GBE | GBE/GBE |
| HFC.1,962. | HFC.1,963. | HFC.1,964. | HSC.4,853. |
| (WEBB-HULL ELEY.No 12 LONDON) | (WEEKES 12 PATENT) | (WEEKES 12 PATENT) | (WEEKES No ? 12 PATENT) |
| | UK patent. | | UK patent. |
| GBE/GBE | IRL | IRL | IRL |
| HSC.4,854. | HSC.4,855. | HFC.2,223. | HSC.4,856. |
| (W.E.EKINS No 12 ADELAIDE) | (W.E.EKINS 12 12 ADELAIDE) | (W.E.EKINS.ADELAIDE No 12 ELEY) | (WERNER 12 GA) |
| W. E. Ekins. 92 Currie Street, Adelaide, S.A. | | | Apc. 12 gauge. |
| AUS | AUS | AUS/GBE | USA |
| HSC.4,857. | HSC.4,858. | HSC.4,859. | HSC.4,860/R. |

| | | | |
|---|---|---|---|
| 12 gauge. | Apc. | Post Ww2. | Pla. 12 gauge. |
| CDN/CDN | CDN/CDN | CDN/CDN | CDN/CDN |
| HSC.4,861. | HSC.4,862. | HSC.4,863. | HFC.1,965. |
| Pla. | Western Cartridge Company. | | |
| USA/USA | USA/USA | USA/USA | USA/USA |
| HSC.4,864. | HFC.1,966. | HFC.1,967. | HFC.4,865. |
| | Western Cartridge Company. | | Manufacturer. |
| | 16. | | |
| USA/USA | USA/USA | USA/USA | USA/USA |
| HSC.4,866. | HSC.4,867. | HSC.4,868. | HFC.2,224. |
| 12 gauge. | Western Cartridge Company. | | 12 gauge. |
| USA/USA | USA/USA | USA/USA | USA/USA |
| HFC.2,225. | HFC.1,968. | HFC.2,226. | HFC.4,869. |

| | | | |
|---|---|---|---|
| 12 gauge. Pla. | Western Cartridge Company. | | 12 gauge. |
| | | 28,20,16,10. | |
| CDN | AUS/AUS | USA/USA | USA/USA |
| HSC.4,870. | HFC.1,969. | HFC.1,970. | HFC.4,871. |
| | | | |
| | Western Cartridge Company. | | |
| 20,16. | | | |
| USA/USA | CDN | AUS/AUS | USA/USA |
| HSC.4,872. | HFC.4,873. | HFC.1,971. | HFC.1,972. |
| | | | |
| Manufacturer. | Gnm. Post Ww2. | Bullet load, Gnm. | Bullet load. Gnm. |
| 28,20,16,10. | | | |
| USA/USA | GBE | GBE | GBE |
| HFC.1,973. | HFC.1,974. | HFC.4,874. | HFC.1,975. |
| | | | |
| 12 gauge. Ejt. | Bullet load, Gnm. | Gnm. | Gnm, 12 gauge. |
| | | | |
| GBE | GBE | GBE | GBE |
| HFC.1,976. | HSC.4,875. | HSC.4,876. | HFC.1,977. |

| | | | |
|---|---|---|---|
| 12 gauge. Gnm. | Gnm. | Gnm. Pre Ww1. | 12 gauge. Gnm. Ejt. |
| GBE | GBE | GBE/GBE | GBE/GBE |
| HFC.4,877. | HFC.4,878. | HSC.4,879. | HFC.1,978. |
| Gnm. Ejt. | Gnm. Ejt. | Gnm. | Gnm. |
| GBE/GBE | GBE/GBE | GBE | GBE/GBE |
| HFC.1,979. | HFC.4,880. | HSC.4,881. | HSC.4,882. |
| Gnm. Eley Bros case. | William Evans, Gnm, Pall Mall, London. | | |
| GBE/GBE | GBE | GBE | GBE/GBE |
| HSC.4,883. | HFC.1,980. | HFC.1,981. | HFC.1,982. |
| 12 gauge. | William Evans, Gnm, Pall Mall, London. | | William Garden, Gnm. |
| GBE | GBE/GBE | GBE/GBE | GBS/GBE |
| HFC.1,983. | HFC.1,985. | HFC.1,984. | HFC.1,986. |

| | | | |
|---|---|---|---|
| W.GARDEN ABERDEEN Kynoch Patent Grouse Ejector No 12 | W.GOLDEN HUDDERSFIELD No 12 | W.GOLDEN HUDDERSFIELD No 12 | W.GRIFFITHS MANCHESTER Kynoch Patent Grouse Ejector No 12 |
| 12 gauge. Gnm. Ejt. | William Golden. Irm. | | Kynoch Ejt case. |
| GBE/GBE | GBE | GBE | GBE/GBE |
| HFC.4,884. | HFC.1,988. | HFC.1,987. | HFC.1,989. |
| W.HAYNES READING No 12 | N.W.HENSMAN BOSTON No 12 | WHITEHOUSE OAKHAM No 12 | N.WHITEHOUSE OAKHAM No 12 |
| Irm. | Gnm. | John Edward Whitehouse. Gnm. | |
| GBE | GBE | GBE | GBE |
| HFC.2,008. | HSC.4,885. | HSC.4,886. | HSC.4,887. |
| N.WHITEHOUSE OAKHAM No 12 | WHITE. NORTHAMPTON & PARIS No 12 | WHITE POWDER No 12 | "WHITLOCK" HOLSWORTHY |
| Gnm. | | | Irm, 12 gauge. |
| GBE | GBE-F/ | USA | GBE/F |
| HFC.4,888. | HFC.2,009. | HSC.4,889. | HSC.4,890. |
| WHITNEY CARTRIDGE | WHITNEY 12 GA CARTRIDGE | PAT. WHITNEY PEND 12 | W.H.JANE. BODMIN No 12 |
| 12 gauge. Apc. | Apc. | Apc. | Wil'm Henry. Irm/Gnm |
| USA | USA | USA | GBE |
| HFC.2,010. | HSC.4,891. | HSC.4,892. | HSC.4,893. |

| | | | |
|---|---|---|---|
| (W. HODGSON No 12 RIPON) | (W. HOOTON SLEAFORD No 12) | (W.H.POLLARD No 12 LONDON) | (W.H.TISDALL No 12 WELLINGTON) |
| William, Gnm. | William, Gnm. | Remains found. | 12 gauge. |
| GBE | GBE | GBE | NZ |
| HFC.2,011. | HFC.2,012. | HFC.2,013. | HSC.4,894. |
| (W.H.TISDALL LTD No 12 WELLINGTON & CHRISTCHURCH) | (W.H.TISDALL LTD ELEY. No 12 WELLINGTON & CHRISTCHURCH) | (WIGGLESWORTH No 12 THIRSK) | (WILKINSON. PALL MALL ? No 12) |
| Also at Auckland and Hamilton. | | Yorkshire. | Gun and sword maker. |
| NZ | NZ/GBE | GBE | GBE |
| HSC.4,895. | HSC.4,896. | HFC.2,015. | HSC.4,897. |
| (WILKINSON No 12 PALL MALL) | (WILKINSON No 12 PALL MALL) | (WILKINSON'S No 12 KYNOCH DURHAM) | (WILKINSON'S No 12 KYNOCH DURHAM) |
| James Wilkinson, | Pall Mall, London. | Irm. | Irm. |
| GBE | GBE | GBE/GBE | GBE/GBE |
| HFC.2,014. | HFC.4,898. | HFC.2,017. | HFC.2,016. |
| (WILLIAM FORD BIRMM No 12 ELEY) | (WILLIAMS PAT No 12 ST. LOUIS) | (WILLIAMS & POWELL L'POOL No 12) | (WILLIAMS & POWELL No 12 LIVERPOOL) |
| 12 gauge. Gnm. | | South Street. Gnm. | 12 gauge. |
| GBE/GBE | USA | GBE | GBE |
| HSC.4,899. | HSC.4,900. | HSC.4,901. | HFC.2,018. |

329

| | | | |
|---|---|---|---|
| 12 gauge. Gnm. | Gnm, Ejt. | Manufacturer. | 12 gauge. |
| GBE/GBE | GBE/GBE | USA/USA | USA/USA |
| HSC.4,902. | HFC.2,019. | HSC.4,903. | HSC.4,904. |
| Manufacturer. | Pla. | Pla. | Pla. |
| USA/USA | USA/USA | USA/USA | AUS/AUS |
| HSC.4,905. | HFC.2,020. | HSC.4,906. | HFC.4,907. |
| Pla. | Pla. | Pla. | Manufacturer. |
| | | AUS/AUS | USA/USA |
| HFC.2,021. | HFC.2,022. | HFC.2,023. | HSC.4,908. |
| 12 gauge, Pla. | Pla. | Manufacturer. | 12 gauge. |
| AUS/AUS | AUS/AUS | USA/USA | USA/USA |
| HFC.2,024. | HFC.2,025. | HSC.4,909. | HFC.2,227. |

| | | | |
|---|---|---|---|
| 12 gauge. | Winchester Repeating Arms Company. | | 12 gauge. |
| | | | 20,16,10,8. |
| USA/USA | USA/USA | USA/USA | USA/USA |
| HFC.2,026. | HSC.4,910. | HFC.2,027. | HSC.4,911. |
| Large cap. | | | Manufacturer. |
| | | 10. | |
| USA/USA | USA/USA | USA/USA | USA/USA |
| HSC.4,912. | HSC.4,913. | HSC.4,914. | HSC.4,915. |
| Manufacturer. | Winchester Repeating Arms Company. | | |
| | | | 12 gauge only. |
| USA/USA | USA/USA | USA/USA | USA/USA |
| HSC.4,916. | HSC.4,917. | HSC.4,918. | HSC.4,919. |
| 12 gauge. | | | 12 gauge. |
| | | 20,16,10. | 20,16,10. |
| USA/USA | USA/USA | USA/USA | USA/USA |
| HSC.4,920. | HSC.4,921. | HSC.4,922. | HSC.4,923. |

| | | | |
|---|---|---|---|
| (Winchester Nublack No 12) | (Winchester Pigeon No W 12) | (Winchester Ranger No 12) | (Winchester Ranger No 12) |
| 12 gauge. | Winchester Repeating Arms Company. | | 12 gauge. |
| | 10. | | |
| USA/USA | USA/USA | USA/USA | USA/USA |
| HSC.4,924. | HSC.4,925. | HFC.4,926. | HFC.2,028. |
| (Winchester Ranger No 12) | (Winchester Repeater No 12) | (Winchester Repeater No 12) | (Winchester Repeater No 12) |
| | | | Manufacturer. |
| | | | 20,16,10. |
| USA/USA | USA/USA | USA/USA | USA/USA |
| HFC.5,455. | HFC.2,030. | HSC.4,927. | HSC.4,928. |
| (Winchester New Rival No 12) | (Winchester Speedload No 12) | (Winchester Super Speed No 12) | (Winchester Super Speed No 12) |
| | Winchester Repeating Arms Company. | | |
| USA/USA | USA/USA | | USA/USA |
| HSC.4,929. | HSC.4,930. | HFC.2,031. | HFC.2,032. |
| (Winchester Super Speed No 12 Made in Italy) | (Winchester Super Speed No 12) | (Winchester Super Speed No 12) | (Winchester Tiro Xpert 12 12) |
| 12 gauge. Pla. | Manufacturer. | Pla. | 12 gauge. |
| I/I | USA/USA | USA/USA | USA/USA |
| HFC.2,033. | HFC.2,034. | HFC.4,931. | HSC.4,932. |

| | | | |
|---|---|---|---|
| WINCHESTER WESTERN | 12 WESTERN GA | 12 WINCHESTER 12 | 12 WINCHESTER 12 |
| 12 ga' on dummy. | Pla. | Pla. | 12 gauge. |
| | | | |
| USA/USA | USA/USA | USA/USA | |
| HFC.4,933. | HFC.2,035. | HFC.2,036. | HFC.4,934. |
| 12 WINCHESTER 12 | No WINCO 12 | No WINNER 12 | 12 WINCHESTER GA WONDER |
| Pla. | Winchester Repeating Arms Company. | | Large cap. |
| | 12 gauge only. | 12 gauge only. | |
| I/I | USA/USA | USA/USA | USA/USA |
| HFC.2,037. | HSC.4,935. | HSC.4,936. | HFC.2,228. |
| No XPERT 12 | 12 XPERT I 12 | No XPERT II 12 | No YELLOW RIVAL 12 |
| Manufacturer. | Pla. Apc. | Pla. | |
| | | | 20,16,14,10. |
| I/I | I/I | | USA/USA |
| HSC.4,937. | HSC.4,938. | HFC.2,038. | HSC.4,939. |
| WITTON No 12 BIRMINGHAM | WITTON No 12 BIRMINGHAM | W.J.FELL No 12 RELIABLE | W.J.FELL No 12 RELIABLE |
| 12 gauge. | G.Kynoch & Company. | | 12 gauge. |
| | | | |
| GBE/GBE | GBE/GBE | AUS | AUS |
| HFC.2,040. | HFC.2,039. | HSC.4,940. | HSC.4,941. |

| | | | |
|---|---|---|---|
| 12 gauge. | Gnm. | Case by U.M.C.Co. | Gnm, 12 gauge. |
| AUS | GBE/F | GBE/USA | GBE |
| HFC.2,041. | HFC.2,042. | HSC.4,942. | HSC.4,943. |
| Gnm. | Extra large cap. | Gnm. | Gnm. |
| GBE | GBE | GBE | GBE |
| HFC.4,944. | HSC.4,945. | HFC.2,043. | HFC.4,946. |
| Gnm. | Gmn. | Eley Bros case. | Gnm. |
| GBE | GBE | GBE/GBE | GBE |
| HFC.4,947. | HFC.4,948. | HFC.2,044. | HFC.4,949. |
| 12 gauge. Gnm. | Gnm. | Gnm, | Eley Bros case. |
| GBE/F | GBE | GBE | GBE/GBE |
| HFC.4,950. | HSC.4,951. | HFC.2,046. | HSC.4,952. |

| | | | |
|---|---|---|---|
| W.J.JEFFERY & Co LONDON No K 12 | W.J.JEFFERY & Co LTD No K 12 LONDON | W.J.JEFFERY LTD & Co 12 MADE IN BAVARIA 12 LONDON | W.J.JEFFERY & Co LTD 12 MADE IN BAVARIA 12 LONDON |
| Case by Kynoch. | Case by Kynoch. | Gnm. | Gnm, 12 gauge. |
| GBE/GBE | GBE/GBE | GBE/D | GBE/D |
| HFC.2,048. | HFC.2,047. | HFC.4,953. | HFC.2,045. |
| W.J.JEFFERY LTD & Co 12 MADE IN BELGIUM 12 LONDON | W.J.JEFFERY & Co LTD No S.F.M 12 MADE IN FRANCE LONDON | W.J.JEFFERY & Co LTD No S.F.M 12 MADE IN FRANCE LONDON | W.J.POWELL No 12 LEISTON |
| Gnm. | Gnm. | Gnm. | Gnm. |
| GBE/B | GBE/F | GBE/F | GBE |
| HSC.4,954. | HFC.4,955. | HSC.4,956. | HFC.2,049. |
| W.KAVANAGH & SON 12 12 DUBLIN | W.KAVANAGH & SON No KYNOCH 12 DUBLIN | WM 12 12 B | W.McILWRAITH & Co No 12 12 ELGIN |
| Gnm. | Gnm, Kynoch case. | | |
| IRL | IRL/GBE | D/D | GBS |
| HFC.2,050. | HFC.2,051. | HSC.4,957. | HSC.4,958. |
| WM.COOK 12 12 LIVERPOOL | WM.EVANS No 12 ELEY LONDON | WM 12 12 FABRIK BISCHWEILER | W.MOORE & GREY.LONDON No 12 |
| 12 gauge. | Gnm, Pre Wwl. | | 12 gauge. Gnm, |
| GBE | GBE/GBE | D/D | GBE |
| HFC.4,959. | HSC.4,960. | HFC.1,990. | HFC.4,961. |

| | | | |
|---|---|---|---|
| Wolff & Co Walsrode 12 | Wolff & Co Walsrode 12 | Wolff & Co Walsrode 12 | Wolff & Co Walsrode 12 |
| 12 gauge. | Manufacturer. | | 12 gauge. |
| D/D | D/D | D/D | D/D |
| HFC.1,991. | HFC.4,962. | HSC.4,963. | HFC.1,992. |
| Wöllersdorf Werke 12 | Wood Salisbury No 12 | Woodward Canada 12 | Woodward London 12 |
| | Fwk. | | Gnm. |
| | GBE | CDN | GBE/? |
| HSC.4,964. | HFC.4,965. | HSC.4,966. | HFC.4,967. |
| Woodward's Canada 12 | Woodward & Sons London 12 | Woolliscroft Leek No 12 Eley | W.P. Jones No 12 Birmingham |
| | Gnm. | Ralph, Irm. | |
| CDN | GBE | GBE/GBE | GBE |
| HFC.4,968. | HSC.4,969. | HFC.1,993. | HFC.4,970. |
| W.P. Jones No 12 Birmingham | W.P. Jones Birmm No 12 Eley | W. Powell & Son Birmm 12 | W. Powell & Son Birmingham No 12 |
| W. Palmer Jones (Guns). | | Gnm. | Gnm, 12 gauge. |
| GBE | GBE/GBE | GBE | GBE |
| HFC.1,994. | HFC.1,995. | HFC.1,996. | HFC.4,971. |

| | | | |
|---|---|---|---|
| 12 gauge. | Gnm. | Gnm. | 12 gauge, Gnm, Ejt. |
| | | | |
| GBE/GBE | GBE/GBE | GBE/GBE | GBE/GBE |
| HSC.4,972. | HFC.4,973. | HFC.1,997. | HFC.4,974. |
| | | | |
| 12 gauge. | Winchester Repeating Arms Company. | | |
| | | | |
| USA/USA | USA/USA | USA/USA | USA/USA |
| HSC.4,975. | HSC.4,976. | HFC.2,229. | HFC.2,230. |
| | | | |
| | Manufacturer. | | Geo Wren. Irm. |
| | 10. | 20,16,10. | |
| USA/USA | USA/USA | USA/USA | GBE |
| HFC.2,231. | HSC.4,977. | HFC.1,998. | HFC.1,999. |
| | | | |
| 12 gauge. | Gnm. | Pre Ww1. | Kynoch Grouse Ejt. |
| | | | |
| GBE/GBE | GBE | GBE/GBE | GBE/GBE |
| HSC.4,978. | HFC.2,000. | HSC.4,979. | HFC.2,001. |

| | | | |
|---|---|---|---|
| (W.RICHARDS KYNOCH'S PATENT CROUSE EJETOR LIVERPOOL No 12) | (W.RICHARDS KYNOCH LIVERPOOL No 12) | (W.RICHARDS PRESTON No 12) | (W.RICHARDS PRESTON No 12 ELEY) |
| Gnm. Kynoch Ejt. | Kynoch made case. | Gnm. | Gnm, 12 gauge. |
| GBE/GBE | GBE/GBE | GBE | GBE/GBE |
| HSC.4,980. | HFC.2,002. | HFC.2,003. | HSC.4,981. |
| (W.R.LEESON ASHFORD No 12) | (W.R.LEESON LTD KYNOCH ASHFORD No 12) | (W.R.PAPE ELEY NEWCASTLE No 12) | (W.R.PAPE KYNOCH NEWCASTLE ON TYNE No 12) |
| | | William Rochester Pape. Gnm. | |
| GBE | GBE/GBE | GBE/GBE | GBE/GBE |
| HFC.2,004. | HSC.4,982. | HFC.2,005. | HFC.2,006. |
| (W.STOVIN GRANTHAM No 12) | (W.T.HANCOCK HIGH HOLBORN No 12) | (W.T.HANCOCK 308 HIGH HOLBORN No 12) | (W.T.HANCOCK ELEY HOLBORN No 12) |
| Wm Stovin. Gnm. | London Gnm. | Gnm. | Gnm, Eley Bros Case |
| GBE | GBE | GBE | GBE/GBE |
| HSC.4,983. | HSC.4,984. | HFC.2,007. | HSC.4,985. |
| (W.URTON KYNOCH CHESTERFIELD No 12) | (W.VARLEY C.H.M.C. HULL No 12) | (W-W 12 GA AA) | (W.WALLAS.WIGTON ELEY No 12) |
| Wm Urton. Gnm. | Cogswll & Harrison. | Manufacturer. | Gnm, 12 gauge. |
| GBE/GBE | GBE/GBE | USA/USA | GBE/GBE |
| HSC.4,986. | HSC.4,987. | HFC.2,054. | HFC.2,055. |

| | | | |
|---|---|---|---|
| 12 gauge, Gnm, Ejt. | Manufacturer. | Gnm. | 12 gauge. |
| GBE/GBE | USA/USA | GBE | GBE |
| HFC.2,056. | HFC.2,053. | HFC.4,988. | HFC.4,989/R. |
| Gnm. | William Wellington Greener. Gnm. | | Gnm. 12 gauge. |
| GBE | GBE | GBE | GBE |
| HFC.4,990. | HFC.4,991. | HFC.4,992. | HFC.2,058. |
| 12 gauge, Gnm. | 12 gauge, Gnm. | 10 gauge. | 10 gauge. |
| GBE | GBE/GBE | USA/USA | USA/USA |
| HFC.2,057. | HFC.2,059. | HSC.4,993. | HSC.4,994. |
| 10 gauge. | Manufacturer. | Manufacturer. | 10 gauge. |
| 12. | 12. | 28,20,16,12. | 20,16,12. |
| USA/USA | USA/USA | USA/USA | USA/USA |
| HSC.4,995. | HSC.4,996. | HSC.4,997. | HSC.4,998. |

339

| | | | |
|---|---|---|---|
| WESTERN MADE IN U.S.A. No 10 SUPER X | WESTERN MADE IN U.S.A. No 10 XPERT | WILLIAMS PAT No 10 ST. LOUIS | WILLIAMS PAT No 10 ST. LOUIS |
| Western Cartridge Company. | | | 10 gauge. |
| 28,20,16,12. | 28,20,16,12. | | |
| USA/USA | USA/USA | USA/USA | USA/USA |
| HSC.4,999. | HSC.5,000. | HSC.5,001. | HSC.5,002. |
| WINCHESTER No 10 | WINCHESTER No 10 BLUE RIVAL | WINCHESTER No 10 LEADER | WINCHESTER No 10 LEADER |
| Manufacturer. | | Large cap. | |
| 20,16,14,12,8,4. | | | |
| USA/USA | USA/USA | USA/USA | USA/USA |
| HSC.5,003. | HSC.5,004. | HSC.5,005. | HFC.2,104. |
| WINCHESTER No 10 LEADER MADE IN U.S.A. | WINCHESTER No 10 METAL LINED | WINCHESTER No 10 NEW RIVAL | WINCHESTER No 10 NEW RIVAL MADE IN U.S.A. |
| | Winchester Repeating Arms Company. | | |
| 12. | | | |
| USA/USA | USA/USA | USA/USA | USA/USA |
| HSC.5,006. | HSC.5,007. | HSC.5,008. | HSC.5,009. |
| WINCHESTER No 10 NUBLACK | WINCHESTER 10 GA NUBLACK | WINCHESTER No 10 NUBLACK MADE IN USA | WINCHESTER No 10 PIGEON |
| 10 gauge. | Winchester Repeating Arms Company. | | 10 gauge. |
| 20,16,12. | 20,16,12. | | 12. |
| USA/USA | USA/USA | USA/USA | USA/USA |
| HSC.5,010. | HSC.5,011. | HSC.5,012. | HSC.5,013. |

| | | | |
|---|---|---|---|
| WINCHESTER RANGER No 10 MADE IN USA | WINCHESTER REPEATER No 10 | WINCHESTER YELLOW RIVAL No W 10 | WOOD 10 |
| Winchester Repeating Arms Company. | | | Waterbury Brass Co, |
| 24,20,16,12. | 20,16,12. | 20,16,14,12. | |
| | USA/USA | USA/USA | USA |
| HSC.5,014. | HSC.5,015. | HSC.5,016. | HSC.5,017. |
| WOOD 10 | WOOD No 10 NEW YORK | W.R.A.Co. No 10 RIVAL | W.R.A.Co. No 10 S.Q. |
| | | Manufacturer. | |
| | 10 gauge only. | | |
| USA | USA | USA/USA | USA/USA |
| HSC.5,018. | HSC.5,019. | HSC.5,020. | HFC.2,236. |
| W.R.A.Co. No 10 STAR | W.R.A.Co. No 10 XX | W.R.A.Co. No 10 XX | W-W 10 GAUGE |
| | Winchester Repeating Arms Company. | | 10 gauge. |
| | 12. | 20,16,12. | 12. |
| USA/USA | USA/USA | USA/USA | USA/USA |
| HFC.2,237. | HSC.5,021. | HSC.5,022. | HSC.5,023. |
| W.W.GREENER No 10 | W.W.GREENER No 10 LONDON | WESTERN SUPER-X No 8 INDUSTRIAL | WESTERN SUPER-X No 8 INDUSTRIAL |
| 10 gauge, Gnm. | 10 gauge, Gnm. | 8 gauge. | 8 gauge. |
| GBE | GBE | USA/USA | USA/USA |
| HSC.5,024. | HSC.5,025. | HFC.2,113. | HFC.2,112. |

| | | | |
|---|---|---|---|
| 8 gauge. | Winchester Repeating Arms Company. | | 8 gauge. |
| USA/USA | USA/USA | USA/USA | USA/USA |
| HSC.5,026. | HSC.5,027. | HSC.5,028. | HSC.5,029. |
| 4 gauge. | Manufacturer. | 4 gauge. | |
| USA/USA | USA/USA | USA/USA | |
| HSC.5,030. | HSC.5,031. | HSC.5,032. | |

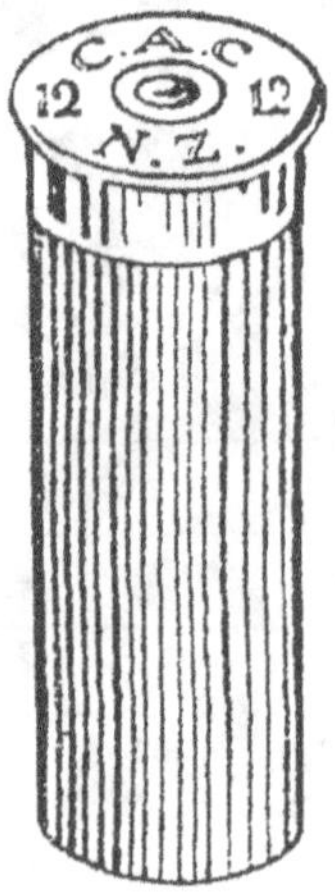

COLONIAL AMMUNITION CO. N.Z. LTD.

# The Championship Cartridge—C.A.C. Match Favourite

**THE GREATEST MATCH WINNING CARTRIDGE USED IN NEW ZEALAND.**

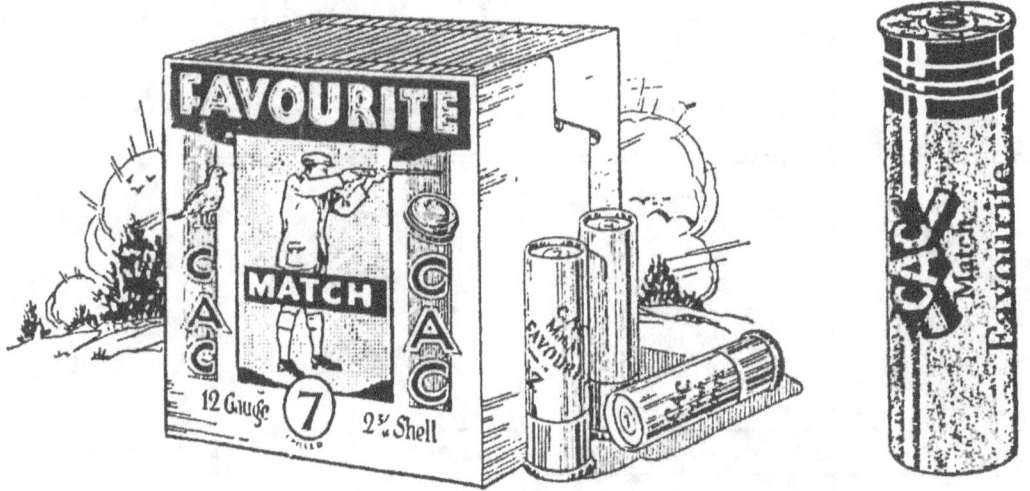

Loaded with Bulk Smokeless Powder and Super-chilled Shot.
No. 167—Price, 25/- per 100; rail extra.

| | | | |
|---|---|---|---|
| (XTRA-RANGE 20 20 C.C.CO.) | (XTRA-RANGE 20 20 S.R & CO.) | (XTRA-RANGE 16 16 C.C.CO.) | (N° XTRA-RANGE 16 16 J.C. HIGGINS) |
| Clinton C.C. | Sears-Rooebuck C. | Clinton C.C. | 16 gauge. |
| 16,12. | | 20,12. | 12. |
| USA | USA | USA | |
| HSC.5,033. | HSC.5,034. | HSC.5,035. | HFC.608. |
| (XTRA-RANGE 16 16 S.R & CO.) | (XTRA-RANGE 12 12 C.C.CO.) | (N° XTRA-RANGE 12 J G HIGGINS) | (XTRA-RANGE 12 12 S.R & CO.) |
| 16 gauge. | Clinton C.C. | | Sears-Roebuck C. |
| 12. | 20,16. | 16. | 20,16. |
| USA | USA | | USA |
| HSC.5,036. | HSC.5,037. | HFC.2,060. | HSC.5,038. |
| (X 10) | | | |
| Delaware C.C. | | | |
| USA | | | |
| HSC.5,039. | | | |

343

| | | | |
|---|---|---|---|
| 20 gauge. | Winchester Repeating Arms Company. | | 14 gauge. |
| 16,14,12,10. | 20,14,12,10. | 20,16,12,10. | |
| USA/USA | USA/USA | USA/USA | |
| HSC.5,040. | HSC.5,041. | HSC.5,042. | HSC.5,043. |
| 12 gauge. | | | 10 gauge. |
| 20,16,14,10. | | 8. | 20,16,14,12. |
| USA/USA | J | | USA/USA |
| HSC.5,044. | HSC.5,045. | HSC.5,046. | HSC.5,047. |

| 8 gauge. |
|---|
| 12. |
| |
| HSC.5,048. |

### KENT & SON,
### Ironmongers, ✣ Wantage,

Have a Large and Assorted Stock of

### SPORTING REQUISITES.

*AGENTS FOR*

### Kynoch's WORLD RENOWNED Cartridges.

*Also Cases & Wadds of every description. Extractors, Cleaning Rods, &c. Cartridge Bags, Belts, &c.*

**GUNS & AMMUNITION**

*Cartridges loaded with Black or any Kind of Smokeless Powders with any size Shot.*

**GUNS & RIFLES LENT ON HIRE.**

| | | | |
|---|---|---|---|
| ZBROJOVKA 16 16 BRNO | ZBROJOVKA 12 SB 12 BRNO | ZENITH 12 12 G.G.&Cº | ZIGOR 12 12 VITORIA |
| 16 gauge. | | | Pla. 12 gauge. |
| CS | CS | | I/I |
| HSC.5.049. | HSC.5,050. | HFC.2,061. | HSC.5,051. |
| ZIGOR 12 12 VITORIA | ZIGOR 12 12 ZIGOR | ZIGOR 12 12 ZIGOR | ZIGOR 12 12 ZIGOR |
| 12 gauge, Apc. | Pla, | Recessed. | Apc. |
| I/I | I/I | I/I | I/I |
| HSC.5,052. | HSC.5,053. | HFC.2,062. | HFC.2,063. |
| ZULU * * 12 | ZULU * * 10 | | |
| 12 gauge. | 10 gauge, dummy. | | |
| 10. | 12. | | |
| HSC.5,054. | HFC.2,105. | | |

CURTISS & HARVEYS AMBERITE SMOKELESS POWDER Made in Great Britain

CURTIS'S & HARVEY'S "RUBY" SMOKELESS POWDER Made in Great Britain

CURTIS'S & HARVEY'S "MARVEL" Smokeless Cartridge Made in Great Britain

AMBERITE

CURTIS'S & HARVEYS SMOKELESS DIAMOND POWDER Made in Great Britain

CURTIS'S & HARVEYS SMOKELESS DIAMOND POWDER Made in Great Britain

# THE BIG BOYS

I freely admit that I do not understand these large gauge sizes. Having drawn them, I am here including them for what they are worth. All the same, I am unable to guarantee that they are all drawn to their correct sizes

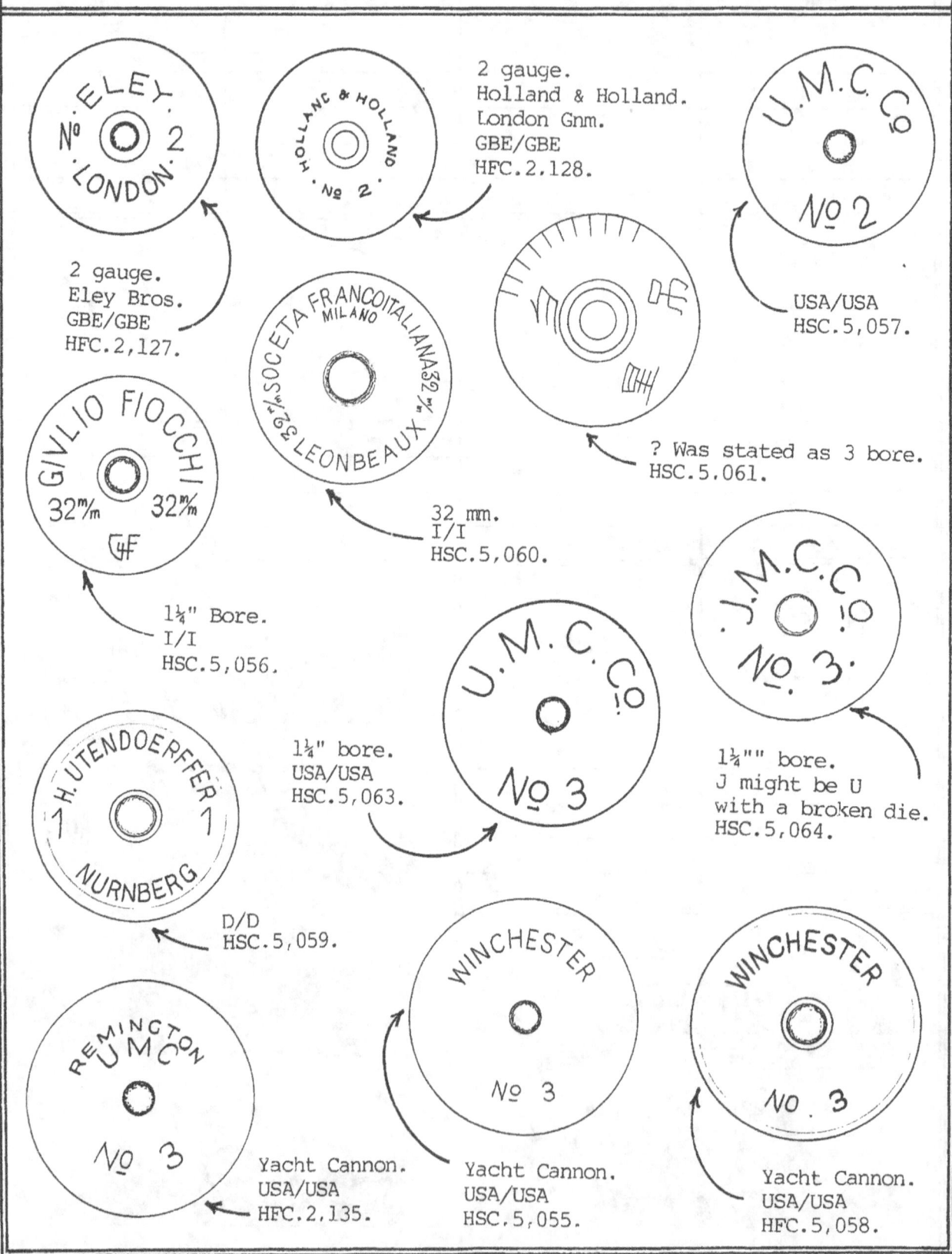

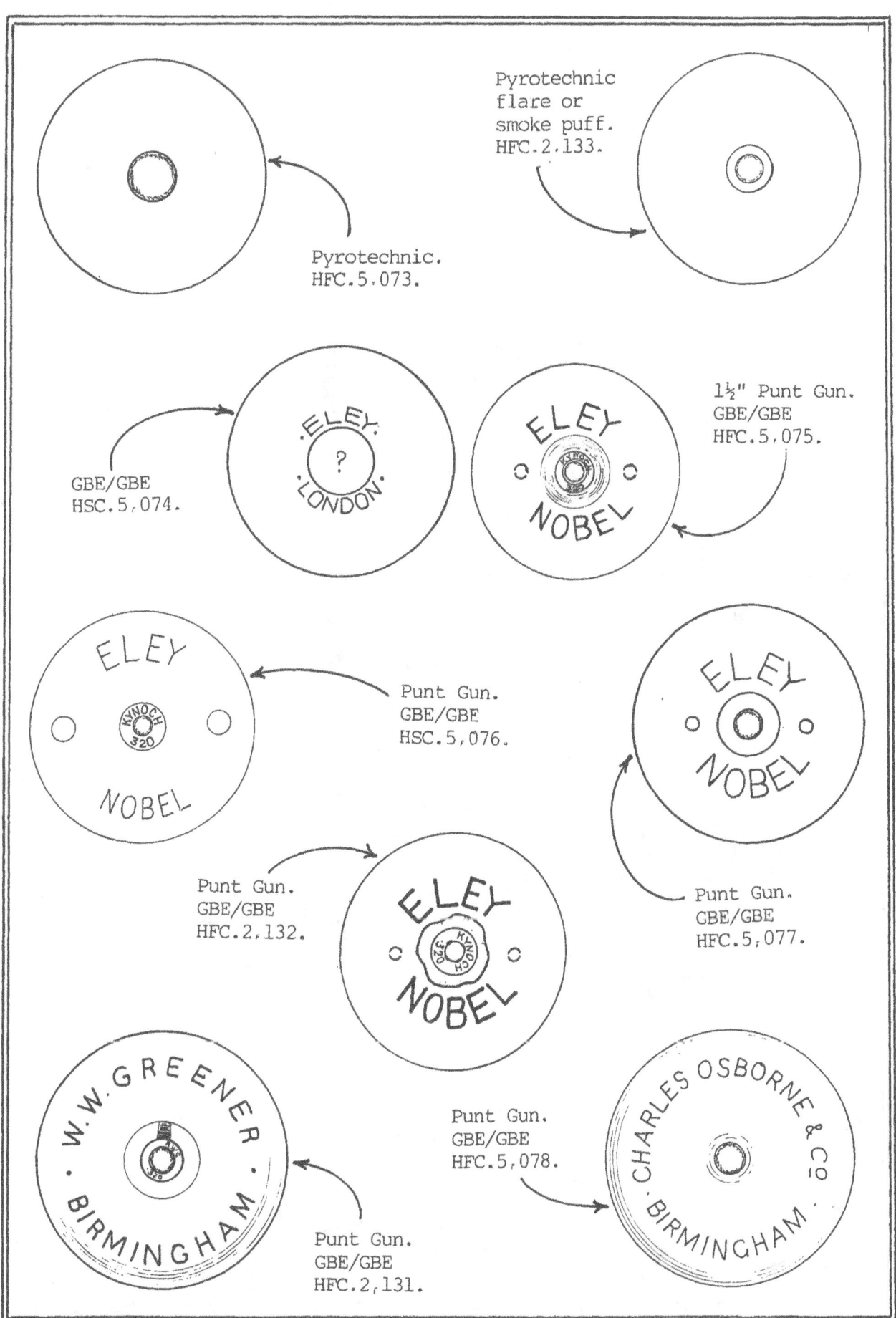

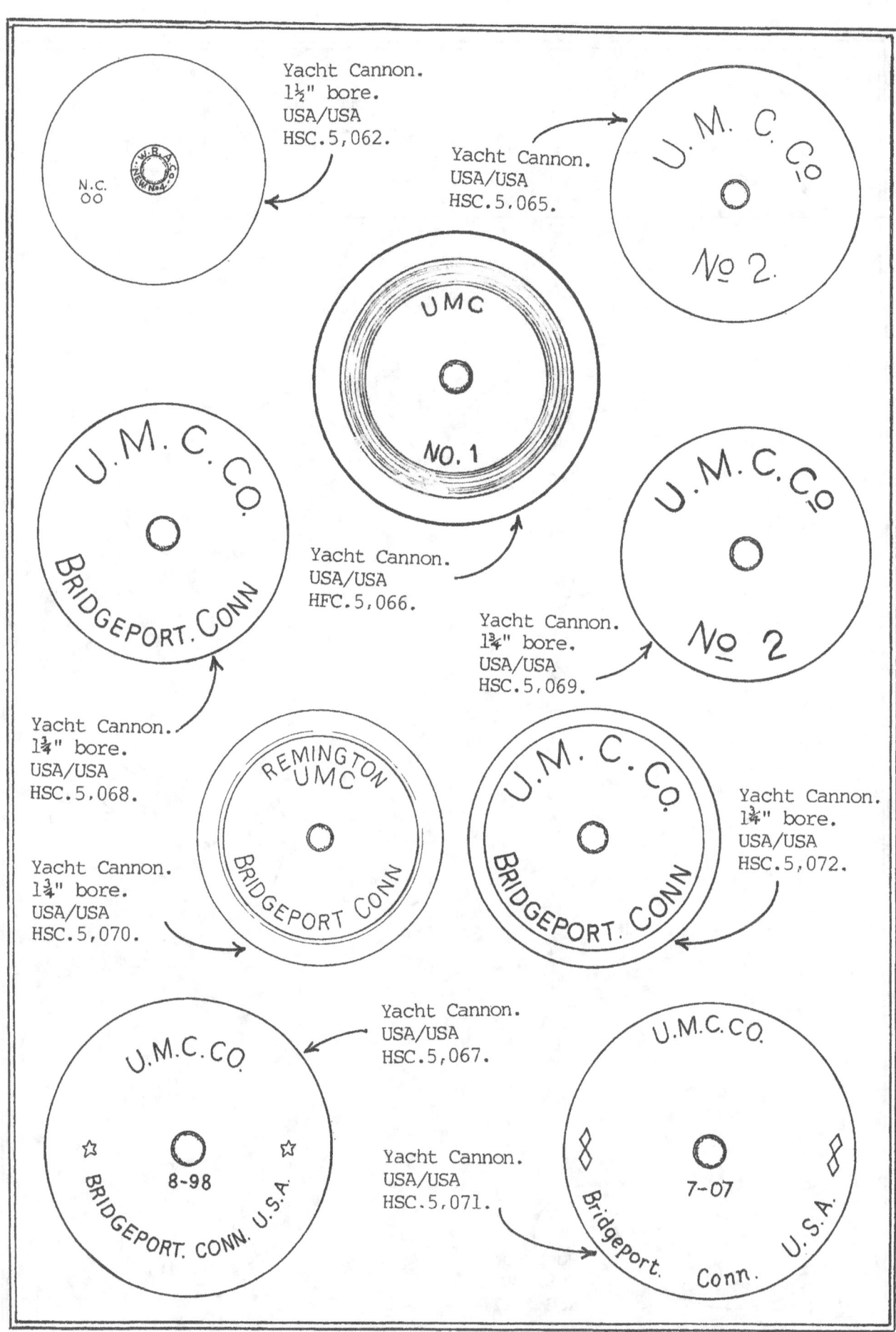

POWDER TRANSPORTATION

These two are by Sellior & Bellot. It was cheaper to ship powders in cases as cartridges than in bulk.

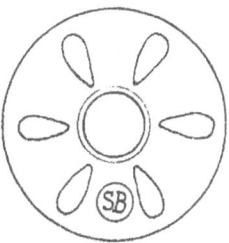

CS/CS
HFN.2,129.

CS/CS
HFN.2,130.

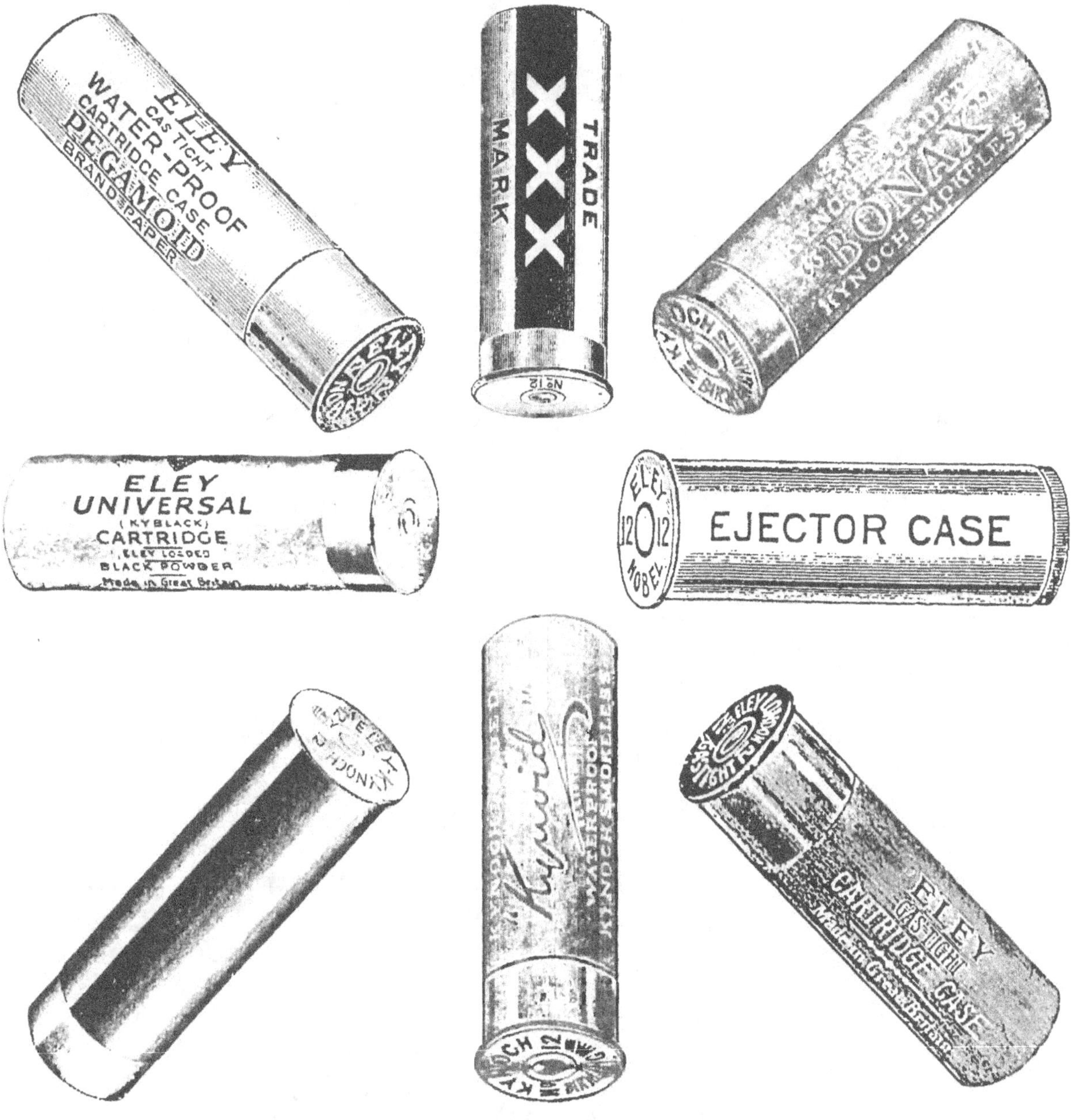

|  ALL STAMPINGS ON THIS PAGE  WILHELM COLLATH & SOHNE  Frankfurt-am-Main, Germany.  All stampings are as, D/D | EQUIVELANTS |
|---|---|
| | No. 0 = 10 gauge.<br>No. 1 = 12 gauge.<br>No. 3 = 14 gauge.<br>No. 4 = 16 gauge.<br>No. 5 = 18 gauge.<br>No. 6 = 20 gauge.<br>No. 7 = 24 gauge.<br>No. 8 = 28 gauge. |

| | | | | |
|---|---|---|---|---|
| HSC.5,461. | HSC.5.468. | HSC.5,237/R. | HSC.5,463. | HSC.5,458. |
| HFC.427. | HFC.428. | HSC.5,462. | HSC.5,467/R. | HSC.5,465. |
| HSC.5,459. | HSC.5,460. | HSC,5,456/R. | HSC.5,464. | HFC.609. |
| HSC.5,466. | HSC.5,469. | HFC.5,239. | HSC.5,240. | HSC.5,460. |
| HSC.5,241/R. | HSC.5,457. | HSC.5,242. | | |

# GREENER POLICE GUN

**THE CARTRIDGE**

- Metal crimp.
- Wadding.
- Bottle neck.
- Paper tube.
- Solid drawn brass case.
- Groove to receive striker horns.

## THE GUN AND ITS CARTRIDGES

The gun is designed on semi-military lines for hard wearing. It will only fire special Greener ammunition and it will not fire standard ammunition. Manufactured as ideal weapons for arming State Forces, Crown Colonies Police, Prison Warders and Custom House Guards. A Mark III/12 gun was chambered to take standard 12 bore 2 inch cartridges.

Most Greener Police Gun cartridges had solid drawn brass cases. Some later cartridges had hard plastic cases. If accidentally dropped, these cases could shatter.

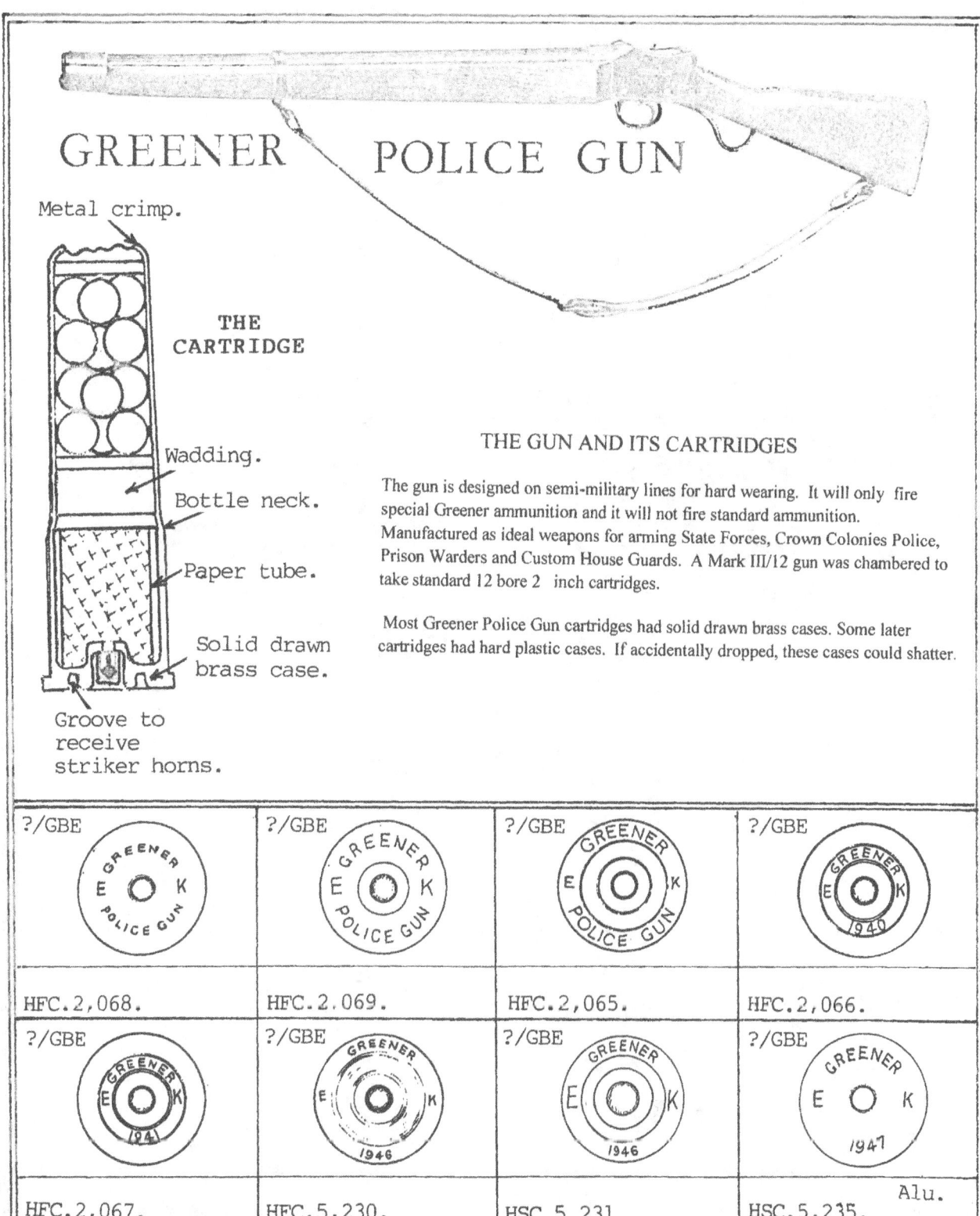

| ?/GBE | ?/GBE | ?/GBE | ?/GBE |
|---|---|---|---|
| HFC.2,068. | HFC.2,069. | HFC.2,065. | HFC.2,066. |
| ?/GBE | ?/GBE | ?/GBE | ?/GBE |
| HFC.2,067. | HFC.5,230. | HSC.5,231. | HSC.5,235. Alu. |
| ?/GBE | ?/GBE | ?/GBE | ?/GBE |
| HSC.5,234. | HFC.5,232. | Old gold Apc. HFC.5,233. | Old gold Apc. HSC.5,236. |

## GARDEN GUN RIM-FIRES

| ☆ | 🧜 | Ⓔ | Ⓔ | Ⓕ | ⚓ |
|---|---|---|---|---|---|
| HFR.208. | HSR.5,470. | HFR.210. | HFR.209. | HSR.5,473. | HSR.5,474. |
| Ⓖ | GF | ICI | MGM | SB | U |
| HFR.211. | HFR.212. | HSR.5,476. | HSR.5,472. | HSR.5,475. | HSR.5,471. |

## SOME ODDITYS

| C.A.C. 11 | WRA No 1 MADE IN USA | W.R.A.CO. No 1 MADE IN USA | W.R.A.CO. No 1 MADE IN USA JET |
|---|---|---|---|
| NZ | USA/USA | 20 gauge for jet engines. USA/USA | USA/USA |
| HSC.5,250. | HSC.5,251. | HSC.5,252. | HSC.5,253. |
| F.V.DREYES 0.70 | COGSWELL & HARRISON LONDON | REMINGTON ELECTRIC 21MM SEISMIC | D & C. 20 SOEMMERDA |
| | GBE/GBE | USA/USA | |
| HFC.5,478. | HFC.5,477. | HFE.2,096. | HFR.5,479. |

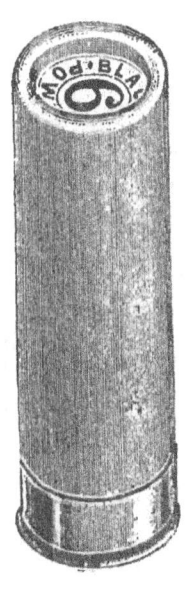

# THE
# SIDE ELEVATIONS

## BRITISH MULLERITE

ONLY BEST "NAMED" POWDERS, "**CLERMONITE**" and "**MULLERITE**" are used in a range of cartridges suitable for every shooting need

The "CHAMPION" SMOKELESS CARTRIDGE. Full load for Game and vermin, 12/6 per 100

YELLOW SEAL Mullerite BRITISH LOADED The Standard Sporting Cartridge. 13/6 per 100

ACE Long Range Original Heavy Load Long Range. 15/- per 100

RED SEAL Mullerite BRITISH LOADED The Standard with deep Brass Shell 15 6 per 100

Note to those interested in shooting economy: It's the **COST PER KILL** not the **PRICE PER 100** that counts

All available in 12, 16, 20, 28 and .410 bores; 2½", 2¾" and 3" lengths; Waterproof 6d. extra

OF ALL DEALERS, or in case of difficulty in obtaining write

**MULLERITE CARTRIDGE WORKS, St. Mary's Row, BIRMINGHAM**

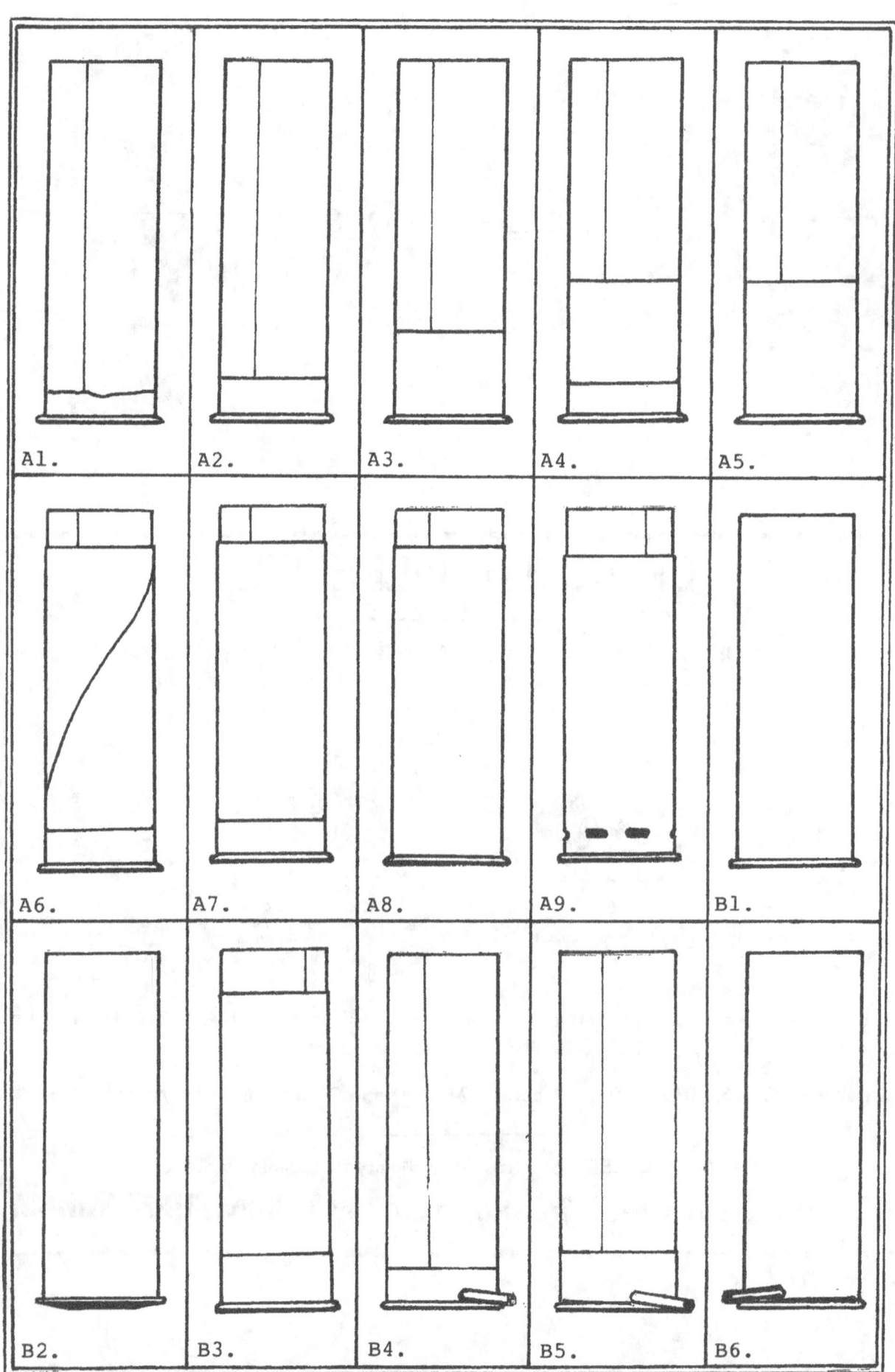

Some general side elevations.

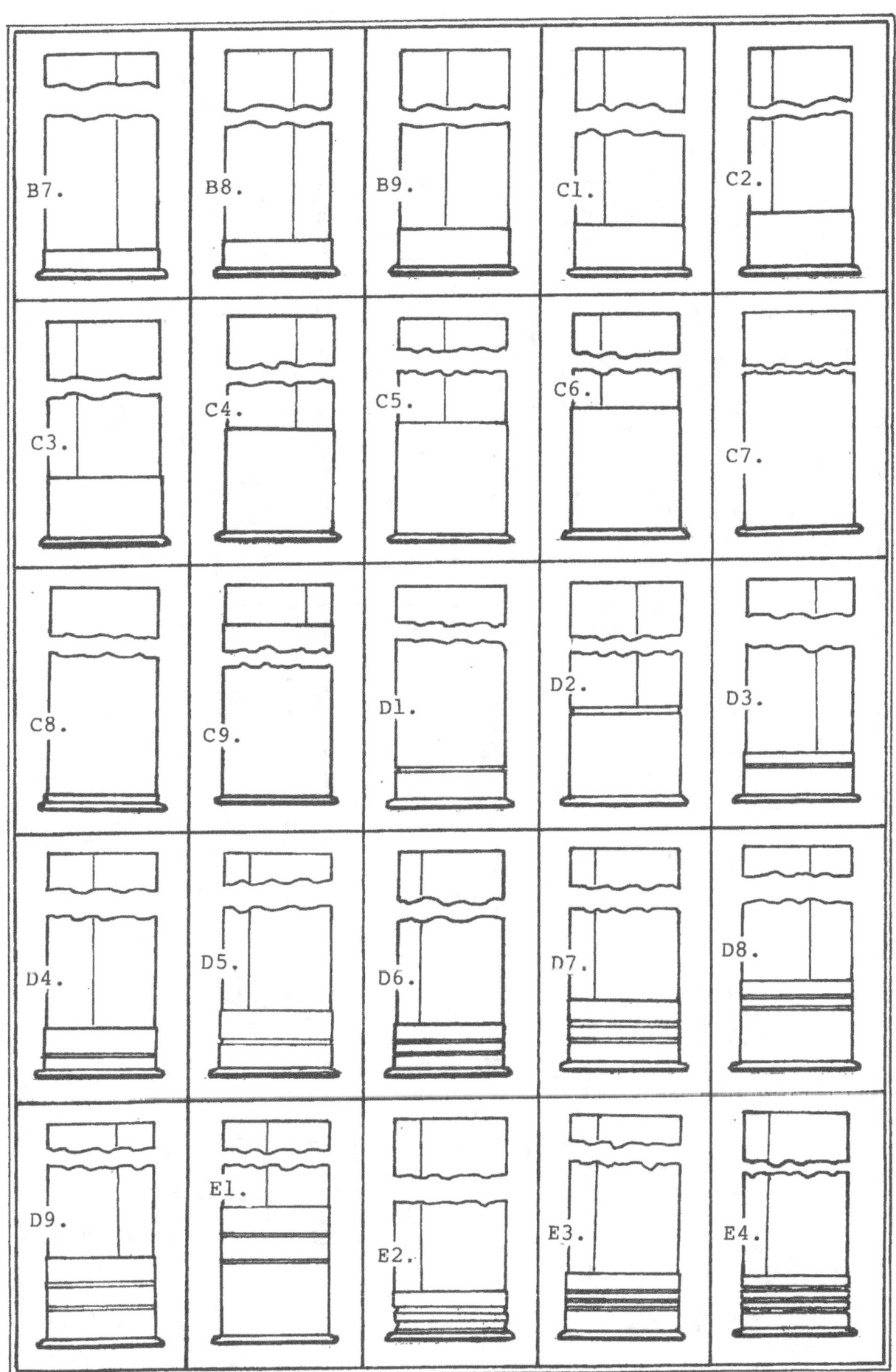

Drawn as paper tubed. Plastic would be seamless.

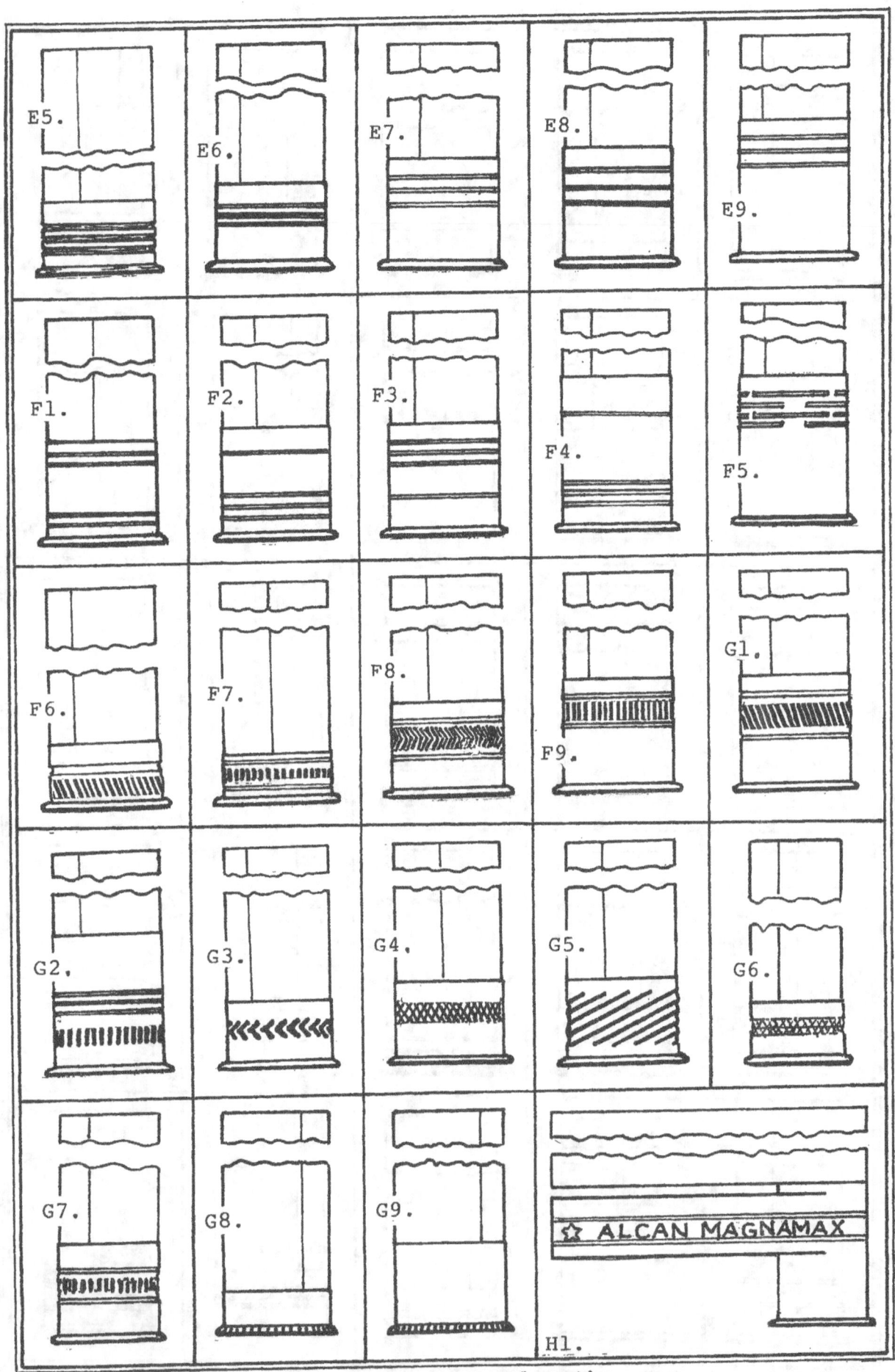

Cartridges come in various case lengths.

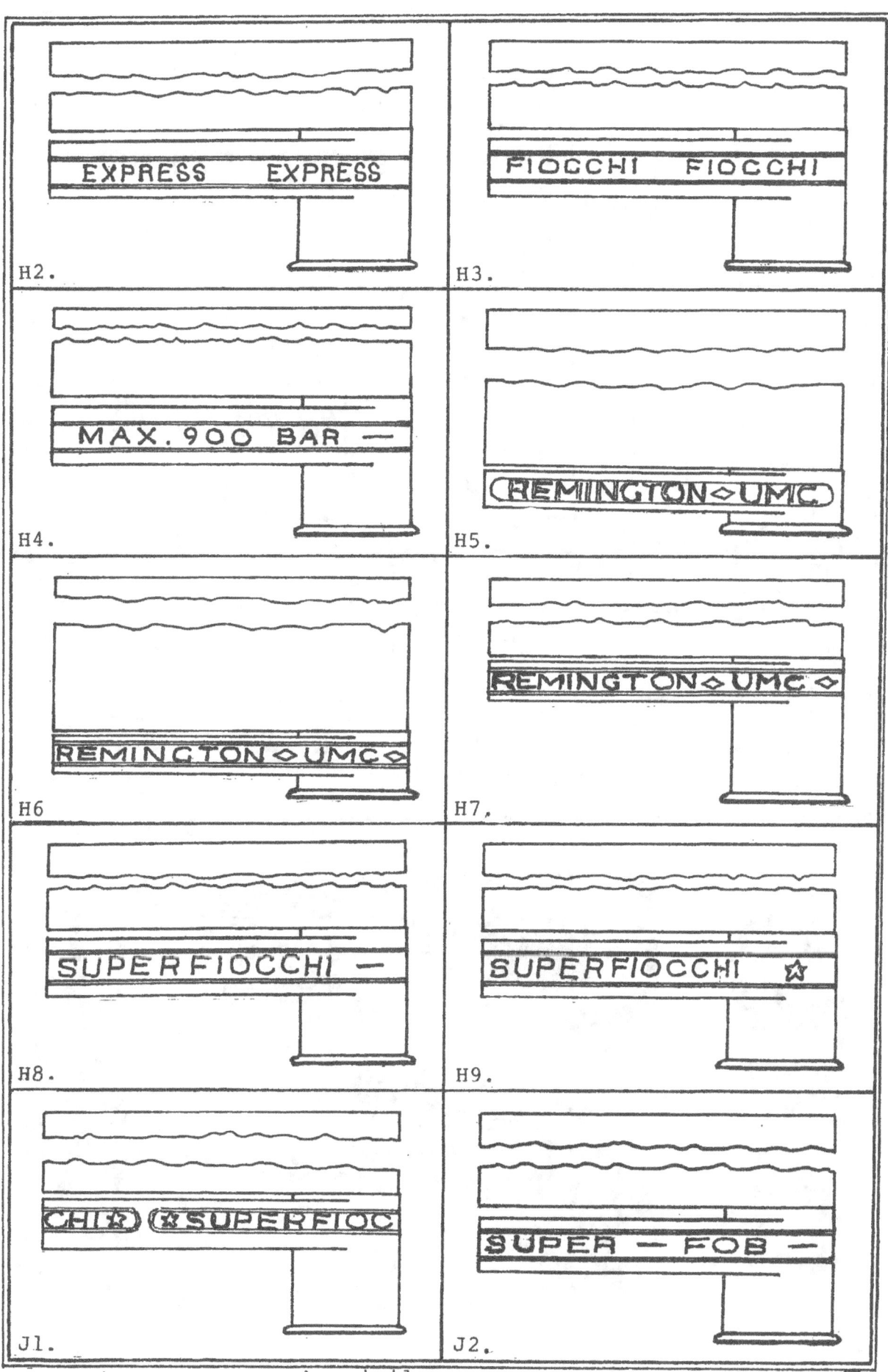

Various gauges maybe similar.

J3.
20g.
J4.
J5.
J6.
J7.
J8.
10g.
J9.
K1.
K2.
K3.

PNEUMATIC
CARTRIDGES
THE MOST EFFICIENT YET EVOLVED
LESS RECOIL
GREATER VELOCITY
LONGER RANGE
CLEAN KILLING
NO GUN HEADACHE
The world's most up-to-date Cartridge
-because
the explosion of the powder charge (A) flattens the domed cards (B) against the cork wad (D) which replaces the old fashioned solid felt wad; the compression of the air within the air chamber (C) expands the walls of the cork wad firmly against the bore of the barrel — making a perfect gas check. Maximum velocity and penetration are therefore ensured, while recoil is reduced 8.3 per cent.

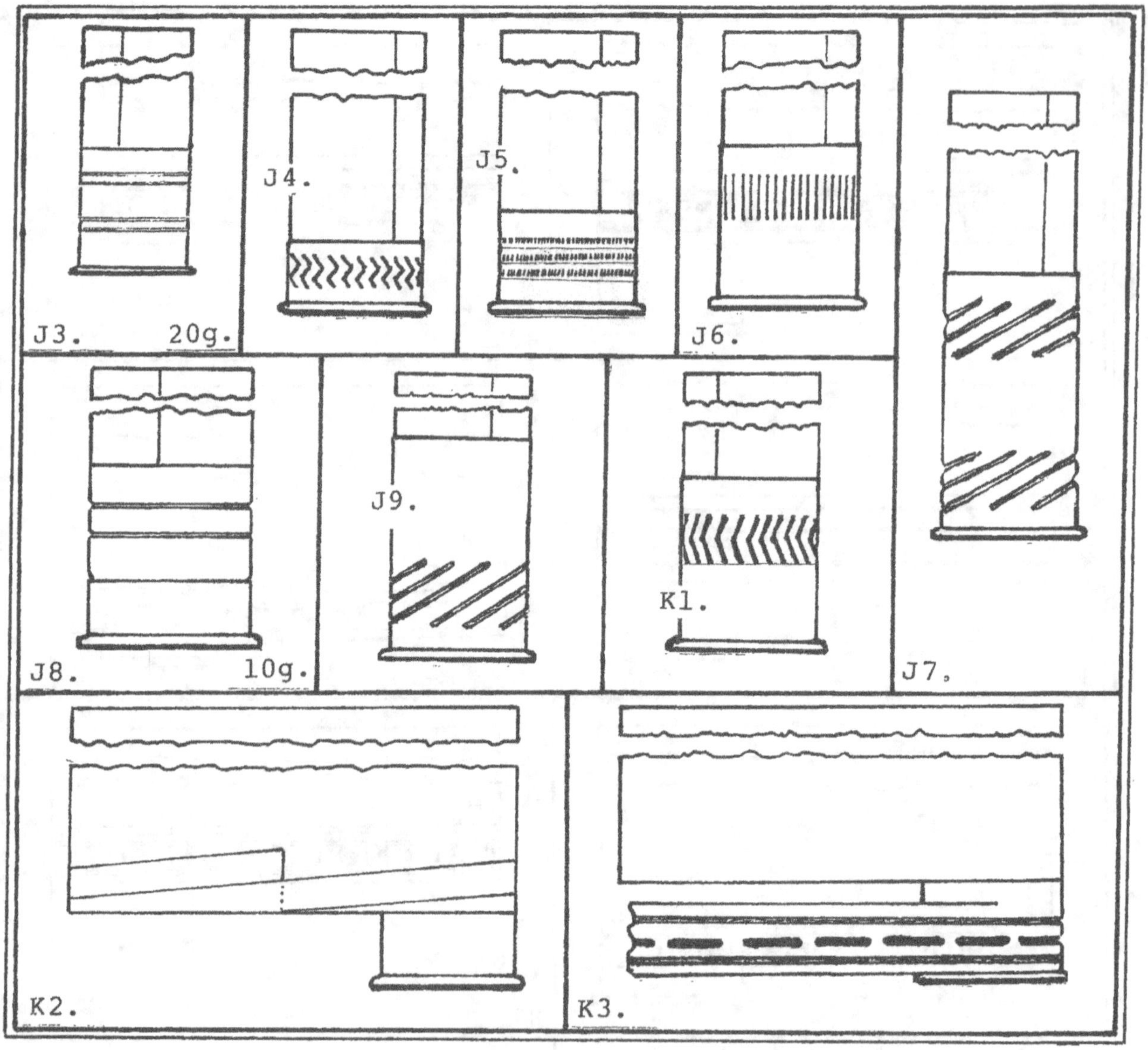

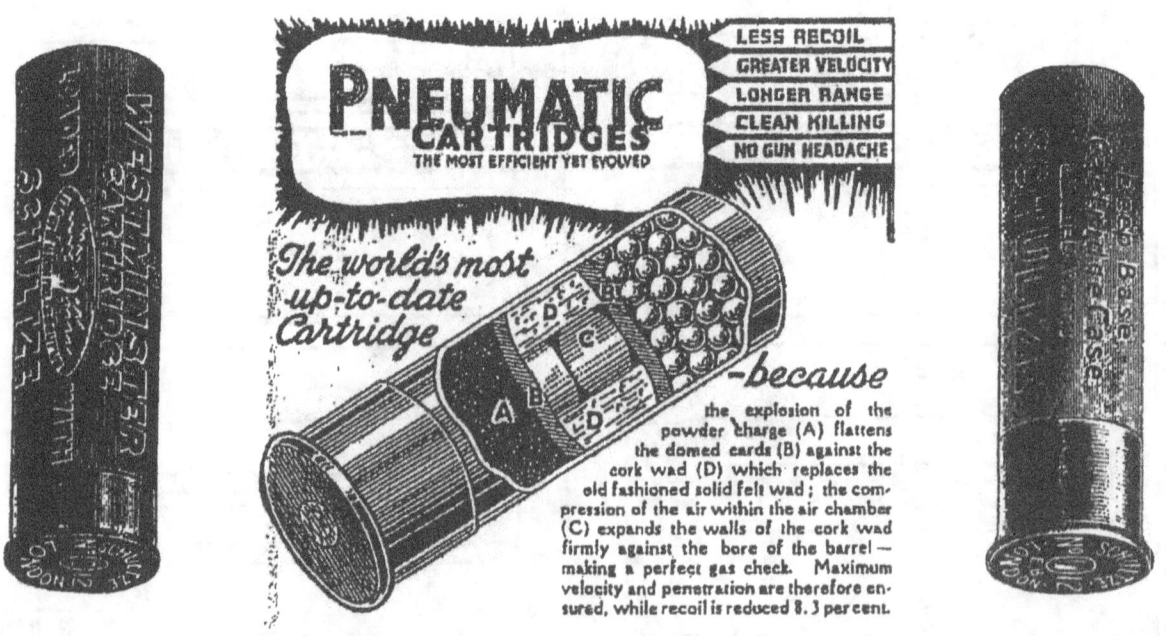

# BELATED ADDITIONS

Due to various reasons, a few drawings have missed their alphabetical slot. Very many others came along later when they were sent to me from various sources. Rather than omit them, I have included them in this section. Within this section all letters are alphabetically grouped and shown in the order from small to large in gauge sizes.

| | | | |
|---|---|---|---|
| 12 gauge. | 12 gauge. | 20 gauge, Gnm. | Joyce made case. |
| | | GBE/GBE | AUS/GBE |
| HFC.5,480. | HFC.5,481. | HSC.5482. | HSC.5,483. |
| 16 gauge.<br>12,10.<br>USA/USA | Gnm.<br><br>GBS | Manufacturer.<br>12.<br>GBE | 16 gauge, Dps.<br><br> |
| HSC.5,254. | HFC.500. | HFC.5,255. | HSC.5,256. |
| 16 gauge.<br>20,12,10.<br>USA/USA | London Gnm.<br>12.<br>GBE/GBE | London Gnm, Ejt.<br><br>GBE/GBE | 15 gauge ?<br>Maybe an error ?<br>GBE/IND |
| HSC.5,257. | HFC.5,258. | HFC.5,259. | HFC.2,152. |
| Kynoch double brass.<br><br>GBE/GBE | Gnm, Ejt.<br><br>GBS/GBE | Gnm.<br><br>GBS/GBE | Gnm.<br><br>GBS/F |
| HSC.5,260. | HSC.5,261. | HSC.5,262. | HSC.5,263. |

| | | | |
|---|---|---|---|
| A.T. Bates Canterbury | Barnett Sturminster | Blissett Liverpool | Boss & Co London |
| 12 gauge, Gnm. | Sturminster Newton. Irm. | 12 gauge. | 12 gauge, Gnm. |
| GBE/F | GBE | GBE | GBE/F |
| HSC.5,485. | HSC.5,499. | HSC.5,498. | HSC.5,497. |
| Browning 12 | Browning 12 GA | Buffalo 12 | Bulcock Burnley |
| 12 gauge. | Manufacturer. | 12 gauge. | J. Bulcock. |
| | | USA | GBE |
| HSC.5,495. | HSC.5,494. | HSC.5,493. | HSC.5,496. |
| Cartoucherie Fse 16 Paris 16 | Cartoucherie Fse 16 Paris 16 | Chambers Cardiff | Comet R.H.P.Co. |
| 16 gauge, Adv. | 16 gauge, Adv. | Septimus, Gnm. | Robin Hood Powder. |
| F/F | F/F | GBW | USA/USA |
| HSP.5,484. | HSC.5,492. | HSC.5,489. | HSC.5,488. |
| Campbell & Sons Leyburn | Charles Lancaster J&Co 12 | Charles Rosson Derby | Churchill 8 Agar St. Strand |
| 12 gauge. | Gnm, Joyce case. | Gnm. | London Gnm. |
| GBE | GBE/GBE | GBE/F | GBE |
| HSC.5,490. | HSC.5,491. | HSC.5,487. | HSC.5,486. |

361

| | | | |
|---|---|---|---|
| (COGSWELL & HARRISON -12-) | (COGSWELL & HARRISON No12) | (COGSWELL & HARRISON E.B. No12) | (COLE.DEVIZES No12 ELEY) |
| London Gnm. 20,16. | London Gnm. | London Gnm. | 12 gauge. Gnm, |
| GBE | GBE/GBE | GBE/GBE | GBE/GBE |
| HSC.5,278. | HSC.5,279. | HSC.5,280. | HFC.5,281. |
| (COLE & SON No 12 ELEY GUNMAKERS) | (W. COOMBS No 12 FROME) | (COOPPAL No 2 No 12 SMOKELESS POWDER) | (COX & CLARKE KYNOCH PATENT No 12 GROUSE EJECTOR SOUTHAMPTON) |
| 12 gauge, Gnm. | Wm. Coombs. | 12 gauge. | Kynoch Ejt. |
| GBE/GBE | GBE | GBE/GBE | GBE/GBE |
| HFC.5,282. | HFC.5,283. | HFC.5,284. | HFC.5,285. |
| (CRAMER & BUCHHOLZ *12*) | (DOMINION No 28 MADE IN CANADA) | (DARLOW No 12 NORWICH) | (D.GRAY & Co. INVERNESS No 12 ELEY) |
| 12 gauge, Adv. | Manufacturer. On other gauges. | Gnm. | 12 gauge, Gnm. |
| D/D | CDN/CDN | GBE | GBS/GBE |
| HSC.5,286. | HSC.5,287. | HSC.5,288. | HSC.5,289. |
| (DOUGALL & SONS No12) | (DICKSON & SON EDINBURGH No 10) | (DYER & ROBSON No 4 LONDON) | (ELEY 24 24 NOBEL) |
| 12 gauge, Gnm. | 10 gauge, Gnm. | 4 gauge. Fwk. | 24 gauge. On other gauges. |
| GBS | GBS | GBE | GBE/GBE |
| HFC.5,290. | HFC.2,071. | HFC.2,115. | HFC.270. |

| | | | |
|---|---|---|---|
| 20 gauge, Ejt. | 20 gauge. | 16 gauge. Adv. | 12 gauge, Gnm. |
| GBE/GBE | B/? | D/D | GBE |
| HFC.5,291. | HSC.5,292. | HSC.5,293. | HFC.5,294. |
| 12 gauge. | Gnm. | Kynoch made case. | Fore St, Okehampton. |
| F | GBE | GBE/GBE | GBE/GBE |
| HSC.5,295. | HFC.5,296/R. | HSC.5,297. | HFC.5,298. |
| Henry C.Squires. | 16 gauge. | 12 gauge, Gnm. | 12 gauge, Gnm. |
| USA/GBE | F/F | GBE | GBE |
| HSC.5,299. | HSC.5,300. | HSC.5,301. | HFC.5,302. |
| Copper head. | Manufacturer. | 12 gauge, Pla. | Irm, 12 gauge. |
| GBE/GBE | GBE/GBE | | GBE/GBE |
| HSC.5,303/R. | HSC.5,304. | HSC.5,305. | HSC.5,306. |

| | | | |
|---|---|---|---|
| Mrs E. Frampton, Gnm | Gnm, loader. | Gnm, loader. | Gnm, 12 gauge. |
| GBE | GBE/B | GBE/B | GBE |
| HSC.5,307. | HSC.5,308. | HSC.5,309. | HFC.5,310. |
| Gnm. | 20 gauge. | Eley Bros. | Gnm, 16 gauge. |
| GBE | F | GBE/GBE | GBE |
| HFC.5,311. | HSC.5,312. | HSC.5,313. | HSC.5,314. |
| 12 gauge. | 12 gauge. | Manufacturer. | Geo Bate, Gnm. |
| F/F | | I/I | GBE |
| HSC.5,315. | HFC.5,316. | HFC.5,317. | HSC.5,318. |
| Geo Bate, Gnm. | Gnm, circa 1885. | 12 gauge, Abc. 16. | Geo Fredk, Irm. |
| GBE | GBE | GBE/? | GBE |
| HSC.5,319. | HFC.5,320. | HSC.5,321. | HFC.5,322. |

| | | | |
|---|---|---|---|
| G.&J.PECK.ELY No.12 ELEY | GOLD No 12 BRISTOL | GOLDEN.BRADFORD No.12 ELEY | GRIFFITHS No 12 MANCHESTER |
| 12 gauge, Irm. | G. E. Gold, Gnm. | Charles Golden, Gnm | W. Griffiths. |
| GBE/GBE | GBE | GBE/GBE | GBE |
| HSC.5,323. | HSC.5,324. | HSC.5,325. | HSC.5,326. |
| H.U. 410 N | HOULLIER.BLANCHARD.PARIS 20 | HOULLIER.BLANCHARD.PARIS 16 | HUSSA 16 |
| .410, Adv. | 20 gauge. | 16 gauge. | 16 gauge, Adv. |
| | 16. | 20. | |
| D/D | F | F | D/D |
| HSC.5,327. | HSC.5,328. | HSC.5,329. | HSC.5,330. |
| H.J.HUSSEY.81.NEW BOND ST. No.16 ELEY | HUTENDOFRFFER 16 NURNBERG 16 | HUTENDOFRFFER 16 NURNBERG 16 | H.ATKIN No 12 2 JERMYN ST.S.W. |
| London Gnm. | 16 gauge, Adv. | 16 gauge, Adv. | London Gnm. |
| GBE/GBE | D/D | D/D | GBE |
| HSC.5,331. | HSC.5,332. | HSC.5,333. | HFC.5,334. |
| H.CLARKE&SON 12 12 LEICESTER | CLARKE.LEICESTER EXPRESS CARTRIDGE No 12 | HELSON MADE IN 12 12 EXETER BELGIUM | HENRY.ATKIN.41.JERMYN ST.S.W. KYNOCH PATENT GROUSE EJECTOR No 12 |
| 12 gauge, Gnm. | Gnm. | 12 gauge. | London Gnm, Ejt. |
| GBE | GBE | GBE/B | GBE/GBE |
| HSC.5,335. | HSC.5,336. | HSC.5,337. | HFC.5,338. |

| | | | |
|---|---|---|---|
| 12 gauge, Gnm. | 32 gauge. | Manufacturer. | 16 gauge, Adv. |
| GBE/GBE | GBE/GBE | GBE/GBE | F/F |
| HSC.5,339. | HSC.5,340. | HSC.5,341. | HSC.5,342. |
| 16 gauge, Adv. | Gnm, Kynoch case. | | 12 gauge, Gnm. |
| F/F | GBE/GBE | GBE | GBS |
| HSC.5,343. | HSC.5,344. | HSC.5,345. | HFC.5,346. |
| Gnm, Kynoch case. | Gnm, Ejt. | Gnm. | Gnm, double brass, |
| GBS/GBE | GBE/GBE | GBE | GBE/GBE |
| HSC.5,347. | HSC.5,348. | HSC.5,349. | HSC.5,350. |
| Joseph Harkom, Gnm. | 12 gauge. | Gnm. | London Gnm, Ejt. |
| GBS/GBE | GBE | IRL | GBE/GBE |
| HSC.5,351. | HSC.5,352. | HSC.5,353/R. | HFC.5,354. |

| | | | |
|---|---|---|---|
| Bailey cap. | 16 gauge, Gnm. | 14 gauge. | 14 gauge. |
| GBE/GBE | GBE | GBE/GBE | GBE/GBE |
| HSC.5,355. | HSC.5,356. | HFC.5,357. | HSC.5,358/R. |
| 12 gauge. | 12 gauge. | Manufacturer. | 10 gauge. |
| | GBE/F | GBE/GBE | GBE/GBE |
| HSC.5,359. | HSC.5,360. | HFC.5,361. | HSC.5,362. |
| London Gnm. | Kynoch made case. | Gnm. | 12 gauge. |
| GBE | GBE/GBE | B/GBE | GBE |
| HSC.5,363. | HSC.5,364. | HSC.5,365. | HSC.5,366. |
| Gnm, 12 gauge. | Gnm, Kynoch Ejt. | Gnm, Joyce case. | Gnm, 28 gauge. |
| GBE | GBE/GBE | GBE/GBE | GBS/GBE |
| HSC.5,367. | HSC.5,368. | HSC.5,369. | HSC.5,370. |

| | | | |
|---|---|---|---|
| 20 gauge. | Gnm, 20 gauge. | 16 gauge. | Gnm, Kynoch case. |
| | | | On other gauges. |
| B | GBE/F | F/F | GBS/GBE |
| HSC.5,371. | HSC.5,372. | HFC.5,373. | HSC.5,374. |
| 12 gauge. | 12 gauge. | Gnm. Adv. | Recessed head. |
| | | | 16. |
| GBS | ?/USA | IND | I/I |
| HFC.5,375. | HSC.5,376. | HSC.5,377. | HFC.1,526. |
| London Gnm. | 12 gauge, Gnm. | Gnm, 12 gauge. | 12 gauge, Gnm. |
| | | | |
| GBE | GBE/F | GBE | GBE/GBE |
| HSC.5,378. | HSC.5,379. | HFC.5,380. | HSC.5,381. |
| Gnm, 12 gauge. | Gnm, 16 gauge. | Post WW2. | Gnm, Kynoch Ejt. |
| | | | |
| GBS/GBE | GBE | GBE/? | GBE/GBE |
| HSC.5,382. | HSC.5,383. | HFC.5,384. | HSC.5,385. |

| | | | |
|---|---|---|---|
| (NOBEL'S No 12 EMPIRE) | (OAKES & Co. LD. MADRAS No 12 ELEY) | (PETERS 410 HV MADE IN USA) | (POLLARD & Co No 16 WORCESTER) |
| Powder Co. | 12 gauge. | .410 | Herbert, Gnm. |
| GBS/GBE | IND/GBE | USA/USA | GBE |
| HSC.5,386. | HSC.5,387. | HFC.236. | HSC.5,388. |
| (P.C.CO 12 G NITRO) | (PETERS 12 G REINFORCED) | (PURDEY No 12) | (PURDEY No 12) |
| Peters C. C. 10. | 12 gauge. 10. | London Gnm. | Gnm, 12 gauge. |
| USA/USA | USA/USA | GBE | GBE |
| HSC.5,389. | HSC.5,390. | HSC.5,391. | HSC.5,392/R. |
| (REM-UMC 410 MADE IN USA) | (REM-UMC No 24 NITRO CLUB) | (ROSSON DERBY & NORWICH 20) | (R.PINTO 16 ? 16 ESTE) |
| .410. | 24 gauge. On other gauges. | Gnm, 20 gauge. | 16 gauge. |
| USA/USA | USA/USA | GBE | I/I |
| HFC.237. | HSC.5,393. | HSC.5,394. | HSC.5,395. |
| (R.W.S. ♥ ♥ 16) | (RWS 16 16 NURNBERG) | (R.CAMBELL & SONS No 12 LEYBURN) | (ROYAL No 12 L.B.&Co.) |
| Rheinische Westfalische Springstoff. | | | |
| D/D | D/D | GBE | |
| HSC.5,396. | HFC.5,397. | HSC.5,398. | HSC.5,399. |

| | | | |
|---|---|---|---|
| R.ROBINSON.HULL No.12 | RUSSELL No 12 MAIDSTONE | RUSSELL KYNOCH'S PATENT No 12 GROUSE EJECTOR MAIDSTONE | SMOKELESS 28 28 GASTIGHT |
| Gnm, 12 gauge. | Gnm, 12 gauge. | Gnm, Kynoch Ejt. | 28 gauge. |
| GBE | GBE | GBE/GBE | |
| HSC.5,400. | HSC.5,401. | HSC.5,402. | HFC.267. |
| SCHULTZE No 20 EB LONDON | SMITH & SONS NEWARK No 20 | STERLING 16 16 LONDON | SELBY 12 12 STANDARD |
| Eley Bros case. 12. | Gnm, 20 gauge. | 16 gauge. | 12 gauge. 10. |
| GBE/GBE | GBE | GBE | USA |
| HSC.5,403. | HSC.5,404. | HSC.5,405. | HSC.5,406. |
| SELLIER & BELLOT 12 | N.S.G.Co No 12 K YEOMAN | SHAPLAND BROS No 12 WELLINGTON | SLINGSBY.LEEDS No.12 |
| Manufacturer. | Schultze Gunpowder. | 12 gauge. | 12 gauge. |
| CS/CS | GBE/GBE | GBE | GBE |
| HFC.5,407. | HSC.5,408. | HSC.5,409. | HSC.5,410. |
| SMITH & SONS NEWARK No.12 ELEY | SMITH MIDSLEY & Co No 12 BRADFORD | SMYTHE KYNOCH'S PATENT No 12 GROUSE EJECTOR DARLINGTON | SQUIBMAN 12 12 XTRAVEL |
| Gnm, Eley case. | Gnm. | Gnm, Kynoch Ejt. | 12 gauge. |
| GBE/GBE | GBE | GBE/GBE | |
| HSC.5,411. | HSC.5,412. | HSC.5,413. | HSC.5,414. |

| | | | |
|---|---|---|---|
| STEPHEN GRANT. LONDON. No 12. ELEY | S. WARRELL No 12 PORTSMOUTH | TAYLOR & SONS No 12 PENZANCE | T. TURNER & SONS. READING. No 12 |
| Gnm, 12 gauge. | Gnm, 12 gauge. | Old brown Pap. | Gnm, 12 gauge. |
| GBE/GBE | GBE | GBE/GBE | GBE |
| HSC.5,415. | HFC.5,416. | HSC.5,417. | HSC.5,418. |
| VULCAIN 16 | WINCHESTER 410 | W.C.CO. No 12 NEW CHIEF | W. DARLOW No 12 NORWICH |
| 16 gauge. | .410. | Winchester C.C. | Gnm, 12 gauge. |
| F/F | USA/USA | USA/USA | GBE |
| HSC.5,419. | HSC.5,420. | HSC.5,421. | HFC.5,422. |
| WESTLEY RICHARDS No 12 KYNOCH BIRMINGHAM | W. RICHARDS No 12 LIVERPOOL | W.W. GREENER No 12 LONDON & B'HAM | "SWIFT" |
| Gnm, 10 mm head. | Gnm. | Gnm, 12 gauge. | |
| GBE/GBE | GBE | GBE | |
| HFC.5,423. | HSC.5,424. | HFC.5,425. | |

THE WESTLEY RICHARDS WATERPROOF PAPER

THE WESTLEY RICHARDS BEST GASTIGHT PAPER

THE WESTLEY RICHARDS CARLTON CARTRIDGE

6½ WESTLEY RICHARDS game load

371

# THE END

I have had an idea that I think should work, though I have never tried it out for myself. It is having fun at the seaside with the children by drawing headstamps in the flat wet sand. To do this you would need to take three small pointed sticks with you and a short length of string. Tie one stick on each end of the string making it look like a small gardening line. Stick one of the sticks in the sand and with the string held taught scribe a circle with the other stick. You will now have made the outer circle of the headstamp. Now wind in the string on this stick and lightly scribe some inner circles. These to write your messages between. Now make your smallest circle to draw in the cap chamber. Use your third stick to write in your message. Let me give you an example.

Having drawn so many headstamps I feel that I must just draw one more for this page and it will be fictitious. I trust that you have enjoyed all of the rest of them and have found them useful.

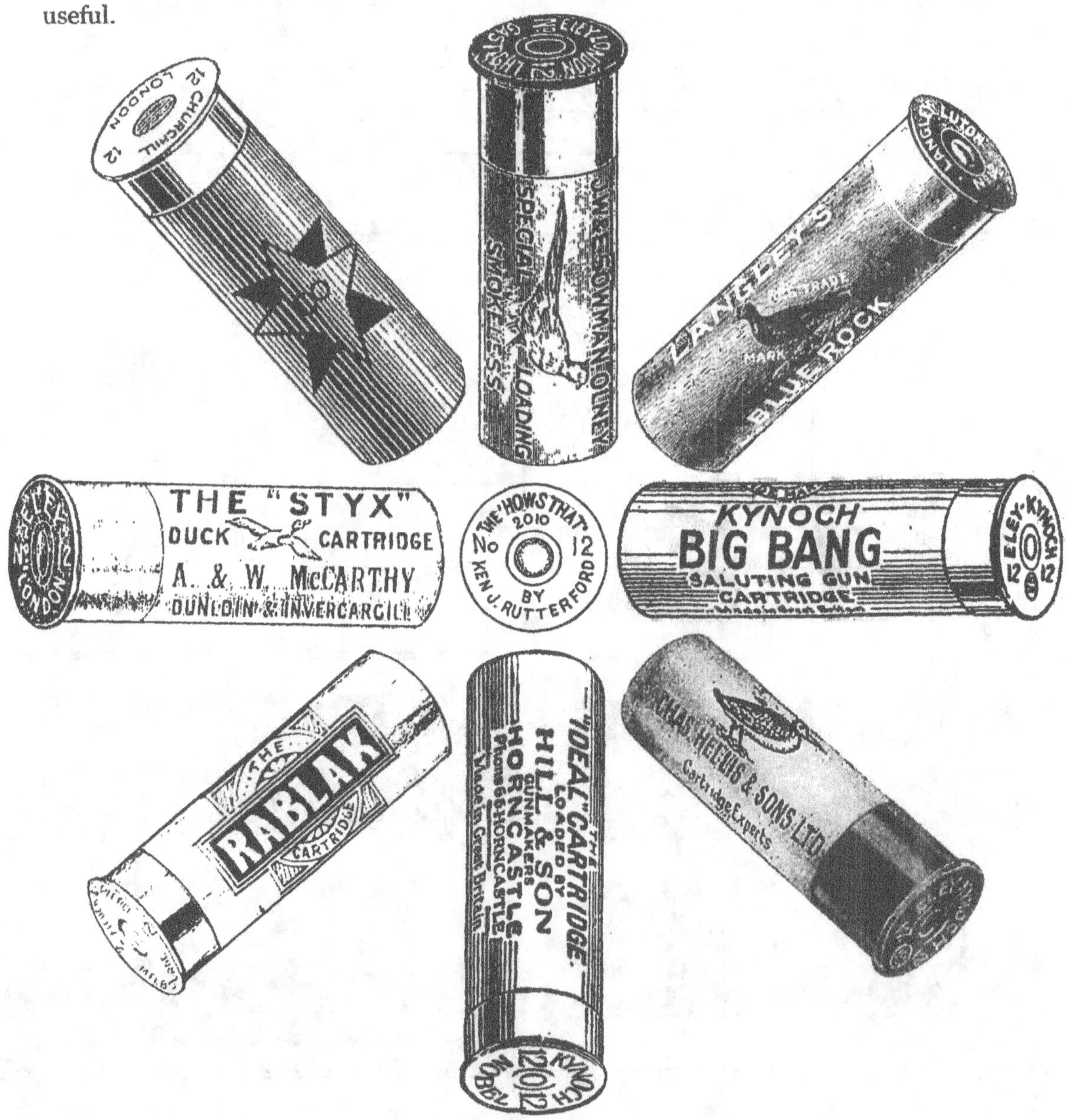

372

For Personal Drawings

For Personal Drawings

For Personal Drawings